HMH SCIENCE DIMENSIONS™

Physics

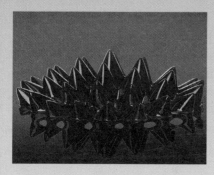 

Physics is the study of energy and matter and how they interact. When ferrofluid interacts with the energy in magnetic fields, the ferrofluid changes shape and position. Other interactions are critical to the technologies that support and provide electrical energy to communities.

This book belongs to

_____

Teacher/Room

_____

Houghton Mifflin Harcourt.
The Learning Company™

John Galisky

Physics Teacher and Science Department Chair
Lompoc High School
Lompoc, California

John Galisky, an Albert Einstein Distinguished Educator Fellow, has taught physics, Earth science, electronics, robotics, and space science at Lompoc High School for 23 years. He established the Space, Technology, and Robotic Systems (STaRS) Academy, an engineering program that integrates core academics in math, science, and language arts with drafting, engineering design, electronics, robotics, and manufacturing. Galisky has worked in partnership with CREATE, a National Science Foundation Advanced Technological Education (ATE) Center in California, to develop and disseminate curriculum related to renewable energy production and distribution.

Jeffrey Rylander, MS Physics

Physics Teacher and Instructional Supervisor for Science
Department of Science
Glenbrook South High School
Glenview, Illinois

Jeffrey Rylander has taught physics since 1990 and has served as the chair of Glenbrook South High School's Science Department since 2006. In addition to overseeing the high school science curriculum, Rylander has served as a consultant to elementary districts adopting the Next Generation Science Standards. Under his leadership, Glenbrook South has developed a four-year sequence of paired science and engineering courses that seeks to prepare the scientists and engineers of tomorrow. Rylander has given presentations on science instruction at several national conferences and has published numerous articles on physics education.

Copyright © 2020 by Houghton Mifflin Harcourt Publishing Company

ISBN 978-0-544-86179-4

3 4 5 6 7 8 9 10 0928 28 27 26 25 24 23 22 21 20

4500797436   C D E F G

ENGINEERING CONSULTANT

Cary I. Sneider, PhD
Associate Research Professor
Portland State University
Portland, Oregon

LAB SAFETY REVIEWER

Kenneth R. Roy, PhD
Senior Lab Safety Compliance Consultant
National Safety Consultants, LLC
Vernon, Connecticut

PROGRAM ADVISORS

Alvin M. Saperstein, PhD
Professor Emeritus of Physics
Wayne State University
Detroit, Michigan

ACCESS AND EQUITY CONSULTANT

Bernadine Okoro
STEM Learning Advocate & Consultant
Washington, DC

Donald E. Simanek, PhD
Professor Emeritus of Physics
Lock Haven University
Lock Haven, Pennsylvania

CLASSROOM REVIEWERS

Jesús Rafael Aguilar-Landaverde
NYOS Charter School
Austin, Texas

Matthew Lindsey
Mosinee High School
Mosinee, Wisconsin

Joseph Sean Moore
Severna Park High School
Severna Park, Maryland

Bhavna Rawal
Harmony School of Excellence and Houston
   Community College
Houston, Texas

Ursula Strojan
Cicely Tyson School of Performing and Fine Arts
   Middle/High School
East Orange, New Jersey

Kelsey Thompson
Independence High School
Independence, Kansas

This tensegrity sculpture uses tension and compression in a stable structure.

A roller coaster gains speed as it rolls downhill.

Plus/Getty Images

Charge builds up as the wheel spins. The force becomes strong enough to produce a spark between the metal balls.

UNIT 4

Electromagnetism and Generators 237

An electric arc is an electric discharge across a medium that is not normally conductive, such as air.

Images Plus/Getty Images

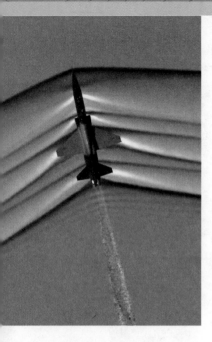

In this photograph of a supersonic jet, areas of different air pressure appear as light and dark regions.

Claims, Evidence, and Reasoning

You likely use claims, evidence, and reasoning in your daily life—perhaps without even being aware of it. Suppose you leave a notebook behind in the cafeteria. When you return later, you see a number of similar notebooks on the counter. You say, "I left my notebook here earlier," and pick up one of them. The cafeteria worker says, "Are you sure that one is yours? They all look pretty much alike." You say, "Yes, my initials are right here on the cover." To confirm the fact, you open the notebook to show your full name inside. You also present your student ID to prove that it's your name.

This encounter is a claims-evidence-reasoning interaction. You claimed the notebook was yours, and you showed evidence to prove your point.

CLAIM

A *claim* is your position on an issue or problem. It answers the question, "What do you know?"

EVIDENCE

Evidence is any data related to your claim that answer the question, "How do you know that?" These data may be from your own experiments and observations, reports by scientists or engineers, or other reliable sources. Scientific knowledge is based on *empirical evidence*, or evidence that is derived from observation or experiment. As you read about science, perform lab activities, engage in class discussions, and write explanations, you will need to cite evidence to support your claims.

REASONING

Reasoning is the use of logical, analytical thought to form conclusions or inferences. It answers the question, "Why does your evidence support your claim?" Reasoning may involve citing a scientific law or principle that helps explain the relationship between the evidence and the claim.

Scientists use claims, evidence, and reasoning—or *argumentation*—for many purposes: to explain, to persuade, to convince, to predict, to demonstrate, and to prove things. When scientists publish the results of their investigations, they must be prepared to defend their conclusions if they are challenged by other scientists.

Here is an example of a claims-evidence-reasoning argument.

CLAIM: Ice melts faster in the sun than it does in the shade.

EVIDENCE: We placed two ice cubes of the same size in identical plastic dishes. We placed one dish on a wooden bench in the sun and placed the other on a different part of the same bench in the shade. The ice cube in the sun melted in 14 minutes and 32 seconds. The ice cube in the shade melted in 18 minutes and 15 seconds.

REASONING: We designed the investigation so that the only variable in the setup was whether the ice cubes were in the shade or in the sun. Because the ice cube in the sun melted almost 4 minutes faster, this is sufficient evidence to support the claim that ice melts faster in the sun than it does in the shade.

Construct your own argument below by recording a claim, evidence, and reasoning. With your teacher's permission, you can do an investigation to answer a question you have about how the world works, or you can construct your argument based on observations you have already made about the world.

CLAIM	
EVIDENCE	
REASONING	

Getty Images

 For more information on claims, evidence, and reasoning, see the online
English Language Arts Handbook.

Using Your
Evidence Notebook

Throughout the units and lessons of **HMH Science Dimensions Physics**, you will see notebook icons that highlight important places for you to stop and reflect. These Evidence Notebook prompts signal opportunities for you to record observations and evidence, analyze data, and make explanations for phenomena.

The Evidence Notebook is your location to gather evidence and record your thinking as you make your way through each lesson. Your teacher may determine a specific format for you to use, such as a digital or paper notebook. Whatever the format, you will record here the evidence you gather throughout the lesson to support your response to the Can You Explain the Phenomenon?/Can You Solve the Problem? challenge. You will also record significant information from the lesson to use as a study tool and to build your own study guide at the end of the lesson.

The following pages from the first lesson in the book will familiarize you with the main types of Evidence Notebook prompts you will see throughout the course.

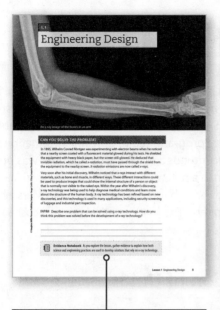

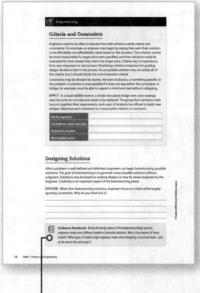

Provides general direction about the evidence to collect related to this phenomenon as you explore the lesson.

Provides a point-of-use opportunity to address the unit project or lesson phenomena.

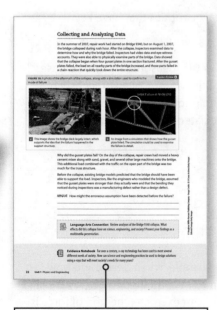

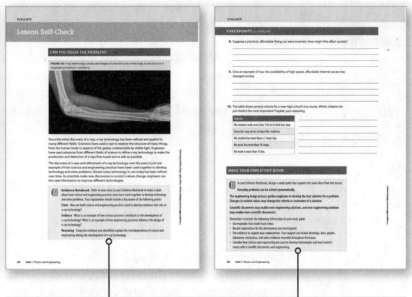

Prompts you to synthesize information from evidence, analysis, models, and other information gathered over the course of an Exploration.

At the end of each lesson, you will also be prompted to use the notes from your Evidence Notebook to construct an explanation and to make your own study guide for the main ideas from the lesson.

Working with
Measurement

FIGURE 1: An artist's rendition of the Mars Climate Orbiter

Clear communication is important for scientific investigation. In 1999, a miscommunication about units of measurement had devastating consequences for NASA's Mars Climate Orbiter, shown in Figure 1. Part of the landing system was programmed to transmit information in one unit of measurement, and the intended receiving component was programmed to receive information in a different unit of measurement. The resulting miscalculation caused the Orbiter to pass too close to Mars and to disintegrate in the planet's atmosphere. The mathematical mistake cost $125 million, and no data were collected.

Standardization of Units

In 1960, scientists established a standard set of units based on the metric system called the *Système International d'Unités* (French for the International System of Units), or SI.

Derived Units and Other Accepted Units

SI has seven base units to describe physical quantities that have key importance in scientific measurements.

ANALYZE Notice that volume is not one of the measures assigned a base unit. Think about how you would calculate the volume of an object such as a cube. Which of the base units in the table could you use to measure volume? Give an example of the units associated with volume based on one of the base units in SI.

Measure	Base unit
Length	meter (m)
Mass	kilogram (kg)
Time	second (s)
Temperature	kelvin (K)
Quantity	mole (mol)
Electric Current	ampere (A)
Luminous Intensity	candela (cd)

_____

_____

_____

_____

In SI, many units are derived from the base units. For example, when describing how fast something is moving, the base units for length and time are combined to give a rate of meters per second, m/s. Some derived units are named. For example, the unit of force is called the newton (N), which is equal to 1 kg·m/s^2.

Liquid volume is commonly measured in liters (L). Though not officially an SI unit, the liter is an accepted unit of measure in SI. Similarly, degree Celsius is an accepted unit to use when measuring temperature. Figure 2 shows the relationship between Kelvin, Celsius, and Fahrenheit temperature scales.

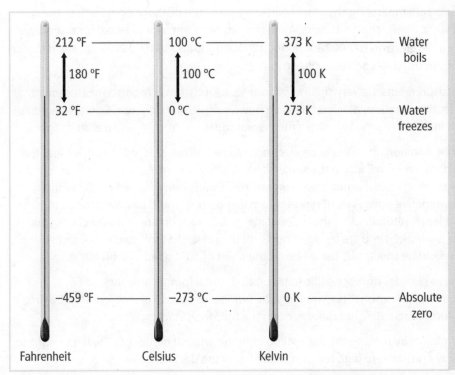

FIGURE 2: A diagram showing the relationships between the Kelvin, Celsius, and Fahrenheit temperature scales, with respect to three key temperatures. Any temperature in one of the scales can be converted to a temperature in the other scales. Though Fahrenheit is common in some parts of the world, it is not an accepted unit for scientific measurement.

Unit Prefixes

The diameter of a single atom ranges from about 0.1 to 0.3 nanometers (nm). If you measure something with a meterstick, you may report its length in centimeters (cm). The distance between two cities may be measured in kilometers (km). By appending a prefix such as kilo- or centi- onto a base unit, it is easier to report measurements for large or small quantities. SI has 20 accepted prefixes that change the magnitude of a unit by a power of 10. For example, 1 kilometer is equal to 1000 meters, and 1 millisecond is equal to 0.001 second.

To convert from the original unit to the modified unit, multiply or divide by the appropriate power of 10 or simply move the decimal the corresponding number of places. For example, to convert from grams to kilograms, divide the number of grams by 1000 or move the decimal three places to the left. Fill in places with zeros if needed. Only one prefix at a time may be appended to a unit.

Factor	Prefix (symbol)
10^{-24}	yocto (y)
10^{-21}	zepto (z)
10^{-18}	atto (a)
10^{-15}	femto (f)
10^{-12}	pico (p)
10^{-9}	nano (n)
10^{-6}	micro (μ)
10^{-3}	milli (m)
10^{-2}	centi (c)
10^{-1}	deci (d)

Factor	Prefix (symbol)
10^{1}	deka (da)
10^{2}	hecto (h)
10^{3}	kilo (k)
10^{6}	mega (M)
10^{9}	giga (G)
10^{12}	tera (T)
10^{15}	peta (P)
10^{18}	exa (E)
10^{21}	zetta (Z)
10^{24}	yotta (Y)

SOLVE Write the correct quantity for each conversion.

1. 38 000 kg = _____ g

2. 6.5 m = _____ mm

3. 4.3 ms = _____ s

4. 0.02 km = _____ cm

Magnitude and Scientific Notation

Imagine you are measuring the mass of an electron or the distance from Earth to the sun. Without some handy shortcuts, you would have to write out a lot of zeros. For example, the mass of an electron is 0. 000 000 000 000 000 000 000 000 000 000 910 9 kg. The distance from Earth to the sun is 149 600 000 000 m.

When measurements are very small or very large, scientists may report a measurement using scientific notation, which is based on powers of 10, or *magnitude*. Scientific notation is written in the form $m \times 10^n$, where the magnitude is $1 \leq m < 10$, and n is an integer.

In scientific notation, the mass of an electron may be written as 9.109×10^{-31} kg, and the average distance from Earth to the sun is about 1.496×10^{11} m. Adding a prefix to a unit is similar to using scientific notation. For example, 1 milligram (mg) $= 1 \times 10^{-3}$ gram (g). Note that negative powers of 10 represent smaller numbers, and positive powers of 10 represent larger numbers. Use the order of magnitude to estimate and help check your work. For example, if you are trying to calculate the mass of a molecule, you know your answer should be small, so it should be on the order of 10^{-23} g rather than 10^{23} g.

To convert a number from scientific notation to decimal form, follow the rules of multiplication and exponents to multiply the number as usual. To convert a number from decimal form to scientific notation, perform the following steps:

1. Determine m by moving the decimal point in the original number to the left or right so that only one nonzero digit remains to the left of the decimal point.

2. Determine n by counting the number of places you moved the decimal point in the first step. If you moved the decimal point to the right, n is negative. If you moved the decimal to the left, n is positive.

EVALUATE Use your knowledge of multiplication and exponents to rewrite the following numbers in either decimal notation or scientific notation.

Decimal notation	Scientific notation
5280	5.28×10^3
4 967 000 000 000 000	
	5.12×10^{12}
0. 000 000 000 000 159	
	9.109×10^{-31}

When it comes to very small or very large numbers, scientific notation reduces errors due to miscounting the number of digits. Numbers written in scientific notation all require approximately the same amount of space regardless of magnitude, making it easier to compare the magnitude of values by looking at the power of 10 in the number. For example, consider the distances 1.5×10^6 m, 3.4×10^6 m, and 9.5×10^{-3} m. The first two distances have the same magnitude, 10^6, and are much larger than the magnitude of the third distance, 10^{-3}. If you add these three distances, the third distance will have little effect on the final sum, even though the leading coefficient 9.5 is larger than the other two coefficients.

SOLVE A measurement may be reported in many different ways. The diameter of Earth is approximately 12 700 km. Match the quantities shown with the appropriate units to show other ways that Earth's diameter may be written.

$$1.27 \times 10^4 \qquad 1.27 \times 10^7 \qquad 1.27 \times 10^{10} \qquad 12.7$$

_____ Mm	_____ km	_____ m	_____ mm

Many calculators and software programs can display results in scientific notation. The letter *E* is used in place of the multiplication. For example, the number 1.689×10^{-15} may be displayed as 1.689E–15 or 1.689e–15. Refer to a calculator's manual to see how to enter numbers in scientific notation and how to configure the calculator to display numbers in scientific notation.

Accuracy and Precision

The tools that scientists use to measure affect how accurately and precisely the measurement can be made. The terms *accuracy* and *precision* are often used interchangeably in everyday conversation. In science, however, these terms have different meanings. *Accuracy* is the closeness of a measurement to the correct or accepted value of the quantity measured. *Precision* is the closeness of a set of measurements of the same quantity made in the same way. Precision may also refer to the number of gradations on a measurement device.

If a balance displayed values that were two grams more than the true mass every time you used it, the balance would be precise but not accurate. Its readings are wrong, but they are consistent. Imagine you have two digital scales and a known 2 kg mass. You use the 2 kg mass to determine how accurate and precise the two scales are. You place the 2 kg mass on each scale 4 different times and record the values shown in the table.

Scale A measurements	Scale B measurements
1999 g	2005 g
2005 g	2004 g
2008 g	2005 g
1994 g	2005 g

In this example, the accuracy of each measurement on scale A varies widely, though, if averaged, the average value is close to the accepted value. The measurements are also not very precise. Scale B gives more precise measurements, but it is still inaccurate. The ideal measuring tool would be both precise and accurate.

ANALYZE Below each image, state whether the points on the target are *accurate* or *not accurate*, and whether they are *precise* or *not precise*.

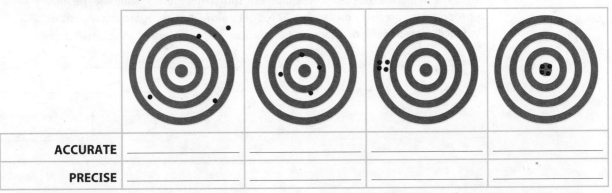

ACCURATE	_____	_____	_____	_____
PRECISE	_____	_____	_____	_____

Describing Accuracy

Consider the following two measurements: the amount of water in a swimming pool and the amount of medicine being administered to a patient. The swimming pool has a volume of 3.75×10^8 mL, and the medicine has a volume of 5.00 mL. Both measurements are 1 mL more than the true volume.

ARGUE All measurements have some error. How do you determine the acceptable level of accuracy for a measurement? Use the measurements of the swimming pool volume and medicine volume to support your claim.

_____

_____

_____

_____

Measuring Precisely

Different pieces of equipment allow for measurements with different levels of precision. Digital measuring devices may specify precision by the smallest digit presented. In the scale example earlier, the scales may be said to have a precision of 1 g, because that is the smallest increment the scales can report (though, as the example shows, that is not their true precision).

FIGURE 3: Left to right, the name and smallest increment marked on each piece of equipment: graduated cylinder (2 mL), Erlenmeyer flask (25 mL), beaker (10 mL).

For analog devices, the precision is related to how many measuring increments or graduations the device has. For example, a graduated cylinder with 0.1 mL increments allows for more-precise measurements than a graduated cylinder with 1 mL increments. The smallest division on the equipment indicates how precisely you can make a measurement using the equipment.

It is appropriate to estimate a value that is 1/10 the size of the smallest division on a measurement tool. If using equipment that clearly indicates the tenths place, you could record a value with an estimated digit in the hundredths place. For example, if a volume appeared to be between 36.2 and 36.3 mL on a graduated cylinder with 0.1 mL increments, the volume could be recorded as 36.25 mL. The 5 in the hundredths place is the estimated digit.

EXPLAIN Which of the pieces of equipment shown in Figure 3 would be the most appropriate for precisely measuring 29 mL of liquid? Explain your reasoning, citing evidence related to the divisions on each tool and the concept of an estimated digit.

_____

_____

_____

_____

Significant Figures

When manipulating and reporting measurements, it is important to know the precision with which the measurements were made. For example, you use a scale with a precision of 0.1 kg to measure the mass of an object three times. The results are 8.5 kg, 8.6 kg, and 8.5 kg. You average the three measurements and get 8.533 333 33 kg on the calculator. If you report the mass as 8.533 333 33 kg this indicates that you measured the mass much more precisely than you really did.

One way to maintain the precision of a measurement is to use significant figures. The *significant figures* in a measurement are all of the digits known with certainty, plus the first uncertain or estimated digit. Recall that the 5 in the hundredths place of the graduated cylinder measurement of 36.25 mL was an estimated digit. The measurement of 36.25 mL has 4 significant figures. The table below shows the rules for identifying significant figures in a measurement. Writing a number in scientific notation can help you see which digits are significant.

Digit	Rule	Examples
1, 2, 3, 4, 5, 6, 7, 8, or 9	Significant	275 m: three significant figures 42.35 mL: four significant figures
0 between nonzero digits (captive zeros)	Significant	40.7 °C: three significant figures 87 009 g: five significant figures
0 before nonzero digits (leading zeros)	Not significant	0.095 807 cm: five significant figures
0 at the end of a number without decimal point (trailing zeros)	Not significant	2000 kg: 1 significant figure, unless otherwise specified
0 at the end of a number with a decimal point (trailing zeros)	Significant	2000. s: four significant figures 25.00 mA: four significant figures

When a calculation is completed, you will often need to round the value to the correct number of significant figures for the problem. If the digit after the place you are rounding to is a 5 or higher, you round up. For example, 27.15 cm rounds to 27.2 cm. But 27.14 cm rounds to 27.1 cm.

SOLVE A calculator displays the number 50 238.450 124. Round this number as described for each row of the table.

Round to . . .	Rounded value
thousandths place	_____
tenths place	_____
3 significant figures	_____
1 significant figure, in scientific notation	_____
4 significant figures, in scientific notation	_____

Mathematical Operations and Significant Figures

Calculators do not account for significant figures, so you must properly manage the precision of reported results. The following sections describe some standard rules that should be used when calculating with measured values to ensure that significant figures are manipulated in a uniform way. If performing a multistep problem, keep track of which figures are significant as you work, but do not round until your final answer. Check with your teacher in case they have any different rules for operations with measurements.

Adding and Subtracting Significant Figures

When adding or subtracting measured values, the resulting number can have no more precision than any of the numbers used in the calculation. Perform the addition or subtraction and then round the result to the appropriate decimal place.

ANALYZE In the right column identify the decimal place, such as *tenths place*, with the most precision for each measurement and the precision of the resulting sum.

	Measured/Calculated value	Most-precise place
Length one	25.1 cm	
Length two	2.05 cm	
Sum	27.2 cm	

Multiplying and Dividing Significant Figures

When multiplying or dividing measured values, the resulting number can have no more significant figures than any of the factors, divisors, or dividends. Perform the multiplication or division, and then round.

ANALYZE In the right column, write the number of significant figures for each measurement and the resulting quotient.

	Measured/Calculated value	Significant figures
Mass	3.05 g	
Volume	8.470 mL	
Density = mass / volume	0.360 g/mL	

Conversion Factors and Counting Numbers

Some quantities—counted numbers, defined values and conversion factors—are considered exact numbers. These quantities have no uncertainty and therefore have infinite significant figures. These quantities do not affect the uncertainty of a calculation. For example, there are exactly 100 cm in 1 m. A measure of 460.8 cm will convert to 4.608 m. Both the original measurement and the converted measurement have 4 significant figures.

Combined Operations

When performing a multistep problem, identify the measurement with the least significant figures before you begin your calculations. The order of operations matters. If the measurement 25.1 m is subtracted from 26.1 m, the result of 1.0 m has 2 significant figures. If this result is then divided by 0.512 s, the result of 1.953125 m/s would need to be rounded to 2 significant figures, 2.0 m/s, even though the original measurements had 3 significant figures.

SOLVE To calculate the rate at which an object moves you subtract Position A, 5.20 m, from Position B, 102.10 m, and then divide by the time it took to move between positions, 4.81 s. Using the rules presented here, what should the final answer be?

○ **a.** 20 m/s   ○ **b.** 20. m/s   ○ **c.** 20.1 m/s   ○ **d.** 20.15 m/s

Dimensional Analysis

It is common to convert units within SI or from non-SI units to SI units. Dimensional analysis is a method that helps you apply conversion factors to convert between units. *Conversion factors* are ratios relating the value of one unit of measure to another. In dimensional analysis, the conversion factors are applied such that when you multiply, all of the units except for the desired units cancel out. For example, a length of 1 foot is equivalent to 0.3048 meters.

$$1 \text{ ft} = 0.3048 \text{ m}$$

This conversion factor may be written as:

$$\frac{1 \text{ ft}}{0.3048 \text{ m}} \quad \text{or} \quad \frac{0.3048 \text{ m}}{1 \text{ ft}}$$

depending on whether you want to convert from feet to meters or meters to feet. To convert a measurement of 3.1 feet to meters, you would do the following:

$$3.1 \text{ ft} \times \left(\frac{0.3048 \text{ m}}{1 \text{ ft}} \right) = 0.94 \text{ m}$$

Notice that the final quantity has 2 significant figures because the original measurement had 2 significant figures; significant figure rules apply during dimensional analysis.

Dimensional analysis may involve multiple conversion factors, so special care must be taken to ensure the conversion factors are placed appropriately. This may be more challenging if you are converting a ratio such as speed.

SOLVE Use the following equivalent values to convert the measurement 55 mi/h into m/s. Make sure to write each conversion factor such that units will cancel when you multiply, leaving only the desired units.

1 mi = 5280 ft   1 ft = 0.3048 m   1 h = 3600 s

_____ m/s

Lab Safety

Before you work in the laboratory, read these safety rules. Ask your teacher to explain any rules that you do not completely understand. Refer to these rules later on if you have questions about safety in the science classroom.

Personal Protective Equipment (PPE)

- PPE includes eye protection, nitrile or nonlatex gloves, and nonlatex aprons. In all labs involving chemicals, indirectly vented chemical splash goggles are required.

- Wear the required PPE during the setup, hands-on, and takedown segments of the activity.

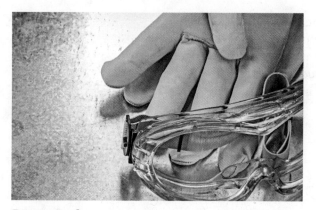

Dress Code

- Secure any article of clothing—such as a loose sweater or a scarf—that hangs down and may touch a flame, chemical, or piece of equipment.

- Wear closed-toe shoes.

- Tie back long hair or hair that hangs in front of your eyes.

- Acrylic fingernails are very flammable and should not be worn when using a flame.

Directions

- Observe all safety icons.

- Know where the fire extinguisher, fire blanket, shower, and eyewash station are located in your classroom or lab, and know how to use them in an emergency.

- Read all directions, and make sure that you understand them before starting the activity.

- Do not begin any investigation or touch any equipment until your teacher has told you to start.

- Never experiment on your own. If you want to try a procedure that the directions do not call for, ask your teacher for permission first.

- If you are hurt or injured in any way, tell your teacher immediately.

Chemical Safety

- If you get a chemical in your eye, use the eyewash station immediately. Flush the eye a minimum of 15 minutes.

- If you get a hazardous chemical on your skin or clothes, use the emergency shower for a minimum of 15 minutes.

- Never touch, taste, or sniff any chemicals in the lab. If you need to determine odor, waft. To waft, hold the chemical in its container 15 cm away from your nose and use your fingers to bring fumes from the container to your nose.

- Take only the amount of chemical you need for the investigation. If you get too much, ask your teacher how to dispose of the excess. Do not return unused chemicals to the storage container; this can cause contamination.

- When diluting acid with water, always add acid to water. Never add water to an acid.

Heating and Fire Safety

- Keep your work area neat, clean, and free of materials.

- Never reach over a flame or heat source.

- Never heat a substance or an object in a closed container.

- Use oven mitts, clamps, tongs, or a test tube holder to hold heated items.

- Do not throw hot substances into the trash. Wait for them to cool, and dispose of them in the container provided by your teacher.

Electrical Safety

- Never use lamps or other electrical equipment with frayed cords or plugs with a missing ground prong.

- Make sure no cord is lying on the floor where someone can trip over it.

- Do not let a cord hang over the side of a counter or table so that the equipment can easily be pulled or knocked to the floor.

- Never let cords hang into sinks or other places where water can be found.

- Only use a Ground Fault Interrupter (GFI) protected circuit receptacle.

Glassware and Sharp-Object Safety

- Use only clean glassware that is free of chips and cracks.

- Use knives and other cutting instruments carefully. Always wear eye protection and cut away from yourself.

Animal Safety

- Never hurt an animal.

- Wear gloves when handling animals or preserved specimens.

- Specimens for dissection should be properly mounted and supported.

Cleanup

- Follow your teacher's instructions for the disposal or storage of supplies.

- Clean your work area, and pick up anything that has dropped to the floor.

- Wash your hands with soap and water after completing the activity.

Safety in the Field

- Be sure you understand the goal of your fieldwork and the proper way to carry out the investigation before you begin fieldwork.

- Do not approach or touch wild animals. Do not touch plants unless instructed by your teacher to do so. Leave natural areas as you found them.

- Use proper accident procedures, and let your teacher know about a hazard in the environment or an accident immediately, even if the hazard or accident seems minor.

Safety Symbols

Safety is the priority in the science classroom. In all of the activities in this textbook, safety symbols are used to alert you to materials, procedures, or situations that could be potentially hazardous if the safety guidelines are not followed. Learn what you need to do when you see these icons, and read all lab procedures before coming to the lab so you are prepared. Always ask your teacher if you have questions.

 ANIMALS Never injure an animal. Follow your teacher's instructions for handling specific animals or preserved specimens. Wash your hands with soap and water after handling animals or preserved specimens.

 APRON Wear a nonlatex apron at all times in the lab as directed. Stand whenever possible to avoid spilling in your lap.

 BREAKAGE Use caution when handling items that may break, such as glassware and thermometers. Always store test tubes in a test tube rack.

 CHEMICALS Always wear indirectly vented chemical splash goggles when working with chemicals. Stand whenever possible when working with chemicals to avoid spilling on your lap. Tell your teacher immediately if you spill chemicals on yourself, the table, or the floor. Never taste any substance or chemical in the lab. Always wash your hands with soap and water after working with chemicals.

 DISPOSAL Follow your teacher's instructions for disposing of all waste materials, including chemicals, specimens, or broken glass.

 ELECTRIC Keep electrical cords away from water to avoid shock. Do not use cords with frayed edges or plugs with a missing ground prong. Unplug all equipment when done. Only use GFI protected electrical receptacles.

 FIRE Put on safety goggles before lighting flames. Remove loose clothing and tie back hair. Never leave a lit object unattended. Extinguish flames as soon as you finish heating.

 FUMES Always work in a well-ventilated area. Do not inhale or sniff fumes; instead, use your fingers to bring fumes from the container to your nose.

 GLOVES Always wear gloves to protect your skin from possible injury when working with substances that may be harmful or when working with animals.

 HAND WASHING Wash your hands with soap and water after working with soil, chemicals, animals, or preserved specimens.

 HEATING Wear indirectly vented chemical splash goggles, and never leave any substance while it is being heated. Use tongs or appropriate insulated holders when handling heated objects. Point any materials being heated away from you and others. Place hot objects such as test tubes in test tube racks while cooling.

 PLANTS Do not eat any part of a plant. Do not pick any wild plant unless your teacher instructs you to do so. Wash your hands with soap and water after handling any plant.

 SAFETY GOGGLES Always wear indirectly vented chemical splash goggles when working with chemicals, heating any substance, or using a sharp object or any material that could fly up and injure you or others.

 SHARP OBJECTS Use scissors, knives, or razor tools with care. Wear goggles when cutting something. Always cut away from yourself.

 SLIP HAZARD Immediately pick up any items dropped on the floor, and wipe up any spilled water or other liquid so it does not become a slip/fall hazard. Tell your teacher immediately if you spill chemicals.

Physics and Engineering

This tensegrity sculpture uses tension and compression in a stable structure.

Gallery/Edwin Remsberg/Alamy

FIGURE 1: When forces change, a structure can become unstable.

Think about stable objects around you. A building's framework directs forces on each part to the foundation. Bridges distribute forces to hold the weight of traffic. Chairs distribute forces so that you don't tumble to the floor. Engineers balance forces to make structures stable. Stability is just as important for structures in motion. Moving vehicles must have the structural integrity to carry a load without falling apart. For example, an airplane must support its own weight and the weight of passengers and baggage. How you control forces and motion is a key part of your interactions with the world around you.

EXPLAIN A stable stack of rectangular blocks collapses when a block is removed. What changed that caused it to collapse?

_____

_____

_____

DRIVING QUESTIONS

As you move through the unit, gather evidence to help you answer the following questions. In your Evidence Notebook, record what you already know about these topics and any questions you have about them.

1. How do engineers analyze and develop solutions to problems?
2. How can an object's motion be described and predicted?
3. How do forces affect motion?
4. How can forces be used to predict stability?

UNIT PROJECT

Go online to download the Unit Project Worksheet to help plan your project.

Design a Support Beam

Some architects try to maximize space by designing very tall buildings. It's a real challenge to find the right mix of strength and weight of materials for constructing these buildings. Not enough strength, or too much weight, and the building can collapse. Design and test different support beams under a load. How can you improve the design of the beam to bear more weight or to support the same force using less mass?

Language Development

Use the lessons in this unit to complete the chart and expand your understanding of the science concepts.

TERM: criterion (plural criteria)

Definition	Example

Similar Term	Phrase

TERM: tradeoff

Definition	Example

Similar Term	Phrase

TERM: acceleration

Definition	Example

Similar Term	Phrase

TERM: vector

Definition	Example

Similar Term	Phrase

TERM: velocity

Definition	Example

Similar Term	Phrase

TERM: force

Definition	Example

Similar Term	Phrase

TERM: friction

Definition	Example

Similar Term	Phrase

TERM: stress

Definition	Example

Similar Term	Phrase

Engineering Design

An x-ray image of the bones in an arm

CAN YOU SOLVE THE PROBLEM?

In 1895, Wilhelm Conrad Röntgen was experimenting with electron beams when he noticed that a nearby screen coated with a fluorescent material glowed during his tests. He shielded the equipment with heavy black paper, but the screen still glowed. He deduced that invisible radiation, which he called *x-radiation*, must have passed through the shield from the equipment to the nearby screen. *X-radiation* emissions are now called *x-rays*.

Very soon after his initial discovery, Wilhelm noticed that x-rays interact with different materials, such as bone and muscle, in different ways. These different interactions could be used to produce images that could show the internal structure of a person or object that is normally not visible to the naked eye. Within the year after Wilhelm's discovery, x-ray technology was being used to help diagnose medical conditions and learn more about the structure of the human body. X-ray technology has been refined based on new discoveries, and this technology is used in many applications, including security screening of luggage and industrial part inspection.

INFER Describe one problem that can be solved using x-ray technology. How do you think this problem was solved before the development of x-ray technology?

_____

_____

_____

 Evidence Notebook As you explore the lesson, gather evidence to explain how both science and engineering practices are used to develop solutions that rely on x-ray technology.

Solving an Everyday Problem

Every day you solve many problems. Most of these problems are small problems, and you consider your options and find a resolution in a very short amount of time. Sometimes, the problem has more serious consequences, so you may carefully consider options before making a decision.

Kai Moves to a New School

FIGURE 1: City buses often have a rack for cyclists to transport their bicycles during a commute.

Kai opens the door of the refrigerator and examines the shelves, looking for something to eat.

Kai's mom enters the kitchen and begins a conversation. "Are you ready to start at your new school on Monday?"

"I guess."

"Have you thought about how you're going to get there?"

"Just take the bus like I did at my old school, right?"

"This school doesn't have yellow school buses. Most people live close to the school, and there are sidewalks and public transit."

"So, I take the regular city bus?"

"That's one option. I could give you a ride, but I leave for work around 8."

"So I would have to get up early, and then sit around waiting for school to open? Never mind. Besides, I like the idea of getting around by myself here," Kai explains. "I'm 15 now."

Kai stops looking for food and looks at the city bus schedule online. "Let's see, classes start at 9," Kai mumbles. "If I catch the 8:40 bus, I should get there in time. With five minutes to walk to the bus stop, I need to leave our apartment by 8:35. That means I get to sleep in compared to my last school."

Kai then looks at the school website to check the rules for taking public transit. "It looks like you can ride the bus for free if you have your school ID." Kai continues looking at the registration forms. "Oh, I just realized that I won't have my ID until Monday, so I won't be able to ride the bus in the morning."

ANALYZE What problem does Kai need to solve?

_____

_____

_____

_____

Kai Evaluates Needs and Wants

"Maybe I could walk, we're not that far away."

Kai resumes looking for food.

"That's a good idea," Kai's mom agrees.

"How long do you think it would take to walk to school?" Kai asks, finally grabbing an apple and some peanut butter.

"We're less than a mile from school, so I think only about 20 minutes. That's almost as fast as the bus, and it could be a good way for you to make some new friends. I think Mr. Suarez's kids walk, maybe you could walk with them."

"Is that the family that lives in the apartment below us? Wouldn't it be weird for me to just join them? I mean we've never even spoken."

"I happened to meet the Suarez family yesterday and we're invited down to visit tomorrow afternoon. So you'll get a chance to meet them before Monday. Why don't we start with that and see how it goes?"

"OK."

Kai peruses maps of the area. "I was just thinking, I have some time now and the weather's nice, maybe we can walk the route and see how long it really takes. Then I can also check out the bus stops, in case I decide to ride the bus."

"OK. Let me find some shoes."

FIGURE 2: Walking is a popular way for students to get to school when they live near the school.

DESIGN What factors (needs, concerns, or desires) can Kai use to help choose the best solution for the problem you identified earlier? List the factors, and then rank them in the second column by order of importance, with 1 being the most important.

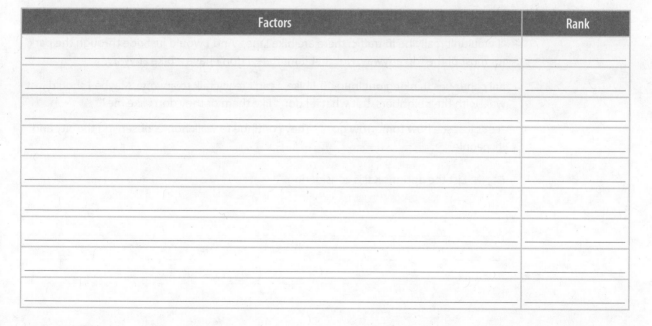

Factors	Rank

Kai Considers Options

As they walk, Kai observes, "The bus stops are covered, so that's nice. Maybe the city bus will be fine."

They look at the bike lanes and the bike trail that goes through the park.

"If I had a bike, that would be something. That trail looks nice. I could get to school in only 10 minutes, I think."

"You never used your last bike," Kai's mom comments with a raised eyebrow.

"I didn't ride because we lived a lot farther from school, and all my friends rode the bus," Kai says, "and also, it snowed for months on end. The weather is a lot nicer here."

Just then, they arrive at the school. "Look—" Kai points, "there are bike racks. My last school didn't have those, so it looks like more students bike here."

FIGURE 3: Many schools have bike racks for students to store their bikes during school hours.

"I'm not sure how I feel about you biking in city traffic," Kai's mom cautioned.

"I wouldn't really be in traffic; there are bike lanes. And I would just ride through the park for most of the trip anyway. Not that it matters, I don't have a bike anyway."

Kai continues thinking out loud, "If I bike, I can't really talk to anyone. Maybe I should just walk with the neighbors, but what if I don't like them or they don't like me?"

"Let's just see how tomorrow goes." They continue to walk home, observing the city and its people.

PLAN List the options Kai is considering.

_____

_____

_____

_____

_____

_____

Kai Simplifies the Problem

Kai's mom recalls, "Hmm . . . I was just thinking, your uncle mentioned the other day that now that your cousin is off at college, they have a spare bike. Since there are bike lanes . . ."

"Can you ask him if I can borrow the bike?"

Kai's mom messages Kai's uncle to ask about using the bike.

As they walk home, Kai continues analyzing options. "I do want to start meeting people. But I also want to be able to get around quickly. If I bike and then decide to walk or take the bus home with someone, can we go pick up my bike later?"

"No, I don't think that's practical," Kai's mom hesitates, "and I don't like the idea of you leaving the bike at school overnight."

FIGURE 4: A bicycle is a cost-effective and energy-efficient mode of transportation.

"True, but it would be nice to have the option to bike. I guess I could just take the bike on the bus or walk with it if I decided to walk with some of the other kids."

Later, as they arrive home Kai realizes "we don't really have much space to keep a bike . . ."

Kai's mom replies, "If you really want to bike, we can find a place."

"You know, after Monday I'll have my ID, and riding the bus will be an easier option. I just need to decide what I want to do Monday morning for now."

The phone dings with Kai's uncle's response.

"Your uncle says he can drop off the bike for you tomorrow. What should I tell him?"

ANALYZE How is Kai simplifying the problem?

_____

_____

_____

_____

Collaborate In a small group, debate the methods Kai could use to get to school on the first day. Together with your group, choose the method that you would recommend to Kai, and explain your choice to the class.

Evidence Notebook People often follow a process similar to Kai's decision process to solve everyday problems. What is the benefit of using a systematic process to solve problems? Describe how a systematic problem-solving process might have led to the application of x-ray technology for medical imaging.

The Engineering Design Process

The engineering design process helps engineers consider all of the relevant information to find the best solution possible. While the process lays out specific steps, engineers may revisit steps whenever needed. As Kai was looking for a solution to the problem of getting to school, Kai followed several steps similar to those in the engineering design process.

Systematically Solving Problems

Engineering design begins by identifying a need or want, and then engineers work to develop a solution to meet the need or want. Engineers systematically develop and test possible solutions to find the best solution possible, given existing constraints. The engineering design process is a formalized process to help guide engineers to develop a solution for any type of problem. While the steps are ordered, they may be revisited at different times during the process when needed.

FIGURE 5: This diagram is a model of the engineering design process. Though steps are usually performed in a particular order, an engineer may return to any previous step any time new information makes it necessary.

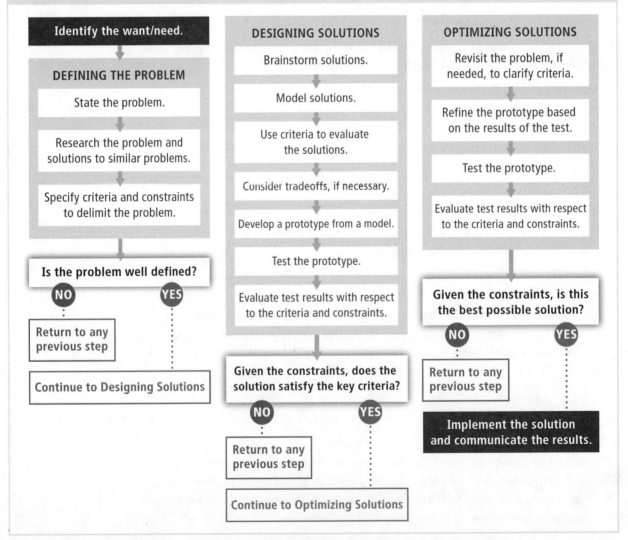

ANALYZE The model of the engineering design process in Figure 5 shows three specific questions engineers use to evaluate their current information and decide whether to return to a previous step or move forward in the process. Are these the only points at which an engineer may evaluate their progress and choose to repeat a previous step? Explain your answer.

_____

_____

_____

_____

Collaborate To *iterate* means to repeat. The engineering design process is iterative because steps can be repeated again and again. Each iteration requires money and time. Which steps of the engineering design process are most likely to be repeated, and why? Compare your views with a partner's.

Defining and Delimiting the Problem

To fully define a problem, an engineer needs to gather as much information as possible about the problem. The engineer might look at the system around the problem, research scientific issues, and find out how other people have solved similar problems.

Language Arts Connection Choose a universal human need, such as access to clean water or food. For your local community, define a problem that is preventing this need from being met. Use multiple sources to gather as much information as possible about the problem. Make a poster to raise awareness for the problem that states, as specifically as possible, the problem that could be solved using the engineering design process.

Engineers delimit a problem, or set the scope for how much of the problem will be solved, by specifying criteria. Criteria (singular *criterion*) are desirable features of a solution. Some criteria may be chosen based on scientific knowledge or desires of the intended user. Other criteria may be set by society. For example, society values clean air, so vehicle designers set criteria to minimize air pollutants emitted from vehicles while they operate.

Constraints are the limitations on a solution. Two of the most common constraints engineers face are budget and time. Constraints prohibit certain solutions. For example, an engine cannot output more energy than it takes in. This is a constraint due to the laws of physics.

When a problem is complex, engineers divide the problem into smaller, more limited problems. These smaller parts of the problem may be solved by several groups working at the same time. Because one group's decisions may affect another group's work, team members must communicate frequently in order to coordinate their work.

DESIGN A team is designing a bicycle. How can this problem be divided into smaller, more limited problems that can be solved simultaneously?

_____

_____

_____

Criteria and Constraints

Engineers need to be able to evaluate how well solutions satisfy criteria and constraints. For example, an engineer may begin by saying they want their solution to be affordable, but affordability varies based on the situation. This criterion would be more measurable if a target price were specified, and then solutions could be evaluated for how closely they match the target price. Criteria vary in importance, from very important to nice to have. Prioritizing criteria is important for guiding design decisions later in the process. An acceptable solution may not satisfy all of the criteria, but it should satisfy the most important criteria.

Constraints may be dictated by society, the laws of physics, or something specific to the problem. A solution is unacceptable if it does not stay within the constraints. A bridge, for example, must be able to support a minimum load without collapsing.

APPLY In a local wildlife reserve, a simple two-plank bridge over a low swampy area has sunk on one side and needs to be replaced. The group that maintains trails has put together their requirements, and a pair of students has offered to build new bridges. Rephrase each statement as a measurable criterion or constraint.

Not too expensive	
Can hold two adults and a dog	
Resistant to weather	
Won't pollute water	

Designing Solutions

After a problem is well defined and delimited, engineers can begin brainstorming possible solutions. The goal of brainstorming is to generate many possible solutions without judgment. Solutions may be based on existing designs or may be newly imagined by the engineer. Creativity is an important aspect of the brainstorming phase.

EXPLAIN When first brainstorming solutions, engineers focus on criteria while largely ignoring constraints. Why do you think this is?

_____

_____

_____

_____

 Evidence Notebook During the design phase of the engineering design process, engineers make many different models of potential solutions. What is the purpose of these models? What types of models might engineers make when designing a structural beam, such as the one in the unit project?

Evaluating Design Solutions

Once engineers have several possible solutions, all of the solutions must be evaluated against the criteria and constraints. Constraints can be used to eliminate solutions—though parts of these solutions may still be considered—remaining solutions can then be judged against the criteria. Solutions that are expected to better satisfy the criteria are more desirable. Parts of different solutions may be combined to better satisfy the criteria.

 Engineering

Tradeoffs

Sometimes, a solution that performs well for one criterion may perform poorly for another criterion or not satisfy all constraints. When this happens, an engineer may need to make a tradeoff, which is when one desired feature is given up in return for another. For example, materials for a more durable bike are more expensive than other materials. In this example, the engineer needs to decide which is more important: a durable bike or a more affordable bike. The engineer needs to make a tradeoff, such as accepting a lower-durability solution in order to make the bike more affordable. Deciding on a tradeoff depends on which criterion is considered more important. Therefore criteria must be carefully prioritized when delimiting engineering problems. Most complex designs may involve making tradeoffs, but not every decision is a tradeoff.

Consider the three different designs for bus stop shelters. Glass's transparency to sunlight might be desirable on cold days but undesirable on hot, sunny days. Both the wood and metal shelters block the sunlight, but the aesthetics (how attractive something is) and durability of these materials differ. Depending on how transparency, durability, and aesthetics are valued, a different material might be seen as a better choice. Aesthetic factors may be difficult to measure.

FIGURE 6: Three bus stop shelters made of different materials

a. wood   b. metal   c. glass

EVALUATE The following describe pairs of characteristics for possible solutions. The criteria are that the bus stop has a long lifetime, low initial price, is low maintenance, and that it looks nice in the neighborhood. Which of the following would be considered tradeoffs? Select all correct answers.

☐ **a.** shorter lifetime / lower initial price

☐ **b.** more attractive / lower initial price

☐ **c.** more maintenance / lower initial price

☐ **d.** more maintenance / higher initial price

☐ **e.** better wind resistance / more attractive

Decision Matrix

A *decision matrix* is a tool engineers use to organize and evaluate how well multiple solutions satisfy each of the criteria. By turning qualitative descriptions, such as *excellent* or *okay,* into numerical values, you can score each solution. The highest overall score should show the best choice among the designs. Each criterion is given a number, called a *weight,* to describe its relative importance. Greater weight means greater importance. Figure 7 shows a decision matrix for three lawnmowers. For this solution, safety is the most important criterion and aesthetics is the least important. Each design is scored from 0–5 depending on how well it meets each criterion—0 means not at all and 5 means perfect. Each score is multiplied by the criterion weight, and then the weighted scores are added to give an overall score that shows how well each design meets the criteria.

FIGURE 7: A decision matrix evaluating three lawnmowers

Design criteria	Weight	Lawnmower 1	Lawnmower 2	Lawnmower 3
Safety	5	4	1	5
Reliability	4	2	3	4
Affordability	2	1	2	1
Aesthetics	1	1	3	0
Total points		31	24	43

EVALUATE Look at the window designs in Figure 8, then complete the decision matrix. Specify two more criteria and assign each criterion a weight. Score each proposed solution and calculate the total points. Compare the designs' scores and then circle the best choice.

Decision matrix for windows in a home				
Design criteria	Weight	Sliding panes	Vertical pivot	Horizontal pivot
Cleanable from inside				
Safety				
Total points				

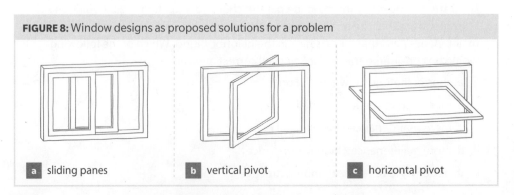

FIGURE 8: Window designs as proposed solutions for a problem

a sliding panes   b vertical pivot   c horizontal pivot

Developing and Testing Prototypes

During the design phase, engineers can model solutions to examine different features. Proposed solutions must be tested because solutions may not perform as expected. A prototype is a model of a solution that can be tested. Prototypes may or may not be made of the same materials as the final product, and they may not be full-scale. When a solution fails to satisfy the criteria and constraints, adjustments must be made, and the solution must be tested again.

ANALYZE Lead is a substance which can be harmful to human health, and is often found in older buildings. A lead test kit should identify lead on wood or drywall accurately at least 95% of the time when the sample is 0.5% or more lead by weight. Which prototypes meet the criteria? Select all correct answers.

- ☐ **a.** Prototype A identifies lead correctly more than 90% of the time.
- ☐ **b.** Prototype B identifies lead correctly 80% of the time on all surfaces.
- ☐ **c.** Prototype C identifies lead correctly 95% of the time on all surfaces.
- ☐ **d.** Prototype D identifies lead correctly 98% of the time on drywall or plaster.
- ☐ **e.** Prototype E identifies lead correctly 97% of the time on drywall, plaster, or wood.

Optimizing Solutions

An engineer may iterate through the testing and modification steps multiple times during the design phase until an acceptable solution is found. Once an acceptable solution is developed, engineers may continue on to optimizing their solution if time and budget permit. To optimize a solution means to make it the best solution possible. An engineer might optimize one part of a design by defining it as a separate problem. When that part is put back into the overall solution, further iterations of the design process may be needed to adjust other parts of the design. With each iteration through the steps of the engineering design process, engineers learn more about the problem and its possible solutions. New information is incorporated in the next iteration; the optimized solution reflects many refinements of the initial design. For example, early x-ray images were blurry and required long exposures. When scientists learned more about the possible damaging effects of x-rays, they looked for ways to limit exposure to the radiation while improving or maintaining the detail of the images.

Communicating a Solution

Communication is an important part of the design process. Engineers communicate with team members, customers, and society in general. Engineers use models, write papers, and use many other methods to communicate their solutions. This helps society and customers understand a solution and allows future solutions to build on earlier solutions.

 Language Arts Connection Present a solution to a problem in two different ways, such as a paragraph and a demonstration. Ask the people to whom you present for feedback on which parts were clear and which parts were hard to follow with each method. Record which types of presentation styles are better for communicating different types of information.

 Evidence Notebook X-ray technology can be used to image industrial parts for inspection as well as the human body. Explain whether these solutions have the same criteria and constraints.

Science, Engineering, and Technology

Scientists investigate aspects of the natural and designed world to understand how they work. Engineers apply science and math to solve problems. Though engineers and scientists have different goals, they share many similar practices, and advances in one field can lead to advances in the other.

Technology

Technologies include human-made products, processes, and systems that people use to achieve a goal. Technology can be as simple as a stick used as a digging tool or as complex as a city's transportation system or a smartphone. Though they have been used for many years, pencils and paper are examples of technologies. Engineers use scientific principles to develop new technologies. As science leads to a deeper understanding of certain phenomena, engineers can apply this new information to improve technology.

The development of x-ray technology enabled scientists and engineers to see structures not usually visible in photo-like images. Scientists have used this technology to learn more about the structures within the human body and other living things. X-ray technology even helped scientists discover the structure of DNA. X-ray technology has also been used to inspect manufactured structures to look for flaws.

Wave-based technologies other than x-ray, such as radar, sonar, ultrasound, gravimetry, and infrared sensing, have enabled scientists in fields from astronomy to zoology to gain a better understanding of the natural world.

EXPLAIN Give an example of a specific technology that has enabled scientists to better understand a phenomenon. How did the technology help?

_____

_____

_____

FIGURE 9: A high-speed camera is capable of capturing several thousand frames per second.

High-speed photography has had many refinements in recent years. Early photos required long exposures and were limited to well-lit static scenes outdoors. As developments in chemistry led to more sensitive film, shorter exposure times became possible, and photos were able to capture quick moments of action. Advances in the field of physics enabled engineers to develop cameras that could record motion too quick to follow with the human eye. This advanced technology altered and improved our understanding of processes that could not be directly observed before.

INFER How might scientists and engineers use high-speed photography differently in their fields? Give examples.

_____

_____

_____

_____

Engineering and Society

A society's needs and wants change over time. The values of society also change; these value changes affect the problems that engineers and other designers address. Even when the problems stay the same, the solutions considered to be acceptable may change.

The relative values of costs, benefits, and risks depend on the community's values and knowledge. They may also depend on scale. For example, burning coal transforms chemical energy into thermal energy, which may be used to warm a home or to warm water in a steam turbine to generate electrical energy in a power plant. In both of these uses, the heat from the burned coal is a desired consequence, a *benefit*. However, burning coal also produces airborne pollution. This airborne pollution is a negative consequence, or *cost*. Initially, the pollution was an acceptable cost, but as coal usage increased and more was learned about its health and environmental effects, burning coal became less desirable to society.

FIGURE 10: The costs, benefits, and risks of using wind turbines to generate electrical energy have changed as technology has improved and society's values have changed.

A *risk* is a cost that may or may not happen. For example, a wind turbine generates electrical energy without directly producing airborne pollution. However, the blades of a wind turbine might disrupt local bat and bird populations, affecting the entire ecosystem of the area. This is a risk.

A community must decide which factors are most important to them and choose a solution that balances the costs, benefits, and risks in a way that is acceptable. Analyzing the relative costs, benefits, and risks of a solution is known as *cost-benefit analysis*, and is another way to analyze and evaluate solutions.

Language Arts Connection Worldwide, electrical energy is produced using different methods, such as geothermal, nuclear, solar, wind, coal, and natural gas. Conduct research about the different methods of generating electrical energy. Evaluate the benefits, costs, and risks of the different methods, taking into consideration society's values. Write a recommendation to the North American Electric Reliability Corporation explaining which sources should be increased in future years and which should be phased out. Provide evidence and reasoning to support your recommendation.

Engineering

3D Printing

Explore Online ▶

FIGURE 11: Complex shapes can be printed with little waste.

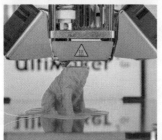

Traditional construction techniques often involve cutting material away from larger pieces to produce the desired forms. The material that is cut away from the larger piece often is unusable for construction, making it wasted material. In contrast, 3D printing only prints out the necessary material to build an object, so less material is wasted.

A 3D-printing machine builds a three-dimensional object in layers, according to coded instructions. Different types of plastic are commonly used in desktop 3D-printing machines. Before scientists understood how to manipulate these plastics, 3D printing with plastics was not a solution available to engineers. Because a variety of specialized shapes can be made without needing to retool the machines used to form them, 3D printing is a popular choice for manufacturing unique items such as prototypes.

IDENTIFY CONSTRAINTS The International Space Station now has a 3D printer. What constraints does this 3D printer work around?

_____

_____

_____

_____

The size of a 3D-printing machine limits the size of object that can be printed. A large 3D printer can even be used to build a house. Normal building materials that can be made fluid, such as concrete, plastic, and mud mixed with straw, can be used to print houses. 3D printing may be quicker than traditional construction methods, saving both time and labor costs. However, the 3D-printing machines necessary to print a house are not common and require a substantial financial investment.

FIGURE 12: A 3D-printed house under construction and completed

Collaborate With a partner, discuss the factors associated with designing and building a 3D-printed home. Compare the social, cultural, and environmental effects of 3D printing to the effects of other methods of construction.

Radiation Poisoning and Radiation Therapy

One of the first applications of x-rays was to form images of bones. The images helped doctors identify problems, such as broken bones or bone spurs, and also helped document human anatomy. In the 1940s and 1950s, x-ray machines were even used in shoe stores to show how well shoes fit a person's foot.

FIGURE 13: Radiation therapy is sometimes used to treat people with cancer.

Over time, scientists realized that repeated exposure to high-energy radiation, such as that used in x-rays, can cause cells to mutate. X-ray technology was refined to minimize the exposure to this radiation while still enabling x-ray images to reveal internal structures. X-ray machines are no longer found in shoe stores. In medical labs, lead aprons and screens are used to limit the exposure of both patients and technicians.

However, radiation's dangerous effects were applied in a new field, using radiation to destroy cancer cells. As concentrated x-rays move through tissue, they have enough energy to cause chemical changes that can damage the DNA in cancer cells.

ANALYZE Identify at least one example of a benefit, a cost, and a risk of using radiation to treat cancer.

_____

_____

_____

_____

Redefining a Problem

Problems are not static. Sometimes new criteria or constraints arise, such as learning more about the possible environmental risks of x-rays. Sometimes no solution meets the original criteria of a problem, such as designing an inexpensive lead test that anyone can use that is accurate on all materials. When new information changes the problem, or no solution works, you redefine the problem.

REVISE Refer to the engineering design process. If you need to redefine your problem, how might this impact your next steps?

○ **a.** Return to defining and delimiting the problem.

○ **b.** Return to brainstorming solutions.

○ **c.** Return to choosing a solution to test.

 Evidence Notebook Scientific discoveries have affected the development of x-ray technology. How has x-ray technology led to solutions related to scientific exploration and engineering?

Case Study: Bridge 9340

Bridge 9340, also called the Interstate 35 West Bridge or the Saint Anthony Falls Bridge, opened in 1967. Bridge 9340 carried traffic across the Mississippi River in downtown Minneapolis. In 2007, the bridge collapsed.

ASK What questions might engineers ask that would help them better understand this failure?

_____

_____

_____

Bridge 9340 Details

FIGURE 14: Bridge 9340 structure from afar and up close

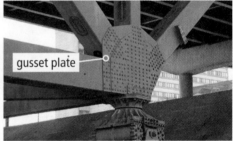

gusset plate

a Overall bridge structure

b Detail showing steel bars connected by a gusset plate

Bridge 9340 (Figure 14a) was a steel truss arch bridge that was about 580 meters (m) long and carried eight lanes of traffic. The section of the bridge over the river spanned 139 m and was supported between hollow concrete columns that rested on the riverbanks.

A bridge must be able to support its own weight plus the weight of any traffic. In a steel truss bridge, straight bars of steel form stable triangles, or trusses. In Bridge 9340, a steel gusset plate held together multiple components at each node. Figure 14b shows how a gusset plate and steel bars were joined using rivets. Trusses are an efficient means of spanning long distances with minimal material—which reduces the weight of the bridge—and are often used in bridge design.

PREDICT Which of the following would help engineers determine the maximum load the bridge would be able to support? Select all correct answers.

☐ **a**. X-ray bridge parts.

☐ **b**. Drive across the bridge.

☐ **c**. Build and test a physical model.

☐ **d**. Perform simulations using physics.

☐ **e**. Take photos of the bridge structure.

Changes over Time

Bridge 9340 operated for 40 years. What types of changes happened in those 40 years? One change was the amount and type of traffic supported by the bridge. Traffic on the bridge had increased, and many vehicles also became larger and heavier. The bridge itself changed due to repairs, weathering, and wear and tear.

FIGURE 15: The pickup truck has been a popular vehicle for many years. This model vehicle shows some of the typical changes vehicles had over the lifespan of the bridge.

a Truck model ca. 1967

b Same model truck ca. 2007

ANALYZE In 1977 the state increased the thickness of the bridge deck, or surface, and in 1998 a median barrier was added. How did these renovations affect the bridge?

○ **a.** made the bridge stronger

○ **b.** made the bridge weaker

○ **c.** increased the load on the bridge

○ **d.** decreased the load on the bridge

In the 1990s, inspections of the bridge found that some elements of the support structure and the deck had weakened. Steel in the joints was found to be corroded, and sections where the bridge deck connects with paved surface roads showed cracks due to fatigue. Bridge 9340 was considered structurally deficient, or in need of repair but not replacement. The bridge was also rated as fracture critical, meaning that a failure in one part could lead to the collapse of the whole.

In the early 2000s, inspection of cracks in the bridge found that they had not grown in the intervening decade. Monitors were attached at various points to collect data about how the load on the bridge was distributed. This information was used to develop a computer model of the bridge, which determined that the main deck was not likely to crack, so it was not recommended that the bridge be replaced. Instead, engineers recommended that the bridge be repaired.

PLAN Think about the technological and societal changes that have happened since 1967. What should engineers consider to ensure that a new bridge design will last for at least 50 years in the future?

_____

_____

_____

_____

_____

Collecting and Analyzing Data

In the summer of 2007, repair work had started on Bridge 9340, but on August 1, 2007, the bridge collapsed during rush hour. After the collapse, inspectors examined data to determine how and why the bridge failed. Inspectors had video data and eye-witness accounts. They were also able to physically examine parts of the bridge. Data showed that the collapse began when four gusset plates in one section fractured. After the gusset plates failed, the load on all nearby parts of the bridge increased, and those parts failed in a chain reaction that quickly took down the entire structure.

FIGURE 16: A photo of the aftermath of the collapse, along with a simulation used to confirm the mode of failure

Explore Online ▶

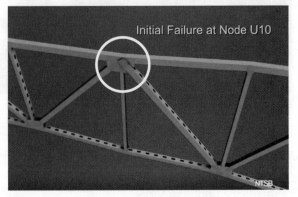

Initial Failure at Node U10

a This image shows the bridge deck largely intact, which supports the idea that the failure happened in the support structure.

b An image from a simulation that shows how the gusset plate failed. The simulation could be used to examine the failure in detail.

Why did the gusset plates fail? On the day of the collapse, repair crews had moved a heavy cement mixer along with sand, gravel, and several other large machines onto the bridge. This additional load combined with the traffic on the open part of the bridge was too much for the truss structure.

Before the collapse, existing bridge models predicted that the bridge should have been able to support the load. Inspectors, like the engineers who modeled the bridge, assumed that the gusset plates were stronger than they actually were and that the bending they noticed during inspections was a manufacturing defect rather than a design defect.

ARGUE How might the erroneous assumption have been detected before the failure?

_____

_____

_____

 Language Arts Connection Review analyses of the Bridge 9340 collapse. What effects did this collapse have on science, engineering, and society? Present your findings as a multimedia presentation.

 Evidence Notebook For over a century, x-ray technology has been used to meet several different needs of society. How can science and engineering practices be used to design solutions using x-rays that will meet society's needs for many years?

Careers in Science

Patent Attorney

Imagine that you spend weeks, months, or even years developing a new invention. You finally are ready to present and sell your invention to customers. However, soon after you start selling, a competitor begins selling an invention almost exactly like the one you designed. You are unable to recoup the investment you made designing your new invention.

To protect your investment in the development of your new process or technology, you may apply for a patent. A patent grants protection to you, the inventor, by legally preventing others from making, using, or selling an invention for a period of time. Patents can be assigned to machines, to processes, to manufactured objects, and to combinations of chemical compounds.

A patent attorney is a type of lawyer that specializes in helping clients complete the legal documents necessary to apply for a patent and defends the client's rights in court if a client's patent is infringed upon. Patent infringement happens when someone who is not the patent owner makes, sells, uses, or even offers to sell something that is equivalent to the process, machine, object, or chemical compound described by the patent.

Patent attorneys must be well versed in both the law and scientific principles so that they are able to evaluate patents and claims of infringement and clearly explain scientific concepts to a jury.

Before earning a law degree, patent lawyers usually study in a science or engineering field for their undergraduate degree. Like other lawyers, patent attorneys must pass the bar exam for the state in which they wish to practice law. For most fields of patent law, they must also pass an exam administered by the U.S. Patent and Trademark Office. Some patent lawyers even work for the government to evaluate new patent applications.

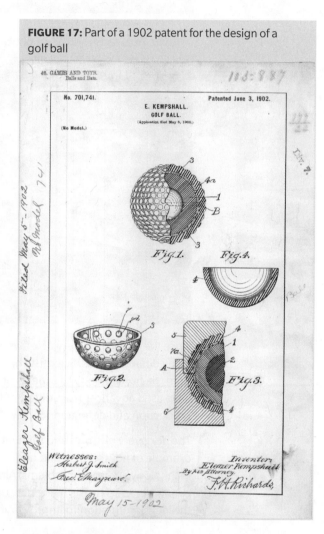

FIGURE 17: Part of a 1902 patent for the design of a golf ball

Language Arts Connection Research and examine the process of applying for a patent. Make a multimedia presentation that explains the requirements for applying for a new patent or defending a patent against infringement, and explain how a patent attorney participates in this process.

LARGE-SCALE ENGINEERING PROJECTS

CIVIL ENGINEERING TEAMS

DEFINE AND DELIMIT A PROBLEM

Go online to choose one of these other paths.

Lesson Self-Check

CAN YOU SOLVE THE PROBLEM?

FIGURE 18: X-ray technology produces images of internal parts of the body to aid doctors in diagnosing medical conditions.

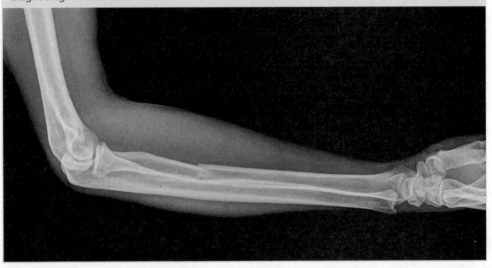

Since the initial discovery of x-rays, x-ray technology has been refined and applied to many different fields. Scientists have used x-rays to explore the structure of many things, from the human body to aspects of the galaxy undetectable by visible light. Engineers have used advances from different fields of science to refine x-ray technology to make the production and detection of x-rays fine-tuned and as safe as possible.

The discovery of x-rays and refinement of x-ray technology over the years is just one example of how science and engineering practices have been used together to develop technology and solve problems. Almost every technology in use today has been refined over time. As scientists make new discoveries or society's values change, engineers use this new information to improve different technologies.

Evidence Notebook Refer to your notes in your Evidence Notebook to make a claim about how science and engineering practices have been used together to develop technology and solve problems. Your explanation should include a discussion of the following points:

Claim How are both science and engineering practices used to develop solutions that rely on x-ray technology?

Evidence What is an example of how science practices contribute to the development of x-ray technology? What is an example of how engineering practices influence the design of x-ray technology?

Reasoning Using the evidence you identified, explain the interdependence of science and engineering during the development of x-ray technology.

CHECKPOINTS

Check Your Understanding

For the next three questions, use the decision matrix for designs of a handheld can opener.

Criteria	Weight	Design 1	Design 2	Design 3
Comfortable to hold while applying force	4	3	4	5
Easy to use	4	5	4	3
Affordable	2	4	5	1
Durable	1	3	2	1
Total points		43	44	35

1. Complete the statements.

   Design 1 | 2 | 3 is the most comfortable.

   Design 1 | 2 | 3 is the easiest to use.

   Design 1 | 2 | 3 is the most affordable.

   Design 1 | 2 | 3 has the best score, even though it is not the most comfortable | affordable.

2. Which claims about the can opener criteria are supported by the decision matrix? Select all correct answers.

   ☐ **a.** Durability is more important than price.

   ☐ **b.** Price is more important than durability.

   ☐ **c.** Comfort is more important than price.

   ☐ **d.** Ease of use is more important than comfort.

3. Which of the following are ways to restate the criterion "Durable" in a way that is measurable? Select all correct answers.

   ☐ **a.** will last at least two years

   ☐ **b.** will not break when dropped

   ☐ **c.** can be used at least 100 times without damage

   ☐ **d.** can be dropped 1 m onto a tile floor without damage

4. Select the correct term to complete the statement.

   The best solution may not satisfy all of the criteria | constraints.

5. A community is building a small footbridge along a trail in a national forest to help people cross a small ravine. The following are expected consequences of this action. Write "B" to identify benefits and "C" to identify costs of this action.

   _____ **a.** people able to enjoy more of the forest

   _____ **b.** wildlife disturbed by pedestrians

   _____ **c.** less disturbance of plants in the ravine

   _____ **d.** trees removed for additional parking

6. Select the correct terms to complete the statements.

   Technology and society influence each other | outside elements. Society frames the practical problems | solutions technology is designed to address. When society adopts a new technology, the society is often | never changed by that technology.

For question 7, use the following criteria for the design of a car.

Criteria
Fuel-efficient
Safe in a collision
Affordable to purchase
Affordable to maintain
Space for four or more adult passengers
Cargo space for four large suitcases

7. The following statements describe an aspect of a new solution compared with a current solution. Select all statements that describe a tradeoff being made for a new solution.

   ☐ **a.** safer in a collision / space for two adults instead of six

   ☐ **b.** cheaper to purchase / less safe in a collision

   ☐ **c.** more expensive to maintain / less safe in a collision

   ☐ **d.** more fuel-efficient / more expensive to maintain

CHECKPOINTS (continued)

8. Suppose a practical, affordable flying car were invented. How might this affect society?

_____

_____

_____

_____

9. Give an example of how the availability of high-speed, affordable Internet access has changed society.

_____

_____

_____

_____

10. The table shows several criteria for a new high school's bus routes. Which criterion do you think is the most important? Explain your reasoning.

Criteria
No students walk more than 150 m to their bus stop.
Every bus stop serves at least five students.
No student has more than a 1-hour trip.
No route has more than 10 stops.
No route is more than 15 km.

_____

_____

_____

_____

_____

MAKE YOUR OWN STUDY GUIDE

 In your Evidence Notebook, design a study guide that supports the main ideas from this lesson:

Everyday problems can be solved systematically.

The engineering design process guides engineers to develop the best solution for a problem. Changes in societal values may change the criteria or constraints of a solution.

Scientific discoveries may enable new engineering solutions, and new engineering solutions may enable more scientific discoveries.

Remember to include the following information in your study guide:
- Use examples that model main ideas.
- Record explanations for the phenomena you investigated.
- Use evidence to support your explanations. Your support can include drawings, data, graphs, laboratory conclusions, and other evidence recorded throughout the lesson.
- Consider how science and engineering are used to develop technologies and how society's values affect scientific discoveries and engineering.

Modeling Motion

A skier's jump is photographed at equal time intervals.

CAN YOU SOLVE THE PROBLEM?

During a ski big air competition, skiers jump off a ramp and fly through the air while doing tricks such as spins and flips. The photo shows part of a skier's jump. The photo is a multiple-exposure photo that captures details of the jump that can be difficult to observe in real time. To produce this photo, a camera recorded images of the skier at equal time intervals, and a computer was used to combine them into one image. The many images taken in a short interval captured the rapid changes in position of the jumping skier and trace the path of the skier over time.

PREDICT This multiple-exposure photo does not show the skier's full jump. What do you think happens to the skier in the rest of the jump?

_____

_____

_____

_____

 Evidence Notebook As you explore the lesson, gather evidence to explain how information about an object's past and present motion can be used to predict its future motion.

Representing Motion

Imagine that you and a friend are planning to meet at the library. You want to meet at the library's door, but you will travel to the library from different locations in the city.

FIGURE 1: A and B are starting positions of two friends on their way to the library.

Collaborate Write a description of the path to the door of the library starting from Position A in Figure 1 while a partner writes a description of the path starting from Position B. Trade descriptions, and follow your partner's directions from your starting point. How does the starting position affect where you end up?

FIGURE 2: Two frames of reference used to describe motion

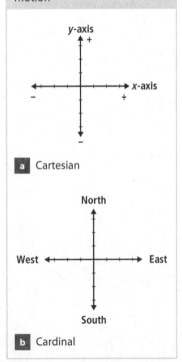

a Cartesian

b Cardinal

INFER Use evidence from your experience to infer what information scientists need to include when communicating about position and motion.

_____

_____

_____

Frame of Reference

Representations of motion, such as a multiple-exposure photo or a graph of position over time, enable scientists to quantify motion and look for patterns. Descriptions of motion should be accurate, and the usage of units should be consistent. Lack of precision can cause confusion. For example, the position description "5 m" might mean a position "5 m above the floor" or a position "5 m left of the door."

Motion is a change in position relative to something else. Motion is described within a frame of reference, which is a system of coordinates that has a fixed origin. Figure 2 shows two common frames of reference that you might use to describe motion and position in science class or in everyday life. Examples of origins might include things such as oneself, the steps in front of the local library, or the bottom left corner of a desk. The observed position and motion of an object depend on the frame of reference of the observer.

Hands-On Lab

Frame of Reference in Motion

When police officers investigate car accidents, they may interview several witnesses. People watching from nearby sidewalks or other cars will make different observations of the motion of the cars in the accident. The officers must interpret each description based on frame of reference of that witness.

In this activity, you will record the same event from various frames of reference, like the example in Figure 3.

RESEARCH QUESTION How does frame of reference change the description of a moving object?

MAKE A CLAIM

How does the location of a camera affect the way motion is captured?

_____

_____

_____

FIGURE 3: Different perspectives of the same car

a Car filmed from the side

b Car filmed from behind

POSSIBLE MATERIALS

- meterstick
- tape
- video-recording device, such as a cell phone
- wind-up or remote-control car

SAFETY INFORMATION

- Wear safety goggles during the setup, hands-on, and takedown segments of the activity.

- If recording the car from above, make sure to attach the camera securely to its support. It should not be placed above shoulder height, and one student in the group should be on-hand to catch the assembly should it begin to fall.

- Immediately pick up any items dropped on the floor so they do not become a slip/fall hazard.

PLAN THE INVESTIGATION

In your Evidence Notebook, develop a procedure to investigate how frames of reference change how you describe the motion of the car. Make sure your teacher approves your procedure and safety plan before proceeding. When developing your procedure, consider the following:

- To compare the same event from different frames of reference, you will need to be able to recreate the car's motion exactly in repeated trials.

- In some trials, the camera will be stationary. Adjust the car's path and the camera's position so that the path fits in the frame of the camera.

- In your plan, include a list of the camera shots that describes the position of the camera and the motion of the car. Also include a description of the camera's motion if it moves during a shot. Plan to perform multiple trials of each shot.

ANALYZE

1. In your Evidence Notebook, draw the experimental setup for at least two of your trials. Label key components, and define your coordinate system.

2. When the camera is stationary, what determines the perceived direction of the car's motion?

_____

_____

3. Suppose you film the car from the side. In one trial, the camera is moving at the same speed in the same direction as the car. In another trial, the camera is moving at the same speed in the opposite direction. If the car's speed is 0.3 meters per second (m/s) relative to its surroundings, what will its apparent speed relative to the camera be in each trial?

_____

_____

_____

4. How does the frame of reference affect how an observer perceives motion? In this lab, the camera is the observer, and the video recording is what an observer would perceive.

_____

_____

_____

DRAW CONCLUSIONS

Write a conclusion that addresses each of the points below.

Claim How does the location of the camera affect the way motion is captured? Was your initial claim correct?

Evidence What evidence from your investigation supports your claim?

Reasoning Explain how the evidence you gave supports your claim. Describe in detail the connections between the evidence you cited and the argument you are making.

_____

_____

_____

_____

_____

_____

Evidence Notebook How might viewing the beam prototypes in your unit project from different frames of reference yield information to help you improve the design?

Position and Changes in Position

If you were to describe your position, you may say "at my desk" or "by the teacher." You would describe your position compared to some other point in space, like the desk or the teacher. In science, the point in space you refer to is the origin in a frame of reference.

Modeling Changes in Position

When something moves or is in motion, how it moves can be described with distance, direction, and time. *Displacement* is a change in position in a frame of reference that describes the distance and direction of an object's final position from its initial position. Examples of displacement include moving right 5 units on graph paper or walking 8 blocks north on a city grid.

Quantities used to describe motion and other quantities in science are either scalars or vectors. A *scalar* is a quantity that has magnitude (duration or size) but no direction, such as 15 minutes (min) or 8.3 meters (m). A *vector* is a quantity that has both magnitude and direction, such as 14 centimeters (cm) forward, 0.09 millimeters per second (mm/s) left, or −15 m, where the negative sign indicates direction in a frame of reference.

Vector variables are given in bold, for example **v**. A scalar that gives the magnitude of a vector but not the direction is indicated using absolute value notation as $|\mathbf{v}|$ or using scalar notation as v. Position is a vector because it has magnitude and direction from the origin in a frame of reference. Displacement, $\Delta\mathbf{x}$, is a

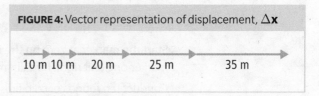

FIGURE 4: Vector representation of displacement, $\Delta\mathbf{x}$

10 m 10 m   20 m   25 m   35 m

vector that represents a change in the position vector **x**, as shown in Figure 4. The symbol Δ is the Greek letter Delta, and it means *change in*. Distance is a scalar quantity. If an object travels in a straight path, the distance, how far it traveled, is the magnitude of its displacement, how much its position changed. For example, the displacement $\Delta\mathbf{x} = -8$ m corresponds to the distance of 8 m. In a 100 m race, runners travel a distance of 100 m, and the displacement is 100 m forward from the starting line.

Vector quantities can be modeled with arrows. The length of the arrow corresponds to the magnitude of the vector, and the orientation of the arrow corresponds to its direction.

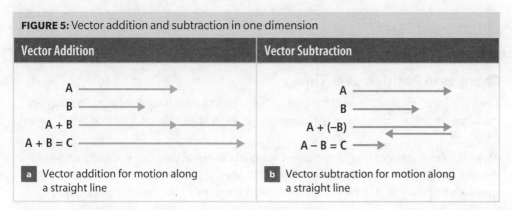

FIGURE 5: Vector addition and subtraction in one dimension

Vector Addition	Vector Subtraction
A ⟶ B ⟶ A + B ⟶ A + B = C ⟶	A ⟶ B ⟶ A + (−B) ⟶ A − B = C ⟶
a Vector addition for motion along a straight line	**b** Vector subtraction for motion along a straight line

Arrow models of vectors can be helpful when adding and subtracting vectors, as shown in Figure 5. To add two vectors, align the head (triangle end) of the first arrow with the tail (flat end) of the second arrow. Draw a new arrow from the tail of the first arrow to the head of the second arrow. This new arrow represents the magnitude and direction of the resultant vector. Subtracting vectors is similar, except that you would align the subtracted arrow −**B** in the opposite direction as the original vector **B**. From there, subtraction is the addition of a negative term, so the head-tail method of vector addition can be applied.

Modeling Displacement

The magnitude of displacement is sometimes but not always equal to the distance an object travels. In this activity, you will model a random path with a number line, a marker, and a coin. You will move the marker one unit with each coin flip, with the direction determined by the coin flip result.

MATERIALS
· safety goggles   · coin   · marker   · number line

SAFETY INFORMATION

· Wear safety goggles during the setup, hands-on, and takedown segments of the activity.
· Immediately pick up any items dropped on the floor so they do not become a slip/fall hazard.

CARRY OUT THE INVESTIGATION

· Start the marker at zero on the number line, and flip the coin. For heads, move the marker one unit right; for tails, move one unit left.
· Conduct ten rounds of coin flips.
· In your Evidence Notebook, use vector arrow models to determine the displacement of your marker after ten coin flips.

ANALYZE

How does the distance traveled by the coin compare to its displacement after ten flips? Compare your results with those of other groups.

_____

_____

_____

Changes in Position over Time

The velocity of an object is a vector giving its speed in a particular direction. The *average velocity* over a time interval is the displacement of the object divided by that time interval.

ANNOTATE A sprinter is photographed at equal time intervals. Draw vectors arrows to indicate the displacement between adjacent images of the sprinter. What happens to the sprinter's displacement between images? What happens to the sprinter's velocity?

Average and Instantaneous Velocity

A dog runs across a field in a straight line, and its motion can be analyzed with a position-time graph (Figure 6). The x-axis shows time, t; the y-axis shows position, **x**. The change in the y-value between any two points gives the dog's displacement over that time interval. Dividing the change in y (position) by the change in x (time) will give the average velocity in that interval.

Place a straight edge between the points for $t = 0$ s and $t = 4$ s in Figure 6. The slope of the line (rise ÷ run) is equal to the runner's average velocity during that segment.

$$\text{average velocity} = \frac{\text{displacement}}{\text{change in time}} = \frac{\mathbf{x}_{final} - \mathbf{x}_{initial}}{t_{final} - t_{initial}} = \frac{\Delta\mathbf{x}}{\Delta t}$$

To find the average velocity in the first 4 s, and over the whole graph:

$$\mathbf{v} = \frac{20\text{ m} - 0\text{ m}}{4\text{ s} - 0\text{ s}} = 5\text{ m/s forward}$$

$$\mathbf{v} = \frac{100\text{ m} - 0\text{ m}}{10\text{ s} - 0\text{ s}} = 10\text{ m/s forward}$$

Over the entire 100 m, the average velocity was 10 m/s forward, but this number does not capture the velocity at each point in the dog's path. The average velocity in the first 2 s was slower, and the average velocity in the last 2 s was faster. The average velocity only conveys the total motion over that interval, not the precise velocity at any single moment. The dog's momentary velocity at one point in time is called the *instantaneous velocity*.

If the graph were a straight line, it would indicate that displacement changed linearly over time, and so velocity was constant. That velocity would be equal to the slope of the line. A curved line on a position-time graph indicates that the velocity is changing over time.

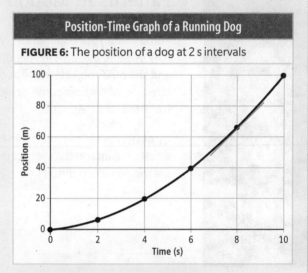

Position-Time Graph of a Running Dog

FIGURE 6: The position of a dog at 2 s intervals

EVALUATE Determine whether the question asks about an average or instantaneous velocity.

	Average velocity	Instantaneous velocity
How fast must you bike to get there in half an hour?	○	○
What is the fastest she can run?	○	○
What is the minimum speed for takeoff?	○	○
How fast did he run the first 5 miles of the marathon?	○	○

 Evidence Notebook Look back at the multiple-exposure photo of the sprinter as well as the position versus time graph for the dog in Figure 6. If the sprinter and dog were instead slowing down, how would the photo and graph look different?

Acceleration in One Dimension

One-dimensional motion is motion along a straight line. A rising elevator, a container lifted by a crane, and the ball in Figure 7 are examples of objects in one-dimensional vertical motion. A moving train car, a person walking down a hallway, and the ball in Figure 8 are examples of objects in one-dimensional horizontal motion.

FIGURE 7: A ball falls freely.

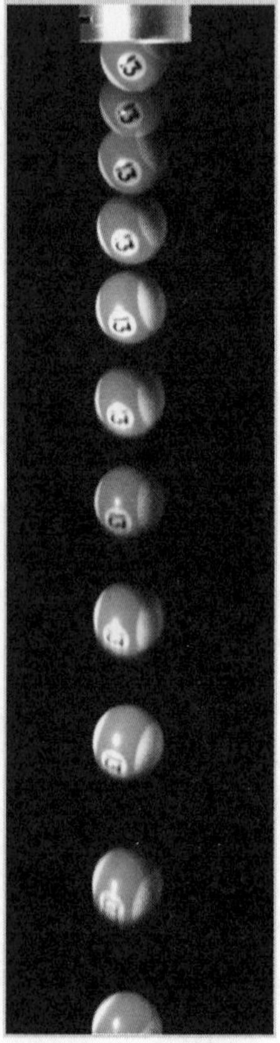

FIGURE 8: A ball rolls across a table.

Patterns

Patterns in Motion

Throughout your experiences, you observe many different patterns in motion. You may observe patterns in speed: some objects speed up, some objects slow down, and still other objects move at constant speeds. You may also observe patterns in direction of motion: some objects move in straight lines, some move in circles, and some follow other paths.

EVALUATE For the images in Figure 7 and Figure 8, the balls were photographed at equal time intervals. What patterns do you see in the motions of the two balls? How are their motions different?

_____

_____

_____

_____

Changes in Velocity

For an object in motion, the object's position is always changing, and its velocity can also change. Acceleration is a change in velocity over time. Like displacement and velocity, acceleration is a vector quantity because it has magnitude and direction. When the acceleration of an object is in the direction of motion, the object speeds up. When the acceleration is in the opposite direction, the object slows down. Acceleration is the rate of change of velocity, $\Delta \mathbf{v}/\Delta t$.

$$\mathbf{a} = \frac{\mathbf{v}_{final} - \mathbf{v}_{initial}}{t_{final} - t_{initial}} = \frac{\mathbf{v}_f - \mathbf{v}_i}{t_f - t_i} = \frac{\Delta \mathbf{v}}{\Delta t}$$

Horizontal Motion

Suppose a ball rolls to the right, moving at constant velocity. The ball hits a spring, and the ball slows as the spring compresses. The ball comes to rest and then accelerates to the left as the spring expands. In this frame of reference, right is defined as the positive direction.

ANALYZE Use the models in Figures 9 and 10 to complete the table. Use only +, −, and 0 to indicate whether the quantity is positive, negative, or zero at that time.

FIGURE 9: The ball's speed decreases as the spring compresses, indicating acceleration opposite to the direction of motion. As the spring expands, it accelerates the ball to the left.

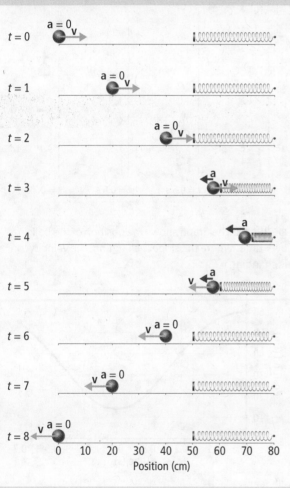

Time, t	Position, x	Velocity, v	Acceleration, a
0 s	0 cm	_____	_____
1 s	20 cm	_____	_____
2 s	40 cm	_____	_____
3 s	57 cm	_____	_____
4 s	67 cm	_____	_____
5 s	57 cm	_____	_____
6 s	40 cm	_____	_____
7 s	20 cm	_____	_____
8 s	0 cm	_____	_____

FIGURE 10: The graph shows the position of the ball over time. Where the slope is changing, the velocity is changing.

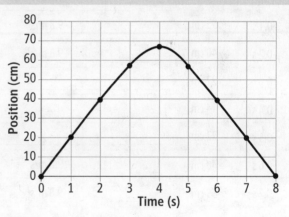

EXPLAIN Describe the acceleration of the ball before, during, and after hitting the spring. How does the spring affect the velocity and acceleration of the ball?

_____

_____

_____

If the spring were removed, the ball would continue moving to the right without slowing, speeding up, or changing direction. This uniform motion would look the same as the motion in Figure 8. Because the ball's displacement would be equal in equal time intervals, its velocity would be constant, and its acceleration would be zero.

Vertical Motion

Suppose that a ball is dropped and falls freely as it is accelerated by gravity. The magnitude of acceleration due to gravity is 9.8 meters per second squared (m/s^2) for a freely falling object near Earth's surface. When the ball hits a spring, the spring slows it until it stops. The spring then pushes upward on the ball until the ball is launched back into the air.

ANALYZE Use the models in Figures 11 and 12 to complete the table. Use only +, –, and 0 to indicate whether the quantity is positive, negative, or zero at that time. In this frame of reference, downward is defined as the negative direction.

FIGURE 11: A ball is held at 60 cm and then dropped onto a spring, compressing the spring. The spring then expands, pushing up on the ball and launching it into the air.

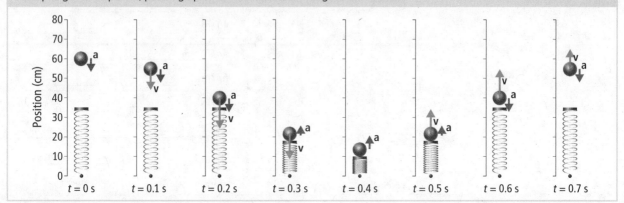

Time, t	Position, x	Velocity, v	Acceleration, a
0 s	60 cm		$-9.8 \ m/s^2$
0.1 s	55 cm		$-9.8 \ m/s^2$
0.2 s	40 cm		$-9.8 \ m/s^2$
0.3 s	22 cm		
0.4 s	14 cm		
0.5 s	22 cm		
0.6 s	40 cm		$-9.8 \ m/s^2$
0.7 s	55 cm		$-9.8 \ m/s^2$

FIGURE 12: The graph shows the position of the ball over time. Where the slope is changing, the velocity is changing.

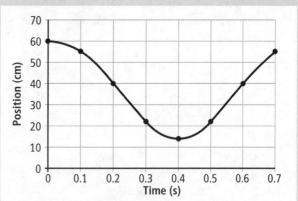

EXPLAIN Order the list to describe the ball's motion as it drops onto the spring.

_____ **a.** The acceleration of the ball decreases as the spring extends.

_____ **b.** The push from the spring exceeds the pull of gravity. The ball momentarily comes to rest.

_____ **c.** The velocity decreases due to gravitational acceleration in the negative direction.

_____ **d.** Acceleration of the ball changes directions from negative to positive due to an upward push from the spring.

__1__ **e.** The ball is dropped from rest and then accelerates in the negative direction.

_____ **f.** The ball leaves the spring with a large velocity in the positive direction. The acceleration due to gravity is in the negative direction.

An object is said to be in free fall when gravity is the only force acting on it. Near Earth's surface, objects in free fall have a constant acceleration downward. Because downward is usually defined as the negative direction, acceleration due to gravity is often shown with a negative sign.

For an object in free fall, the vertical component of the object's motion exhibits constant acceleration and thus a changing velocity. Rising objects have a velocity in the positive direction that is decreased by gravity over time, and falling objects have a velocity in the negative direction that is increased by gravity over time.

 Hands-On Activity

Falling Objects

In this activity, you will explore the effect of mass on the acceleration of falling objects.

MATERIALS

· safety goggles   · two or more objects of different masses

SAFETY INFORMATION

- Wear safety goggles during the setup, hands-on, and takedown segments of the activity.
- Immediately pick up any items dropped on the floor so they do not become a slip/fall hazard.

CARRY OUT THE INVESTIGATION

- Align the bottoms of two objects that have different masses and drop them. Do they hit the ground at about the same time, or at different times? Repeat several times with different objects and from different starting heights.
- In your Evidence Notebook, describe what happened in terms of the objects' masses. Does more mass make an object hit the ground first, or does mass have no effect?

ANALYZE

In a vacuum chamber with no air resistance, would a feather and hammer dropped from the same height hit the ground at the same time? Explain your reasoning with evidence from your investigation.

_____

_____

_____

_____

 Evidence Notebook Compare the motion of the ball falling and rolling horizontally in Figures 7 and 8 with the motion of the skier. Describe the velocity and acceleration of each ball and of the skier. Define up and right as positive.

Motion in Two Dimensions

FIGURE 13: The ball on the left falls freely with no horizontal velocity, and the ball on the right is launched with an initial horizontal velocity and then falls freely.

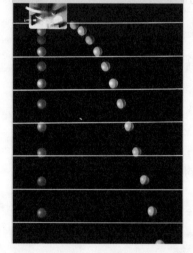

What do a thrown ball, a falling branch, and a rocket in flight that has burned all its fuel have in common? All three objects are projectiles, which are objects acted on only by gravity.

ANALYZE Compare the motions of the projectiles in Figure 13. How does the vertical motion of the ball on the left compare to the vertical motion of the ball on the right? What about the horizontal motions of the projectiles?

_____

_____

_____

_____

Components of Two–Dimensional Motion

The two-dimensional motion of an object can be broken into horizontal and vertical components. The basketball in Figure 14 is a projectile, launched into the air with an initial diagonal push. At the end of the push, the ball is moving diagonally upward, and then the ball traces a path according to its initial motion and the effect of gravity.

FIGURE 14: The motion of the basketball is broken down into horizontal and vertical components.

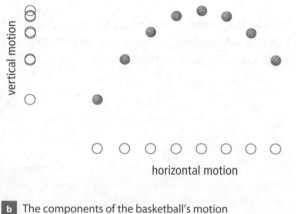

a The basketball in motion

b The components of the basketball's motion

The horizontal component of the motion looks like that of a ball rolling across a table; it moves to the right at constant velocity. The vertical component of the motion looks like a ball thrown straight upward, accelerating in free fall. Combining the horizontal and vertical motions yields a curved path.

The basketball's motion can be described using vectors that specify its position, velocity, and acceleration at any point or overall. To practice representing and analyzing two-dimensional motion with vectors, consider an example of navigating your community.

MODEL Starting at the door of the town hall, you travel to the door of the library, staying on the roads. Use vector arrows to model your path. Because vectors only indicate motion in a straight line, start a new vector arrow each time you change direction. Once you have modeled your full path from the town hall door to the library door, draw another vector arrow to represent your total displacement.

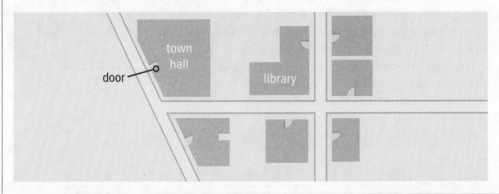

As shown in Figure 15, any vector can be described by a pair of vectors giving the horizontal and vertical components. However, if the vector aligns with the x-axis, the vertical component is zero, and if the vector aligns with the y-axis, the horizontal component is zero. The first vector arrow in your model, starting at the door of the town hall, has both a vertical and horizontal component. The second has only a horizontal component, and the third vector, ending at the door of the library, has only a vertical component. Just like the vectors in Figure 15, you can combine the horizontal and vertical components of your path vectors to find your overall displacement vectors in the x- and y-directions. Combining the x- and y-vectors yields your total displacement vector, starting at the town hall door and ending at the library door. Notice that vector arrows are always combined with the tail (flat end) of one vector arrow B_x connected to the head (triangle end) of the previous arrow B_y.

FIGURE 15: To combine vectors in two dimensions, **A** is broken into a horizontal portion A_x and a vertical portion A_y. The same is done to **B**. These horizontal and vertical components are combined to yield **C**, called the resultant.

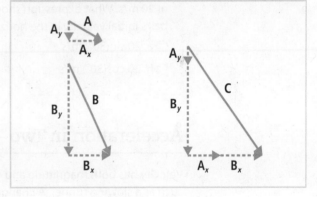

APPLY Draw the horizontal and vertical components of vectors **B** and **C,** as shown for vector **A.** Label the components. Check that your component vectors are arranged head to tail.

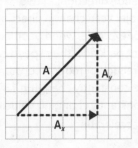

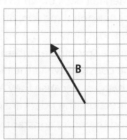

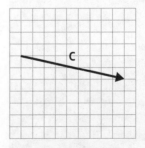

Trigonometry and Vectors

Trigonometry is the branch of mathematics concerned with the relationships between sides and angles of triangles. Physicists use trigonometry to calculate the components of an object's velocity based on its speed and direction. Horizontal and vertical component vectors form right triangles as in Figure 16, so the trigonometric ratios in Figure 17 can be used to find the lengths of the vectors and the angles between them. The symbol θ is the Greek letter theta, representing the size of an angle.

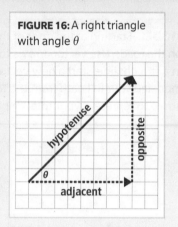

FIGURE 16: A right triangle with angle θ

FIGURE 17: The basic trigonometric relationships for a right triangle

$\sin\theta = \dfrac{\text{opposite}}{\text{hypotenuse}}$	$\cos\theta = \dfrac{\text{adjacent}}{\text{hypotenuse}}$	$\tan\theta = \dfrac{\text{opposite}}{\text{adjacent}}$

For a vector **A** that makes an angle θ with the horizontal, the magnitude of the horizontal component is given by $|\mathbf{A}|\cos\theta$ and the vertical component by $|\mathbf{A}|\sin\theta$.

EVALUATE A student kicks a soccer ball upward at a 30° angle with an initial speed of 20 m/s. What expression should the student use to calculate the magnitude of the ball's initial velocity in the horizontal direction?

○ **a.** 20 sin(30°) m/s

○ **c.** 20 tan(30°) m/s

○ **b.** 20 cos(30°) m/s

○ **d.** 20 m/s

Acceleration in Two–Dimensional Motion

Velocity has both magnitude and direction. A change in velocity can be a change in speed, such as a slowing runner. A change in direction is also a change in velocity, such as a bicyclist turning. Acceleration is any change in velocity: magnitude, direction, or both.

FIGURE 18: People on a spinning ride move at constant speed but are also constantly changing direction.

Change in Direction

Picture a ball thrown straight up in the air. Traveling in only one dimension, the ball had to slow, stop, and then fall back down to change direction. In two-dimensional motion, an object can change direction without slowing down. For example, when people ride a spinning amusement park ride, their speed can be constant while their direction of motion constantly changes. Because they are constantly changing direction, the riders are constantly changing velocity and therefore constantly accelerating.

Change in Speed and Direction

If the acceleration of an object is parallel to the direction of the object's motion, the object will slow down or speed up. If the acceleration is not parallel to the direction of the object's motion, the object will turn in the direction of the acceleration.

A projectile launched with a horizontal velocity shows both effects of acceleration. The vertical component of the motion is parallel to the acceleration and shows a change in speed. The horizontal component of the motion, perpendicular to the acceleration, does not change its speed. The projectile curves in the direction of the acceleration, downward.

FIGURE 19: In projectile motion, the path can be broken into two parts. The vertical motion shows an acceleration, while the horizontal motion is at constant speed. A downward acceleration means that the vertical speed of a horizontally fired projectile increases, leading to a curved path. Compare the projectile's path with the horizontal path it would follow in the absence of gravity.

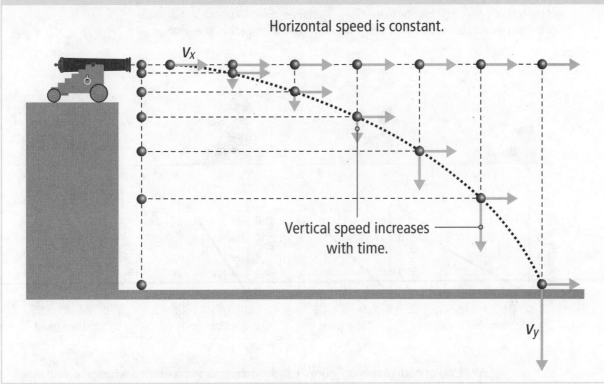

Horizontal speed is constant.

V_x

Vertical speed increases with time.

V_y

As shown in Figure 19, a projectile moves horizontally at a constant speed; near Earth's surface, it will accelerate downward at a constant rate of acceleration. The result of the two motions is a parabolic curve, a specific mathematic type of curved path where horizontal position changes linearly and vertical position changes as the square of time.

PREDICT Look at Figure 20. Predict the path of the fire retardant after it is dropped from the plane. In your prediction, state any assumptions you made about the fire retardant's acceleration and velocity.

_____

_____

_____

_____

_____

_____

FIGURE 20: An aircraft is dropping a fire retardant onto a wildfire.

Motion on a Ramp

An object placed on a horizontal surface will not move if it is not pushed or pulled. If you lift one end of the surface to make a ramp, the object starts to slide. As the angle of the ramp increases, the object's motion approaches that of an object in free fall. Consider the objects sliding down ramps in Figure 21, and examine the graphs of their velocities.

Velocity Graphs for Ramps at Different Angles

FIGURE 21: The graphs show the velocity of each object over time, where the direction of the object's velocity is parallel to the ramp. The slope of each line, calculated as the change in velocity divided by the change in time, is the magnitude of acceleration.

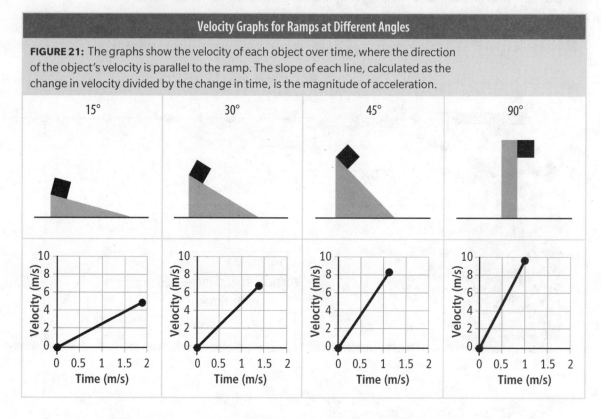

APPLY For each graph in Figure 21, is the acceleration constant or changing with time? Explain your reasoning using evidence.

_____

_____

ANALYZE How does the angle of the ramp affect the acceleration of the object?

_____

_____

EVALUATE Calculate the acceleration of the object on each ramp. How does the magnitude of each object's acceleration compare to the acceleration due to gravity?

_____

_____

_____

_____

Calculating with Acceleration

FIGURE 22: The basketball is in projectile motion, which is a combination of accelerating and non-accelerating motion.

Examine the basketball's motion shown in Figure 22. The basketball, once the player has thrown it, is an example of an object in projectile motion.

EXPLAIN Suppose a basketball player is passing the ball. Her teammate wants to know where the ball will land so he can catch it. What do you need to know about the ball's motion to calculate where it will land?

_____

_____

_____

You likely identified that you would need information about the ball's initial position, velocity, and acceleration. With these pieces of data, you could use the following equations to make a mathematical model of the basketball's flight. The subscripts *i* and *f* indicate *initial* and *final* conditions, respectively. The subscripts *x* and *y* represent components of velocity or acceleration in the horizontal and vertical directions, respectively, just as the variables *x* and *y* represent position in the *x* and *y* directions.

Non-accelerating motion	Accelerating motion
$x_f = x_i + v_{i,x}t$ $y_f = y_i + v_{i,y}t$	$x_f = x_i + v_{i,x}t + (1/2)\,a_x t^2$ $y_f = y_i + v_{i,y}t + (1/2)\,a_y t^2$

Projectile motion can be broken into horizontal and vertical components, so the equations can be used to analyze each component separately. Because these equations only consider one dimension at a time, direction can be indicated with positive and negative signs according to the frame of reference. The variables *v* and *a* represent the magnitudes of velocity and acceleration, and they can be entered into the equations as negative or positive based on their direction.

ANALYZE Which expression would you use to calculate the final vertical position of a projectile, like the basketball?

○ **a.** $x_f = x_i + v_{i,x}t$

○ **b.** $y_f = y_i + v_{i,y}t$

○ **c.** $x_f = x_i + v_{i,x}t + (1/2)\,a_x t^2$

○ **d.** $y_f = y_i + v_{i,y}t + (1/2)\,a_y t^2$

For projectiles moving only under the influence of gravity, the horizontal motion will be non-accelerating motion, with constant velocity. The acceleration due to gravity is only in the vertical direction, so it will not change the horizontal speed. The vertical motion will be accelerating motion, with velocity increasing at the rate of acceleration due to gravity.

Evidence Notebook Analyze the motion of the basketball in Figure 22 by considering the horizontal and vertical components separately. How does this motion compare to the skier's motion? Sketch an analysis of the skier's motion similar to that in Figure 14b. How are one-dimensional and two-dimensional motion related?

Engineering

Motion of Humanitarian Airdrop Packages

FIGURE 23: Relief organizations sometimes use airdrops to deliver aid.

After natural disasters or during conflicts, delivering food and medical supplies to people who need them can be difficult. Relief organizations may deliver supplies using airdrops, operations where an aircraft drops a package that lands at a target location.

Use a Mathematical Model

Suppose that a time-sensitive medication needs to be delivered to an isolated community. Engineers evaluate two delivery methods. The first is a hover drop, where the package drops from an aircraft that hovers directly over the target. The second is a fly-by drop, where the package drops from an aircraft as it flies by the target.

SOLVE Use the equations for accelerating and non-accelerating motion as appropriate to calculate the time needed for each package to land. Report to two significant figures.

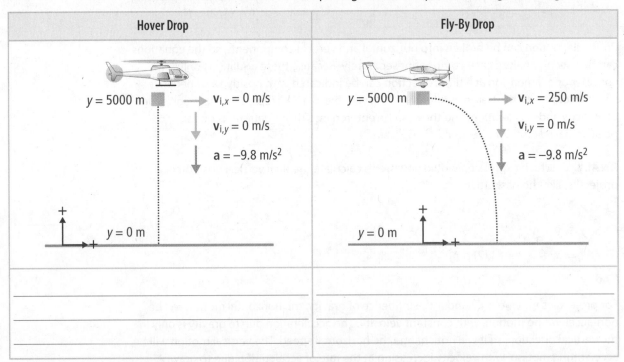

Hover Drop	Fly-By Drop
$y = 5000$ m $v_{i,x} = 0$ m/s $v_{i,y} = 0$ m/s $a = -9.8$ m/s^2 $y = 0$ m	$y = 5000$ m $v_{i,x} = 250$ m/s $v_{i,y} = 0$ m/s $a = -9.8$ m/s^2 $y = 0$ m

ANALYZE For each method, how precisely does the drop need to be timed to hit the target? Why does precision matter in implementing the solution?

Evaluating Solutions

When engineers evaluate solutions to a design problem, they consider a broad range of factors, which may be criteria or constraints. To identify these criteria and constraints, engineers may do background research and talk to customers or end users.

 Language Arts Connection Research a situation in which people needed humanitarian aid. Use information from news sources, geographical resources, and humanitarian organizations to identify at least three criteria and two constraints that were important when developing a solution to deliver humanitarian aid. Write a short summary.

EVALUATE Imagine you are tasked with developing a solution to deliver aid in the situation you researched. Choose two possible solutions to evaluate. Use the decision matrix and the results of your research to evaluate the two solutions. Assign each criterion a weight between 1 and 5, with higher weights assigned to more important criteria. For each design solution, rate on a scale of 1–5 how well it satisfies each criterion, with higher ratings assigned to solutions that satisfy the criterion well. Calculate the total points, and compare the designs to identify the best choice.

Decision Matrix			
Design Criteria	Weight		
Total points			

ARGUE Which solution would you recommend engineers prototype and test? Justify your choice based on the decision matrix and how each solution satisfies the constraints.

_____

_____

_____

EXPLAIN Few engineering solutions are perfect. Explain what tradeoffs you made when deciding which solution was best for the situation you researched.

_____

_____

_____

 Evidence Notebook Think about how the path of an airdrop package relates to the path of the skier. How can information about a falling object's motion be used to determine where it will land? How can you design an object's path to hit a target?

Hands-On Lab

Hitting the Mark

A ski jumper awaits her turn at the top of a jump. She sees the landing area several meters beyond the jump on the ground below. She must land between two lines painted on the snow in order to receive a qualifying score.

Think about what ski jump designers must know in order to determine the landing area for the jumper. The ski jumper follows a projectile path through the air. The jump designers might need to estimate the jumper's initial velocity off the ramp and the time the jumper is in the air to determine how far the jumper travels parallel to the ground before landing. The engineer might use equations like these to analyze the skier's motion:

- Vertical displacement: $\Delta y = v_{i,y}t + \frac{1}{2}a_y t^2$
- Horizontal displacement: $\Delta x = v_{i,x}t$
- Acceleration: $\mathbf{a} = \frac{\Delta \mathbf{v}}{t}$

In these formulas, Δx and Δy represent change in position in the horizontal and vertical directions, respectively, a_y represents the magnitude of acceleration in the vertical direction, and $v_{i,x}$ and $v_{i,y}$ represent the magnitude of initial velocity in the horizontal and vertical directions, respectively.

In this lab, you will determine the launch speed of a projectile and then use this value to predict where it will land when launched horizontally from some height. You will work with a simplified model, assuming that the skier represented by your toy projectile only has initial velocity in the horizontal direction. Can your group be the first to "hit the mark"?

RESEARCH QUESTION How can physics principles be applied to predict future motion?

- -

MAKE A CLAIM

How can you apply knowledge of velocity and acceleration to launch a toy to hit a target?

_____

_____

_____

- -

MATERIALS

- safety goggles
- desk or table
- metersticks (2)
- paper plate
- toy, spring-loaded
- video-recording device, such as a cell phone

- -

SAFETY INFORMATION

- Wear safety goggles during the setup, hands-on, and takedown segments of the activity.
- Immediately pick up any items dropped on the floor so they do not become a slip/fall hazard.
- Mark off the area where the projectile will fly. Do not allow anyone to stand in the path of the projectile.
- Wash your hands with soap and water immediately after completing this activity.

Part I: Finding Initial Velocity

PLAN THE INVESTIGATION

1. Figure 24 shows a ball launched with an initial vertical velocity. Think about how the time it takes to rise to its maximum height compares to the time for its fall to the ground. Also, think about how the ball's initial velocity compares to its final velocity. In your Evidence Notebook, explain how to find the ball's initial vertical velocity using the maximum height that the ball reaches. Your explanation should include an equation.

2. Plan an investigation to determine the height a toy rises into the air. You may choose to record video of this motion to help with accuracy. Think about how you might place a meterstick within the view frame of the camera so that it can help you measure the height that the toy rises into the air. You should also decide where to place the camera, if you choose to use one. In your Evidence Notebook, write a method to measure the maximum height the toy rises. Make sure your teacher approves your procedure and safety plan before proceeding.

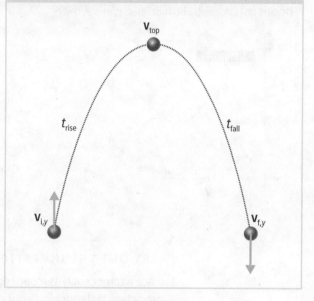

FIGURE 24: A ball launched with an initial vertical velocity is shown at the beginning, middle, and end of its path. The width of this path has been exaggerated to illustrate the ball's rise and fall.

3. Launch a spring-loaded toy projectile *vertically*, and record the height to which it rises as accurately as possible using the method you planned in Step 2. Then use the equation you wrote in Step 1 to find the initial velocity. Is the value you calculated reasonable? If not, return to your method, make adjustments, and perform another trial. Once you calculate a reasonable value, consult with your teacher to confirm your method for calculating the initial velocity.

CARRY OUT THE INVESTIGATION

1. Launch a spring-loaded toy projectile vertically and record the height to which it rises in the data table or in a spreadsheet. Complete at least three trials, but do as many as needed to obtain a consistent measure of the height. You may need to perform several different trials to ensure the consistency of your launcher's performance. Use your data and calculations to complete the data table.

2. Calculate the initial velocity of your projectile for each trial. Record your results in the data table.

Trial	Maximum height	Initial velocity
average		

Part II: Hitting The Mark

PLAN THE INVESTIGATION

1. Figure 25 shows two balls, one that is dropped and another that is launched horizontally. Think about whether or not the two balls hit the ground at the same time. In your Evidence Notebook, use the equations for accelerating and non-accelerating motion to write an equation to find the time it takes the launched ball to fall to the ground.

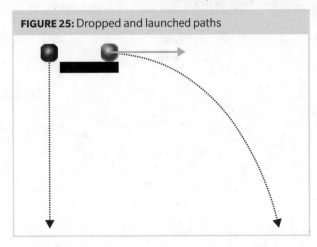

FIGURE 25: Dropped and launched paths

2. The horizontally launched ball maintains its velocity in the *x*-direction even while falling. Explain how to determine the landing location of the launched ball, and identify any measurements you need to make.

3. Choose the surface to launch your toy horizontally from. Complete the measurements that you identified. Use motion equations to predict where the toy lands. Record your work in your Evidence Notebook.

4. Plan an investigation to determine if your prediction is accurate. Consider how you will measure where the projectile lands. Have your teacher approve your procedure and safety plan before proceeding.

CARRY OUT THE INVESTIGATION

1. Place a target such as a paper plate at the predicted landing location. Test your prediction by launching your projectile. You may try the launch three times. Mark where the toy lands, then measure the distance from this point to the base of the launching surface and record your data.

_____

_____

_____

_____

2. If your toy did not hit the mark during any of the tests, evaluate what you need to change in your method to determine its landing spot. Recalculate using a corrected method and then retest your launch. Explain what happens.

_____

_____

_____

_____

ANALYZE

1. Why were you able to use the projectile's initial velocity from Part I in Part II?

_____

_____

_____

2. Reflecting on the accuracy of your prediction, identify one to three specific sources of error. Identify which error sources were the result of errors in your measurements, then explain whether each source produces a predictable (systematic) error or a random error.

_____

_____

_____

_____

CONSTRUCT AN EXPLANATION

What method should a ski jump engineer use to determine the approximate landing distance of a ski jumper? What measurements would the engineer need to make? What calculations would the engineer need to perform? Make the same simplifying assumption that the ski jumper only has initial velocity in the horizontal direction.

_____

_____

_____

_____

DRAW CONCLUSIONS

Write a conclusion that addresses each of the points below.

Claim How can you apply knowledge of velocity and acceleration to hit a target? Explain whether or not you correctly predicted where the toy projectile would land. Was your initial claim correct?

Evidence What evidence from the investigation supports your claims?

Reasoning Explain how the evidence you gave supports your claims. Describe in detail the connections between the evidence you cited and the arguments you are making.

_____

_____

_____

_____

_____

_____

| ANIMATOR | INVESTIGATING FREE FALL | ROTATIONAL MOTION SOLUTIONS | Go online to choose one of these other paths. |

Lesson Self-Check

CAN YOU SOLVE THE PROBLEM?

MODEL Use what you learned in this lesson to model the path of the athlete's motion, extending the path to the right.

Now that you have learned about projectile motion, observe how the skier's motion follows a curved path. Your drawing should show the horizontal and vertical motion of the skier and both components of displacement for each interval. Consider how the changes in the skier's motion relate to other examples you have analyzed in the lesson.

 Evidence Notebook Refer to your notes in your Evidence Notebook to make a claim about how determining position, velocity, and acceleration can be used to predict the path of a moving object. Your explanation should include a discussion of the following points:

Claim How can information about an object's past and present motion be used to predict its future motion?

Evidence What evidence supports your claim about predicting future motion?

Reasoning How does the evidence you provided support your claim about predicting future motion?

CHECKPOINTS

Check Your Understanding

1. The stage directions for a play requires an actor to walk 5 steps forward, 9 steps left, and 2 steps backward to be standing over the trap door. What are the components of the actor's displacement from the starting position?

   ○ **a.** 7 steps left and 2 steps forward

   ○ **b.** 7 steps left and 2 steps backward

   ○ **c.** 9 steps left and 3 steps backward

   ○ **d.** 9 steps left and 3 steps forward

2. Complete the statement.

Near Earth's surface, the acceleration due to gravity is constant | changing and directed upward | downward | sideways. Using the formula $\mathbf{v} = \mathbf{a}t$, you can find the instantaneous | average velocity of an object dropped from rest at any time in its journey.

3. You toss a ball at an angle 45° above the horizontal. After the ball leaves your hands, its motion can be described in terms of displacement, velocity, and acceleration. For each item, is the quantity constant, changing linearly, or changing nonlinearly during consecutive time intervals?

_____ horizontal displacement

_____ horizontal velocity

_____ horizontal acceleration

_____ vertical displacement

_____ vertical velocity

_____ vertical acceleration

4. Complete the statement.

Assume that positive in the horizontal direction is to the right, and positive in the vertical direction is upwards. In projectile motion, the horizontal component of velocity is constant | changing and the vertical component of velocity is constant | changing. The acceleration is zero | positive | negative horizontally and zero | positive | negative vertically.

5. The vectors show the car's velocity before and after a time *t*, while the dots show the car's position at equal time intervals. Positive velocity is to the right, and negative velocity is to the left. The images of the car indicate its final position in each of the situations. In each case, label the velocity and the acceleration as positive or negative, using + or −.

_____ velocity, _____ acceleration

_____ velocity, _____ acceleration

_____ velocity, _____ acceleration

_____ velocity, _____ acceleration

6. Which of these scenarios describe acceleration? Select all correct answers.

   ☐ **a.** a graph of position versus time that shows a horizontal line

   ☐ **b.** a graph of position versus time that shows a parabola

   ☐ **c.** a graph of position versus time that shows a diagonal line

   ☐ **d.** a racecar moving around a circular track at constant speed

   ☐ **e.** a racecar slowing down to a stop as it comes into the pit stop

   ☐ **f.** a racecar with an instantaneous velocity of 120 km/h east on a straight section

CHECKPOINTS (continued)

7. A soccer field is 90 m long and 45 m wide. For this coordinate system, the origin is in the bottom left corner of the field, and up and right are defined as positive directions. Player 1 starts at (25 m, 14 m). Player 2 starts at (30 m, 65 m). The players meet at (10 m, 50 m) at the same time. Draw the starting positions of the players, and draw the vectors showing their displacement as they run to the meeting point. Label the x- and y-components of each player's displacement vector, and label the magnitude of each component.

8. Consider the players in the previous question. If Player 1 runs with an average speed of 6.0 m/s, determine the average speed of Player 2 if Player 2 arrives at the meeting point at the same time. Report your final answer using the correct number of significant figures.

_____

_____

_____

_____

9. At $t = 0.0$ s, a runner is moving forward (in the positive direction along the x-axis) at a speed of 7.0 m/s. For 2.0 s the runner accelerates to his left at 0.50 m/s^2 and backward at 1.0 m/s^2. What is the runner's position at $t = 2.0$ s in terms of the component directions (forward/back and left/right)?

_____

_____

_____

_____

MAKE YOUR OWN STUDY GUIDE

 In your Evidence Notebook, design a study guide that supports the main ideas from this lesson:

Motion can be described with velocity, acceleration, and a frame of reference.

Motion in two dimensions can be analyzed as the combination of different motions in one dimension.

Remember to include the following information in your study guide:
- Use examples that model main ideas.
- Record explanations for the phenomena you investigated.
- Use evidence to support your explanations. Your support can include drawings, data, graphs, laboratory conclusions, and other evidence recorded throughout the lesson.

Consider how the vector descriptions of motion represent an underlying pattern.

Effects of Forces

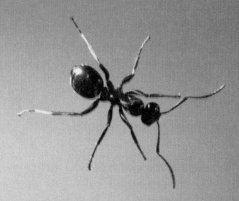

A small creature such as an insect can fall from a great height and walk away unharmed.

CAN YOU EXPLAIN THE PHENOMENON?

You have studied how objects moving only under the influence of gravity fall with the same downward acceleration. Yet you know of real-world examples that show more complex motion, such as the fall of a leaf or a sheet of paper.

Think about an acorn and an ant, each falling from the same high branch of a tree. As the acorn hits the ground, it produces a sound loud enough to hear. The ant hits almost silently and walks away unharmed.

INFER Use the impact of the ant and the acorn with the ground as a way of comparing their motion just before impact. Describe a likely way the ant's motion differs from the acorn's motion.

_____

_____

_____

_____

_____

Evidence Notebook As you explore the lesson, gather evidence to explain the factors that can cause the motion of the falling ant and the acorn in the example to differ.

Representing Forces

In everyday language, "to force" can mean *to cause something to happen*; in science, a force is a push or a pull exerted by one object on another. In the International System (SI) of Units, the unit for force is the newton (N), which is equal to 1 kg·m/s^2. Force is a vector quantity because it has direction as well as magnitude.

> **Collaborate** With a partner, compare and contrast the everyday and scientific meanings of force. In your discussion, address these questions: Can there be a force if nothing happens? How might the units (kg·m/s^2) be related to the scientific definition?

FIGURE 1: Spring scales are used to measure force.

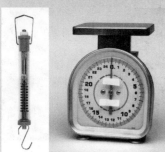

Identifying Forces

Think about the downward pull due to gravity. Scientists distinguish between weight, the gravitational force acting on an object, and mass, a measure of the amount of matter. The mass of an object can be measured by comparing it to known masses using a balance; mass is not a force.

Weight and other forces can be measured—for example, by how much they push or pull a spring in a spring scale. These tools work because an object's weight is balanced by another force. A kitchen or bathroom scale can be used to measure the downward force (weight) that is balanced by an upward supporting force, such as from a table or the floor. This supporting force is perpendicular to a surface and is called the normal force.

INFER For each type of force in the table, match the example description with the vector image of the force.

Force	Description
air resistance	Air exerts a force against the moving box in a way that increases with the box's speed.
friction	Two sliding surfaces produce a force that acts opposite to the direction of the relative motion of the surfaces.
gravitational force	Earth exerts a force of attraction on the box.
normal force	An object exerts a force on the box in a direction perpendicular to the surfaces in contact.

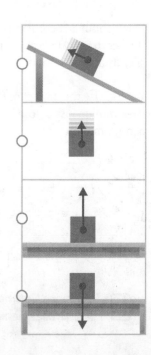

Exploring Friction

When an object is pushed or pulled across another object, small points of the surfaces in contact push against each other and resist motion. This effect and several other effects, together, produce friction. Friction is a force that opposes motion between two surfaces that are in contact. The box in Figure 2 stays in place because *static friction* resists the force that would make it slide down the ramp. Static friction occurs when the two surfaces are not sliding. When the box slides along the surface, *kinetic friction* resists—but does not prevent—the motion. The force of kinetic friction is less than the maximum value of static friction.

FIGURE 2: The surfaces of the box and the ramp resist motion between them.

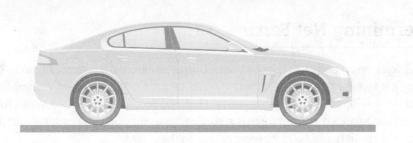

Unlike air resistance, static and kinetic friction do not typically depend on speed or on the area of contact. They are each proportional to the force pushing the surfaces together, which is usually characterized by the normal force. The normal force is in a direction perpendicular to a surface, so it is not always vertical.

 Language Arts Connection Use the two types of friction to describe what happens as you slide a heavy box across a table. You might also research the coefficient of friction. Prepare an explanation to present to the class.

Using Diagrams to Analyze Force

The normal force and static friction tend to oppose other forces, while forces acting in the same direction produce a greater force. Forces combine as vectors, in the same way velocities or accelerations combine. To make calculations, however, you have to determine which vectors to add together.

APPLY Use vector arrows to draw the forces you expect to be present when a car is parked on flat pavement. Treat the car as a single object.

Compare the vectors you drew with those of a classmate. Each of you may have represented the car's weight, for example, in different ways. Perhaps you drew gravitational force pulling down on the car or the heavy car pressing down on the pavement. Look at the forces on a single object: the car. You can combine these forces. It is less useful to combine the forces that act on different objects.

A *free-body diagram* is a way to model a situation by looking at only one object and the external forces that act on it. Figure 3a shows some forces on the car and forces on the pavement. Figure 3b includes the car's weight but not the forces on the pavement.

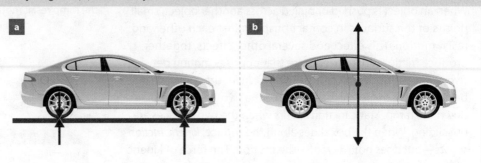

FIGURE 3: The first model (a) shows forces on both the car and the ground. The second, free-body diagram (b) shows only forces on the car.

In a free-body diagram, each force on an object is represented by a vector arrow. This model treats all forces as if they were acting at a single point, called the *center of mass* of the object. The center of mass is usually represented as a dot and may not be exactly at the center of the object. In Figure 3b, the free-body diagram of the car, the normal force is shown as a single vector pointing upward from the center of mass. Compare Figure 3a, in which the normal forces from the ground are represented as two vectors at the tires.

ANALYZE Select the correct label for each vector in the free-body diagrams. A label can be used more than once.

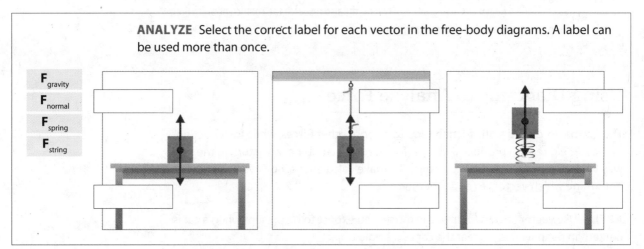

$F_{gravity}$

F_{normal}

F_{spring}

F_{string}

Determining Net Force

The net force on an object, F_{net}, is the vector sum of all external forces acting on it. You may also see net force written as ΣF, where the capital sigma, Σ, indicates a summation. In each of the free-body diagrams that you labeled, two forces are balanced. When forces on an object are balanced, the net force is zero. The forces may be large or small, but if they balance, the result is as if no force were acting on the object.

INFER What can you infer about the net force when an object is unmoving—at rest? Explain your reasoning.

_____

_____

_____

PREDICT Next to each diagram, draw a vector to represent the direction and approximate magnitude of the net force. Then describe what you think will happen to the motion of the box.

Scenario	Free-body diagram	Predicted motion
box falling in air		
box on a spring		

If forces act in one dimension—that is, along a single line—they can be represented as positive and negative numbers. For example, a force of 10 N down and a force 8 N up can be written as $-10\,\text{N} + 8\,\text{N} = -2\,\text{N}$, a net force of 2 N downward.

When forces are in two dimensions, you can look separately at the forces in perpendicular directions, such as vertical and horizontal forces. Because frictional forces are parallel to surfaces in contact and normal forces are perpendicular to the surfaces, you might choose a coordinate system oriented with one axis along the surface. In Figure 4, one axis would be parallel to the ramp and the other would be perpendicular to the ramp and parallel to the normal force on the box.

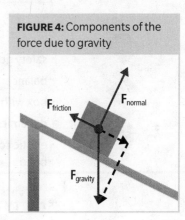

FIGURE 4: Components of the force due to gravity

You can often determine the normal force by analyzing the other forces. Suppose gravitational force is the only force pressing the object to the surface. For an object at rest on a horizontal surface, the normal force equals the weight of the object supported by the surface. For a slanted surface, such as a ramp, the normal force equals the component of the force due to gravity perpendicular to the surface.

APPLY Suppose you place a coin on a book; the book's cover acts as a ramp. You open the cover slowly until static friction is overcome. The coin begins to slide. What happens to the forces on the coin as the angle of the cover changes? Select all correct answers.

☐ **a.** A component of the frictional force begins pushing the coin and book together.

☐ **b.** The frictional force decreases suddenly as the coin starts to slide.

☐ **c.** The gravitational force increases.

☐ **d.** The component of gravitational force along the surface increases.

☐ **e.** The component of gravitational force perpendicular to the surface decreases.

☐ **f.** The normal force decreases slowly, which produces a slow decrease in static friction.

 Evidence Notebook Construct a free-body diagram for the falling ant and the falling acorn in the example, just before each hits the ground. Use the lengths of the vectors to show your estimate of the relative magnitudes.

Hands-On Lab
Exploring Force and Motion

In this lab, you will explore two ways of producing constant forces and the effects of constant forces on motion. Then you will use a more formal setup to determine the effects of constant forces on the motion of objects that are initially at rest and initially moving.

RESEARCH QUESTION How is force related to motion?

MAKE A CLAIM

After completing Part I, use your hypothesis to help you address this question: Suppose the frictionless system shown in Figure 7 is tested with equal masses. What will happen if the system is given a small initial motion—one mass moving upward, one downward?

POSSIBLE MATERIALS

- safety goggles
- balance
- box with a flat bottom
- dynamics cart
- elastic cord or rubber band

- mass set and/or objects of known mass
- mass hangers and slotted mass set
- pulley with clamp for table edge

- ring stand
- spring scale or other force meter
- stopwatch or other timing device
- string
- surfaces, assorted
- tape, masking

SAFETY INFORMATION

- Wear safety goggles during the setup, hands-on, and takedown segments of the activity.
- Immediately pick up any items dropped on the floor so that they do not become a slip/fall hazard.
- Wash your hands with soap and water immediately after completing this activity.

FIGURE 5: Use a spring scale to ensure a steady applied force.

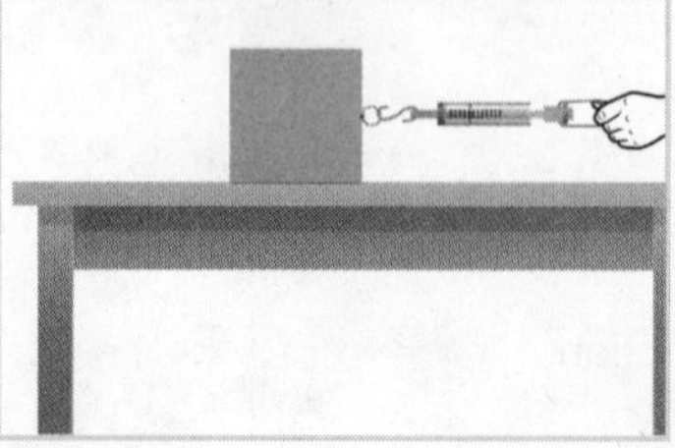

PART I: Testing Constant Forces

CARRY OUT THE INVESTIGATION

In Part I, you will first explore the relationship between applied force and net force. Later, you will need to decide which force to use in your hypothesis. Then you will use a setup in which a gravitational force is approximately the same as the net force on a system. As you work, you will need to determine and record details of your procedure based on the materials available, your ongoing results, and your judgment.

Use three or more values of an independent variable (such as force applied or mass of the moving object) to make a rough graph as you work. Try to determine whether the variable has no effect (a horizontal line), a linear effect (a straight line), or a nonlinear effect (a curved line). If you can't tell, gather more or better data before you put away the equipment.

Procedure

Record details of your procedure and your observations in your Evidence Notebook. You might design tables to record multiple trials and multiple values of independent variables.

1. Record the type and mass of the box you use. Tie a loop of string around the box. Place the box flat on a table or the floor, and hook the force meter to the string loop. Add a known amount of mass to the box.

2. Gently pull the spring scale with different amounts of force but without moving the box. Record the range of forces you can apply and the static friction you infer.

3. Gently pull the box along the table using the spring scale. Try to keep the force constant as the box slides. Optimize the mass in the box and the applied force to find a range for which you can keep your applied force constant. Then describe the relative velocity and acceleration for different applied forces, as well as an estimated net force.

   • You can use the stretch of an elastic cord as another way to estimate the applied force.

   • Vary the sliding surfaces or the mass of the box to increase or reduce friction in order to help you pull the box with a constant force. For example, you can put strips of tape along the surface or the bottom of the box.

4. Set up a low-friction system as shown in Figure 6. The hanging weight (b) provides a constant force as it drops. Check that the string's length enables the maximum motion. Prevent the cart and hanging weight from hitting anything at the end of each run.

5. Experiment with different masses in the cart and different hanging weights to find a range that gives good results. Ignore friction and assume the hanging weight is the net force. Then test enough values of force to develop a hypothesis about the effect of force on motion. Record your measurements or estimates of velocity and acceleration, along with any qualitative observations of motion for each trial run.

FIGURE 6: Use a hanging weight (b) to provide a steady force on the object (a), but include its mass as part of the system in motion.

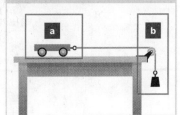

ANALYZE

1. List the relationships that were clearly linear or clearly nonlinear.

   _____

   _____

   _____

   _____

2. Do you think the applied force, the frictional force, or the net force has the strongest relationship to motion? Use a free-body diagram to help you determine your answer.

   _____

   _____

   _____

3. Think about how varying the force you chose affects velocity and acceleration. Write a hypothesis that summarizes how force affects motion.

   _____

   _____

   _____

PART II: Testing Your Hypothesis

PLAN YOUR INVESTIGATION

Use your hypothesis from Part I to make a claim about the setup shown in Figure 7. Then use your experiences from Part I to develop a plan to test your hypothesis about force and motion. Consider these suggestions as you plan your procedure:

- Use or adapt one of the two setups from Part I. Draw a free-body diagram of the system to help ensure that you will be able to measure or calculate all significant forces.
- Design a procedure to test and refine your hypothesis about how force affects motion.
- Plan to determine whether the effect of force has a linear relationship to an object's velocity or acceleration. If not, find a way to describe the relationship.
- Test enough values of force to provide evidence of the relationship. Also test several values of mass to ensure that the relationship holds for different objects.
- If you can, test a setup in which there is zero net force and a small initial velocity.

Make sure your teacher approves your procedure and safety plan. Then carry out your procedure and record your observations in your Evidence Notebook.

ANALYZE

1. Based on your experiment, is the effect of force more closely related to an object's velocity or its acceleration? Is the relationship linear? Give details of the relationship.

_____

_____

2. How well does your answer to the first question apply if you use a different mass?

_____

_____

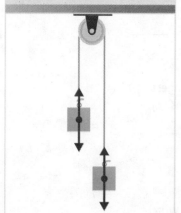

FIGURE 7: A string passing over a pulley supports two objects.

DRAW CONCLUSIONS

Write a conclusion that addresses each of the points below.

Claim Suppose the frictionless system shown in Figure 7 is tested with objects of equal mass (zero net force). What will happen if the system is given a small initial motion, such that one mass moves up and the other moves down?

Evidence Present your hypothesis tests and other evidence to support your claim.

Reasoning Explain how your evidence applies to the system in Figure 7.

_____

_____

_____

_____

_____

 Evidence Notebook Apply what you have learned about the effect of force on motion to form a hypothesis about the difference between the falling ant and acorn.

Connecting Force and Motion

 Collaborate With a partner, choose a scenario such as sliding a table across the floor. Discuss the effect of the force you apply, such as by pulling or pushing the object. Then discuss the effect of net force. Which force would you use to predict the object's motion?

Analyzing Force and Motion

ANALYZE For each example, describe the car's motion by determining whether velocity and acceleration are zero, positive, or negative. Then try to do the same for net force.

Example	Velocity	Acceleration	Net force
A car is parked.			
A car moves at a constant speed of 100 km/h on a straight roadway.			
A car slows in a school zone.			
A car that was stopped at a red light begins to move when the light turns green.			
A car turns a corner at a constant speed of 10 km/h.			

When two balanced forces are exerted on an object, such as an object's weight and the normal force from the floor beneath it, the effects of the forces tend to cancel each other. To predict motion, scientists typically use net force.

In Figure 8, two objects hang by a single string that runs over a pulley. The device, called Atwood's machine, shows how net force affects motion. Each object is pulled down by gravity and up by the string.

EVALUATE Select the correct terms to complete the statements about the forces in Figure 8.

- The forces from the string, $F_{1,string}$ and $F_{2,string}$, have magnitudes that are the same | different and directions that are the same | opposite | perpendicular, whether or not the system is in motion.

- If the masses are equal and unmoving, the net force on each object must be upward | zero | downward.

Suppose the masses of the objects are equal and the masses of the string and the pulley are small enough to be ignored. If the objects are at rest, they stay at rest. However, if the system is initially moving, it continues moving steadily until something stops it. One object moves up and the other moves down, each at constant velocity, until an object reaches the pulley or the ground.

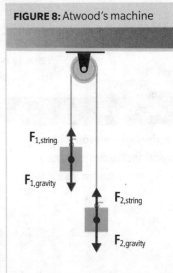

FIGURE 8: Atwood's machine

$F_{1,string}$

$F_{1,gravity}$

$F_{2,string}$

$F_{2,gravity}$

Effect of Balanced Forces on Motion

In many everyday experiences, moving objects tend to slow down or stop unless something keeps them moving. For example, if you tap a pencil to make it slide along a table, it slows down and comes to a stop. You may not notice that frictional force acts on the pencil; it represents a net force in the direction opposite to the pencil's velocity. Gravitational force and friction are part of most of your everyday experiences. If you have experiences with objects sliding on ice or other nearly frictionless surfaces, you may have noticed that objects can move at a constant velocity for a long time without anything pushing on them.

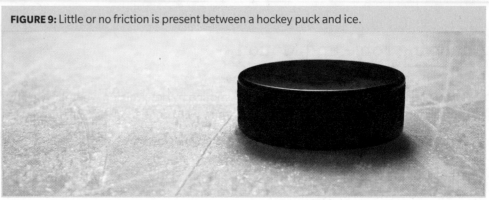

FIGURE 9: Little or no friction is present between a hockey puck and ice.

INFER Draw the free-body diagram for the hockey puck when it is not moving (a), and when it is moving steadily to the right (b).

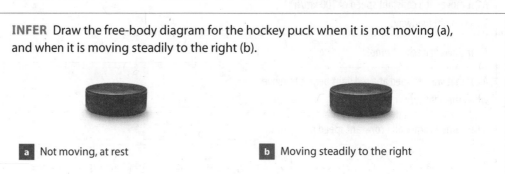

a | Not moving, at rest

b | Moving steadily to the right

Apply the idea of net force to everyday experiences in which you exert a force to keep an object moving. Suppose you pull an object just hard enough to oppose friction, so $F_{net} = 0$. If you reduce friction, such as by using a slippery surface, less force is needed to keep the object in motion. If you could reduce friction all the way to zero, an object sliding across the surface would continue to slide at its initial velocity without any applied force. You would not have to continue pulling to keep it moving. The same thing happens with Atwood's machine and with an ideal hockey puck; an object can move at a constant velocity when $F_{net} = 0$. When a moving object slows, it is because of a net force, such as friction, acting on it.

Explore Online ▶

Hands-On Lab

Exploring Newton's Laws
Explore the factors that cause a change in the motion of an object.

You can summarize the two effects of zero net force: An object at rest remains at rest and an object in motion continues in motion with constant velocity unless the object is subject to a net external force. This relationship is called *Newton's first law of motion*. Remember that an object at rest has zero velocity. In other words, when net force is zero, an object remains at constant velocity (which may be zero); it does not accelerate.

Language Arts Connection Find a video, simulation, or physical situation that shows an example of Newton's first law of motion. You might instead be able to demonstrate an example. Describe the example and draw a free-body diagram that represents it.

Effect of Unbalanced Forces on Motion

As you may have inferred, an object's velocity changes when the net force on it is not zero. The object may slow down, speed up, or turn; the force causes this change in motion.

 Data Analysis

Magnitude of Net Force

MODEL Graph the simulated data from the table, which show the effect of different forces on a 2 kg object, or make a graph of data from an experiment or a simulation. Then draw the curve or straight line that best represents the points.

Model	m (kg)	a (m/s²)	F_{net} (N)
	2	2.5	5
	2	5	10
	2	10	20
	2	15	30

Force (N)

0

0

Acceleration (m/s²)

ANALYZE Select the correct terms to complete the statements.

The points lie along a straight line | simple curve | complex path, so the relationship between acceleration and force is linear | geometric | exponential.

The magnitude of the acceleration **a** is directly proportional to | inversely proportional to | the inverse square of the magnitude of the force **F**.

The overall slope represents the velocity | rate of change in acceleration | mass.

If you push on an object at rest, static friction may prevent it from moving: the net force is zero. If you push hard enough, the object starts moving—accelerates—in the direction of the net force. Explore the relationships between net force, velocity, and acceleration when the object does not start from rest.

INFER The dots show the car's position at equal intervals of time. The vectors show the car's initial and final velocities. For each example, first determine whether the car is speeding up or slowing down, then infer the direction of the net force.

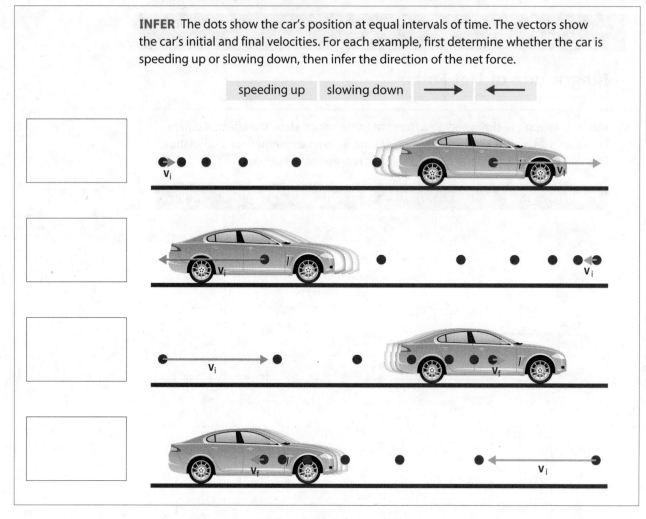

Notice how the direction of net force can be different from the direction of an object's motion. For example, when you slide an object across a floor, the force of kinetic friction is opposite to the velocity and tends to slow the object.

APPLY Select the correct terms to complete the statements for an object acted upon by a nonzero net force.

The direction of acceleration is the same as | opposite to the direction of net force.

A force in the direction of motion causes an object to slow down | speed up | turn.

A force opposite the direction of motion causes an object to slow down | speed up | turn.

A force at a 90° angle to the direction of motion causes an object to slow down | speed up | turn.

Relating Force, Mass, and Acceleration

You have seen how acceleration is related to the net force, but it also depends on an object's mass. Think about how objects of different masses accelerate if pushed with the same force; imagine the objects on ice or another low-friction surface.

Effect of Mass on Acceleration

MODEL The table shows the results of a simulation in which force is held constant. Graph the results to find out how an increase in mass affects acceleration.

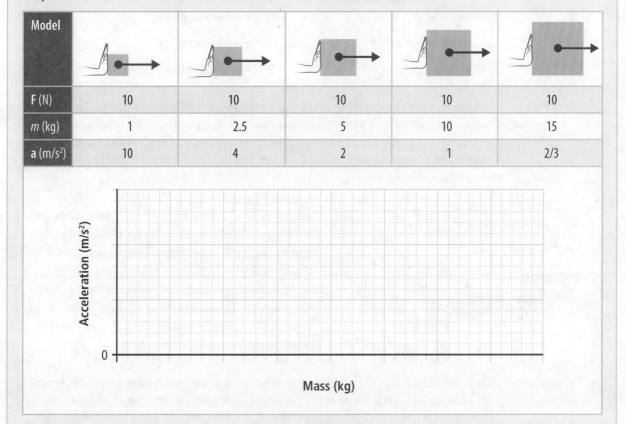

Model					
F (N)	10	10	10	10	10
m (kg)	1	2.5	5	10	15
a (m/s²)	10	4	2	1	2/3

ANALYZE Select the correct terms to complete the statements.

A more massive object acted on by the same net force as a less massive object has a smaller | the same | a greater acceleration.

The tangent to the curve at each point has positive | zero | negative slope.

There is a direct | an inverse | a complex relationship between the mass of an object and its acceleration—**a** is proportional to m | $1/m$.

Suppose you gave pushes of equal force to a small child on one swing and an adult on a second swing. The force has less effect on the adult's greater mass. To achieve the same acceleration of the greater mass, you must apply a greater force.

SOLVE The relationships between $\mathbf{F}_{net}$, acceleration $\mathbf{a}$, and mass m can be summarized in an equation. Place each variable in the equation.

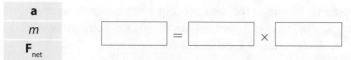

$$\boxed{} = \boxed{} \times \boxed{}$$

The equation can be rewritten to show how acceleration depends on both force and mass: $\mathbf{a} = \mathbf{F}_{net}/m$. This relationship is known as *Newton's second law of motion*. Constant acceleration is the result of a constant net force acting on an object, such as when gravity alone acts on a falling object near Earth's surface.

APPLY Match the change in the force or mass to the change in the acceleration of an object.

As the net force increases slightly, ◯	◯	the acceleration decreases slightly.
When the net force doubles, ◯	◯	the acceleration doubles.
As the mass increases slightly, ◯	◯	the acceleration halves.
When the mass doubles, ◯	◯	the acceleration increases slightly.

The mass in the equation is the total mass of the system being accelerated. For two objects connected by a (massless) string over a pulley, both objects contribute to the system's mass. If you use a descending weight to provide a constant force, or if you set up Atwood's machine with different masses, the net force is the unbalanced part of the gravitational force.

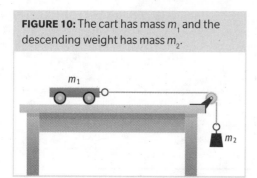

FIGURE 10: The cart has mass m_1 and the descending weight has mass m_2.

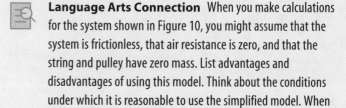

Language Arts Connection When you make calculations for the system shown in Figure 10, you might assume that the system is frictionless, that air resistance is zero, and that the string and pulley have zero mass. List advantages and disadvantages of using this model. Think about the conditions under which it is reasonable to use the simplified model. When might you need to include more detail in your calculations? Summarize your conclusions in a flow chart.

Think about how this relationship applies to situations with different amounts of friction. On a frictionless surface or in space, an object accelerates as soon any force is applied. In contrast, a heavy object on a high-friction surface does not move until the applied force becomes great enough. It then moves suddenly as the force due to static friction is exceeded and kinetic friction begins.

On a frictionless surface or in space, a more massive object takes greater force to speed up, to turn, or to stop. Its mass resists the change in velocity. In situations with significant friction, the amount of friction often depends on an object's weight, which is proportional to its mass. A more massive object takes greater force to accelerate both because its mass resists acceleration and because its weight produces greater friction.

Evidence Notebook Think about the motion of the ant and acorn just before each hits the ground; assume the acorn hits at a greater velocity. Infer the relative accelerations, compare the net forces on the ant and acorn, and then review the free-body diagrams you made.

Analyzing Action and Reaction

Language Arts Connection Think about a toy that jumps when a spring is released, as in Figure 11. An upward force causes acceleration at the start of the jump, yet the spring presses downward on the table. Use a labeled diagram to identify the unbalanced force that accelerates the toy.

FIGURE 11: A jumping toy

Analyzing Paired Forces

A free-body diagram models only the forces acting on a single object or system treated as a point. A different model is needed to analyze the forces between objects. The car in the visual exerts a forward force as it hits the wall; this force can be considered an action force. The car's speed decreases suddenly, so you can infer that the wall pushes backward on the car. This force can be considered a reaction force. Unlike the forces in a free-body diagram, action and reaction forces act on different objects.

ANNOTATE Label the action and reaction forces shown. Draw and label vectors for other forces in this situation, such as the force pairs that include friction.

Forces in the universe occur in pairs. For every action force, there is a reaction force of equal magnitude in the opposite direction. This relationship is known as *Newton's third law of motion*. Each force in the pair acts on a different object, so these forces cannot balance one another. The forces are equal even when one or both objects accelerate.

Collaborate With a partner, make a list of examples of action-reaction force pairs you have observed. Compare your list with other groups.

The car slows to a stop because of a reaction force to the left, exerted on the car by the wall. In turn, the wall produces a force to the right on the ground, which produces a reaction force to the left on the wall. You can also model the wall and ground as if they were a single object. Think of a swimmer pushing off the wall of a swimming pool; action and reaction forces are always equal, opposite, and exerted on different objects.

Mathematical Models of Newton's Laws

The observations about force discussed in this lesson are collectively known as *Newton's laws of motion.*

First law: An object will remain at rest or in uniform straight-line motion unless acted on by a net external force.

Second law: An object acted on by a net external force will accelerate in the direction of that force according to the equation $\mathbf{F}_{net} = m\mathbf{a}$.

Third law: For every action force, there is an equal and opposite reaction force.

 Evidence Notebook How do the laws apply to the example of the ant and the acorn? Be careful to distinguish between balanced forces and action-reaction pairs.

Analyzing Internal Forces

Suppose a cardboard tube from a roll of paper towels is lying on a table. The normal force from the table balances the weight of the tube, and the tube does not accelerate. If you press down on the tube with your hand, then the tube, in turn, presses down on the table. The upward normal force from the table, a reaction force, increases as the total downward force increases. The forces on the cardboard tube remain balanced, and the tube still does not accelerate.

However, the downward and upward forces on the tube may cause the cardboard to deform. The cross-section of the tube may become oval rather than round, or a dent in the side may form. As the external forces from your hand and the table are transferred through the tube, they produce internal forces. Action-reaction force pairs occur between adjacent particles and are, together, called stress. Stress is also the name of a variable, σ, that has units of force per unit area. Scientists and engineers classify stresses into three types: compression, tension, and shear stress.

EVALUATE Use your knowledge of root words to label the three types of stress. The dotted outline shows the shape of an object before the forces were applied. The solid shapes show the deformation, or strain, resulting from each stress.

tension

shear stress

compression

Aligned forces
push inward

Aligned forces
pull outward

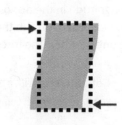

Nonaligned forces
may push or pull

Hands-On Lab
Model Stresses

You will explore the deformation and failure of a material from different types of stress.

RESEARCH QUESTION How do materials show the effects of balanced external forces?

MAKE A CLAIM

Describe how you think the material will respond when subject to different stresses produced by balanced external forces. Will the deformations or breaks be symmetric?

_____

_____

POSSIBLE MATERIALS

- safety goggles, nonlatex apron, nonlatex gloves
- sticky sand, compressible clay, or similar material
- ruler, metric, or similar tool

SAFETY INFORMATION

- Wear safety goggles, a nonlatex apron, and nonlatex gloves during the setup, hands-on, and takedown segments of the activity.

- Immediately clean up any water, sand, or clay spilled on the floor so it does not become a slip/fall hazard.

CARRY OUT THE INVESTIGATION

1. Wearing gloves, shape the material into blocks.

2. Use gloved hands to produce moderate amounts of stress of each type within a block; reshape the material as needed. Try increasing the stress both quickly and gradually. Record your detailed procedure and observations in your Evidence Notebook.

DRAW CONCLUSIONS

Write a conclusion that addresses each of the points below.

Claim Do materials show symmetry when balanced external forces are applied?

Evidence Give specific evidence from your observations to support your claim.

Reasoning Explain how your evidence supports your claim. Give details of the connections between the evidence you cited and the argument you are making.

_____

_____

_____

_____

Evidence Notebook Think about the force pair between a falling object and air. Take into account that air resistance varies with speed. Construct a diagram showing the force pairs for an ant at the beginning, in the middle, and near the end of its fall.

Forces and Stresses in Engineering

 Collaborate With a partner, choose an item you can examine, such as a retractable pen. Discuss how you would evaluate the forces on and within the object.

Analyzing Structures

One strategy for analyzing complex systems or structures is to look at one part at a time. An engineer might make a free-body diagram as if a selected part were a separate object. For a structure to be stable, there must be a way for the expected forces on each part to be balanced by reaction forces ($F_{net} = 0$). A supporting column of a bridge must provide an upward force to match the combined downward weight of the bridge and vehicles.

An engineer may separate the external forces needed to address the design problem—the load—from the forces due to the structure itself. The weight of vehicles might be a bridge's main load. A highway bridge must be designed for a greater load than a pedestrian bridge. Horizontal forces due to wind are also part of the load on a bridge.

Engineering

In a truss—the structure shown—the segments may bend slightly under the weight. The top is typically compressed and the bottom is typically stretched. You can model the weight of each segment as a point mass at the center of the segment.

INFER For each of the two locations marked by a dot, draw a free-body diagram of the forces acting at that point ($F_{net} = 0$). Use the space below the diagram.

— compression
— tension

 Evidence Notebook How might you use ideas from the design of a truss to help you test designs for a beam in your unit project?

Hands-On Lab

Testing a Bridge

RESEARCH QUESTION How does the distribution of a load affect the forces and stresses on a structure?

- -

MAKE A CLAIM

How might the paper bridge in Figure 12 respond differently to a line of pennies across the span of paper and to a stack of pennies in the middle?

FIGURE 12: A piece of paper forms a bridge between books.

_____

_____

- -

POSSIBLE MATERIALS

- safety goggles
- books, matching (2)
- paper, sheets (3)
- pennies or other small masses (50)

- -

SAFETY INFORMATION

- Wear safety goggles during the setup, hands-on, and takedown segments of the activity.
- Immediately pick up any items dropped on the floor so they do not become a slip/fall hazard.
- Wash your hands with soap and water immediately after completing this activity.

- -

CARRY OUT THE INVESTIGATION

Fold a piece of paper to make a bridge, such as in Figure 12, and place it on two books. Test the bridge by placing pennies, one at a time, and recording the maximum number before the bridge fails. Make sure that none of the pennies are resting on the books. After each failure, build a new bridge using fresh paper. Test three distributions of pennies.

Center of bridge: Spread along length: One end of bridge:

_____   _____   _____

- -

DRAW CONCLUSIONS

Write a conclusion that addresses each of the points below.

Claim What load distribution is most likely to cause the model bridge to collapse?

Evidence Give specific evidence from your observations to support your claim.

Reasoning Describe, in detail, how the evidence you cited supports your argument.

_____

_____

_____

_____

- -

EXTEND

Test different bridge designs, such as a simple flat sheet or a sheet cut to resemble a truss.

Using Forces in Designs

For a structure to stay stable or moving as intended, it must withstand the expected forces. An umbrella, for example, must withstand the weight of precipitation. It must withstand the forces that cause it to open and close. An umbrella should also withstand the forces as a person hangs onto the umbrella during a light gust of wind.

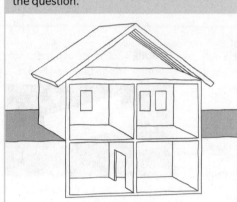

FIGURE 13: Use this house design to answer the question.

APPLY Suppose wind blows on the house in Figure 13 from the left and also produces an upward force on the roof. What reaction forces are needed to support the weight of the roof and counteract forces from the wind?

_____

_____

_____

_____

A designer may first look at the external forces on a structure, such as those shown in a free-body diagram. If wind blows on one side of the house in Figure 13, the reaction force you identified comes from the structure of the house. The structure pushes on the ground on the opposite side, which, in turn, opposes the force. The structure of the house must transfer the force from one side to the other without breaking. A designer might add stiff braces, rigid triangles, or tight wires to the structure to balance possible forces.

In any building design, many different forces are involved. An engineer uses equations for balanced forces and action-reaction force pairs to break the problem into solvable parts and then puts the parts together to find an overall design solution. For example, to reduce the forces on a support beam or other structure, a designer might choose components that weigh less. Yet the designer might need to widen a support or add more supports to provide greater reaction forces, and so may have to make tradeoffs.

 Collaborate Analyze the external forces acting on a chair, such as one in which you sit. Think about how forces are transferred through different parts the chair to the floor. With a partner, discuss ways to add support for someone who likes to rock from side to side.

Calculating Stress

External forces produce stress inside a material. The effect depends, in part, on the area over which the forces act. Think of poking a balloon with a finger and with a pin using equal forces. The balloon is more likely to break with the pin because the force is concentrated into a smaller area. As the area decreases, the stress increases. Designers often seek ways to distribute forces and to reduce stress. They generally avoid having a large force through one narrow part. They may use larger pieces, use more pieces, change the angles, or use curved pieces.

SOLVE How does stress (σ) depend on force (**F**) and area (A)?

○ **a.** $\sigma = FA$ ○ **b.** $\sigma = \dfrac{1}{FA}$ ○ **c.** $\sigma = \dfrac{F}{A}$ ○ **d.** $\sigma = \dfrac{A}{F}$

Using Stresses in Designs

One measure of a material's strength is the maximum amount of stress that can be applied before the material breaks or deforms an unacceptable amount. Tensile, compressive, and shear strengths describe how a material stands up to tension, compression, and shear stresses, respectively. The megapascal (MPa) is a unit of strength equal to 10^6 N/m^2, roughly equal to the weight of a 10 kg object pressing on 1 cm^2.

SOLVE An engineer is deciding whether to replace a bar made of an aluminum alloy with steel of tensile strength 500 MPa. A bar of the aluminum alloy 2 cm across (square cross section) can withstand pulling up to about 120 000 N. What is the tensile strength of the aluminum alloy, and how would a steel bar of equal tensile strength compare?

○ **a.** about 600 MPa; an equivalent steel bar would be thicker

○ **b.** about 300 MPa; an equivalent steel bar would be thinner

○ **c.** about 60 MPa; an equivalent steel bar would be much thinner

In the example, the steel also has much greater density than the aluminum alloy. A steel replacement bar would also have a greater mass. Other parts would need to support a greater weight. Engineers and other designers must consider tradeoffs among strength, size, and weight as well as other factors such as cost and ease of use.

FIGURE 14: Donghai Bridge near Shanghai and a simplified model of stresses in beam bridges

 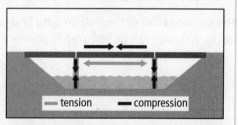

— tension — compression

Think about the tradeoffs for the large beam bridge shown in Figure 14. It has supporting columns that reduce the lengths of the unsupported horizontal parts, or spans. The weight causes each span to bend slightly. A material is needed that can support compression in the top surface and tension in the bottom surface. A choice of material might be good for longer spans but require stronger columns, while a different choice might require shorter spans and more columns.

EVALUATE Measurements of strength depend on many factors; example values and ranges are listed in the table. Of the materials listed, recommend a material to use for the beam bridge's vertical supporting columns and a material to use for the horizontal spans.

Material	Concrete	Steel (structural)	Wood (pine)
Compressive strength (MPa)	20–40	300	30–50
Tensile strength (MPa)	2–5	400–500	40
Shear strength (MPa)	6–17	300–400	6–10
Approximate density (kg/m^3)	2400	7900	350–590
Recommended use(s) in a beam bridge	_____ _____	_____ _____	_____ _____

FIGURE 15: Stresses in truss bridges (Astoria Bridge connecting Oregon and Washington)

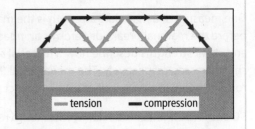

A truss bridge typically has a framework of triangles, a shape that can resist stress in different directions. As with a beam bridge, the top is compressed and bottom stretched. Diagonal pieces support compression or tension, as needed. The height or thickness of the truss helps provide these extra reaction forces. The open framework results in less weight and less force from the wind than a solid design.

EVALUATE Suspension and cable-stayed bridges have cables under tension, as shown in Figure 16. Study the figure, and select all correct statements.

☐ **a.** Cables are used where the design calls for both compression and tension.

☐ **b.** Vertical columns support the weight of the span through compression.

☐ **c.** Vertical columns are pulled upward by tension from the cables.

☐ **d.** Tension acts horizontally as well as vertically.

The curved cables of the Golden Gate Bridge (Figure 16a) change the direction of some forces. A design can be adjusted to produce different stresses. A designer can then make use of different materials, such as those used in the four bridges in Figures 14, 15, and 16.

FIGURE 16: Stresses in suspension bridges (a) and cable-stayed bridges (b)

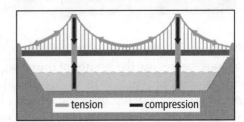

a Golden Gate Bridge, San Francisco

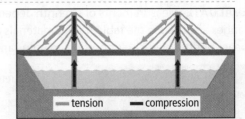

b Vasco da Gama Bridge near Lisbon

Evidence Notebook Use the forces you have inferred for the ant in the example to evaluate the stresses. Explain the type(s) of stress you expect as the ant falls.

Guided Research

Accelerometers

FIGURE 17: A micromechanical accelerometer, used in vehicle stability systems

Library/Science Source

An accelerometer is a device to measure acceleration. It may consist of a mass suspended in a casing on a spring. When the accelerometer is at rest or moving at constant velocity, the mass doesn't shift. When the device accelerates along the axis of the spring, the mass compresses or stretches the spring. The displacement of the mass is often measured electronically, such as by compressing a material that responds by producing electric current.

Think about your motion when riding in a car, bus, or other vehicle. When the vehicle accelerates forward from rest, you are pressed back in your seat briefly and then move at the velocity of the vehicle. When the vehicle brakes, you continue forward; when it turns, your body slides in the opposite direction. However, from a point of view outside of the car, your body tends to continue moving in a straight line. Your body is acting like the mass in an accelerometer.

Accelerometers are used in many fields to determine changes in motion. For example, they measure the motion of spacecraft and cars, the orientation of cell phones, and the motion of artificial limbs.

Language Arts Connection Research the design of a simple one-dimensional accelerometer that you can make with household materials. Build and calibrate a working prototype. Use it to measure acceleration in two or more situations, such as the following tests:

- Ride as a passenger in a bus as it speeds up, slows down, and makes turns.
- Use the device in an elevator or on an amusement park ride.
- Move the device upward or downward quickly, such as by standing rapidly or jumping off a step.
- Explore circular motion, such as turning or moving the device in an arc.

Develop an instruction manual.

- Identify the parts of the device.
- Give step-by-step instructions for how to use the device.
- Explain the physical principles behind its function. Why does it work?
- Compare the device you built to a commercial device, such as the sensors of a cell phone. How accurate is your device?

| PULLEYS | TYPES OF FRICTION | MEASURING IN SPACE | Go online to choose one of these other paths. |

Lesson Self-Check

CAN YOU EXPLAIN THE PHENOMENON?

FIGURE 18: An acorn and an ant fall from a branch at the same time. The insect hits the ground more gently. Use these details as evidence when you construct your explanation.

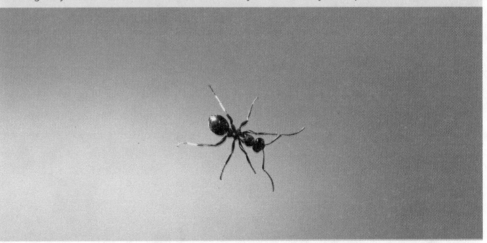

The effect of gravity on a steel ball, a rubber ball, and an iron ball is similar—all fall with a constant acceleration of 9.8 m/s^2. A leaf is also subject to the force due to gravity, yet it may fall with a different pattern of motion.

In this lesson, you have learned how forces affect motion. You have also learned some of the factors that affect the magnitudes and directions of different types of forces. For example, frictional force depends on the normal force but not on area or speed of the object, while air resistance depends on both the area and the speed of the object moving through air. Apply your knowledge to the example of an acorn and an ant, each falling from the same high branch of a tree. Recall that the acorn makes an audible sound as it hits the ground, while the ant hits almost silently and walks away unharmed.

Evidence Notebook Refer to your notes in your Evidence Notebook to explain the factors that affect the motion of falling objects. Your explanation should include a discussion of different forces that can act on a falling object, net force, and acceleration due to force.

Claim Explain the factors that can cause the motion of the falling ant and the acorn in the example to differ. Put your claim in terms of physical quantities such as force, mass, and acceleration.

Evidence List the information given about the ant and acorn, observations you have made in labs and other situations, physical laws, and any other information that you are using as evidence to support your claim.

Reasoning Explain how the evidence supports your claim. Use free-body or force-pair diagrams to compare the falling ant and acorn. If either or both depart from an acceleration of 9.8 m/s^2, explain why.

CHECKPOINTS

Check Your Understanding

Use the following description to answer the next three questions.

A book of mass 0.8 kg is pushed left across a table with a force of 2.0 N. Kinetic friction provides a force of magnitude 0.2 N.

1. Use a free-body diagram to analyze the forces on the object. In what direction is the net force?
   - ○ **a.** Net force is down.
   - ○ **b.** Net force is up.
   - ○ **c.** Net force is to the left.
   - ○ **d.** Net force is to the right.
   - ○ **e.** Net force is at a diagonal.

2. What is the magnitude of the net force on the book?
   - ○ **a.** 0 N
   - ○ **b.** 1.8 N
   - ○ **c.** 2.0 N
   - ○ **d.** 2.2 N
   - ○ **e.** 7.8 N

3. What is the magnitude of the acceleration of the book?
   - ○ **a.** 0 m/s^2
   - ○ **b.** 2.3 m/s^2
   - ○ **c.** 2.5 m/s^2
   - ○ **d.** 9.8 m/s^2

4. Select the correct terms to complete the sentence about force and acceleration. Ignore friction.

   When a bowling ball hits a bowling pin of lesser mass, it exerts a forward force on the pin. The pin exerts a forward | backward force on the ball. This force is less than | more than | equal to the force of the ball on the pin. The ball accelerates forward | backward, and the magnitude of the ball's acceleration is less than | more than | equal to the magnitude of the pin's acceleration.

5. Two ice skaters stand facing each other. The first skater has a mass of 100 kg and the second has a mass of 50 kg. They push each other away. During this push, the first skater accelerates at 3 m/s^2 to the left. The second skater accelerates at

   _____ m/s^2 to the _____.

Use the diagram to answer the next two questions. Assume the pulley and string are massless and the system is frictionless.

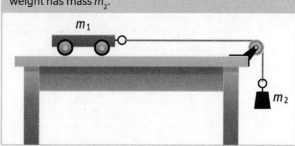

FIGURE 19: The cart has mass m_1 and the descending weight has mass m_2.

6. Select the correct terms to complete the statements about the diagram.

   The tension in the vertical part of the string is less than | greater than | the same as the tension in the horizontal part of the same string.

   The net force on the cart-string-weight system is $m_1g \,|\, m_2g \,|\, (m_1 + m_2)g \,|\, (m_2 - m_1)g$.

7. Suppose that for trial 1, $m_1 = 0.2$ kg and $m_2 = 0.5$ kg. For trial 2, $m_1 = 0.4$ kg, double the initial value. How will the acceleration of trial 2 compare to that measured in trial 1?
   - ○ **a.** Acceleration will double.
   - ○ **b.** Acceleration will be halved.
   - ○ **c.** Acceleration will increase by less than a factor of 2.
   - ○ **d.** Acceleration will decrease by less than a factor of 2.

8. An engineer wants to increase the load that the legs of a wooden stool can support. Which of the following changes would meet that goal? Select all correct answers.
   - ☐ **a.** Add more legs.
   - ☐ **b.** Make the legs thicker (larger diameter).
   - ☐ **c.** Use stronger wood of the same density.
   - ☐ **d.** Use taller legs.
   - ☐ **e.** Make the stool smaller in every dimension.

CHECKPOINTS (continued)

9. A box sits at rest on a ramp. Draw a free-body diagram to model the forces on the box. Then explain how you could change the system so that the box would slide down the ramp.

_____

_____

_____

_____

_____

_____

_____

10. What is the distinction between weight and mass? How would each affect the acceleration of an object pushed horizontally?

_____

_____

_____

_____

_____

_____

MAKE YOUR OWN STUDY GUIDE

 In your Evidence Notebook, design a study guide that supports the main ideas from this lesson:

The net force is the vector sum of all external forces acting on an object.

If the net force is zero, the object continues at rest or in straight-line motion at constant velocity.

If the net force is not zero, the object accelerates according to $a = F_{net}/m$.

Forces come in equal and opposite pairs, which act on different bodies.

Engineers balance external forces and design structures that make use of stresses in order to produce stable structures or desired motion.

Remember to include the following information in your study guide:
• Use examples that model main ideas.
• Record explanations for the phenomena you investigated.
• Use evidence to support your explanations. Your support can include drawings, data, graphs, laboratory conclusions, and other evidence recorded throughout the lesson.

Think about how Newton's laws explain how force affects motion.

Life Science Connection

A Very Long Jump The muscles in the grasshopper's legs store energy through tension, just as a spring stores energy. The energy is released when the legs push against the ground. The reaction force of the ground pushes the insect forward rapidly. Grasshoppers can jump many times the length of their bodies in a single leap.

> Research how far a typical grasshopper can jump. Compare the relative length of the grasshopper's leap to that of a champion human athlete. Make a poster that compares the scales of the two motions and relates the different forces acting in and on the organisms.

FIGURE 1: This grasshopper's legs are ready to exert force.

Art Connection

More Powerful than a Locomotive In a movie, TV show, or graphic novel, you might find the laws of physics set aside. Characters fly through the air. They stop moving objects with no hint of a force pushing back and maybe even catch bullets in their hands. Buses fly impossible distances. These abilities and events make for interesting stories, but they do not reflect the physical laws that describe the world around you.

> Research fictional characters who live and operate by their own rules of nature. Make a chart to compare the assumptions that the authors of the fictional characters had to make that do not match what you know about physics.

FIGURE 2: Forces in action movies do not always strictly follow the laws of physics.

Architecture Connection

Floating Structures Tensegrity structures often appear to break rules of common sense about how structures stay together. However, they do not violate the rules of physics. In these structures, the skeletal parts, such as sticks, are held in place by forces that compress them from both ends. The parts do not touch one another. They are held in position by other elements, such as strings or cables that have forces of tension pulling them tight. The result is a stable structure that always looks like it is on the edge of collapse.

> Research tensegrity structures. Identify how forces work together to make them stable. Then use common items such as sticks or rods along with string or rubber bands to build your own structure. Design an infographic that includes a sketch of your structure. Label all of the forces that you can.

FIGURE 3: At a casual glance, it is hard to understand why the structure does not collapse.

A BOOK EXPLAINING
COMPLEX IDEAS USING
ONLY THE 1,000 MOST
COMMON WORDS

TALL ROADS
Roads that help people walk over deep holes

You know that all structures have forces acting on them—and that forces always exist in pairs. What forces must engineers consider when designing and building a bridge? As you read this explanation of how bridges are built, keep Newton's third law of motion (action-reaction forces) in mind.

RANDALL MUNROE
XKCD.COM

THE STORY OF GETTING FROM HERE TO THERE

THE EARTH'S PULL HOLDS PEOPLE TO THE GROUND.

HEY, GET BACK HERE!

WE LIKE TO WALK AROUND, BUT SOMETIMES THE GROUND GOES PLACES WE DON'T WANT TO GO, LIKE INTO A DEEP HOLE.

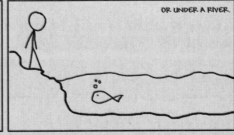

OR UNDER A RIVER.

WE CAN'T GET PAST THOSE PLACES BECAUSE WE HAVE TO FOLLOW THE GROUND.

(BIRDS DON'T, SINCE THEY CAN FLY BY PUSHING ON THE AIR. SOMEONE IN A MOVIE ONCE SANG, "IF BIRDS FLY OVER THE SKY, WHY CAN'T I?" THE ANSWER IS, "YOU ARE TOO BIG AND DON'T HAVE WINGS.")

If we want to go somewhere, we can make a road that goes straight across, high above the ground. Making short roads over holes and rivers is pretty easy, but making long ones can be very hard.

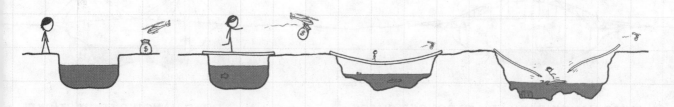

HOLE
Sometimes, you want to walk somewhere, but you don't want to go where the ground goes.

ROAD
If the hole is small enough, you can put a board over the hole to make a new road. Then you can walk across the board.

LONG ROAD
If you find a bigger hole, you can try to find a bigger board. Bigger boards are longer and stronger, but they're also heavier—and bigger things get heavier faster than they get stronger.

LONGER ROAD
All boards bend a little, and longer boards bend more. A long enough board will break under your weight, and a very long board will break under its *own*.

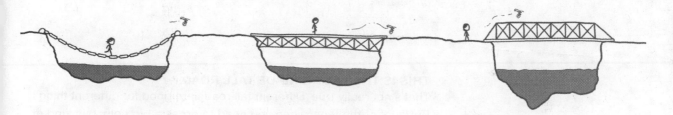

BENDY ROAD
You can cross a larger hole with a road that's allowed to bend. If you tie many small boards together and let it hang, bending won't hurt it, and that will let it hold more weight.

This kind of road gets stronger the more you let it hang down, but it also gets harder to walk across. If it hangs down *too* far, it's no better than just walking down into the hole.

THICK ROAD
You can cross a bigger hole if you make the board thicker. Thicker things are harder to bend, so this kind of road is stronger.

TALL ROAD
It might seem like it would make more sense to put the extra-thick part below the road, because it's "holding" the road up, and we usually hold things from below.

But if it's strong mostly because it's thick, then it works just as well if you add the thickness above the road.

TALL ROADS

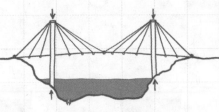

ROAD HANGING UNDER A STRONGER SHAPE
Since all this stuff you're adding is just there to hold the road up, that stuff doesn't need to be near the road. You can make a strong metal piece that goes high up over the hole—which gives it a stronger shape, but would be harder to walk on if the road went that way—and then use strong metal lines to hang the road straighter across under it.

HANGING ROAD PROBLEMS
When you hold up a road by hanging it, you have to be very careful. These tall roads keep the road from being moved by the Earth's pull—which is always straight down—but wind can make the road swing side-to-side.

Some roads have fallen down because the builders didn't understand wind well enough.

ROAD HANGING FROM STICKS
Another way to hold up a road is to build very strong sticks, then hang the road from the top ends of the sticks. The lines need to be a little stronger than the lines in the other hanging road, and the sticks need to be *really* strong. On the other hand, there are only two sticks, so that can make building easier.

THIS IS THE BEST KIND OF TALL ROAD.
That's not really true. Different tall roads are good for different things.

But a lot of the time, when you need to cross a big hole, this kind of shape will let your road reach farther than any other shape would.

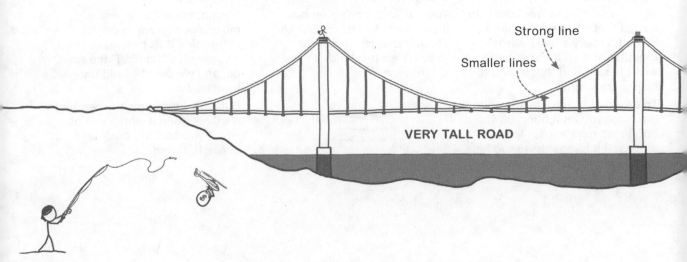

Strong line

Smaller lines

VERY TALL ROAD

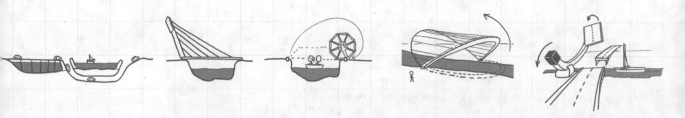

TALL ROADS ON OTHER WORLDS

A very bright person (who was known for calling the Earth a "pale blue point") once said something interesting about these kinds of roads in one of his books.

He pointed out that everything about the shape of very tall roads is decided by the laws of space and time—the laws that say how a world's weight pulls things—and those laws are the same everywhere.

That means that if there's life on other worlds, the road shape that works best for them should be the same one that works best for us. Our tall roads may look familiar to them.

Maybe that's true; maybe it's not. We don't know if there's life on other worlds, and if there is, maybe they don't build roads at all. Maybe their way of living is different from ours in ways we can't even think about.

But if they have holes they need to get across. . .

. . . and if, in their world, they build things out of different shapes, like us . . .

. . . and if they have problems with holding their roads up . . .

. . . then they very well may build tall roads that look just like ours.

I like that idea, because now, when I look at one of these tall roads, I always feel a little happier. It makes me think about how maybe, somewhere far across space and time, there's someone looking at another tall road, thinking about how the shape might be found across many worlds, and—maybe—wondering about me.

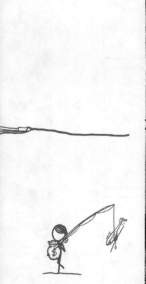

A BOOK EXPLAINING
COMPLEX IDEAS USING
ONLY THE 1,000 MOST
COMMON WORDS

RANDALL MUNROE
XKCD.COM

LIFTING ROOM
Boxes that carry people up and down

You've learned about both horizontal and vertical one-dimensional motion. A classic example of vertical one-dimensional motion is an elevator. Here's an explanation of how elevators work—and why they are a safe way to travel up and down.

THE STORY OF LIFTING ROOMS

A LIFTING ROOM IS A BOX THAT CARRIES PEOPLE UP AND DOWN IN A BUILDING.

TODAY'S CITIES WOULDN'T MAKE SENSE WITHOUT LIFTING ROOMS. IF WE HAD TALL BUILDINGS WITHOUT THEM, EVERYONE WOULD WANT TO STAY ON THEIR OWN FLOOR, BECAUSE GOING UP OR DOWN WOULD TAKE A LOT MORE WORK THAN GOING THE SAME DISTANCE TO THE SIDE.

TALL BUILDINGS MIGHT HAVE TO JOIN UP WITH EACH OTHER, AND PEOPLE WOULD MOSTLY MOVE BETWEEN THEM WHILE STAYING ON THEIR OWN FLOORS.

MOST LIFTING ROOMS GO STRAIGHT UP AND DOWN.

A FEW GO TO THE SIDE WHILE GOING UP AND DOWN, TO TAKE PEOPLE TO THE TOP OF A HILL.

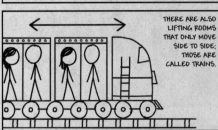

THERE ARE ALSO LIFTING ROOMS THAT ONLY MOVE SIDE TO SIDE; THOSE ARE CALLED TRAINS.

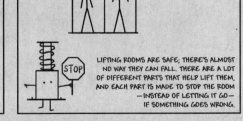

STOP

LIFTING ROOMS ARE SAFE; THERE'S ALMOST NO WAY THEY CAN FALL. THERE ARE A LOT OF DIFFERENT PARTS THAT HELP LIFT THEM, AND EACH PART IS MADE TO STOP THE ROOM —INSTEAD OF LETTING IT GO— IF SOMETHING GOES WRONG.

LIFTER

These lifters usually sit in a machine room above the top floor the lifting room can visit. They use power to turn a big wheel that pulls a line running between the room and a weight.

WEIGHT

This weight makes it easier for the puller to lift the room. It hangs down on the other end of the line holding the room, so when the puller at the top lifts the room, it's also lowering the weight.

PULLING LINES

Lifting rooms are held and lifted by a big group of metal lines. There are usually around four to eight of them, but it can be more or less than that.

These lines are very strong. Usually, even just one of them would be enough to hold the whole room on its own, but we use more just to be safe.

GRABBERS

If the fall feeler pulls on the line, these grab the metal stick really hard and stop the room from moving.

FALL FEELER

This wheel is joined to the room's stopping grabbers by a line. As the room moves up and down, the wheel turns.

If the room starts going down fast, the wheel starts spinning fast, and the little arms in the middle of the wheel swing out and catch onto the teeth around them. This makes the wheel stop turning, which makes the room suddenly pull on the line—setting off the room's stopping grabbers.

METAL STICK

LIFTING ROOM

PRETEND CONTROLS

There are controls on the inside of a lifting room that you use to tell it where you want to go. Some of these controls, like the one marked "DOOR CLOSE," don't always seem to do anything.

Some people say that those controls don't even go anywhere, because the lifting room's computer knows when to open and close the door better than you do.

This is half true. On some new lifting rooms, the DOOR CLOSE control might not normally do anything. This is different in different buildings; it's up to the person who owns the building to decide whether to make these controls work.

But the DOOR OPEN control *is* always joined to the lifting room's systems, in case fire fighters need to take full control of the lifters—by putting a special key into the control place—to use them while fighting a fire.

LIFTING ROOM

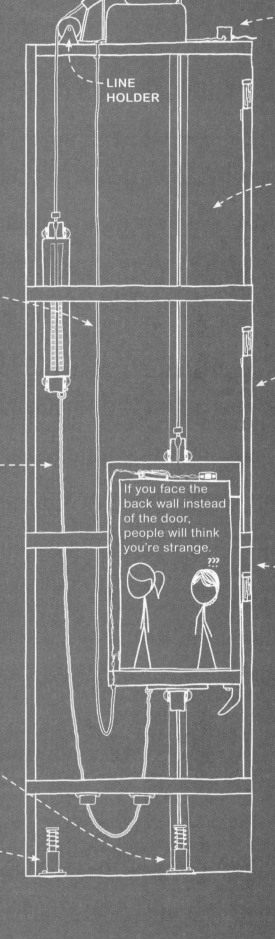

LINE STOPPER - - -
This thing listens to the different parts of the machines, sometimes with the help of a computer, and grabs the line if anything goes wrong.

The line stopper also grabs the line when the room stops at a floor to make sure it doesn't move while people get on and off. It's made so it will keep holding on if the power goes out.

LINE HOLDER

POWER LINE - - -
This line brings power for the lights and controls in the lifting room. It sometimes runs to the top of the hallway, where the pulling machines are, or sometimes to the side of the wall part of the way up the hallway.

WEIGHT LINE - - - - - - - - - - -
This line is used in the lifting rooms in tall buildings to help keep the weight on the puller even.

When a room is all the way at the top or bottom, the lines holding it add to the weight on one side. When that happens, most of the weight of this line hangs on the other side, which keeps things even.

If you face the back wall instead of the door, people will think you're strange.

CATCHER - -
If a lifting room does fall, these catchers hit a metal plate on the bottom of the room and make the landing a little softer.

There's a second catcher for the weight. - - -

Go online for more about *Thing Explainer*.

POWER FROM BUILDING

Lifting rooms use a lot of power, but the lights and air systems in the building use even more.

TALL HALLWAY

The lifting room sits inside a long hallway that goes up and down instead of to the side. It can be longer than any of the normal hallways in the building, but most people never see it.

DOORS

These doors line up with the doors on the room. When the lifting room stops, both doors open together.

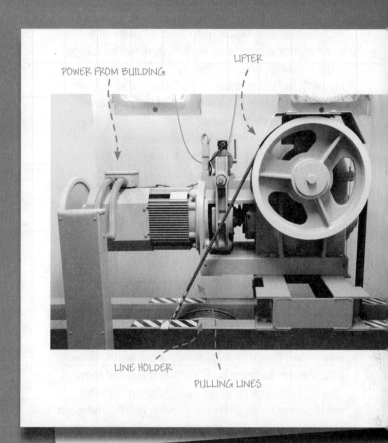

POWER FROM BUILDING

LIFTER

LINE HOLDER

PULLING LINES

EMPTY ROOM

Lifting rooms are usually empty. People don't put chairs or tables in them except to move those things to other floors. If you tried to use one of these rooms as an office, someone would probably yell at you.

DING!

HI, CAN I HELP YOU?

Modeling a Building Design

Architects design buildings to meet a variety of aesthetic and functional criteria. In each design, the buildings must be stable and safe for use. To achieve this stability, buildings must be constructed such that forces are balanced in each part of the structure. The buildings must be able to withstand weather and geologic conditions for the area, as well as any other conditions required by the use of the building.

Build and use a model to explore how forces might be balanced in a building design. Consider how real-world buildings might use balanced forces or more complex designs to achieve stability.

FIGURE 4: A building that includes a cantilever design

1. DEFINE THE PROBLEM

The building in Figure 4 has a cantilever, which is a part that projects out and is unsupported on one end. Examine Figure 4 or another building with an interesting structure and identify what aesthetic or functional criteria the building was designed to meet. Describe why the building was designed with the cantilever or other interesting characteristic and what challenges the construction team might have faced.

2. DEVELOP A MODEL

Use simple materials—a stack of matching books or blocks—to build an interesting, stable structure that includes at least one cantilever. Consider the following questions when designing your structure.

- How far out horizontally from the base can you extend the structure?
- What are different ways to achieve an overhanging part of the structure?

3. USE A MODEL

Draw a diagram or take a photo of the most interesting or successful model structure developed using the stacked books or blocks. On the diagram or photo, label various measurements, including the height of the structure and how far out from the base the structure extends. Describe the characteristics of the materials used. Draw force vectors showing how forces balance on three different objects within the structure.

4. COMMUNICATE

Make a poster or digital presentation that includes the labeled diagram of the model and a real-world building design. For both the model and the real-world design, describe how forces are balanced at different places on the structure. Describe how the model is relevant to the real-world design, and then identify challenges and criteria the real-world design had to meet that cannot be represented in the model.

CHECK YOUR WORK

Once you have completed this task, you should have the following:

- a labeled diagram or photo of the stacked book/block building model
- a poster or digital presentation describing both the model and a real-world design, and the relationship between them
- an explanation of challenges and criteria that architects encounter when designing an interesting structure

Name _____ Date _____

SYNTHESIZE THE UNIT

In your Evidence Notebook, make a concept map, other graphic organizer, or outline using the Study Guides you made for each lesson in this unit. Be sure to use evidence to support your claims.

When synthesizing individual information, remember to follow these general steps:
- Find the central idea of each piece of information.
- Think about the relationships among the central ideas.
- Combine the ideas to come up with a new understanding.

DRIVING QUESTIONS

Look back to the Driving Questions from the opening section of this unit. In your Evidence Notebook, review and revise your previous answers to those questions. Use the evidence you gathered and other observations you made throughout the unit to support your claims.

PRACTICE AND REVIEW

1. Complete the statement about force pairs.

   1/20   equal to   20 times

   A 100 kg person throws a 5 kg bowling ball. The force of the person on the ball is _____ the force of the ball on the person and opposite in direction. If there is no friction with the floor to hold the person in place, the acceleration of the ball is _____ the acceleration of the person and opposite in direction.

2. A toy rocket is launched into the air at an angle of 75° relative to the ground. Which statements about the motion of the rocket are true, assuming air resistance to be zero and there is no thrust on the rocket after launch? Select all correct answers.
   - ☐ a. The acceleration of the rocket is positive as it rises and negative as it falls.
   - ☐ b. The downward acceleration of the rocket is 9.8 m/s² throughout its flight.
   - ☐ c. The average horizontal velocity of the rocket through the entire flight is zero.
   - ☐ d. The instantaneous velocity of the rocket just before it hits the ground is the same as it was just after launch.

3. A train is moving on a track with an upward gradient at a constant speed. Which of the following statements are true?
   - ○ a. The net force on one of the train cars is zero.
   - ○ b. The only force acting on the train is the pull of the engine.
   - ○ c. There is no normal force because the train is moving.
   - ○ d. The net force on the train is in the direction of its motion.

4. How is the engineering design process different from the scientific inquiry process?
   - ○ a. Engineering design is an iterative process.
   - ○ b. Engineering design is focused on solving a defined problem.
   - ○ c. Engineering design does not have to adhere to scientific principles.
   - ○ d. Engineering design processes have many steps, but they are flexible.

5. A bridge over a small river washes out, disrupting local traffic. Within a week, a new temporary bridge is placed next to the washed-out one. Over the next ten months, a second bridge is constructed where the old one stood. Which criterion likely received the most weight when choosing the design for the temporary bridge?
   - ○ a. price   ○ c. durability
   - ○ b. time   ○ d. environment

6. A small rubber ball is rolling quickly on a table. When it reaches the edge of the table, it falls to the floor. Describe the motion of the ball after it rolls off the table, and identify the force(s) acting on it.

_____

_____

_____

_____

_____

7. A tractor is dragging a large object across a field at a constant speed using a chain. Draw a free-body diagram to model the forces on the object. Then explain how the system could be changed to move the object faster.

_____

_____

_____

_____

_____

_____

8. How does a decision matrix help engineers determine what design is most likely to be the best solution to a problem?

_____

_____

_____

_____

UNIT PROJECT

Return to your unit project. Prepare a presentation using your research and materials, and share it with the class. In your final presentation, show how you compared beam designs and how you evaluated their strength.

Remember these tips while evaluating:

- Explain how the cross section of the design affects its strength.

- Describe your test and how it provides data for comparison of different designs.

- Evaluate different aspects of your design and other designs from the class to determine which design elements increase strength the most.

Energy and Motion

YOU SOLVE IT

**How Can You Select Materials
for Colliding Objects?**

**How Can Thermal
Energy Transfer between
Two Components?**

To begin exploring this unit's concepts,
go online to investigate ways to solve a
real-world problem.

A roller coaster gains speed as it rolls
downhill.

Images Plus/Getty Images

FIGURE 1: A meteor glows as it disintegrates in Earth's atmosphere.

A fragment of an asteroid crossing the space between planets has kinetic energy. When the rock enters Earth's atmosphere, it compresses the air in front of it. Friction between the air and the rock increases the temperature of both. The rock becomes so hot it glows and vaporizes, becoming a meteor that can be seen as a streak of light in the sky. The meteor may cause a shock wave and a sonic boom. People have reported hearing sizzling sounds as meteors pass overhead. While the source of these sounds is unclear, one possible explanation is that the glowing rock gives off electromagnetic energy, which affects objects on the ground.

EXPLAIN What does it mean to transfer energy? How does a meteor transfer energy?

_____

_____

_____

DRIVING QUESTIONS

As you move through the unit, gather evidence to help you answer the following questions. In your Evidence Notebook, record what you already know about these topics and any questions you have about them.

1. How can you predict the outcome of a collision?
2. How are momentum and kinetic energy related?
3. How do system models help us understand the transfer of energy?
4. How is energy related to temperature?

UNIT PROJECT

Go online to download the Unit Project Worksheet to help plan your project.

Impractical Machines

When would you want to make a process as complex as possible, rather than simplify it? Rube Goldberg was a Pulitzer Prize–winning cartoonist with a degree in engineering. His cartoons show designs for multistep, overly complicated processes to perform simple tasks, such as buttering toast or wiping one's mouth with a napkin. One device triggers the next in a cascade of steps. Research Rube Goldberg designs, both the original cartoons and videos of physical machines. Then design and build such a device, using as many different steps and as many types of energy as feasible.

Language Development

Use the lessons in this unit to complete the chart and expand your understanding of the science concepts.

TERM: momentum

Definition	Example

Similar Term	Phrase

TERM: impulse

Definition	Example

Similar Term	Phrase

TERM: system

Definition	Example

Similar Term	Phrase

TERM: kinetic energy

Definition	Example

Similar Term	Phrase

TERM: potential energy

Definition	Example

Similar Term	Phrase

TERM: work

Definition	Example

Similar Term	Phrase

TERM: heat

Definition	Example

Similar Term	Phrase

TERM: temperature

Definition	Example

Similar Term	Phrase

2.1

Momentum and Collisions

In an accident, the airbag rapidly inflates to protect the driver.

CAN YOU EXPLAIN THE PHENOMENON?

For many years, seat belts were the main protection for drivers and passengers in cars. Airbags were added to cars to make them safer in an accident. An airbag is similar to a large balloon. During a car crash, the airbag inflates in an instant to cushion the driver and passengers before they would hit the steering wheel or dashboard.

EXPLAIN A car collides with a tree, causing the airbag in the steering wheel to deploy. Describe what happens to the driver and passengers as the airbag deploys and their car suddenly comes to a stop.

_____

_____

_____

_____

_____

_____

 Evidence Notebook As you explore the lesson, gather evidence to explain how cars are designed to minimize the impact on drivers and passengers in a collision.

Quantifying Momentum

The car and truck in Figure 1 are both moving. If the vehicles needed to stop quickly, each driver would apply their brakes. Consider what happens as each vehicle tries to stop.

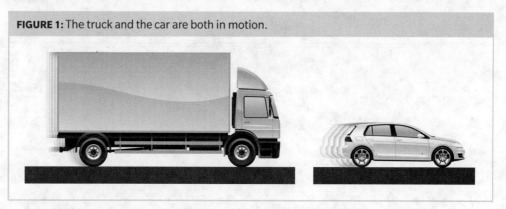

FIGURE 1: The truck and the car are both in motion.

PREDICT Will the car or the truck in Figure 1 be more difficult to stop? What additional information would you need to answer the question?

_____

_____

_____

Momentum

Have you ever tried to stop or slow a moving object? Newton's first law describes that an object in motion tends to stay in motion unless acted upon by an unbalanced force. However, every object is not affected by forces in the same way. A running dog can be slowed down by pulling on its leash, but pulling on a moving car with the same force might barely affect its motion.

Moving objects all have a property called momentum, which can be used to quantify how hard it is to change their motion. The momentum of an object is related to the amount of force needed to change the object's motion in a given amount of time. The symbol used in physics for momentum is the variable **p**. The units of momentum are kilogram meters per second, kg·m/s.

MODEL Momentum is calculated using an object's velocity (**v**) and mass (m). Express momentum as an equation with the variables **p**, m, and **v**. Use the units of momentum to help develop and check your equation.

_____

_____

_____

Momentum Comparisons

FIGURE 2: The truck has twice the mass of the car, but it is moving at only half the speed of the car.

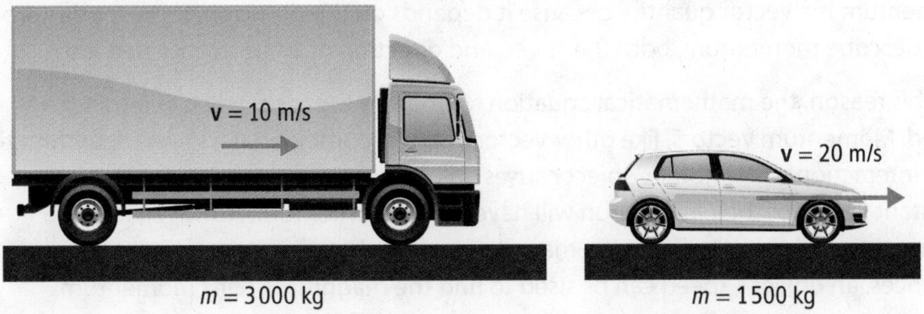

$v = 10$ m/s

$v = 20$ m/s

$m = 3\,000$ kg

$m = 1\,500$ kg

ANALYZE In Figure 2, the truck has a mass of 3000 kg and a velocity of 10 m/s, and the car has half the mass of the truck (1500 kg) but twice the velocity (20 m/s). What is the relationship between the momentum of the car and the momentum of the truck? Which vehicle would be harder to stop?

_____

_____

_____

The momentum of an object is directly proportional to both that object's mass and its velocity. If two objects have the same momentum but different masses, then the object with the smaller mass must have a greater velocity.

FIGURE 3: These balls, viewed from above, are rolling across the floor from left to right. The balls have the same momentum.

Explore Online ▶

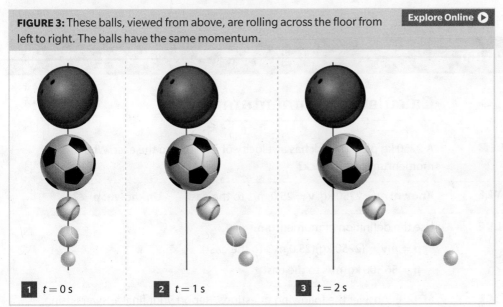

| 1 | $t = 0$ s
| 2 | $t = 1$ s
| 3 | $t = 2$ s

EXPLAIN How do the masses and the velocities of the balls in Figure 3 compare to each other? Describe how the mass of a ball plays a role in its momentum.

_____

_____

_____

Momentum as a Vector

The momentum of an object can be represented as a vector, just as velocity and force vectors can be used to represent movement and forces associated with an object. Momentum is a vector quantity because it depends on the direction of the motion. To fully describe momentum, both the speed and direction of an object are needed.

For this reason, the mathematical equation for momentum uses velocity rather than speed. Momentum vectors, like other vectors, can be combined using vector arithmetic. If an interaction with another object causes an object to change its momentum, the resultant vector of their interaction will have a new momentum. However, it is also common to only need to know the magnitude of an object's momentum. In these instances, an object's speed can be used to find the magnitude of its momentum.

ANALYZE A ball was moving with a velocity $\mathbf{v}_1$. After interacting with a second object, its velocity became $\mathbf{v}_2$. Draw a vector to show the momentum transfer from the second object that was needed in order to change the ball's momentum from $m\mathbf{v}_1$ to $m\mathbf{v}_2$.

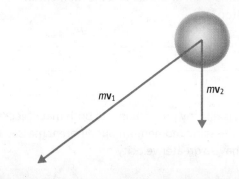

$m\mathbf{v}_1$

$m\mathbf{v}_2$

Problem Solving

Calculating Momentum

SAMPLE PROBLEM

A 2250 kg pickup truck has a velocity of 25.0 m/s to the east. What is the momentum of this truck?

ANALYZE   **Known:** $m = 2250$ kg, $\mathbf{v} = 25.0$ m/s to the east   **Unknown: p = ?**

SOLVE   Use the definition of momentum.

$\mathbf{p} = m\mathbf{v} = (2250$ kg$)(25.0$ m/s to the east$)$

$\mathbf{p} = 56\,300$ kg·m/s to the east

PRACTICE PROBLEM

SOLVE Answer the following questions. Report your final answers using the correct number of significant figures.

1. A deer with a mass of 146 kg is running south at 17.0 m/s. Find the momentum of the deer.

   _____

2. What velocity must a 1210 kg car have in order to have the same momentum as the pickup truck from the Sample Problem?

   _____

Conservation of Momentum

The championship of ice skating is about to begin. Two ice skaters stand facing each other, hands pressed together. The music starts, and one skater pushes on the hands of the other skater. How will the skaters move? Does the mass of each skater affect how they move?

You can use spring-loaded carts to model a similar situation. Like a skater pushing off of another skater, a cart with a spring-loaded plunger can push on another cart.

RESEARCH QUESTION What patterns of motion exist when one ice skater pushes on another skater?

MAKE A CLAIM

When one ice skater pushes another skater, how do they move? How can you predict the specific motion that will occur?

MATERIALS

- safety goggles
- balance

- equipment to find the speeds of moving carts

- carts, 1 with a spring-loaded plunger (2)
- set of masses

SAFETY INFORMATION

- Wear safety goggles during the setup, hands-on, and takedown segments of the activity.
- Secure loose clothing, remove loose jewelry, wear closed-toe shoes, and tie back long hair.
- Immediately pick up any items dropped on the floor so they do not become a slip/fall hazard.
- Wash your hands with soap and water immediately after completing this activity.

PLAN THE INVESTIGATION

Part 1: Qualitative Observations

Consider two carts at rest next to each other. One cart has a spring-loaded plunger that, when released, will push the other cart. In your Evidence Notebook, design a simple experiment to make qualitative observations of the carts' motions after the spring is released. Design a data table to organize your observations. Make sure your procedure includes observing the following situations:

- Case 1: Carts loaded with equal masses
- Case 2: Carts loaded with unequal masses
- Case 3: Carts loaded to have an even greater difference in mass

Part 2: Quantitative Observations

Develop a procedure to collect the data needed to calculate the momentum of multiple carts. Record your procedure and data table in your Evidence Notebook. Repeat each of the three test cases from Part 1 using your procedure to gather the necessary data.

Show your procedures and data tables to your teacher for approval before conducting your experiments.

COLLECT DATA

Organize your observations and data using tables in your Evidence Notebook.

CALCULATE

For Part 2, perform any calculations that might be helpful in predicting the velocities of the carts after they separate. Show all your calculations in your Evidence Notebook. Include an explanation of how you are making use of data from your multiple tests.

CONSTRUCT AN EXPLANATION

1. What patterns do you observe in the motion of the carts during Part 1? How did their velocities compare? How can you predict which cart will move faster?

_____

_____

2. What patterns do you observe in the velocities of the carts during Part 2? How can you predict the exact velocity of one cart given the velocity of the other cart?

_____

_____

DRAW CONCLUSIONS

Write a conclusion that addresses each of the points below.

Claim How do ice skaters move when one ice skater pushes another skater? How can the motion of the skaters be predicted? Make both qualitative and quantitative claims.

Evidence What evidence from your investigation supports your claim?

Reasoning Explain how the evidence you gave supports your claim. Describe, in detail, the connections between the evidence you cited and the argument you are making.

_____

_____

_____

_____

_____

 Evidence Notebook In your evidence notebook, describe the factors that affect the momentum of a car. How could this momentum be changed?

Collisions

Have you ever felt the impact of catching a fly ball, watched a drummer bang out a song using drumsticks, or simply set a book down on a table? All of these actions involve objects striking one another. Physicists call each of these events a collision. Collisions are crashes, bumps, impacts, and hits where two or more objects exert forces on one another over a relatively short period of time.

Systems and Collisions

When objects collide, momentum can be transferred between them. If the objects colliding are defined as a system where there are no unbalanced, external forces acting on the objects, momentum will be conserved during the collision. The total momentum of the objects in these systems will be the same before and after the collision. Collisions can be analyzed by comparing each object's initial momentum to its final momentum. For example, Figure 4 shows two billiard balls colliding. In this system, the force of friction between the balls and table can largely be ignored due to the short duration of the collision. During the collision, the balls apply a force to one another, and these forces transfer momentum. The change in momentum of one ball will be equal and opposite to the change in momentum of the other.

FIGURE 4: Two billiard balls hitting each other is a collision.

 Collaborate With a partner, use a large piece of paper and pens of different colors to model conditions before and after a collision. Generate the ideas of what the system is in terms of what forces are acting on the objects in the system.

 Systems and System Models

Constraints of a System

A system is a way of looking at a phenomenon by limiting the number of interactions considered. This method can make a phenomenon much easier to analyze. For example, the collision between the two billiard balls can be simplified by defining the system to only include the two balls. Considering other factors such as the table or the air around the balls could make a model more accurate, but could also make the system too complicated to analyze well.

ANALYZE Describe a situation in which the momentum of two billiard balls would not be conserved. Your description should include the limits of the system.

_____

_____

_____

_____

Momentum in a System

ANALYZE The white ball is moving toward the stationary red ball. The white ball and red ball comprise a system. Draw arrows to show all the forces acting on the two components of the system at the moment the collision occurs.

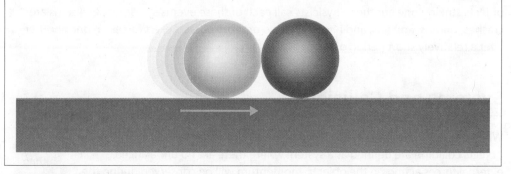

INFER Even though the white ball exerts a force on the red ball, causing the white ball to lose momentum during the collision, we can consider the two balls as a system with no net external forces acting on it. How is this possible?

_____

_____

_____

 Systems and System Models

Conservation of Momentum

When a collision between two objects occurs in a system with no net external forces acting on it, the total momentum of the objects before the collision is equal to the total momentum of the objects after the collision. The momentum lost by one object is equal to the momentum gained by the other object. Because this will always occur, it is called the *law of conservation of momentum*. Within the system, the total momentum is constant.

 Collaborate With a partner, describe three examples in which conservation of momentum can be used to determine the final momenta of objects involved in a collision.

Conservation laws result in a quantity staying constant in a system over time. Momentum is always conserved for collisions when the external forces are balanced. The total momentum before the collision will equal the total momentum after the collision.

When the white ball collides with the stationary red ball, momentum is transferred from the moving white ball, and the stationary red ball moves. The momentum of both billiard balls before the collision will always equal the momentum of both balls after the collision because there are no net external forces acting on any of the balls.

Objects from Rest to Motion

FIGURE 5: Two people push away from each other.

a Before   b After

MODEL In Figure 5, two people on roller skates are facing each other and touching hands. At the same time, they push against each other and roll away from each other in opposite directions. Write equations to represent the initial and final momentum of the system of the two skaters. Are $\mathbf{p}_i$ and $\mathbf{p}_f$ equal to each other?

_____

_____

_____

_____

Colliding Objects

FIGURE 6: A moving ball is about to hit a stationary ball and transfer all of its momentum.

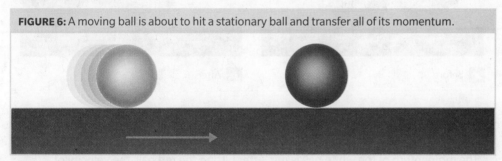

PREDICT A system comprised of two balls of equal mass is shown. One ball, the red ball, is stationary, and the other ball, the white ball, is in motion and heading directly toward the red ball. Which statement describes what most likely happens just after the white ball collides with the stationary red ball?

○ **a.** Both balls move to the right, but the red ball moves faster.

○ **b.** The balls move to the right together.

○ **c.** The white ball becomes stationary, and the red ball moves to the right.

○ **d.** The white ball moves to the left, and the red ball moves to the right.

 Evidence Notebook Define a part of the Rube Goldberg machine in the unit project as a system, and describe how forces affect the objects within that system.

Types of Collisions

ANALYZE Think about examples of collisions that you have seen in games, sports, or toys. Briefly explain what happens to the objects during the collision.

_____

_____

While each object might collide in a slightly different way, most collisions can be sorted into three broad categories. These categories are defined by what happens to the kinetic energy, the energy due to motion, of the colliding objects. Despite what may happen to energy in the collision, each type of collision still follows the conservation of momentum.

Elastic Collisions

Collisions where objects bounce off of one another and kinetic energy is conserved are called elastic collisions. In an elastic collision, there is no loss of velocity and the objects return back to their original shapes after impact. Momentum is conserved for elastic collisions. When there is no loss of kinetic energy, the total kinetic energy of the objects before the collision equals the total kinetic energy of the objects after the collision.

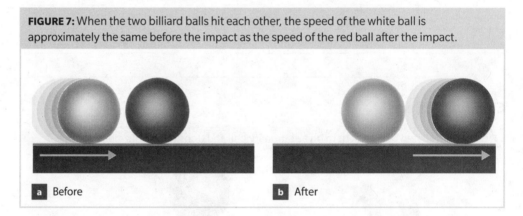

FIGURE 7: When the two billiard balls hit each other, the speed of the white ball is approximately the same before the impact as the speed of the red ball after the impact.

a Before

b After

SOLVE Select the correct terms to complete the paragraph. Assume the usual convention: positive direction is from left to right.

The momentum of the white ball is $m\mathbf{v}$. After hitting the red ball, the velocity of the white ball changes from positive to zero | positive to negative. As a result, the momentum of the red ball changes from zero to positive | negative to positive. Momentum during the collision is conserved | not conserved. For the elastic collision of the two balls, kinetic energy is conserved | not conserved.

Inelastic Collisions

Collisions between billiard balls are often used as an example of elastic collisions. However, during the collision of billiard balls, some kinetic energy is actually lost. On the macroscopic scale, elastic collisions do not truly exist. Some collisions, such as those between billiard balls, lose little enough energy that modeling them as elastic collisions still produces very accurate results. Most collisions observed in everyday life are actually inelastic collisions. In an inelastic collision, two objects bounce off of one another, and while momentum is still conserved, kinetic energy is not. In these collisions, energy is often lost from the system through some combination of deformation, friction, and sound.

Perfectly Inelastic Collisions

Suppose a student is moving along a sidewalk on a skateboard. Without pausing, the student picks up a backpack. In this collision, the objects are not bouncing off of each other, so it cannot be modeled as an elastic or inelastic collision. Instead, this situation can be analyzed as a perfectly inelastic collision. In a perfectly inelastic collision, two objects stay together after colliding. Momentum is conserved, but kinetic energy is not.

FIGURE 8: A collision between a skateboarder and a backpack

Explore Online ▶

APPLY What do you expect to happen after the collision of the skateboarder and the backpack?

○ **a.** The skateboarder will stop.

○ **b.** The skateboarder will move backward.

○ **c.** The skateboarder will move in the same direction, but slower.

○ **d.** The skateboarder will move in the same direction, but faster.

Before the skateboarder picks up the backpack, the skateboarder has a certain amount of momentum, and the bag has zero momentum. When the skateboarder picks up the backpack, the skateboarder and the backpack move together. The momentum of the combined skateboarder and backpack is equal to the momentum of the skateboarder before picking up the backpack because momentum is conserved.

EXPLAIN Two billiard balls hitting one another can be modeled as an elastic collision, and a skateboarder picking up a backpack can be modeled as a perfectly inelastic collision. Summarize the differences between elastic, inelastic, and perfectly inelastic collisions using these examples to help illustrate the differences.

_____

_____

_____

_____

 Language Arts Connection Consider the following scenario: An ice skater accidentally collides with another skater who is standing on the ice. Is it possible for both skaters to be at rest immediately after the collision? Develop a model to demonstrate the situation, and write a brief summary describing how your model supports your conclusion.

Problem Solving

Collisions Using Momentum

SAMPLE PROBLEM A roller skater of 61 kg moving with a velocity of 12 m/s to the east picks up a basket of 5.0 kg. What is the final velocity of the person traveling with the basket?

ANALYZE **Known:** $m_1 = 61$ kg and $m_2 = 5.0$ kg $v_1 = 12$ m/s to the east $v_2 = 0.0$ m/s

Unknown: $p_f = ?$

SOLVE Use the definition of momentum to find the initial momentum of the system.

$$\mathbf{p} = m\mathbf{v} = (61 \text{ kg})(12 \text{ m/s to the east}) + (5.0 \text{ kg})(0.0 \text{ m/s}) = 720 \text{ kg·m/s to the east}$$

Use the law of conservation of momentum.

$$\mathbf{p}_f = \mathbf{p}_i$$

$$\mathbf{p}_f = 720 \text{ kg·m/s to the east} = (61 \text{ kg} + 5.0 \text{ kg}) \, \mathbf{v}_f$$

$$\mathbf{v}_f = 11 \text{ m/s to the east}$$

PRACTICE PROBLEMS **SOLVE** Answer the following questions. Report your final answers using the correct number of significant figures.

1. A 1500 kg car traveling at 15 m/s to the south collides with a 4500 kg truck that is initially at rest at a stoplight. The car and the truck stick together and move together after the collision. What is the final velocity of the two-vehicle mass?

   _____

2. A grocery shopper tosses a 9.0 kg bag of rice into a stationary 18 kg grocery cart. The bag hits the cart with a horizontal speed of 5.5 m/s toward the front of the cart. What is the final speed of the cart and the bag?

   _____

3. A 47.4 kg student runs down the sidewalk and jumps with a horizontal speed of 4.2 m/s onto a stationary skateboard. The student and skateboard move down the sidewalk with a speed of 3.95 m/s. Find the following:

   a. the mass of the skateboard

   _____

   b. how fast the student would have to run initially to have a final speed of 5.0 m/s

   _____

4. A boy on a 2.0 kg skateboard initially at rest tosses an 8.0 kg jug of water in the forward direction. If the jug has a speed of 3.0 m/s relative to the ground and the boy and skateboard move in the opposite direction at 0.60 m/s, find the boy's mass.

   _____

5. A 150 kg bumper car moves forward at +10.0 m/s. It collides with a stationary, 200 kg bumper car. After the collision, the 200 kg bumper car moves forward at 8.57 m/s. What is the 150 kg bumper car's velocity after the collision? Report your answer to 3 significant figures.

   _____

Moving Objects Colliding

While some collisions occur when only one object is moving, many collisions are between multiple moving objects. The same equations from the situations with a stationary object and a moving object can be used to determine momentum of multiple moving objects.

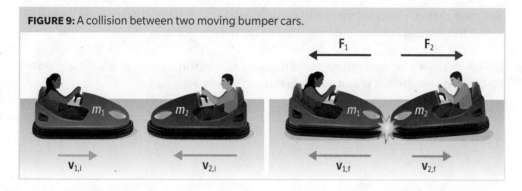

FIGURE 9: A collision between two moving bumper cars.

APPLY What happens to the total momentum of the system of the two bumper cars after this collision? Select all correct answers.

☐ **a.** The total momentum of the system is $m_1\mathbf{v}_{1,i} + m_2\mathbf{v}_{2,i} = m_1\mathbf{v}_{1,f} + m_2\mathbf{v}_{2,f}$.

☐ **b.** The momentum of the bumper car m_1 has the same magnitude but opposite direction as the momentum of the bumper car m_2.

☐ **c.** The change in the total momentum of the system is twice its initial momentum.

PREDICT A person driving a bumper car will feel a jolt during a collision. Based on your knowledge of momentum and collisions, in which type of bumper car collision will the driver experience the biggest jolt: colliding with another bumper car moving in the same direction, colliding with a stationary bumper car, or colliding with a crash barrier?

_____

_____

Explore Online ▶

YOU SOLVE IT

How Can You Select Materials for Colliding Objects?
Investigate how varying materials can affect collisions.

 Energy and Matter

Energy Loss During Collisions

If two lumps of clay stick together after being thrown at each other, the collision could be modeled as a perfectly inelastic collision. The combined lump moves in the direction that the more massive lump was traveling, but slower than its initial velocity. The lump's mass is now greater, and the momentum is constant and conserved. The deformation of the clay does transform some kinetic energy into thermal energy, so the kinetic energy of the system is not conserved.

 Language Arts Connection Make a list of several inelastic collisions you have observed. Identify how energy may be lost in each collision. Make a presentation, including diagrams, that describes each collision and how you think energy is lost.

 Evidence Notebook How do elastic, inelastic, and perfectly inelastic collisions apply to car crashes? When would a crash be classified as each of the different types of collisions?

Relating Impulse and Momentum

You have probably noticed that a ball moving very fast stings your hands when you catch it. This ball exerts a force on your hand over a short period of time.

INFER Baseball players try to minimize the force exerted on their hand when catching a ball. How do you think a player could do this?

_____

_____

_____

Combinations of Force and Time

An unbalanced force is required to change the motion of an object. Applying a force to an object to change its velocity will change the object's momentum. However, forces can be applied in many different ways. Applying a strong force over a short period of time and applying a weak force over a long period of time can produce similar changes in momentum.

An unbalanced force acting on an object over a period of time (Δt) is called an impulse, or a change in momentum. The impulse of the object can be expressed as $I = F\Delta t = \Delta p$—where I is the impulse (a vector quantity), F is the force acting on an object (a vector quantity), and Δt is the time interval during which the force acts on the object (a scalar quantity). However, like momentum, it is also common to discuss only the magnitude of an impulse.

FIGURE 10: The pitcher throws the ball toward the catcher, and the batter tries to hit the ball with the bat.

PREDICT Imagine the pitcher has thrown the ball toward the batter. How does the velocity of the softball before it hits the bat compare to after it hits the bat?

_____

_____

_____

Many different combinations of F and Δt can produce the same impulse (I). A ten newton force acting on an object for five seconds produces the same magnitude of impulse as a twenty-five newton force acting on an object for two seconds.

The time required to stop an object using a constant force is $\Delta t = \Delta p / F$. The same change of an object's momentum can be produced by either decreasing the force while increasing the time interval or increasing the force while decreasing the time interval.

Newton's Second Law and Impulse

Newton's second law of motion is often expressed as $\mathbf{F} = m\mathbf{a}$, but when Newton initially expressed the second law, he wrote it as $\mathbf{F} = \Delta\mathbf{p}/\Delta t$. This equation is equivalent to $\mathbf{I} = \mathbf{F}\Delta t$, but is simply in a different arrangement. According to Newton's second law of motion, the acceleration of an object is directly proportional to the net force acting upon the object and inversely proportional to the object's mass.

SOLVE Select the correct expressions, and order them to show how $\mathbf{F} = \Delta\mathbf{p}/\Delta t$ is equivalent to the more commonly used expression $\mathbf{F} = m\mathbf{a}$.

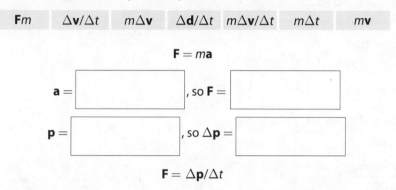

| $\mathbf{F}m$ | $\Delta\mathbf{v}/\Delta t$ | $m\Delta\mathbf{v}$ | $\Delta\mathbf{d}/\Delta t$ | $m\Delta\mathbf{v}/\Delta t$ | $m\Delta t$ | $m\mathbf{v}$ |

$$\mathbf{F} = m\mathbf{a}$$

$\mathbf{a} = \boxed{}$, so $\mathbf{F} = \boxed{}$

$\mathbf{p} = \boxed{}$, so $\Delta\mathbf{p} = \boxed{}$

$$\mathbf{F} = \Delta\mathbf{p}/\Delta t$$

Impulse and Momentum in Sports

According to Newton's second law, any change in an object's motion is closely related to the force applied. When a catcher catches a baseball, the interaction between the mitt and the baseball is a type of collision. Three things are the same for both the mitt and the ball—the magnitude of the force exerted, the time over which the force acts, and the magnitude of the impulse delivered. Recall that impulse is equal to the change in momentum.

FIGURE 11: The catcher catches the ball with a mitt.

ANALYZE Which of the following interactions occur between the ball and catcher's mitt? Select all correct answers.

☐ **a.** The ball exerts a force on the catcher's mitt.

☐ **b.** The catcher's mitt exerts a force on the ball.

☐ **c.** The force on the ball cancels the force on the mitt.

☐ **d.** During the interaction, Δt is the same for the ball and for the mitt.

☐ **e.** During the interaction, Δt is twice as long for the ball as it is for the mitt.

The ball in this example will always require the same impulse to stop. However, the catcher has the ability to vary the amount of force and the amount of time that this force is applied. The catcher can increase the time that the force is exerted over by moving their hand back as they catch the ball. Even though the impulse of the interaction is the same as when the catcher does not move their glove, the force exerted on the catcher's mitt will be reduced by increasing the time during which the force acts.

Force and Impulse

SAMPLE PROBLEM   A baseball with a mass of 0.145 kg travels toward a catcher at a speed of 30.0 m/s. The catcher's mitt brings the ball to rest in 0.20 s. Find the force exerted on the ball by the mitt.

ANALYZE   **Known:** $m = 0.145$ kg

$\quad\quad\quad$ $\mathbf{v}_i = 30.0$ m/s toward the catcher

$\quad\quad\quad$ $\Delta t = 0.20$ s

$\quad\quad\quad$ $\mathbf{v}_f = 0.0$ m/s

Unknown: F = ?

SOLVE   Use the impulse-momentum theorem.

$$\mathbf{F}\Delta t = \Delta\mathbf{p}$$

$$\mathbf{F} = \frac{m\mathbf{v}_f - m\mathbf{v}_i}{\Delta t}$$

$$\mathbf{F} = \frac{(0.145 \text{ kg})(0.0 \text{ m/s}) - (0.145 \text{ kg})(-30.0 \text{ m/s})}{0.20 \text{ s}}$$

$$\mathbf{F} = \frac{4.35 \text{ kg·m/s}}{0.20 \text{ s}}$$

$\mathbf{F} = 22$ N in the direction from the mitt to the ball

---

CHECK YOUR WORK   Since vectors toward the mitt were assigned to be negative (why the $\mathbf{v}_i$ is negative), the force of the mitt on the ball is +21.75 N. Substituting the force back into the impulse-momentum theorem:

$$\mathbf{F}\Delta t = \Delta\mathbf{p}$$

$(21.75 \text{ N})(0.20 \text{ s}) = (0.145 \text{ kg})(0.0 \text{ m/s}) - (0.145 \text{ kg})(-30.0 \text{ m/s}) = 4.35 \text{ kg·m/s}$

Be sure to check your work for each of the Practice Problems below by substituting your final answer into the impulse-momentum theorem to see if both sides of the equation are in agreement.

PRACTICE PROBLEMS   **SOLVE** Answer the following questions. Report your final answer using the correct number of significant figures.

1. A 0.40 kg football is thrown with a velocity of 15 m/s to the right. A stationary receiver catches the ball and brings it to rest in 0.20 s. What is the force exerted on the ball by the receiver?

_____

2. An 82 kg man on a diving board drops from rest 3.0 m above the surface of the water and he comes to rest 0.55 s after reaching the water. What is the average net force on the diver as he is brought to rest? Remember to first find the velocity of the man after he falls 3.0 m off of the diving board.

_____

Stopping Distances and Times

Momentum and impulse are useful for modeling the movement of objects, even when two objects are not colliding. For example, the velocity of a vehicle is an important factor in how much time it takes the vehicle to stop. Stopping distance includes both the distance traveled before the driver reacts and applies the brakes and the braking distance. If we consider only the impulse-momentum theorem, we can infer that the braking distance for a vehicle is related to the resistive force of the brakes, the amount of time that the brakes are applied, and the change in the speed of the vehicle over that given time.

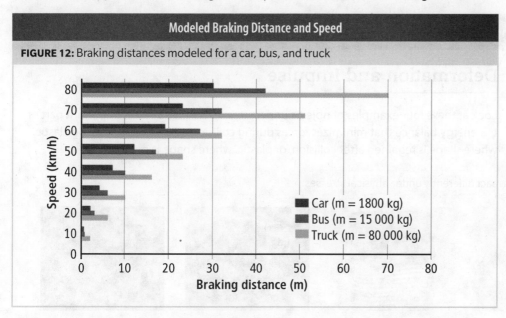

Modeled Braking Distance and Speed

FIGURE 12: Braking distances modeled for a car, bus, and truck

- Car (m = 1800 kg)
- Bus (m = 15 000 kg)
- Truck (m = 80 000 kg)

ANALYZE Compare and contrast the relationships between momentum, impulse, and braking distance as shown in the bar graph for the car, bus, and truck in Figure 12.

Stability and Change

Braking and Momentum

When a car brakes, it is able to slow down without another object colliding with it. Since the car is able to slow seemingly without simply transferring its momentum to another object, it would appear at first glance that a braking car does not obey the law of conservation of momentum.

EXPLAIN Considering the car as the system, why is the car's momentum not conserved over the process of coming to rest? Are there external forces involved?

External Forces in Collisions

When an external force acts on a system, the total momentum of the system will change and momentum will not be conserved. An external force can be applied to increase or decrease the momentum of a system. For example, the system of a car can be defined as the body of the vehicle. This means that the forces from the road, such as frictional forces, are external. When the brakes are applied, the wheels stop turning easily and the external, frictional forces from the road act to slow the car. When external forces act on a system, momentum is not conserved.

Deformation and Impulse

Look at these four examples of objects under stress. *Deformation* is an important part of the energy balance that minimizes forces during collisions. Deformation can be elastic, where shape is regained after collision, or plastic, where shape is not restored.

FIGURE 13: Objects react differently under physical stresses.

a   Rubber bands stretch.
b   Cans bend.
c   Vases fracture.
d   Balls bounce.

PREDICT Some newer cars have crumple zones. These areas of the car are designed to deform plastically, similar to the can in Figure 13b. Why might this be safer than a car that holds it shape during a collision?

_____

_____

_____

EXPLAIN Some materials will crumple or break under very strong forces but hold their shape under weaker forces. How could you change the momentum of objects made with these materials without changing their shape?

_____

_____

_____

 Evidence Notebook Describe the differences between how the momentum of a car changes when it is stopped through braking and when it is stopped by a collision.

Engineering Lab

Modeling Impact Protection

In this activity, you will design a device that can protect an egg in a cart during a collision. Similar to an egg in a cart, car crashes can be modeled to provide safety information about the protection of passengers in the car.

DESIGN CHALLENGE

Design, build, test, and optimize a device that protects an uncooked egg in a cart during a collision with a concrete wall.

POSSIBLE MATERIALS

- safety goggles, nonlatex apron, nonlatex gloves
- eggs, uncooked
- open cart, small

- materials such as packing peanuts, bubble packing, plastic bags, and newspaper
- set of masses

SAFETY INFORMATION

- Wear safety goggles, a nonlatex apron, and nonlatex gloves during the setup, hands-on, and takedown segments of the activity.
- Immediately pick up items dropped on the floor so they do not become a slip/fall hazard.
- Wash your hands with soap and water immediately after completing this activity.
- Never eat any food items used in a lab activity.

CONDUCT RESEARCH

1. What materials and structures do engineers use to build safe cars? How do the properties of these materials and structures help to protect passengers?

_____

_____

_____

2. How do impulse and momentum relate to passenger safety during a collision? What variables do engineers manipulate when designing car safety features?

_____

_____

_____

DEFINE THE PROBLEM

1. Write a statement identifying the problem you are designing a solution for.

_____

2. What are the criteria and constraints for this protective device?

_____

_____

ANALYZE

Evaluate the performance of your design. Did the collision device successfully protect the egg? How did the structures and materials function to protect the egg? What are the weaknesses and strengths of the design? Explain how the design of your device relates to the concepts of momentum and impulse.

_____

_____

_____

_____

OPTIMIZE

1. Revise your design to improve its performance and describe your modifications. In your Evidence Notebook, draw a detailed diagram of your modified design and show your new design to your teacher. Once you have approval for the improved design, construct and test a new prototype following the same procedure as you used to test your original device.

_____

_____

_____

2. Describe the performance of your modified design. Did your design modifications improve the function of your device? Explain the evidence that supports your claims.

_____

_____

_____

COMMUNICATE

Summarize what you learned from your investigation. What factors determine how well a device protects a passenger (egg) from damage during a collision?

_____

_____

_____

_____

_____

_____

_____

 Evidence Notebook Compare the design of your device to an airbag in a car. What strategies used to protect your egg could also help to protect passengers in a car?

Careers in Engineering

FIGURE 14: Hunjoo Kim (left) and Ashley Karp (right) of NASA Jet Propulsion Laboratory, attach heat sensors to the Peregrine Hybrid Rocket Engine prior to its test at the Outdoor Aerodynamic Research Facility at NASA's Ames Research Center.

Rocket Engineer

Rocket engineers work on the design and manufacture of rocket-propelled spacecraft. They can specialize in particular fields such as fuel systems, acoustics, aerodynamics, or guidance systems. Some rocket engineers specialize in quality control inspections.

Rocket engineers who specialize in fuel systems evaluate design specifications to determine the amount of thrust that rocket engines produce. The product of force and time is the impulse. The impulse provided by the rocket engine is critical in causing a stationary rocket to start moving as it lifts off the launch pad and flies. A rocket engineer evaluates information from many different sources to help select criteria for choosing a rocket engine with enough thrust while keeping design constraints such as cost, mass, and availability in mind.

Engineering in Your Community Engineers from diverse backgrounds are responsible for many advances in the fields of rocket science and propulsion. Research an engineer whose work has benefited your community.

Language Arts Connection
Gather information about model rocket engines, the amount of thrust they produce, and the mass of the rocket they can launch. Use the following questions to guide your research:
- What is the range of mass of the model rocket?
- How are model rocket engines rated based on thrust and mass of the rocket?
- What other considerations are necessary when choosing a model rocket engine?

Next, use the Internet to gather charts or tables of model rocket engine data. Include examples from different manufacturers of model rocket engines.

Last, write a brief essay that explains the selection criteria for at least two model rocket engines. As you write, be sure to address the following points:
- the specifications of the model rocket engines selected
- the criteria used to evaluate the suitability for model rocket engines
- the manufacturer and model numbers for the model rocket engines you chose

| SATELLITE LAUNCH | CRASH TESTS | PROTECTING AN EGG | Go online to choose one of these other paths. |

Lesson Self-Check

FIGURE 15: In an accident, the airbag rapidly inflates to cushion and protect the driver.

Car seat belts and airbags are safety features designed to protect the driver and passengers in a collision. Car manufacturers include other ways to make cars safer. Materials used in crumple zones undergo plastic deformation. Parts with elastic deformation regain their shape after impact, while parts with plastic deformation do not.

Momentum is a key concept engineers use when designing car-safety features. Most cars have an electronic sensor that detects sharp decelerations and sends a signal to inflate an airbag. In a collision, the airbag rapidly inflates to protect the driver and passengers. The airbag acts as a pillow between the driver and passengers, and the steering wheel and windshield. Mechanical and chemical engineers work together to design airbags. Properly engineered airbags must work in the space between the driver and the steering wheel, inflate quickly and deflate at the right time, and deploy only during moderate- or high-impact collisions.

 Evidence Notebook Refer to your notes in your Evidence Notebook to make a claim about how a car is designed to minimize the impact on drivers and passengers in a collision. Your explanation should include a discussion of the following points:

Claim How are cars designed to minimize the impact on drivers and passengers in a collision?

Evidence What evidence supports the claim that these design features are useful for protecting drivers and passengers in a collision?

Reasoning How does the evidence you provided support your claim about the usefulness of design features to protect drivers and passengers in a collision?

CHECKPOINTS

Check Your Understanding

1. What is the magnitude of the momentum of a 1000 kg car traveling at 5 m/s?
   - ○ **a.** 200 kg·m/s
   - ○ **b.** 1000 kg·m/s
   - ○ **c.** 5000 kg·m/s

2. What happens to an object's momentum if its mass is reduced by half but its velocity remains the same?
   - ○ **a.** The momentum doubles.
   - ○ **b.** The momentum remains the same.
   - ○ **c.** The momentum is reduced by one half.

3. Which of the following have a greater momentum than a 10 kg ball moving at 10 m/s? Select all correct answers.
   - ☐ **a.** a 1 kg ball moving at 50 m/s
   - ☐ **b.** a 5 kg ball moving at 25 m/s
   - ☐ **c.** a 20 kg ball moving at 10 m/s
   - ☐ **d.** a 50 kg ball moving at 5 m/s
   - ☐ **e.** a 100 kg ball that is stationary

4. Select all of the statements that are true about momentum.
   - ☐ **a.** Two objects with the same mass have the same momentum.
   - ☐ **b.** An object at rest has zero momentum.
   - ☐ **c.** Momentum is a vector quantity.
   - ☐ **d.** Two objects with different velocities but the same mass have the same momentum.
   - ☐ **e.** An object's momentum varies with velocity.

5. Which is true about the momentum of a system of two objects colliding together with no net external forces acting on them?
   - ○ **a.** The total momentum is the same before and after the collision.
   - ○ **b.** The total momentum is less before the collision than after the collision.
   - ○ **c.** The total momentum is greater before the collision than after the collision.

6. A bumper car with a mass of 86 kg is traveling at 3.6 m/s. A bumper car with a mass of 98 kg is traveling at 1.6 m/s in the opposite direction. After the collision, the 86 kg bumper car travels at −0.5 m/s. What is the speed of the 98 kg bumper car after the collision?
   - ○ **a.** 3.1 m/s
   - ○ **b.** 2.0 m/s
   - ○ **c.** 1.8 m/s
   - ○ **d.** 1.1 m/s

7. What happens when a moving bumper car collides with a stationary bumper car?
   - ○ **a.** The stationary bumper car gains momentum.
   - ○ **b.** The moving bumper car gains momentum.
   - ○ **c.** Momentum is not transferred between the bumper cars.
   - ○ **d.** The total momentum after the collision is less than the total momentum before the collision.

8. A baseball with a mass of 0.165 kg travels toward the outfield at a speed of 47 m/s. The outfielder's glove brings the ball to rest in 0.20 s. What is the average force exerted on the ball by the glove?
   - ○ **a.** 1.6 N
   - ○ **b.** 23 N
   - ○ **c.** 39 N
   - ○ **d.** 57 N

9. Which of the following are examples of impulse acting on a baseball? Select all correct answers.
   - ☐ **a.** the catcher catching a ball with the catcher's mitt
   - ☐ **b.** an outfielder throwing the ball to the pitcher
   - ☐ **c.** the batter swinging and missing the ball
   - ☐ **d.** the shortstop scooping up a rolling ball
   - ☐ **e.** the pitcher throwing the ball into the pitcher's own glove

CHECKPOINTS (CONTINUED)

10. Describe how it is possible for a very small force to provide a very large change in the momentum of a moving object.

_____

_____

_____

_____

_____

11. Describe how two objects with different masses can have the same momentum.

_____

_____

_____

_____

12. When a baseball batter hits a baseball, describe what happens to the velocity and momentum of the ball.

_____

_____

_____

_____

_____

MAKE YOUR OWN STUDY GUIDE

 In your Evidence Notebook, design a study guide that supports the main ideas from this lesson:

Momentum is a vector quantity that is the product of mass and velocity.

In a system of colliding objects, with no net external forces acting on them, the total momentum is conserved.

An impulse is produced by a force exerted over a period of time.

The impact during a collision can be minimized if forces are applied over longer periods of time.

Remember to include the following information in your study guide:
- Use examples that model main ideas.
- Record explanations for the phenomena you investigated.
- Use evidence to support your explanations. Your support can include drawings, data, graphs, laboratory conclusions, and other evidence recorded throughout the lesson.

Consider how momentum is conserved in a system when investigating or describing a collision.

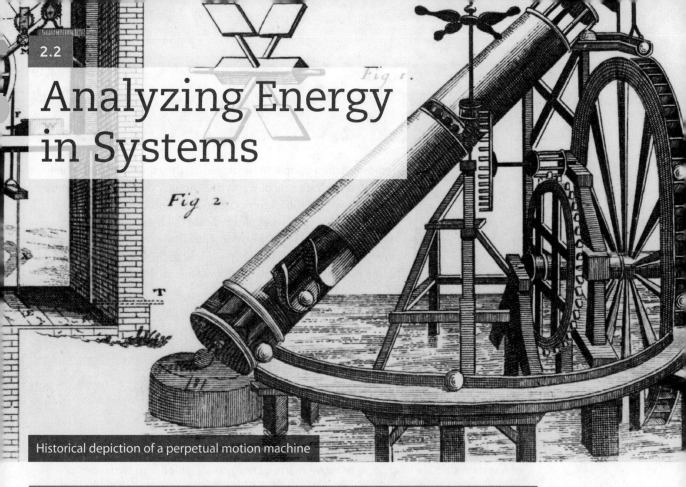

Analyzing Energy in Systems

Historical depiction of a perpetual motion machine

CAN YOU EXPLAIN THE PHENOMENON?

Since the Middle Ages, people have been captivated by the dream of "free energy." Inventors have sought to design machines that could provide unlimited energy; these machines are called perpetual motion machines. In the 12th century, Indian mathematician Bhaskara designed a wheel he claimed could spin forever. In the 17th century, Robert Fludd, an English physician, designed a closed water cycle gristmill that he claimed would continue to run forever. And in the 20th century, an American inventor claimed to have invented a DC motor device that produced more energy than the electrical energy he put in. All of these machines were intended to function indefinitely on their own, but none of them were successfully built.

ANALYZE Look at the machine depicted in the image. How do you think the machine in the image is designed to function?

_____

_____

_____

_____

_____

_____

Evidence Notebook As you explore this lesson, gather evidence to explain why inventors have not successfully built a perpetual motion machine.

Plus/Getty Images

Energy and Systems

FIGURE 1: A car moves past a traffic light.

Typically, when people think of energy, they think about the fuel used to drive their cars or warm their homes; the electrical energy used to energize their lamps, cell phones, and computers; or the food they eat. These examples indicate the many different forms that energy can take. At any moment in time, a system may have energy in one or more forms. It is useful to think of energy as a single quantity that is a sum of its various forms.

 Collaborate With a partner, look at the photo in Figure 1. List as many types and forms of energy in the photo as you can. Discuss your results with another group.

Types and Forms of Energy

The concept of energy has been known to scientists for centuries. Energy is a measure of a system's ability to change or move matter. Energy is classified into two types of energy, each with several forms. Kinetic energy is the type of energy due to the motion of an object. The form of kinetic energy associated with the macroscopic movement of a system is called mechanical kinetic energy. However, the term *kinetic energy* is often used to describe the mechanical form of kinetic energy without specifying "mechanical." The microscopic motion of particles is also kinetic energy. Kinetic energy may be transferred between objects during a collision.

The energy of a system due to its position or state is called potential energy. Potential energy may be associated with the energy in a field—such as a gravitational, magnetic, or electric field—or the state of a system—such as a stretched rubber band. Nuclear energy is an example of potential energy. In a nuclear fission power plant, the bonds in the nucleus of an atom are broken, and the energy from the nuclear bonds transforms into kinetic energy, which warms water into steam to turn a turbine. This turbine turns a generator, which transforms the mechanical kinetic energy into electrical energy. The fact that energy can change form, or transform, is important for systems from cars to light bulbs.

APPLY Consider whether each form of energy is related to motion, or the position/state of a system, and then sort the following forms of energy into the correct type of energy.

chemical   elastic   gravitational   radiant   sound

Kinetic Energy	Potential Energy

Energy and Matter

Fireworks and Energy

A firework is a projectile that is launched into the air, where it then explodes in a colorful display. A firework is an example of how energy and matter interact.

INFER Consider a firework rising into the sky. What forms of energy does the firework have? Support your answer with evidence.

_____

_____

Defining and Analyzing Systems

A system is any portion of the universe that one can select to study. Systems may be simple or complex. The analysis of a complex system can be simplified by dividing the system into subsystems. A system can be used to make energy analysis easier to study by limiting the scope of the analysis.

Systems and System Models

System Boundaries

The extent of a system is defined by its boundaries. Boundaries may be physical or theoretical depending on what is being studied. To see an example of the different types of boundaries, consider how a car can be analyzed as a system. To further simplify the energy analysis of the car, subsystems within the car system can be defined. A car engine is a subsystem of the whole car. A car engine contains cylinders in which pistons move due to the combustion of fuel. The cylinder walls are boundaries of the combustion chamber. These cylinder walls are real, physical boundaries for the expanding gas. The products of combustion exit the system as exhaust. This system boundary does not have a physical counterpart, but makes analyzing the flow of energy in the system easier.

ANALYZE How could you define the system boundaries to analyze the scenario in Figure 3? Explain your answer.

_____

_____

_____

_____

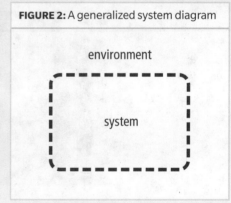

FIGURE 2: A generalized system diagram

environment

system

FIGURE 3: A kicked soccer ball

Gravitational potential energy (GPE) is a form of potential energy that a mass has due to its position in a gravitational field. If the mass is allowed to move freely, the force of gravity will cause the object to move, transforming GPE into kinetic energy. The amount of potential energy the object has is measured relative to a zero position. The zero position is chosen by the scientist performing the analysis and depends on the system being analyzed.

FIGURE 4: Two objects held above a surface

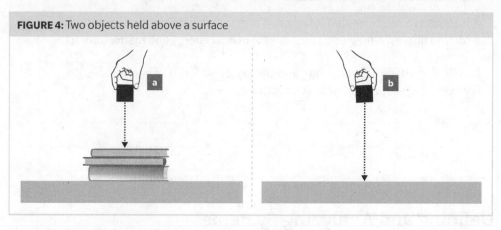

EXPLAIN In Figure 4, two identical objects are held the same distance above the ground. A small stack of books sits under one of them. Do the objects have the same potential energy? Explain why or why not.

FIGURE 5: An apple dropped 1 m

Explore Online ▶

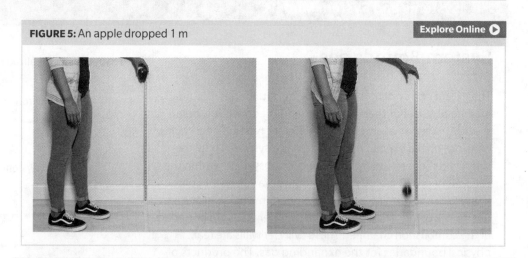

MODEL Make a model showing the relative amounts of kinetic and potential energy in the apple system shown in Figure 5, just before the apple is dropped and just before it hits the floor.

Energy in Systems

Recall that systems can have different types of boundaries. These boundaries describe how the system does or does not interact with the environment outside of the system. A system in which neither matter nor energy crosses the boundaries anywhere may be called a closed system (or when discussing thermodynamics, an isolated system). When defining a system, it is necessary to specify whether or not matter or energy may cross the system's boundaries. A system could be closed to both matter and energy, closed to only matter, closed to only energy, or open to both.

A system may also have boundaries that are open or closed to matter and energy in different ways. In a car engine, gases produced by combustion pass through open valves to the exhaust system but do not pass through the cylinder walls or the piston head.

ANALYZE Consider the system shown in Figure 7. Which of the following statements are true if the boundaries of the system are defined as the exterior surface of the ball. Select all correct answers to complete the statement "The boundaries are . . ."

☐ **a.** open to matter, because the ball loses mass after each bounce.

☐ **b.** closed to matter, because the ball maintains its mass.

☐ **c.** open to energy, because the ball loses energy after each bounce.

☐ **d.** closed to energy, because the ball maintains its energy.

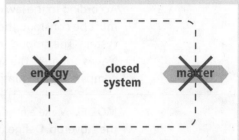

FIGURE 6: Neither energy nor matter may enter or exit a closed system.

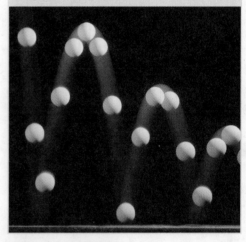

FIGURE 7: A bouncing ball loses some height with each bounce.

Energy and Matter

Conservation of Energy

Though a system may lose energy, that energy is not destroyed; it is transferred out of the system. When energy moves between systems, or between objects within a system, it is called a transfer of energy. The law of conservation of energy states that energy is neither created nor destroyed and is a key concept in physics. Transfers and transformations of energy in a system can be analyzed by applying this law.

Consider a system where the boundaries are closed to both matter and energy along with concepts of conservation of mass and conservation of energy. In this type of system, the amount of mass and energy in the system will remain constant.

EVALUATE For a system closed to energy and matter, which equation models the relationship between the kinetic energy (KE) and potential energy (PE) in the system at two different times, 1 and 2?

○ **a.** $KE_1 + KE_2 = PE_1 + PE_2$

○ **b.** $KE_1 + PE_2 = KE_2 + PE_1$

○ **c.** $KE_1 + PE_1 = KE_2 + PE_2$

Analyzing Energy of a System

According to the law of conservation of energy, the amount of energy in a closed system must be constant, though it can change form or be transferred to different parts of the system. The amount of energy in an open system may change when energy (or matter) leaves or enters the system. To determine the total change in energy of a system, you compare the amounts of energy that leave and enter the system.

MODEL Make a model of a pot of water boiling on a stove as it is being warmed by the stovetop. Define the system boundaries, and show whether matter or energy crosses the boundaries as clearly as possible. Identify the forms of energy where possible.

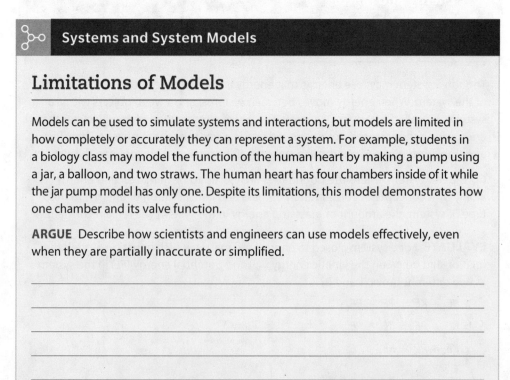

Systems and System Models

Limitations of Models

Models can be used to simulate systems and interactions, but models are limited in how completely or accurately they can represent a system. For example, students in a biology class may model the function of the human heart by making a pump using a jar, a balloon, and two straws. The human heart has four chambers inside of it while the jar pump model has only one. Despite its limitations, this model demonstrates how one chamber and its valve function.

ARGUE Describe how scientists and engineers can use models effectively, even when they are partially inaccurate or simplified.

_____

_____

_____

_____

_____

Energy in Real-World Systems

As demonstrated by the bouncing ball example in Figure 7, what typically occurs in real life does not always appear to follow the law of conservation of energy. Recall, however, that energy can change form, and some energy transformations are not obvious.

FIGURE 8: This figure shows how the gravitational potential energy of a box system transforms as the box falls through air. In (a), the box starts at rest above the ground. In (b) and (c), the box is falling and its speed is increasing.

system energy

a

■ PE
■ KE
▨ thermal energy

system energy

b

■ PE
■ KE
▨ thermal energy

system energy

c

■ PE
■ KE
▨ thermal energy

ANALYZE For the system model shown in Figure 8, which of the statements best describe what happens to the energy in the system? Select all correct answers.

☐ **a.** The gravitational potential energy of the system decreases as it falls.

☐ **b.** The kinetic energy of the system increases as it falls.

☐ **c.** All of the gravitational potential energy transforms into kinetic energy.

☐ **d.** Some of the gravitational potential energy transforms into thermal energy.

As shown in Figure 8, when an object falls through air, not all of the energy transforms into kinetic energy. Friction with the air causes some of the energy to transform into thermal energy. In real-world systems, friction is an unavoidable consequence when systems or objects within a system interact. Friction can be between two objects in contact or may be in the form of drag when an item moves through air or water. Friction often transforms kinetic energy into thermal energy. In practice, it is impossible to prevent thermal energy from transferring into or out of a system.

EVALUATE Drag increases with speed. Racecars, such as the one shown in Figure 9, move at speeds much faster than an average vehicle. Would a vehicle driven at a low speed be more or less efficient at transforming the energy from its fuel or battery into kinetic energy than if it were driven at a great speed? Explain.

FIGURE 9: Racecars move very quickly, and drag must be considered in their design.

_____

_____

_____

_____

_____

 Evidence Notebook For a perpetual motion machine to exist, what would need to be true about energy transfers and transformations in the system and the amount of energy in the system?

Hands-On Lab

Energy Transfer in a Collision

Scientists analyze data to look for trends. They use these trends to identify relationships between variables and predict how a change in one of the variables changes the other.

In this activity, you will develop and carry out a procedure to identify whether or not there is a relationship between the height a ball is raised on a ramp and the distance the ball will move a plow after they collide. You will also predict and test whether the mass of the ball changes this relationship.

RESEARCH QUESTION How is energy related to the distance the cardstock plow moves after its collision with the ball?

MAKE A CLAIM

What factors determine the distance that the plow and ball will travel after the ball rolls down the ramp?

_____

_____

_____

MATERIALS

- safety goggles
- balance
- balls, about 1 cm diameter (1 glass, 1 metal)
- cardstock, 2 cm × 8 cm
- dominoes (9) or 3 identical books, 2–5 cm thick
- meterstick or measuring tape
- ruler, 30 cm, with a channel down its center
- tape, masking
- video camera

SAFETY INFORMATION

- Wear safety goggles during the setup, hands-on, and takedown segments of the activity.
- Immediately pick up any items dropped on the floor so they do not become a slip/fall hazard.
- Wash your hands with soap and water immediately after completing this activity.

PART I: Glass Ball Pushing the Plow

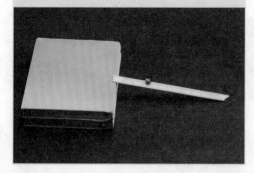

FIGURE 10: The plow should touch the bottom of the ruler.

PLAN AND CARRY OUT THE INVESTIGATION

In your Evidence Notebook, develop a procedure for your investigation. Make sure your teacher approves your procedure and safety plan before proceeding.

1. Use books or dominoes and a ruler to form a gently sloped ramp.

2. Develop a test procedure to collect data relating the height a ball is placed on the ramp and how far the plow and ball move after they collide.

3. Carry out your test procedures. Record your data in your Evidence Notebook.

ANALYZE

1. Make a graph or chart of your data.

2. Identify the relationship between where the ball is placed on the ramp and how far the ball and plow move after they collide.

_____

_____

_____

3. Once you have analyzed your data, show your analysis to your teacher. Your teacher will give you a distance, and you will predict where on the ramp to release the ball from to make the plow travel that distance. Test your prediction. How accurate was your prediction? Explain any discrepancies between your prediction and your test results.

_____

_____

_____

_____

PART II: Metal Ball Pushing the Plow

CARRY OUT THE INVESTIGATION

1. Make a prediction about how far the plow will travel if a more massive metal ball is used instead of the glass ball. Will the results be the same or different than when you used the glass ball? Write your prediction and explanation in your Evidence Notebook.

2. Using your original procedure, repeat your tests with the metal ball instead of the glass ball. Record your data in your Evidence Notebook.

ANALYZE

Compare and contrast the data for the metal ball with the data for the glass ball.

_____

_____

_____

CONSTRUCT AN EXPLANATION

1. Consider the boundaries of the system in this investigation. Does the energy of the system change? If so, how does it change? Explain your answer.

_____

_____

_____

2. Think about the energy of the system. How would the collision change if a different ball or plow were used? What would you need to know about the system in order to predict the result of the collision?

_____

_____

_____

_____

DRAW CONCLUSIONS

Write a conclusion that addresses each of the points below.

Claim What determines the distance that a plow travels when it is pushed by a ball that rolls down a ramp?

Evidence Give specific evidence from your investigation to support your claim.

Reasoning Given your understanding of systems and energy transfer, offer reasoning as to why your evidence supports the claim that you have made.

_____

_____

_____

_____

_____

_____

_____

 Evidence Notebook How does the system in this lab relate to a possible perpetual motion machine? How is energy being added to or removed from this system?

Quantifying Energy

INFER When Clark lifts a stack of books, he changes the energy of the system. How might this change in energy be determined?

_____

_____

_____

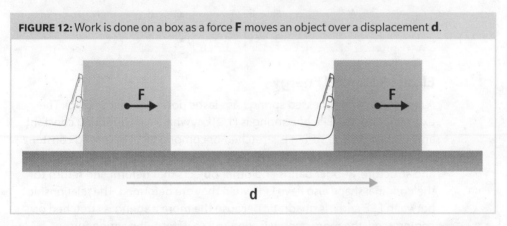

FIGURE 11: Clark picks up a stack of books.

Work and Energy

When an external force acts on a system, the force transfers energy to or from the system. Work is a measure of the energy transfer that happens when an object is moved by an external force. Work is only done if an object moves. Though you may get tired holding a heavy object above the ground, according to physics you are not doing work on the object if it doesn't move. Work and energy are both measured in joules; a joule (J) is equivalent to 1 N·m or 1 kg·m^2/s^2.

FIGURE 12: Work is done on a box as a force **F** moves an object over a displacement **d**.

Force and displacement are both vectors, but work is a scalar. The amount of work done by a force can be calculated using the equation $W = F \bullet d$. If force and displacement vectors are only partly aligned, only the component of the force in the same or opposite direction as the displacement vector does work on the object. Work can be positive or negative depending on whether it increases or decreases the energy of the object.

EXPLAIN A 5 N force stops a hockey puck (on a frictionless surface) over a distance of 1 m. Is the work done on the puck positive or negative?

○ **a.** positive because the force increases the kinetic energy of the puck

○ **b.** positive because the force decreases the kinetic energy of the puck

○ **c.** negative because the force increases the kinetic energy of the puck

○ **d.** negative because the force decreases the kinetic energy of the puck

> **Evidence Notebook** In the unit project, you design an overly complex machine known as a Rube Goldberg machine. How might the concept of work be used to predict how objects can be moved in a Rube Goldberg machine?

Images/Getty Images

Potential Energy

Recall that potential energy is the energy of a system due to its position or state. Potential energy can be quantified by analyzing how much work is needed to place the object in its current position or state.

Gravitational Potential Energy

Gravitational potential energy (GPE) is potential energy that an object has due to its mass and its position in a gravitational field. When Clark holds the books above the ground, they have GPE. The amount of potential energy a mass has is equal to the amount of work gravity will do on the mass when the force of gravity moves the mass (it falls).

The acceleration of most objects near Earth's surface due to gravity, g, varies less than 0.5%. Thus, the magnitude of g can be treated as a constant of 9.8 m/s^2 in most situations, and the force pulling down on an object, mg, is proportional to the object's mass.

APPLY The work equation can be adapted to find an object's GPE. Write the corresponding variables in each space to generate an equation for calculating the GPE of a mass. Recall that g is the acceleration of an object due to gravity, m is the mass of the object, and h is the object's height above a zero point.

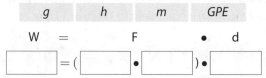

| g | h | m | GPE |

$$W \quad = \quad\quad F \quad\bullet\quad d$$

$$\boxed{} = (\boxed{} \bullet \boxed{}) \bullet \boxed{}$$

FIGURE 13: A stretched rubber band has elastic energy.

Elastic Potential Energy

A stretched or compressed spring has elastic potential energy (EPE). The expression for the EPE of a spring is $(1/2)kx^2$, where k is the spring constant and x is how far the spring is stretched or compressed. The spring constant is a measure of a spring's stiffness, and it depends on the spring's material and structure. Rubber bands and other objects that deform and return to their original shape also have EPE when they are deformed. The relationship between EPE and x is quadratic because the more a spring is stretched or compressed, the more energy is required to deform the spring further.

⚛ Engineering

Potential Energy in Clocks

Some early clocks, such as grandfather clocks, harnessed GPE to keep time. Later clocks, such as pocket watches, harnessed the EPE of springs to keep time.

IDENTIFY CONSTRAINTS Compare the different types of timekeeping devices. Could a device like a pocket watch be run by GPE? Explain.

_____

_____

_____

Kinetic Energy

Recall that kinetic energy is the energy of motion and that energy cannot be created or destroyed, but it can change form.

SOLVE The table shows the height and velocity of a 4.0 kg mass as it falls in a vacuum. Use the equation $PE = mgh$ and $g = 9.8 \text{ m/s}^2$ to calculate the GPE of the mass at each height. Use your knowledge of the conservation of energy to calculate the mass's kinetic energy at each height. Report your answers using two significant figures.

Height (m)	Velocity (m/s)	PE (J)	KE (J)
5.0	0.00	_____	0
4.0	4.43	_____	_____
3.0	6.26	_____	_____
2.0	7.67	_____	_____
1.0	8.85	_____	_____

ANALYZE Look at the table. Are an object's kinetic energy and its velocity related linearly or in some other relationship? Explain how you determined the relationship.

_____

_____

_____

_____

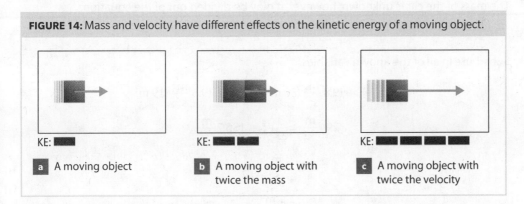

FIGURE 14: Mass and velocity have different effects on the kinetic energy of a moving object.

KE: ▬

a A moving object

KE: ▬ ▬

b A moving object with twice the mass

KE: ▬ ▬ ▬ ▬

c A moving object with twice the velocity

As shown in Figure 14, when mass of an object is doubled, the kinetic energy of the object also doubles. Figure 14c shows that doubling the object's velocity quadruples the object's kinetic energy. The concept of work and Newton's second law of motion can be used to derive an equation for kinetic energy:

$$KE = \frac{1}{2}mv^2$$

In this equation, m is the object's mass and v is its velocity. Kinetic energy—like potential energy and work—is a scalar. The magnitude, but not the direction, of an object's velocity affects its kinetic energy. Notice that the result of squaring either a negative or positive velocity results in a positive value, so kinetic energy will be positive regardless of the direction in which an object is moving. Compare the equation for kinetic energy with your analysis of the relationship between an object's velocity and its kinetic energy.

Problem Solving

Using Energy Equations

SAMPLE PROBLEM

A roller coaster car sits at rest at the top of a hill that is 30 m above the ground. The car slides down the track to a smaller hill that is 19 m above the ground. What is the velocity of the car as it reaches the top of the 19 m hill? Ignore friction and air resistance. Report your final answer using two significant figures.

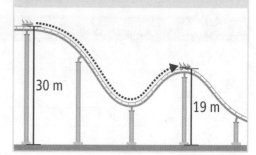

FIGURE 15: A car moves on the rails of a roller coaster track.

30 m

19 m

ANALYZE

Known: $v_1 = 0$ m/s

$h_1 = 30$ m

$h_2 = 19$ m

$g = 9.8$ m/s^2

Conservation of energy equation: $KE_1 + PE_1 = KE_2 + PE_2$

Unknown: $v_2 = ?, m = ?$

PLAN

Apply the conservation of energy equation to the car.

$$KE_1 + PE_1 = KE_2 + PE_2$$
$$\frac{1}{2}mv_1^2 + mgh_1 = \frac{1}{2}mv_2^2 + mgh_2$$

The mass of the car is unknown; however, it may be divided out of the equation.

$$\frac{1}{2}v_1^2 + gh_1 = \frac{1}{2}v_2^2 + gh_2$$

SOLVE

Substitute in all of the known variables.

$$\frac{1}{2}\left(0\ \frac{m}{s}\right)^2 + \left(9.8\ \frac{m}{s^2}\right)(30\ m) = \frac{1}{2}v_2^2 + \left(9.8\ \frac{m}{s^2}\right)(19\ m)$$

$$294\ \frac{m^2}{s^2} = \frac{1}{2}v_2^2 + 186.2\ \frac{m^2}{s^2}$$

$$107.8\ \frac{m^2}{s^2} = \frac{1}{2}v_2^2$$

$$215.6\ \frac{m^2}{s^2} = v_2^2$$

$$\sqrt{215.6\ \frac{m^2}{s^2}} = v_2$$

$$15\ \frac{m}{s} = v_2$$

PRACTICE PROBLEM

SOLVE A sled rider is given a push at the top of an icy hill, giving her an initial speed of 1.0 m/s. If the hill is 4.0 m tall from its base, how fast is the sled rider moving at the bottom of the hill? Assume that the icy hill is frictionless and air resistance is negligible.

Energy and Collisions

When objects collide, they apply a force on each other. These forces transfer energy between the objects. Some of this energy may cause the objects to deform temporarily or permanently. Notice how the golf ball in Figure 16 is flattened where it is being hit by a golf club. The ball deforms during this collision but then returns to its original shape after the collision. Some of the energy may be transformed into thermal energy.

GATHER EVIDENCE Look at the photo of the golf ball being hit by a golf club. What forms of energy are represented in the photo, and what evidence supports your statements?

FIGURE 16: A golf ball is flattened when hit by the club.

_____

_____

_____

_____

Elastic Collisions

Kinetic energy is conserved in an elastic collision. The result of an elastic collision can be predicted by analyzing the energy and momentum transfers that happen during the collision. Though real-world collisions are not elastic, assuming a collision is elastic can sometimes help analyze nearly elastic collisions.

FIGURE 17: A Newton's cradle uses several hard masses that interact in nearly elastic collisions when they collide.

APPLY Which of the following statements about an elastic collision are true? Select all correct answers.

☐ **a.** The total amount of momentum before and after the collision is the same.

☐ **b.** The total amount of kinetic energy before and after the collision is the same.

☐ **c.** The kinetic energy of each object before and after the collision stays the same.

☐ **d.** Kinetic energy is conserved, but momentum is not.

☐ **e.** Most real-world collisions can be considered to be elastic collisions.

Evidence Notebook When analyzing systems, scientists often assume energy transfers and transformations lose no energy. How would this impact a proposed perpetual motion machine?

(bl) ©zentilla/iStock/Getty Images Plus/Getty Images

Case Study: Energy for Vehicles

In the early 1900s, self-powered vehicles became popular around the world, replacing many horses and buggies. One of the most popular vehicles, the gasoline-powered Ford Model T, had a top speed between 65 and 70 km/h (40–45 mph) and a fuel efficiency of between 5.5 and 8.8 km/L (13–21 mpg). Early versions of this vehicle were made of materials such as cast iron and steel, and lacked safety features such as windshield wipers and seat belts. Even though modern cars use materials less dense than steel, such as aluminum, many modern cars are only slightly more fuel efficient than the Model T.

EXPLAIN Engineers have continually improved vehicle designs to make them safer, faster, and more fuel efficient. How might vehicle mass and speed affect the fuel efficiency of a vehicle? How can engineers address these effects?

_____

_____

_____

FIGURE 18: The radiator at the front of a car transfers excess heat away from the engine.

Fuel type	Approximate energy density (MJ/kg)
diesel	45.7
gasoline	47.5
propane	46.4
compressed natural gas	48.6

Internal Combustion Engines

The internal combustion engine was designed to contain combusting fuel inside the engine itself. The chemical energy of the fuel is transformed into both mechanical kinetic energy and thermal energy as the fuel combusts. The mechanical kinetic energy moves pistons to turn the crankshaft, which drives the wheels. To keep the engine from overheating due to excess thermal energy, these engines require radiators to transfer excess energy to the environment. When the weather is cold, some of this excess energy can be used to warm passengers. Internal combustion engines have been refined over the past century to transform as much of the chemical energy of the fuel as possible into vehicle motion.

The distance a vehicle can travel before refueling, range, is an important feature of any vehicle. One of the key factors in determining a vehicle's range is the total amount of potential energy it can carry. One way to measure a fuel's energy density is by measuring the energy that can be released per unit of mass, for example, megajoules per kilogram (MJ/kg). The more energy dense a fuel is, the less fuel is needed to carry an equivalent amount of energy. Some vehicles are designed to use fuels with higher energy density than gasoline.

DESIGN The table shows the typical energy density of some common vehicle fuels. What other factors must be considered in choosing a fuel to run a vehicle?

_____

_____

_____

Electric and Hybrid Vehicles

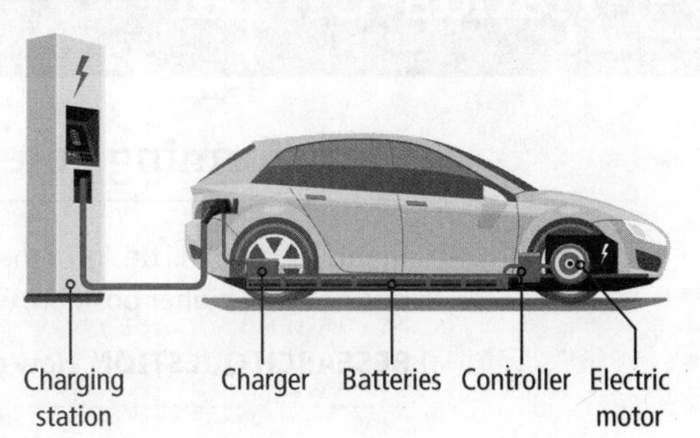

Over time, society has become more aware of the negative consequences of burning fossil fuels, such as gasoline, to move vehicles. People looking for alternatives to fossil fuel–powered vehicles may choose fully electric vehicles or hybrid vehicles. Hybrid vehicles use regenerative braking and electric motors to improve the efficiency of an internal combustion engine. Regenerative braking is a method where an electric motor functions as a generator to transform the kinetic energy of the wheels into electrical energy that is then stored in the batteries for later use. Electric vehicles also use regenerative braking to extend vehicle range, but while hybrid vehicles get energy from a fuel, electric vehicle batteries must be charged by an external source of energy. Electric vehicles generate no exhaust while running, but their "cleanliness" depends on the source of the electrical energy used to charge the batteries. Electric vehicle range depends on how much energy can be stored in the batteries and how efficiently that energy is converted to motion.

FIGURE 19: Electric vehicles require large batteries to store the energy needed for practical use.

Charging station | Charger | Batteries | Controller | Electric motor

Language Arts Connection Research how the energy efficiency of these different types of electric and internal combustion vehicles can be compared. Make a visual guide using digital media that summarizes your research and explains how consumers can compare these vehicles' efficiencies.

Math Connection

Vehicle Range

Fuel efficiency may be reported as range (distance) per amount of fuel or amount of fuel to go a specific distance, such as 100 km. Car A is listed as having an efficiency of 10 km/L. Car B has an efficiency of 9 L/100 km. Which vehicle is more efficient?

ANALYZE	**Known:** Car A: $\dfrac{10 \text{ km}}{\text{L}}$, Car B: $\dfrac{9 \text{ L}}{100 \text{ km}}$ Car A: $\dfrac{1 \text{ L}}{10 \text{ km}} = \dfrac{x \text{ L}}{100 \text{ km}}$	**Unknown:** Car A efficiency
SOLVE	Cross-multiply to solve for x. Car A has an efficiency of 10 L/100 km. Since Car B uses only 9 L of fuel to go 100 km, Car B is the more efficient vehicle.	
PRACTICE PROBLEM	**1.** If a vehicle has a fuel efficiency of 10 km/L and a fuel tank that holds 95 L, how far can the vehicle go on a single tank? Report two significant figures.	

Evidence Notebook Could one make a solar-powered vehicle that could run forever? If so, would that vehicle be considered a perpetual motion machine?

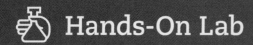

Hands-On Lab

Transforming Potential Energy

In this lab, you will design a machine that uses a pulley system to lift a marble from a lower position to a higher position, where the marble then travels on a track.

RESEARCH QUESTION How can potential energy be transformed to complete a task?

MAKE A CLAIM
How does the energy of the marble at the top of the track compare to the initial energy in the machine?

_____

_____

POSSIBLE MATERIALS

- safety goggles
- box lined with padding material
- building materials and tools
- clamp

- cups, various types
- elastic bands, nonlatex
- hanging mass set
- meterstick

- marble
- pulleys
- ring stand
- string

SAFETY INFORMATION

- Wear safety goggles during the setup, hands-on, and takedown segments of the activity.
- Immediately pick up any items dropped on the floor so they do not become a slip/fall hazard.
- Use caution when using sharp tools, which can cut or puncture skin.
- Remember that falling masses can cause injuries. Use a padded box below your device to catch and contain the falling mass.
- Wash your hands with soap and water immediately after completing this activity.

PLAN THE INVESTIGATION

Build a raised track for your marble, with a height of at least 0.5 m. After you set your device in motion, it should raise the marble to the height of the track without your assistance. The device should be able to be used in multiple trials.

MODEL Make a sketch or series of sketches that depicts the energy transformations required to lift the marble and its holder as well as to tip the marble onto the track.

CARRY OUT THE INVESTIGATION

1. Design a lightweight carrier that can carry the marble up to the track when attached to a pulley system. The machine should be able to tip the marble onto the track.

2. Calculate the potential energy that the marble and carrier should have once raised to the track height, and calculate the minimum amount of mass the counterweight needs to raise the marble and carrier.

3. Build and test your pulley system to see if it functions as expected. Make adjustments and retest if needed to get the desired performance.

ANALYZE

1. What energy transfers and transformations occur in the machine you designed?

_____

_____

_____

_____

_____

2. Compare the initial amount of energy in the system with the energy in the system just before the ball tips onto the ramp. Explain how you know whether all of the energy was transferred to the marble and carrier or if some energy was lost to the environment.

_____

_____

_____

DRAW CONCLUSIONS

Write a conclusion that addresses each of the points below.

Claim How does the energy of the marble at the top of the track compare to the initial energy in the machine?

Evidence What evidence supports your claim?

Reasoning Explain how the evidence you gave supports your claim. Describe in detail the connections between the evidence you cited and the argument you are making.

_____

_____

_____

_____

 Evidence Notebook The machine you design in this lab can be incorporated into the Rube Goldberg machine you design in the unit project.

| KINETIC ENERGY AND MOMENTUM | ENERGY ON EARTH | SOLVE AN ELASTIC COLLISION | Go online to choose one of these other paths. |

Lesson Self-Check

FIGURE 20: Historical depiction of a perpetual motion machine

Since the Middle Ages, people have dreamed of and attempted to design devices that could run forever on a set amount of energy or even produce more energy than they used. Any device that makes either of these claims is called a perpetual motion machine. Even the great artist and inventor Leonardo da Vinci pondered the mechanics of such a machine and sketched several devices that are believed to show his fleeting dreams of perpetual motion.

 Evidence Notebook Refer to your notes in your Evidence Notebook to explain the connection between energy and the implementation of a perpetual motion machine.

Claim Why have inventors not successfully built a perpetual motion machine?

Evidence Provide evidence to support your claim. Observations from your own experiments, observations of real-life systems, or scientific laws can serve as evidence.

Reasoning Use your evidence to support your claim. Make clear connections between the evidence you provide and the argument you are making. Include what conditions are necessary for a perpetual motion machine to be possible.

CHECKPOINTS

Check Your Understanding

1. Which of the following changes would reduce an object's kinetic energy to 1/4 its value? Select all correct answers.
   - ☐ **a.** Decrease the object's mass to 1/4 its original value.
   - ☐ **b.** Decrease the object's velocity to 1/4 its original value.
   - ☐ **c.** Decrease the object's mass by 1/2.
   - ☐ **d.** Decrease the object's velocity by 1/2.

2. Which of the following changes would increase an object's gravitational potential energy to 8 times its value? Select all correct answers.
   - ☐ **a.** Increase the object's mass by a factor of 8.
   - ☐ **b.** Decrease the object's height above the ground by a factor of 8.
   - ☐ **c.** Increase the object's mass by a factor of 4 and increase the height by a factor of 2.
   - ☐ **d.** Decrease the object's mass by a factor of 1/2 and decrease the height by a factor of 1/4.
   - ☐ **e.** Increase the object's mass by a factor of 16 and decrease the height by a factor of 1/2.

3. Position 1 is at the bottom of a frictionless inclined track. A toy car is given an initial velocity up the track. At Position 2, the top of the track, the car almost stops but then continues down the opposite side of the track, which has a rough surface. The car passes through Position 3 at the bottom. Rank the car's kinetic energy from smallest (1) to largest (3) at the three positions.

Rank	Position
_____	position 1 kinetic energy
_____	position 2 kinetic energy
_____	position 3 kinetic energy

4. A human cannonball act uses springy bungee cords to launch a person through a long cylindrical tube into the air. If a cannon is capable of launching a 55 kg test dummy 11 m into the air when launched straight up, what is the minimum amount of energy stored in the bungee cords?
   - ○ **a.** 540 J
   - ○ **b.** 610 J
   - ○ **c.** 3000 J
   - ○ **d.** 5900 J

5. A physics student rides a burlap sack down a slide at the state fair. She starts at rest at the top of the slide. At the bottom of the slide, she notices that the burlap sack is warmer than when she started. Which equation below models the energy of the burlap sack at the top (position 1) and bottom (position 2) of the hill? E_{th} is thermal energy.
   - ○ **a.** $\frac{1}{2}mv_1^2 = mgh_2 + E_{th}$
   - ○ **b.** $mgh_1 = \frac{1}{2}mv_2^2 + E_{th}$
   - ○ **c.** $\frac{1}{2}mv_1^2 + E_{th} = mgh_2$
   - ○ **d.** $mgh_1 + E_{th} = mgh_2$

6. Two balls collide in an elastic collision. The first ball has 20 J of energy before the collision and 50 J after the collision. Which of the following statements about the collision must be true? Select all correct answers.
   - ☐ **a.** Ball 2 gains 30 J of energy.
   - ☐ **b.** Ball 2 loses 30 J of energy.
   - ☐ **c.** Ball 2 was moving faster than ball 1 before the collision.
   - ☐ **d.** Ball 2 is more massive than ball 1.
   - ☐ **e.** Ball 2 had more energy than ball 1 before the collision.

7. A cyclist rides a bicycle. When the brakes are applied, rubber pads press against the wheels of the bicycle to bring the bicycle to a stop. What happens to the kinetic energy of the bicycle?
   - ○ **a.** It is transferred to the cyclist.
   - ○ **b.** It is transformed into thermal energy.
   - ○ **c.** It is transformed into chemical energy.
   - ○ **d.** It is destroyed.

CHECKPOINTS (continued)

8. Suppose a fly and an eagle have the same amount of kinetic energy. Explain under what conditions this statement could be true.

_____

_____

_____

_____

_____

_____

9. Write an argument supporting or denying the claim "A system always has potential energy."

_____

_____

_____

_____

_____

_____

_____

_____

MAKE YOUR OWN STUDY GUIDE

In your Evidence Notebook, design a study guide that supports the main ideas from this lesson: **Energy cannot be created or destroyed. It may transform between different forms of energy such as radiant, gravitational, thermal, sound, and others.**

Energy may transfer into and out of systems or move to different parts within a system.

In real-life scenarios, friction usually transforms some energy into thermal energy, which then transfers from a system to the environment in the form of heat.

Engineers work to optimize energy transformations and transfers to make the most efficient machines possible.

Remember to include the following information in your study guide:

- Use examples that model main ideas.
- Record explanations for the phenomena you investigated.
- Use evidence to support your explanations. Your support can include drawings, data, graphs, laboratory conclusions, and other evidence recorded throughout the lesson.

Consider how energy is conserved even in cases in which it is transferred from a system to the environment.

Transferring Thermal Energy

Water boils in this paper cup when held over a flame.

CAN YOU EXPLAIN THE PHENOMENON?

Paper is often used as kindling to start fires because it ignites easily. However, the widespread use of paper as currency or for recording important information means that there are many situations in which paper burning would be a disaster. Banks and other businesses must store important papers in fireproof containers.

In the photo above, a paper cup is held over a burner. An empty paper cup would quickly catch fire. This paper cup, though, is filled with water. Observe that while the water is boiling, the cup has not yet caught fire.

EXPLAIN What conditions are necessary for water to boil? How do these compare to the conditions necessary for paper to catch fire?

_____

_____

_____

_____

_____

Evidence Notebook As you explore the lesson, gather evidence to explain how energy transfers and transformations cause the water to boil before the paper cup catches fire.

Temperature and Particle Motion

INFER Imagine two glasses of water. One glass has been sitting on a table for several hours. The other has been warmed in a microwave until the water is warm but not boiling. At the particle level, what is different about the water in the two glasses?

_____

_____

_____

Particles in Motion

Kinetic energy can be understood at the microscopic (small, not directly-observable) and macroscopic (large, directly-observable) levels. At both scales, kinetic energy is related to the motion of particles and objects. Particles in warm substances move more and have more kinetic energy than particles in cool substances. When moving particles collide, energy transfers between particles, just like in macroscopic collisions.

 Hands-On Activity

Coat Hanger Energy

In this activity, you will explore energy transfer and transformation by repeatedly bending a hardened wire or a wire coat hanger.

MATERIALS

- safety goggles, gloves   · hardened 12-gauge wire, or wire coat hanger

 SAFETY INFORMATION

- Wear safety goggles and gloves during the setup, hands-on, and takedown segments of the activity.

- Use caution when handling the wire, as the sharp ends might cut or puncture skin.

 **CARRY OUT THE INVESTIGATION**

Hold the wire firmly with both hands, and bend the wire back and forth 10–15 times. Look and feel for changes in the wire, noting observations in your Evidence Notebook.

ANALYZE

Use your knowledge of energy transfers and transformations to explain your observations.

_____

_____

_____

What Is Thermal Energy?

FIGURE 1: Molecules move differently at different temperatures. The arrows represent the velocities of the molecules.

a   Cold water

b   Warm water

ANALYZE In the photos in Figure 1, what is the difference between the molecules of the cold water and the warm water?

○ **a.** the speeds of the molecules

○ **b.** the shapes of the molecules

○ **c.** the masses of the molecules

EXPLAIN Describe what happens to molecules in Figure 1b as energy in the form of heat is added to the system of the pot and water.

_____

_____

_____

The particles of warm water in Figure 1b are moving more quickly on average than the particles of cold water in Figure 1a, so the particles of warm water have more average kinetic energy. Assume the two samples of water in Figure 1 have the same mass. The samples have the same number of particles, but the particles of the warm water have more average kinetic energy than the particles of the cold water. So, the sample of warm water has more total particle-level kinetic energy—more thermal energy—than the sample of cold water in Figure 1a. The total kinetic energy of the particles in a substance is described as thermal energy. Thermal energy is related to the motion and therefore to the kinetic energy of an object's atoms or molecules. A higher thermal energy represents a greater amount of particle-level kinetic energy in a sample.

Imagine a third sample of water that is at the same temperature as the warm water in Figure 1b but has more mass. This sample would have the same average kinetic energy per particle as the warm water, but it would have more particles. So, this third sample would have more thermal energy than the sample in Figure 1b.

Thermal energy can affect states of matter. When water boils on a stove, the stove continues to add energy to the water. However, the water's temperature does not increase because the thermal energy goes into changing the state from a liquid to a gas. Systems undergoing state changes take in or release energy without changing temperature.

Temperature and Thermal Energy

Scientists often find temperature to be a more useful measurement than thermal energy. Temperature is a measure of the average kinetic energy of the particles in a sample, so it does not depend on the amount of mass present. In contrast, thermal energy is the sum of the kinetic energies of every particle in a sample. So, two liters of water will have twice as much thermal energy as one liter of water at the same temperature.

In addition to being independent of mass, temperature corresponds to a scale that allows comparisons between samples and a known value. For example, scientists know that any sample of water at 98 °C is close to its boiling point. The Celsius scale relates temperature to water's freezing point (0 °C) and water's boiling point (100 °C).

ANALYZE Read each statement, and then mark *T* or *F* to indicate if the statement is true or false for temperature and thermal energy. Ignore state changes.

Statement	Temperature	Thermal energy
depends on kinetic energy of particles	_____	_____
depends on mass present	_____	_____
increases when energy is added to a sample	_____	_____
corresponds to a specific scale	_____	_____

Thermal Energy and Heat

FIGURE 2: Energy in the form of heat can be transferred in different ways.

a Boiling water: convection   b Stove coil: conduction   c Heat lamp: radiation

The term *heat* is common in everyday language and generally refers to warm conditions. In science, *heat* has a specific meaning. Heat is energy transferred between objects at different temperatures. As such, an object cannot possess heat, but an object can transfer energy in the form of heat to its surroundings or receive energy in the form of heat from its surroundings. Scientists measure energy transferred as heat in joules (J). Energy may be transferred as heat by convection, conduction, and radiation. Convection transfers energy throughout liquids and gases (Figure 2a). Conduction transfers energy through direct contact (Figure 2b). Radiation transfers energy through electromagnetic waves (Figure 2c).

 Collaborate Work with a partner to make a comic strip illustrating the various ways energy is transferred in the form of heat.

These three modes by which energy can be transferred as heat involve different mechanisms. Convection occurs as portions of a liquid or gas circulate between areas of different densities. Conduction transfers energy between colliding particles. Radiation, including infrared and visible light, can be given off and absorbed by matter without requiring physical contact. In Figure 2c, energy is transferred to the birds by electromagnetic waves emitted from the heat lamps. Because waves of electromagnetic radiation do not depend upon the movement of matter, radiation can occur even in a vacuum.

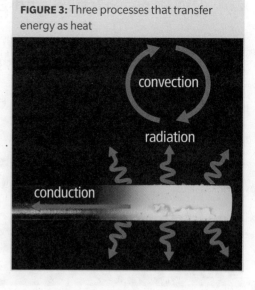

FIGURE 3: Three processes that transfer energy as heat

APPLY A chef's face warms when smelling a pot of boiling soup. Describe the energy transfers that cause the chef's face to warm when it is over the pot.

_____

_____

_____

Energy Transfer by Fluid Motion

Convection can be observed in a pot of boiling water, such as in Figure 2a. Convection is a mode of energy transfer that works primarily by groups of particles in fluids moving from place to place. _Fluid_ is a term that refers to both liquids and gases. When energy is transferred to a fluid, the particles that absorbed the energy begin to move faster. The increasing speed of the particles causes them to spread out, which lowers the density of that portion of the fluid. The cooler, more dense fluid above sinks down, displacing this warmer, less dense fluid. As long as there is a temperature difference between regions of the fluid, there will be a density difference, and this process will repeat. Continuous convection will spread energy throughout the fluid.

Energy Transfer by Particle Collisions

The transfer of energy by conduction involves collisions between particles with different amounts of energy. When two particles collide, the particle with more energy transfers energy to the particle with less energy. Conduction can occur in solids, liquids, and gases. Energy transfer by conduction can occur within a single object or between objects in contact as long as a temperature difference exists. Imagine placing a large empty pot on the coil in Figure 2b. Consider the system of the coil and the pot to be closed to energy transfer with the environment. Particles in the high-temperature coil will collide with particles at the base of the room-temperature pot, transferring energy and causing the base of the pot to warm. Conduction will also transfer energy throughout the pot, as particles in the warm section of the pot collide with lower-energy particles in the cooler parts of the pot. Macroscopic energy transfer would stop if the coil and all portions of the pot were to reach the same temperature.

EXPLAIN Compare and contrast how energy is transferred as heat through convection and conduction.

_____

_____

_____

Friction and Energy

Friction is a force that acts in the opposite direction of an object's motion. Friction occurs whenever objects in contact are pushed or pulled in opposing directions.

FIGURE 4: The brakes of a racecar emit heat and light.

INFER The kinetic energy of a braking car is transformed into which forms of energy? Select all correct answers.

☐ **a.** potential energy   ☐ **c.** light energy

☐ **b.** sound energy   ☐ **d.** thermal energy

When friction resists the motion of an object, it lowers the object's kinetic energy. In the case of the braking car in Figure 4, some of the car's kinetic energy is transformed into thermal energy, sound energy, and light energy. The car's velocity is lowered, but the energy of the car and its environment is conserved.

Friction is the result of interactions between particles on the surfaces of materials in contact. Forces between particles cause them to move and collide as the surfaces move against each other, resulting in energy transfers and transformations. Some of the kinetic energy of the moving macroscopic objects is transformed into thermal energy. This increased particle-level kinetic energy is transferred between the surfaces and to the environment in the form of heat. Exposed particles on rough surfaces interact more than those on smooth surfaces, producing greater friction and greater energy transformation. Engineers often work to decrease the friction between surfaces to minimize energy loss in the form of heat in moving systems.

Energy and Matter

Regenerative Brakes

Some systems transform kinetic energy into forms that are more easily stored and reused. This stored energy can then later be converted back into kinetic energy. In some hybrid and electric cars, an electric generator recovers a portion of the kinetic energy that would otherwise be lost when the driver applies the brakes. This charges the batteries, storing electrical energy that can be used to power the car.

FIGURE 5: An energy monitor in a hybrid car

APPLY Do you think it is possible to transform all of the car's kinetic energy into electrical energy? Why or why not?

_____

_____

 Evidence Notebook Use your knowledge of thermal energy, temperature, and modes of energy transfer to explain how energy is transferred in system of the burner, paper cup, and water.

Energy in Real-World Systems

When steaming coffee is poured into a room-temperature mug, the mug warms, and at the same time, the coffee cools. An ice-cold drink warms when placed in a room-temperature glass. At the same time, the glass cools. Real-world systems tend toward a uniform distribution of energy.

Thermal Equilibrium

SOLVE Red-hot metal is dipped into cold water. In the moments after this photo was taken, what temperature changes would you expect for the metal and for the water?

temperature increases temperature decreases

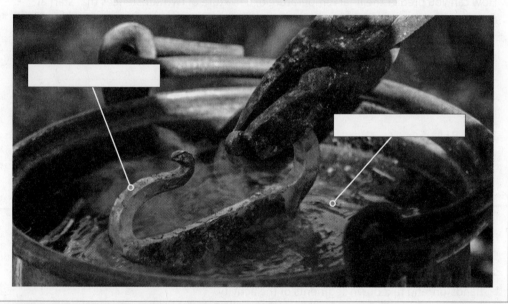

PREDICT The red-hot metal in the photo is placed in the water and then left there for a long time. Which statement describes the final temperature of the water and metal system? Assume that no energy is lost to the environment.

○ **a.** somewhere between the initial temperatures of the metal and water

○ **b.** warmer than the initial temperature of the metal

○ **c.** cooler than the initial temperature of the water

When the red-hot metal came in contact with the water, energy was transferred until they reached the same temperature between their initial temperatures. This new state, in which the system's final temperature is between the starting temperatures of the metal and the water, is called thermal equilibrium. Thermal equilibrium applies when running water for a bath. Define the system as the water in the tub. When you add warm water, you add energy to the system, which increases its equilibrium temperature. When analyzing systems, scientists often ignore short-term energy transfer to the environment. Within a system, energy tends toward a uniform distribution, like the state of thermal equilibrium. This is referred to as the second law of thermodynamics. The first law of thermodynamics describes conservation of energy.

Explore Online ▶

YOU SOLVE IT

How Can Thermal Energy Transfer between Two Components?
Investigate how energy transfers between materials in a system.

Hands-On Lab

Predicting Temperature

A blacksmith quenches a red-hot horseshoe in a pail of cold water. The final temperature of the water and the horseshoe is somewhere between the two extreme starting temperatures. Why? Why does the warmer object become cooler and the cooler object become warmer? Is there a way to predict the final temperature of the mixture? In this lab you will investigate these questions as you predict temperatures. Define the system as the mixture of your samples, and assume no energy transfer with the environment.

RESEARCH QUESTION What factors must be measured in order to accurately predict the final temperature of a mixture of two substances?

MAKE A CLAIM

How can you predict the final temperature of a mixture of two substances that start at different temperatures?

MATERIALS

- safety goggles, nonlatex apron, heat-resistant gloves
- beakers (3)
- balance
- heating vessel, metal
- hot plate
- samples of various metals in shot or bead form
- stirring rod
- thermometer (2)

SAFETY INFORMATION

- Wear safety goggles, a nonlatex apron, and heat-resistant gloves during the setup, hands-on, and takedown segments of the activity.
- Use caution when working with hot plates, which can cause skin burns or electric shock. Never leave a hot plate unattended while it is turned on.
- Secure loose clothing, wear closed-toe shoes, and tie back long hair.
- Do not heat glassware that is broken, chipped, or cracked. Use tongs or a mitt to handle heated metal, glassware, and other equipment because hot equipment does not always look hot. Allow all equipment to cool before storing it.
- Use caution when working with glassware, which can shatter and cut skin.

CARRY OUT THE INVESTIGATION

Design an investigation that will allow you to determine the final temperature of a mixture of two samples of water that start at different temperatures. You may want to start with two samples that contain the same amount of water and then progress to trials involving different amounts of water. Describe your experiment in your Evidence Notebook along with a blank data table that represents the trials that you plan to perform. Have your teacher approve your procedure and safety plan before you proceed.

ANALYZE

1. What patterns did you uncover that you can use to help you predict the final temperature after two different samples of water are mixed?

_____

_____

_____

2. Develop a mathematical equation or set of equations that relates the changes in temperature for two samples of water. Does the mass of the water play a role in this relationship?

_____

_____

_____

CONSTRUCT AN EXPLANATION

How does the principle of conservation of energy relate to your observations?

_____

_____

_____

DRAW CONCLUSIONS

Write a conclusion that addresses each of the points below.

Claim How can you determine the final temperature of a mixture of two different samples of water that start at different temperatures? Was your initial claim correct?

Evidence Give specific examples from your data to support your claim.

Reasoning Explain how the evidence you gave supports your claim. Reference the conservation of energy and the second law of thermodynamics in your reasoning.

_____

_____

_____

_____

_____

EXTEND

Suppose you mixed a sample of water at one temperature with a sample of a different material, like metal, at another temperature and waited until the system reached thermal equilibrium. Does your equation for predicting the final temperature still apply? If so, why? If not, how would you modify it to account for the two different materials? In your Evidence Notebook, design an investigation to test your ideas.

Factors in Thermal Equilibrium

Mass is one of the factors you must consider when thinking about thermal equilibrium between two objects. Objects with greater mass require a greater transfer of energy to change their temperature. Material composition also affects equilibrium temperature.

FIGURE 6: Blocks of lead and silver at different temperatures are put into contact until they reach equilibrium. The block of silver is slightly larger because silver is slightly less dense than lead. The two blocks form a system that is closed to energy transfer with the environment.

20 °C — 1 kg lead   30 °C — 1 kg silver

a before

27 °C — 1 kg lead   27 °C — 1 kg silver

b after

EXPLAIN Based on the illustration in Figure 6, why is the equilibrium temperature closer to the starting temperature of the block of silver than to that of the block of lead?

○ **a.** The block of silver has more surface area than the block of lead.

○ **b.** Silver requires a greater energy transfer to change its temperature.

○ **c.** The block of silver has a higher initial temperature.

In Figure 6, the thermal equilibrium reached by the two blocks was closer to the initial temperature of the silver than that of the lead. This occurs because different materials can store different amounts of thermal energy per unit of mass, a property called *specific heat capacity*, c_p. A substance with a higher specific heat capacity requires a greater energy loss or gain to change its temperature. Silver has a higher specific heat capacity than lead. As a result, the initial temperature of the silver block had a greater effect on the equilibrium temperature of the system.

Systems and System Models

Initial Conditions

When investigating systems, scientists must understand the boundaries and initial conditions in order to conduct analysis. The initial conditions of the system include the masses, specific heat capacities, temperatures, and orientations of objects. This information can be used to understand the final thermal equilibrium. Climate scientists use system models to understand the melting of Arctic sea ice. These models must consider how ice levels vary between months, years, or even decades.

APPLY What initial conditions should climate scientists consider when modeling how the ice would respond to atmospheric and oceanic temperature changes?

_____

_____

_____

Energy Flows into and out of a System

SAMPLE PROBLEM   A 15 kg lead block is dropped 65 cm by a Joule's apparatus, causing a stirrer to spin in a sealed chamber filled with 0.25 L of water. Assuming no energy is lost to the environment, determine the temperature change of the water.

FIGURE 7: Joule's apparatus is a device that converts kinetic energy to thermal energy.

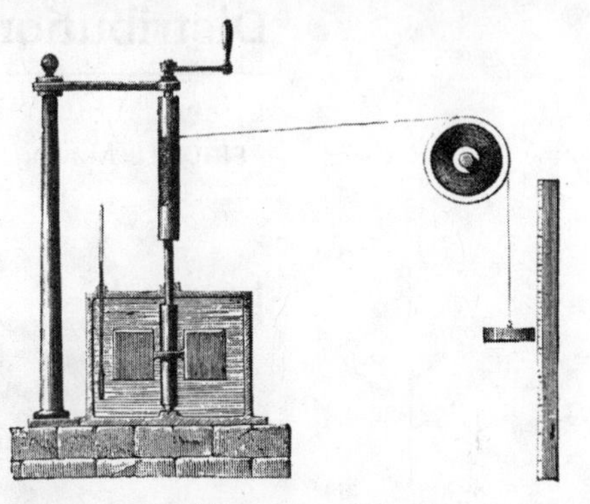

ANALYZE   In this scenario, the change in the potential energy of the lead block is equal to the thermal energy gained by the water. The change in thermal energy is related to the temperature increase, ΔT.

Potential energy $= PE = m_{block} gh$

Energy gained by water $= Q = m_{water} c_p \Delta T$

Known: density of water $= 1.0$ kg/L, volume of water $= 0.25$ L, $m_{block} = 15$ kg, $h = 0.65$ m, $c_p = 4186$ J/kg·°C

Unknown: ΔT

PLAN   Input the mass of the lead block, the height of the block, the mass of the water, and the specific heat of the water into the equation. Solve for the temperature change.

SOLVE   Start by applying the conservation of energy to the problem:

Potential energy change of lead block $=$ Thermal energy gained by water

$$m_{block} gh = m_{water} c_p \Delta T$$

Next, determine the mass of water using the given density. Then solve for the unknown (ΔT). Substitute the known quantities (m_{block}, m_{water}, g, h, c_p), and evaluate:

$$\Delta T = \frac{m_{block} gh}{m_{water} c_p}$$

$$\Delta T = \frac{(15 \text{ kg}) (9.8 \text{ m/s}^2) (0.65 \text{ m})}{(0.25 \text{ kg}) (4186 \text{ J/kg·°C})}$$

$$\Delta T = 0.091 \text{ °C}$$

PRACTICE PROBLEM   **SOLVE** If 301 J of energy is transferred to a sample of water by a Joule's apparatus, from what height must a 10.0 kg block be dropped to deliver this energy? _____

CHECK YOUR WORK   Develop a spreadsheet or other computational model of the relationships in a Joule's apparatus. Use your model to verify your results.

 Evidence Notebook Use what you have learned about thermal equilibrium to explain the energy transfers in the system of the burner, paper cup, and water.

Getty Images

Useful Energy in Heat Engines

When discussing energy, scientists and engineers sometimes describe it in terms of its utility. Different types of energy may or may not be useful depending on the context. In some cases, thermal energy may be an unwanted byproduct. In other cases, such as with a heater, it is the intended product.

Distribution of Energy

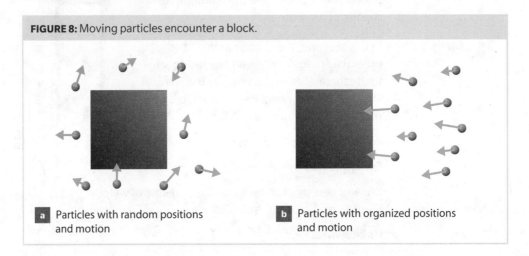

FIGURE 8: Moving particles encounter a block.

a Particles with random positions and motion

b Particles with organized positions and motion

APPLY Based on the diagrams in Figure 8, which model would be more useful for transferring mechanical energy to move the block? Give a reason for your answer.

_____

_____

Energy concentrated in one area or focused in one direction tends to be more useful than unorganized energy. For example, both blocks in Figure 8 are surrounded by the same number of particles with similar average kinetic energy per particle. However, one block is more likely to move. The particles in Figure 8a are moving in random directions and are unlikely to do work on the block. On the other hand, the particles in Figure 8b are all moving toward the block; their energy is concentrated in one direction, making it more likely that the particles will do work on the block and cause it to move. Wind causes a leaf to move because the wind's kinetic energy is concentrated in one direction. This energy would be considered more useful than the dispersed energy in the air on a still day.

Energy can be organized to affect objects in predictable ways. When energy is spread out or is not focused in one direction, it is much harder to make use of. Energy in less organized distributions is often used less efficiently and is often lost to the environment.

 Evidence Notebook How can considering organized and unorganized distributions of energy help you design your Impractical Machine in the unit project? Where in your machine should energy be concentrated? Where in your machine will energy be dispersed?

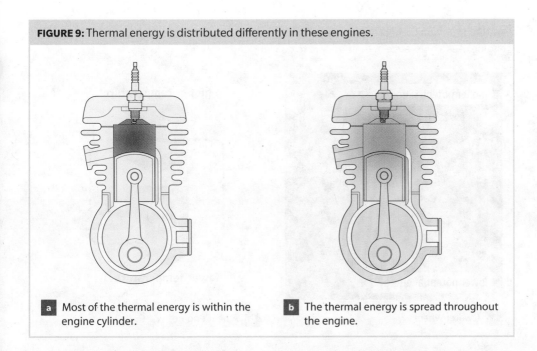

FIGURE 9: Thermal energy is distributed differently in these engines.

a Most of the thermal energy is within the engine cylinder.

b The thermal energy is spread throughout the engine.

EVALUATE Which diagram in Figure 9 shows a cylinder in which the concentration of energy would be most likely to make the piston move? Explain your answer.

_____

_____

_____

Energy tends to be considered useful when it is organized in such a way that it can make something move predictably. In the engine in Figure 9, burning fuel adds energy to the engine. However, it is only in Figure 9a that the energy is concentrated and would cause a predictable result, expanding the gas to push the piston downward and turn the engine. In Figure 9b, the energy is dispersed and unlikely to do work or cause predictable motion.

Heat Engines

PREDICT Would you expect the piston in Figure 10 to move up or down?

_____

_____

An *engine* takes in energy and transforms it into mechanical energy. This mechanical energy might move a car, an elevator, an electric generator, or any number of other devices. To run continuously, engines are designed to go through a cycle so that they return to their initial condition. For the piston and cylinder in Figure 10, the cycle involves warming the gas, pushing the piston out, letting the gas cool, and letting the piston return to its original position.

This cycle is used in steam engines, which use water vapor as the gas. A steam engine is an example of a *heat engine*, which is a system that inputs energy as heat and outputs work and energy as heat. The inputs and outputs are reversed in a *heat pump*, which inputs work and energy as heat and outputs energy as heat. Heat pumps are used in refrigerators and air conditioners.

FIGURE 10: The gases inside and outside the cylinder are both at 30 °C.

piston

30 °C   30 °C

FIGURE 11: A water wheel uses a difference in gravitational potential energy to do work. A heat engine uses a difference in temperature to do work.

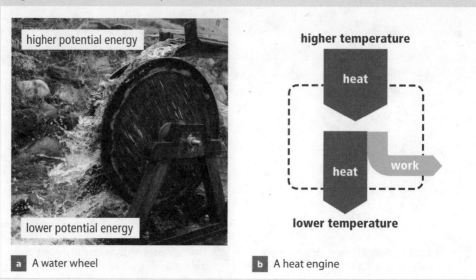

a A water wheel

b A heat engine

A water wheel uses the kinetic and potential energy of falling water to do work. A heat engine uses a difference in temperature to do work; energy as heat enters the engine from a high-temperature area. Some of this energy transforms into mechanical energy, such as a piston's motion, and the remaining energy returns to the environment as the gas cools.

Heat engines and heat pumps are practical systems that use cycles to transfer energy between areas of high and low temperature. A perfectly efficient heat engine would convert all heat to work. In practice, some energy is lost to the environment as waste heat. If a heat engine were 100% efficient, it would be able to do work without losing any energy to its environment, which would violate the second law of thermodynamics.

FIGURE 12: A heat pump takes in work and energy as heat and outputs heat.

Engineering

Engine Efficiency

Engines give off considerable waste heat. Reducing this waste heat makes the engine more efficient because more work is output for the same input of energy. Engineers try to make engines more efficient to reduce the needed energy input. In gasoline engines, reducing the need for energy reduces the amount of fuel needed. Furthermore, burning gasoline produces pollutants that harm air quality and contribute to climate change. Solutions that improve engine efficiency reduce the pollutant production because less fuel is burned.

 Language Arts Connection Conduct research to compare the fuel efficiency and pollutant levels of cars and motorcycles. In a report, cite multiple reliable sources to support a claim about how engine size and complexity can affect these factors.

Energy in Systems

SAMPLE PROBLEM   Energy is required to squeeze a stress ball. Some of the energy is lost as heat as the stress ball is squeezed. A system consisting of a stress ball has 22 J of total energy. Squeezing the ball does 5 J of work on the system. At the same time, 3.5 J are lost as heat. What is the new total energy of the system? In the diagram in Figure 13, label the action that did work on the system and where the energy as heat was transferred to.

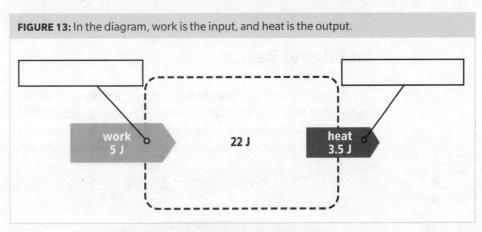

FIGURE 13: In the diagram, work is the input, and heat is the output.

work 5 J   22 J   heat 3.5 J

ANALYZE   Work done by squeezing the stress ball, ΔW, causes an increase in the energy of the system. The heat lost to the environment, ΔQ, decreases the energy of the system. ΔW is an energy input, and ΔQ is an energy output.

Known: $E_f = E_i + \Delta W + \Delta Q$, initial energy $E_i = 22$ J, $\Delta W = +5$ J, $\Delta Q = -3.5$ J

Unknown: final energy E_f

PLAN   Add any changes in energy, such as work added by squeezing the stress ball or heat lost when the ball is squeezed, to E_i.

SOLVE   Work done on the system is the input, and heat is the output. Substitute the known values for each variable, and solve the equation.

$E_f = E_i + \Delta W + \Delta Q = 22$ J $+ 5$ J $- 3.5$ J $= 23.5$ J, rounded to 24 J

PRACTICE PROBLEMS   SOLVE   Answer the following questions:

1. A rolling cart has an initial energy of 85 J. Pushing the cart adds 21 J of energy to the system, and some energy is lost. The system now has 98 J of total energy. What was ΔQ?   _____

2. When a balloon is left in a hot car, it expands. Suppose that the balloon receives 0.20 J of energy in the form of heat and does 0.10 J of work by expanding. If the initial energy of the system was 1.3 J, what is the final energy?   _____

 Evidence Notebook   Think again about the system of the burner, paper cup, and water. How is energy distributed in this system? Where is energy in the system concentrated or dispersed?

Case Study: Jet Engine Improvements

PREDICT Gases within jet engines reach temperatures higher than the melting point of the materials used to build the engines. How do the engines operate without melting?

_____

_____

_____

Jet Engine Basics

The invention of the airplane changed society, allowing people to travel long distances much faster than they could before. Powerful engines accelerate a plane through the air. A jet engine does this work by accelerating air through turbines, as shown in Figure 14. The air ejected from a jet engine pushes back on the plane, accelerating the plane forward.

FIGURE 14: This jet engine model shows the interior structures with simulated airflow.

As shown in Figure 15, jet engines consist of several subsystems. A fan at the front of the engine pulls air in from the plane's surroundings. The air enters a compressor, which is a second fan with many small blades. The small blades spin rapidly, squeezing the air into a smaller volume and raising both its pressure and temperature. The engine sprays fuel into the compressed, hot air. When the engine first starts, it produces a small electric spark to ignite the fuel mist. After the initial spark, the combustion keeps going as air and fuel continuously enter the chamber. This combustion produces expanding gases that burst out through the turbine and nozzle at the back of the engine. As the gases flow through the turbine, the turbine extracts some energy to drive the compressor so that the engine operation continues. The gases leaving the nozzle do work on the plane to propel it forward.

EXPLAIN Jet engines take in fuel and air as matter inputs. They eject exhaust gases as matter outputs. What are the energy inputs and outputs of a jet engine system?

_____

_____

_____

The matter inputs and outputs of a jet engine are connected to the energy transformations that take place as the engine functions. The energy input is equal to the sum of the work done on the plane plus the waste heat output. The engine inputs kinetic energy from fast-moving air and chemical energy from fuel and air, and the engine outputs kinetic energy and thermal energy. The exhaust gases do work on the plane, pushing it forward.

EVALUATE Consider the various simplifications in the model in Figure 15. What factors are not represented that might affect real-world jet engine performance?

_____

_____

FIGURE 15: This model shows matter flows through the five sections of the jet engine system.

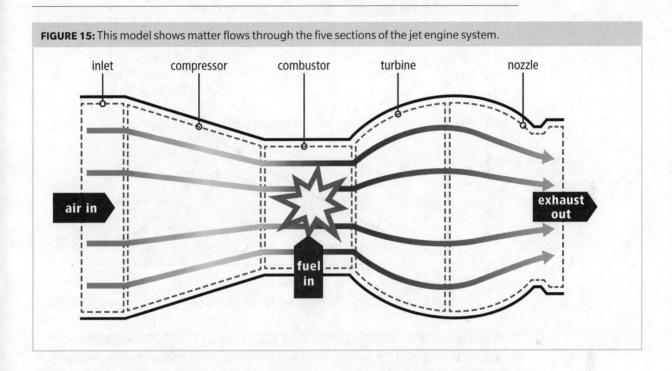

 Language Arts Connection Write a summary describing how jet engines work for an audience of eighth-grade students, using information from the text and the Figure 15 model.

Jet Engines and Temperature

Engineers strive to make jet engines more efficient. Engine efficiency can be measured by how much work the engine does for the amount of fuel it consumes. More efficient engines use less fuel, which reduces operating costs. Temperature within the combustion chamber is one factor that influences jet engine energy efficiency. Not all of the energy is used to do work on the plane; some is lost to the environment as waste heat. Keeping the combustion temperature high allows more fuel to ignite and the engine to do more work.

To accelerate a plane through the air, exhaust gases leaving the engine must be at high pressure. The pressure of the exhaust gases is directly related to the thrust force that pushes back on the engine to move the plane forward. High temperatures help maintain the high pressures needed. In the engine, compression warms the air entering the combustion chamber to temperatures above 500 °C. Combustion of this hot air produces exhaust gases at temperatures that can exceed 1500 °C. The temperatures involved in combustion are high enough to melt the metals used to build the combustion chamber!

Analyze Jet Engine Performance

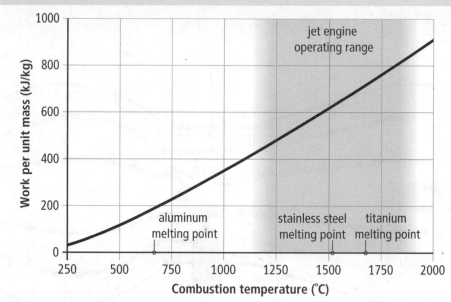

Model of Ideal Jet Engine Performance

FIGURE 16: This graph shows work versus the temperature of gases within the combustion chamber for an ideal jet engine. Under real conditions, jet engine performance would lie somewhere below this curve due to approximations in the model.

As shown in Figure 16, the high temperature in a jet engine's combustion chamber could melt the metal of the engine. To prevent melting, many engine components are built using heat-resistant superalloys and use sophisticated cooling techniques. One such technique is to divert cool air from the intake along the chamber walls. Some of the thermal energy is transferred as heat from the high-temperature exhaust to the cooler air, which reduces the amount of energy that is transferred to the metal of the chamber.

EXPLAIN Explain how you think design features in a jet engine use the transfer and transformation of energy to prevent the metal walls of the engine from melting.

_____

_____

_____

Language Arts Connection Imagine that you are an engineer that builds airplane engines. Conduct research and propose a design change for a jet engine. You might change the engine's materials, fuel, or some other design feature. Develop a presentation using digital media tools that explains how the change improves engine performance.

Evidence Notebook Compare what happens to thermal energy in the system of the burner, paper cup, and water with the thermal energy in the jet engine combustion chamber. What keeps the cup from catching fire? What keeps the metal walls of the engine from melting?

Guided Research

Heat Engines

FIGURE 17: The jet engine in this photo is a type of heat engine.

A steam engine is a type of heat engine in which water is boiled. Within the engine, the water vaporizes and expands, and later the water vapor condenses and contracts. This expanding and contracting produces mechanical motion. Steam engines were first described over 2000 years ago, but they were not widely used until the 1760s, when James Watt developed an efficient version that produced continuous motion. This engine used steam to push a piston and turn a shaft. The steam engine was used to run trains, ships, and factory machinery. Steam engine use declined after the internal combustion engine was developed.

Most vehicles on the road today use internal combustion engines. An internal combustion engine ignites fuel inside a chamber. The burning fuel produces gases that expand and push on a piston to produce rotary motion similar to that produced by a steam engine. Unlike steam engines, which need large amounts of water, internal combustion engines use relatively small amounts of fuel. As a result, internal combustion engines are small enough to easily fit in a vehicle and still do large amounts of work.

A jet engine is another type of engine that converts the chemical energy stored in fuel into mechanical energy. A jet engine does not move a piston to do work. Instead, the engine burns fuel in a pressurized chamber, allowing the expanding gases to escape from one end. Because every action has an equal and opposite reaction, these gases produce thrust that can push airplanes or other vehicles at very high speeds.

 Language Arts Connection Research a modern heat engine, and make a diagram to explain its function. Describe how energy flows through the engine and what the inputs and outputs are. You may want to include text or other forms of media to help explain the engine.

 **BUILD A HEAT ENGINE** | **FIREFIGHTER** | **FREEZING DISCREPANCY** | Go online to choose one of these other paths.

Lesson Self-Check

CAN YOU EXPLAIN THE PHENOMENON?

FIGURE 18: This paper cup is not catching fire, even though the flame below it causes the water to boil.

You can apply what you have learned about the transfer and transformation of thermal energy to explain how a flame can cause water to boil in a paper cup before the cup catches fire. Use your understanding of how energy behaves in a system to explain the phenomenon. Remember to consider how particle-level energy transfers and transformations relate to the conservation of energy on the macroscopic scale.

 Evidence Notebook Refer to your notes in your Evidence Notebook to make a claim about the energy transfers and transformations that occur such that the water boils before the paper cup catches fire. Your explanation should include a discussion of the following:

Claim How do energy transfers and transformations cause the water to boil before the paper cup catches fire?

Evidence What evidence supports your claim about the energy transfers and transformations in this system?

Reasoning How does your evidence support your claim about the energy transfers and transformations in this system?

CHECKPOINTS

Check Your Understanding

1. When two materials at different temperatures are in contact with each other, what factors influence their final temperature? Select all correct answers.

   ☐ **a.** the volume of each material

   ☐ **b.** the mass of each material

   ☐ **c.** the initial temperature of each material

   ☐ **d.** the specific heat capacity of each material

2. A rider pedals a bike uphill, accelerating from 5 km/h to 10 km/h. Which of the following are considered useful energy? Select all correct answers.

   ☐ **a.** the increased kinetic energy of the bike

   ☐ **b.** the increased kinetic energy of the rider

   ☐ **c.** the heat produced by the rider

   ☐ **d.** the heat produced by the friction between wheels and road

   ☐ **e.** the sound the bicycle makes

3. A heat engine absorbs 75 J of heat. Complete the table of possible energy outputs.

Output	
Work (J)	**Heat (J)**
20	_____
35	_____
_____	75

4. Select the correct terms to complete the statement.

   Both thermal energy and temperature depend on the kinetic energy of particles. Temperature measures the total | average kinetic energy of particles in a substance. In contrast to temperature, thermal energy does | does not depend on the mass present.

5. A closed chamber is filled with an ideal gas for an experiment at room temperature. At some point in the experiment, the gas particles in the chamber changed their motion and began to travel at faster speeds. What could have been done to cause this change in particle motion?

   ○ **a.** The chamber was placed in an ice bath.

   ○ **b.** More gas was pumped into the chamber.

   ○ **c.** The chamber was warmed with a hot plate.

6. The mass of a Joule's apparatus drops, decreasing its potential energy by 95 J. The system loses 8.0 J of energy to the environment due to friction in the system. What is the maximum amount of energy available to transfer to the sample of water?

   _____ J

7. Which statements are true about energy transfer through conduction? Select all correct answers.

   ☐ **a.** Conduction occurs when materials are at the same temperature.

   ☐ **b.** Conduction occurs when materials are at different temperatures.

   ☐ **c.** Conduction occurs mainly by particle collisions.

   ☐ **d.** Conduction occurs by groups of particles moving from place to place.

   ☐ **e.** Conduction between materials stops when they are in thermal equilibrium.

8. The temperature of combustion gases in a jet engine exceeds the melting point of the combustion chamber's metal walls. What keeps the metal walls from melting?

   ○ **a.** The chamber walls and the gases are at thermal equilibrium.

   ○ **b.** No thermal energy transfers between the gases and chamber walls.

   ○ **c.** Engineered materials and cool air draw thermal energy away from the metal walls.

   ○ **d.** The metal walls transfer thermal energy poorly, so they remain cool.

CHECKPOINTS (continued)

9. A child places a bowl of soup into the refrigerator because it is too warm to eat. Describe the energy transfers and transformations that take place in the system of the soup, the bowl, and the air in the refrigerator at the directly observable level and the particle-level. Ignore energy transfers between this system and the environment. What will be the condition of this system after several hours?

_____

_____

_____

_____

_____

_____

10. A heat engine is a device that is engineered to use a change in temperature to produce work. In some internal combustion engines, these energy transformations take place in the engine cylinders. Using the example of a car, describe the energy transfers and transformations that lead from the energy within the gasoline to the kinetic energy of the car.

_____

_____

_____

_____

_____

_____

MAKE YOUR OWN STUDY GUIDE

 In your Evidence Notebook, design a study guide that supports the main ideas from this lesson:

Temperature and thermal energy are different measures of particle motion.

Real-world systems tend toward thermal equilibrium.

Engines transform matter and energy inputs into work.

Jet engine design relies on energy transfers and transformations.

Remember to include the following information in your study guide:
- Use examples that model main ideas.
- Record explanations for the phenomena you investigated.
- Use evidence to support your explanations. Your support can include drawings, data, graphs, laboratory conclusions, and other evidence recorded throughout the lesson.

Consider how energy inputs and outputs must be analyzed at the particle level and the directly observable level to describe or model a real-world system, like an engine.

Engineering Connection

Designing Brakes to Capture Energy When a driver brakes from 70 kilometers per hour to a stop, the kinetic energy of the vehicle has to go somewhere. In most cars, it is transformed into thermal energy through friction, mostly between the brake components. Regenerative brakes, used in some electric and hybrid cars, use some of that kinetic energy to generate electrical energy, which is stored in a battery and can later be used to propel the car.

> Research how regenerative brakes capture energy. Develop an infographic in which you describe the system, focusing on the flow of energy between different parts.

FIGURE 1: Regenerative brakes capture some of the energy used to brake, rather than letting it all dissipate as heat.

Art Connection

Kinetic Sculptures A kinetic sculpture is one in which movement is an integral element of the design. This movement is an output by the pieces of the sculpture. The energy input needed can be introduced as kinetic energy by the movement of wind or water in the environment, by an electric motor, or from other sources.

> Research kinetic art. Choose one piece for which there is a video of the piece in motion. Include the video in a presentation in which you explain how energy is input, transferred and transformed through the piece, and output.

FIGURE 2: A kinetic sculpture, such as this one in Los Angeles, includes movement as an essential part of the design.

Environmental Science Connection

Designing Communities to Capture Energy Modern urban planning grew out of frustration. In the late 19th century, new industrialization was laid atop preindustrial city plans. Urban planners attempt to design functional, efficient, and aesthetically pleasing environments for dense populations. One aspect of efficiency is reducing the energy needed per person for various tasks, such as moving one person one kilometer.

> Research methods cities use to decrease their energy use. Choose one existing method and one method that is proposed or just starting to be developed. Write a blog post in which you explain how each method makes the city's design more efficient or functional. In your post, consider whether or not the methods you describe would be effective in your community. If not, describe a plan that would fit the needs of your community.

FIGURE 3: A transport corridor is a main line for travel, such as a train track or road. This elevated rail system carries passengers along the same course as a highway.

(cr) ©FG/Bauer-Griffin/GC Images/Getty Images; (br) ©ZUMA Press, Inc./Alamy

A BOOK EXPLAINING COMPLEX IDEAS USING ONLY THE 1,000 MOST COMMON WORDS

SKY BOAT PUSHER
Machines that push other machines through the air

You've learned about momentum and how it is conserved. How does a jet engine increase an aircraft's momentum, moving it forward? Here's an explanation in simple language.

RANDALL MUNROE
XKCD.COM

THE STORY OF MOVING MACHINES THROUGH AIR

SKY BOATS, LIKE CARS AND SEA BOATS, ARE PUSHED BY MACHINES THAT BURN FIRE WATER. FIRE WATER NEEDS AIR TO BURN, AND SKY BOAT PUSHERS USE SPECIAL BLOWERS THAT USE THE AIR THEY'RE MOVING THROUGH TO FEED THEIR FIRE.

MOST MACHINES THAT BURN FIRE WATER USE THESE FOUR STEPS:

FIRST, PULL AIR IN.

WHY DID I THINK THIS WAS THE BEST IDEA?

SECOND, PUSH THE AIR TOGETHER.

THIRD, BURN FIRE WATER IN THE AIR, HEATING IT AND MAKING IT GET BIGGER.

LAST, USE THAT GROWING AIR TO PUSH ON SOMETHING.

SKY BOAT PUSHERS USE THE FORCE FROM THE HOT AIR IN TWO WAYS: THEY LET IT FLY OUT THE BACK, PUSHING THEM LIKE A SPACE BOAT, BUT THEY ALSO USE IT TO TURN THEIR OWN BLOWERS, PULLING IN MORE AIR AND KEEPING THEMSELVES RUNNING.

KINDS OF PUSHERS

Small sky boats and large ones all work by pushing air, but different kinds of sky boats use different kinds of pushers.

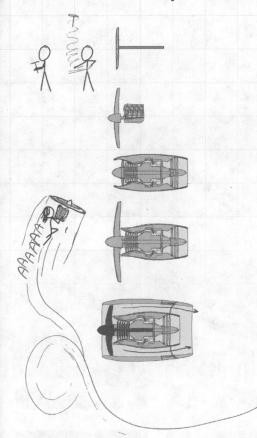

SIMPLE PUSHER
These are fun to play with, but if you try to push any kind of boat with them, your arms get tired.

POWERED PUSHER
These are even more fun to play with (though you probably want to put them on a sky boat first).

FIRE PUSHER
These are used to push fast boats, like the kind that fight in wars. They go fast, but use more fire water than other kinds.

FIRE-POWERED BLOWER
These are like the fire pushers, but with a big blower added to the front. This kind of pusher is very good if you don't want to go too fast. They're very loud.

BIG SKY BOAT PUSHER
These are like fire-powered blowers, but they have a wall around the whole thing to control how the air goes through. They only work well when you're going slower than sound, which is why almost no big sky boats go faster than that.

HOW DO THEY WORK?

To understand how air pushers work, it can help to start by looking at space pushers.

To make a fire, you need air and something to burn. Space boats pour fire water and air into a little room that's open on one side. Then the water and air is set on fire. The fire blows up and flies out the hole, pushing the boat.

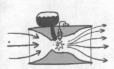

Since there's no air in space, but fires need air, a space boat has to carry air with it. Sky boats can use the air around them, so they only need to carry the fire water. They can take in air, add fire water to it, and burn it.

You can make the pusher better by using a blower in the front to force more air together into the burning room. If there's more air, the fire can burn faster and hotter.

Running the blower in front takes power. You could get that power by burning fire water in a different machine and running power to the blower with power lines. But it's better to just use a little of the power from the fire you're already making.

If you put a blower in back, in the path of the fire, it can turn a stick that turns the blower in the front. This blower slows down the burning air so it doesn't push you as well. But the blower makes the fire work so much better that it more than makes up for it.

There's one last idea that makes this work better. Instead of just using the hot air to power the blowers that press the air into the burning room, you can also use it to power a big blower.

This big blower (which sometimes has a wall around it) is what really pushes the sky boat. Once you add this blower, all the rest of the parts are just there to get lots of air together, start a fire, and get power from it.

SKY BOAT PUSHER

STEP ONE: GET AIR
Air comes in from this side, the first step in making power.

STEP TWO: PUSH
These blowers push the air into a smaller and smaller space, which will help the fire burn faster and hotter.

STEP THREE: BURN
The air from the pushers comes into this burning room, where little drops of fire water are thrown into it and set on fire.

The fire water and air get hot and blow up. The walls make it hard to blow up in any direction except out the back, so that's where the burning air goes.

BLOCKER
If there's stuff in the air, like sticks or rocks, it gets pushed through here so it doesn't hurt the blowers.

POINT
This thing helps to start pushing the air together before it goes inside.

BIG BLOWER
The fire in the back turns this big blower using the stick in the middle. This blower is what really does most of the work of pushing a big sky boat; everything else is just there to turn it.

Not all sky boats have a big blower like this. Some of them just use the hot air itself, which works well for very fast boats. But for boats going slower than sound, it turns out that using the hot air to power big blowers takes less fire water than using the air itself as a pusher.

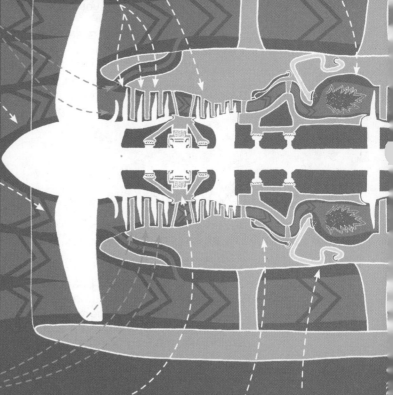

SPIN STOPPERS
The blowers that push the air together all work by spinning, but since they're all spinning in the same direction, they can start the air spinning around instead of going toward the burning room. To keep that from happening, there are little wings in between each blower to make the river of air go straight and keep it from turning too much.

POWER MAKER
This machine uses the turning stick to make a little extra power for the rest of the sky boat to use (for things like lights and computers).

AIR GETTER
The air up high is too thin to breathe. This thing grabs some of the air that the blowers pushed together and sends it to the inside of the sky boat so people can breathe.

FIRE-WATER CARRIERS
These carry fire water into the burning room.

STEP FOUR: MAKE POWER

The force of the air coming out would help push the sky boat on its own, but sky boat pushers do something cooler: They put extra blowers in the path of the air. Instead of turning those blowers to push air, they let the *air* turn the *blowers*. The blowers turn the stick in the middle of the pusher, which turns all the blowers at the start, powering the machine.

That might seem like it shouldn't work, since it's using a blower to power another blower. But the power is coming from the burning fire water pushing its way out. These blowers are just a cool way to use some of that fire to keep the machine running.

WAIT A SECOND!

One thing a lot of people wonder is "How does the force from the fire know to go out the back? Why doesn't it push on the blowers in front just as much, and slow them back down?"

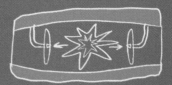

The answer is that the shape of the room and the size of the blowers make it so the easier way out is through the back. It just has to push through a few blowers on the way.

BACK PUSHER

If the sky boat needs to stop, it can use these doors to send the air out the sides and toward the front, which makes it push back instead of forward.

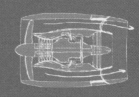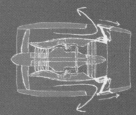

POINT

BIG BLOWER

A BOOK EXPLAINING COMPLEX IDEAS USING ONLY THE 1,000 MOST COMMON WORDS

RANDALL MUNROE
XKCD.COM

UNDER A CAR'S FRONT COVER

How a fire box turns the wheels that move a car

You've learned about complicated cyclic processes, such as those in internal-combustion engines. A car's internal-combustion engine uses heat from combustion to do work. Here's a look at all the parts and what they do.

THE STORY OF WHAT MAKES CARS MOVE

THERE'S LOTS OF STUFF UNDER THE FRONT COVER OF A CAR.

THE BIGGEST THING IS USUALLY THE FIRE BOX, WHICH TURNS THE WHEELS TO PUSH THE CAR.

BUT THERE'S A LOT OF OTHER STUFF, TOO, AND EVEN SOMEONE WHO KNOWS A LOT ABOUT CARS CAN HAVE A HARD TIME TELLING WHAT EVERY PART IS.

This picture shows some of the things you might see if you open a car's front cover.

NOTE: Before opening the car to look under the cover, you should stop driving.

FIRE BOX

This fire box is the car's pusher. Like sky boat pushers, it makes power by burning fire water using air from outside.

To get pushing power from the fire water, the car burns it in little closed boxes. When the water burns, it gets hot, which makes it get bigger and push on the walls of the box. One of the walls of the box can move, and it has a stick that joins it to a wheel.

When the sides of the little boxes move, their sticks push their wheels around. Those wheels are all joined by a turning stick. That stick turns more wheels, and those wheels turn the wheels that touch the ground.

POWER BOX

This box holds power to run different parts of the car. To start the fire box turning, you need a lot of power at once, so this power box is built to let out its power very fast.

You have to be careful, because if you let the two lines from the power box touch, they will let out all their power at once. This is enough power to start a fire or turn a small piece of metal to water.

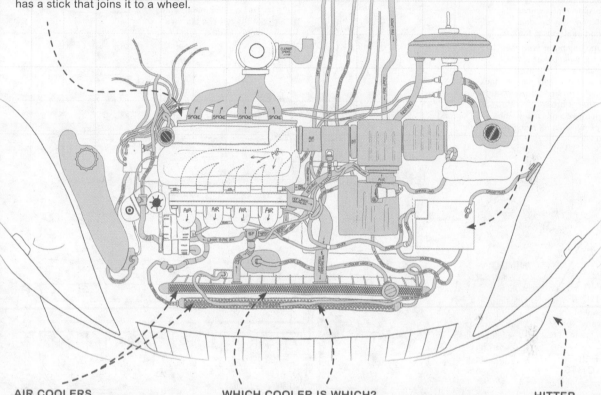

AIR COOLERS

These things cool down hot stuff by letting air blow over them. The air comes in from holes in the front of the car as it moves, but there are also blowers that pull air through the coolers even if you're not moving very fast.

WHICH COOLER IS WHICH?

There are two coolers here. The one in back cools the fire box, and the one in front cools the cooling water for the people in the car. (The people-cooler is in front because you need colder air to cool people. A fire box is so hot that warm and cold person-air are almost the same to it.)

HITTER

If the car runs into something, this part hits it first.

HOW COOLERS WORK

Some coolers work by just using water to carry away heat from hot things. But some machines can use power to make things colder than the air around them.

You need some cooling stuff. The best kind of cooling stuff is something that's air when it's as warm as a room, but turns to water when it gets cold. There are a few kinds of air that work for this.

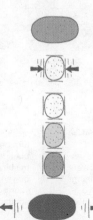

The cooling air starts off as warm as the air outside.

To start the cooling, first you push the air into a smaller space. This makes it get hot ("Making air smaller makes it hotter" is an important air law). For some coolers, this turns them to water.

Next, you let the stuff cool down while holding it in the smaller space. When it's done cooling, it's back to being as warm as the air again, but it's smaller.

Last, you let it get big again. (If it's water now, it will turn back to air.) Because of the air law, this means it will get colder, just like making it smaller made it hotter. You use the cold air to cool things down. You keep doing this until it warms back up, then send it back and do the whole thing again.

UNDER A CAR'S FRONT COVER

FIRE STARTERS (INSIDE)
These use power to make little flashes that light the fire water.

SLIDING WATER
This water helps the parts of the fire box spin without getting stuck. If you run out of it, your engine stops turning, and sometimes the parts get stuck together and it can never turn again.

This water gets dirty, so you have to change it sometimes.

SLIDE FIXER
If you stop too hard, your wheels can stop turning and start to slide. Once wheels start sliding, they become less good at stopping the car.

When the computer feels that one of the wheels has started sliding, this box lifts the stoppers away from the wheel enough that it grabs the ground and starts turning again. Then it presses the stopper back down. It can do this many times each second. This box makes cars much, much better at stopping.

SMOKE BURNER
When cars burn fire water, the smoke it makes has lots of stuff in it that can make people and animals sick. This machine helps the smoke finish burning so it turns to air and water.

(The kind of air it turns into isn't good for the world, either, but at least it's better than the kinds in the smoke.)

OUT THE BACK
This line takes the cleaner smoke and sends it out through a hole in the back of the car.

POWER CHANGERS
These sit on top of the fire starters. They take the kind of power made by the power box and turn it into a kind of power that works better for starting tiny fires in the fire box.

LINE FROM COOLER IN SEAT AREA

SMOKE CARRIER
This carries the air out of the fire box after it's done burning.

WINDOW CLEANING WATER HOLE
If you run out of cleaning water, you can pour more in here.

FRONT LIGHTS
These let you see the road when it's dark.

TURNING LIGHTS
These tell other cars that you're about to turn. A few moments before you turn, you should pull the stick that makes the lights flash.

Some people seem to have a hard time with this idea.

WINDOW CLEANING WATER
This holds the water that pours onto your windows when you pull on the cleaning control.

CLEANING WATER PUSHER

FIRE BOX

CIRCLE LINE
This line goes around the fire box's turning stick, then goes around a lot of other wheels in the car that power different machines—like the thing that makes power for the power box. That way, the fire box can turn them all while it's also turning the ground wheels.

Sometimes this breaks. When that happens, your fire box can only turn the ground wheels. Your car can keep driving, but it won't be able to cool down, so you'll only be able to drive for a few minutes before the car gets too hot and turns itself off.

THING THAT PUSHES AIR INTO A SMALL SPACE
This is what makes the cold air blowers work. It cools things the same way your home ice box does.

STARTER
Once the stick in the fire box starts turning, it keeps itself turning with its own power, but it needs this spinner to start it turning. This is powered by the power box. If your power box is empty, this spinner can't spin, which is why your car won't start.

POWER MAKER
This thing uses the fire box's spinning stick to make power. That power is used to keep the power box full.

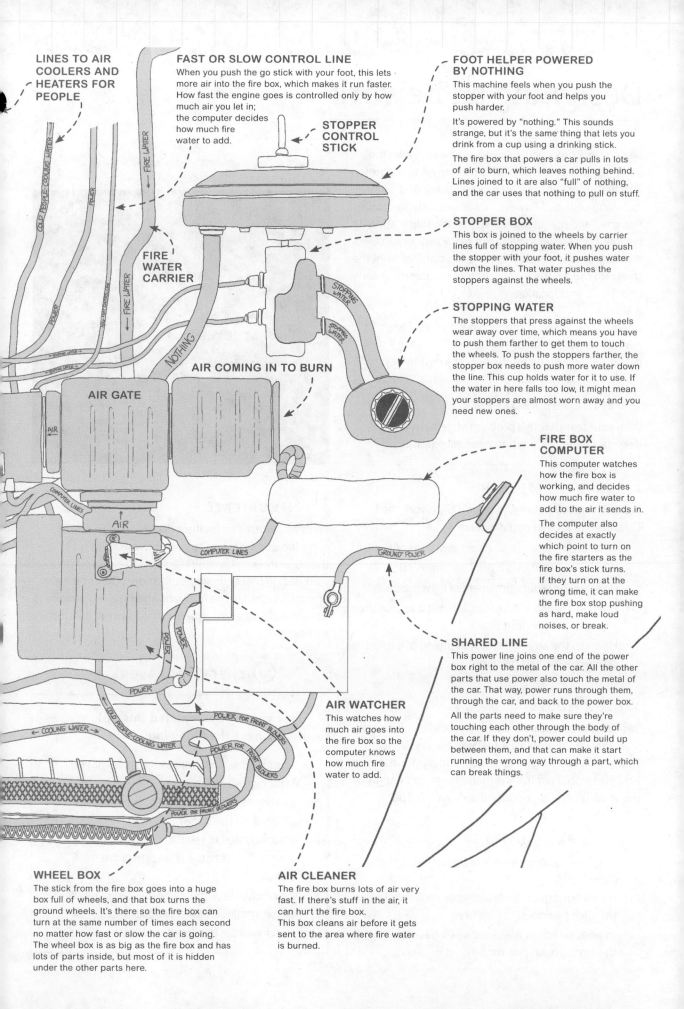

LINES TO AIR COOLERS AND HEATERS FOR PEOPLE

COLD PEOPLE-COOLING WATER

POWER

FIRE WATER

POWER

HOT PEOPLE-HEATING WATER

FIRE WATER

FAST OR SLOW CONTROL LINE

When you push the go stick with your foot, this lets more air into the fire box, which makes it run faster. How fast the engine goes is controlled only by how much air you let in; the computer decides how much fire water to add.

STOPPER CONTROL STICK

FIRE WATER CARRIER

NOTHING

STOPPING WATER

STOPPING WATER

AIR COMING IN TO BURN

AIR GATE

AIR

COMPUTER LINES

AIR

COMPUTER LINES

POWER

POWER

POWER

COOLING WATER

COLD PEOPLE-COOLING WATER

POWER FOR FRONT BLOWERS

POWER FOR FRONT BLOWERS

POWER FOR FRONT BLOWERS

GROUND POWER

FOOT HELPER POWERED BY NOTHING

This machine feels when you push the stopper with your foot and helps you push harder.

It's powered by "nothing." This sounds strange, but it's the same thing that lets you drink from a cup using a drinking stick.

The fire box that powers a car pulls in lots of air to burn, which leaves nothing behind. Lines joined to it are also "full" of nothing, and the car uses that nothing to pull on stuff.

STOPPER BOX

This box is joined to the wheels by carrier lines full of stopping water. When you push the stopper with your foot, it pushes water down the lines. That water pushes the stoppers against the wheels.

STOPPING WATER

The stoppers that press against the wheels wear away over time, which means you have to push them farther to get them to touch the wheels. To push the stoppers farther, the stopper box needs to push more water down the line. This cup holds water for it to use. If the water in here falls too low, it might mean your stoppers are almost worn away and you need new ones.

FIRE BOX COMPUTER

This computer watches how the fire box is working, and decides how much fire water to add to the air it sends in.

The computer also decides at exactly which point to turn on the fire starters as the fire box's stick turns. If they turn on at the wrong time, it can make the fire box stop pushing as hard, make loud noises, or break.

SHARED LINE

This power line joins one end of the power box right to the metal of the car. All the other parts that use power also touch the metal of the car. That way, power runs through them, through the car, and back to the power box.

All the parts need to make sure they're touching each other through the body of the car. If they don't, power could build up between them, and that can make it start running the wrong way through a part, which can break things.

AIR WATCHER

This watches how much air goes into the fire box so the computer knows how much fire water to add.

WHEEL BOX

The stick from the fire box goes into a huge box full of wheels, and that box turns the ground wheels. It's there so the fire box can turn at the same number of times each second no matter how fast or slow the car is going. The wheel box is as big as the fire box and has lots of parts inside, but most of it is hidden under the other parts here.

AIR CLEANER

The fire box burns lots of air very fast. If there's stuff in the air, it can hurt the fire box.
This box cleans air before it gets sent to the area where fire water is burned.

Designing a Firework

The key to a successful fireworks show is to awe the audience with a colorful display. Energy is transformed into flashes of light that look like a variety of shapes, including balls and flowers. The firework shells must be designed and manufactured so that the shape appears reliably. Each firework shell holds many explosives called *stars* that produce the flashes. As each star flies from the shell into the air, the momentum of the star must carry it to the correct location.

Imagine you are an engineer working for a fireworks manufacturer. Design a firework shell to make a new pattern. How will the solution meet a customer need?

1. DEFINE THE PROBLEM

With your team, write a problem statement that describes what the solution must accomplish.

2. CONDUCT RESEARCH

Research what you need to design a firework shell. Questions to answer could include:

- What are the standard shapes and sizes of shells?
- Why are most firework displays symmetric?
- How are individual streamers of light produced?
- How are the individual stars arranged so that they all appear at the right time?
- How can the arrangement and timing of explosions produce a desired pattern?

3. USE A MODEL

Based on your research, design a model of a firework shell that could produce a shape in the sky. Indicate how the stars would be arranged, and demonstrate how you would control the momentum and energy of the various parts to produce the desired shape.

4. DESIGN A SOLUTION

Use evidence to support your reasoning for a particular design.

- How are momentum and energy conserved when the shell explodes?
- In what direction will the stars fly based on the structure of your model?

FIGURE 4: Designers arrange the parts of the shell carefully to make the desired pattern.

5. COMMUNICATE

Prepare a written or multimedia report with one or more labeled diagrams to present your solution to the fireworks display operators and to explain how your design meets their specifications. Describe how energy is stored in the firework, and how that energy is transferred and transformed as the firework is launched and explodes.

 CHECK YOUR WORK

Once you have completed this task, you should have the following:

- a clearly defined problem statement that will lead to the suggested solution
- background information about how fireworks are designed and constructed
- a physical model or a sketch of your design solution along with a description of the pattern that it will produce
- a conclusion that explains how your design accounted for conservation of momentum and indicates how energy would be transferred and transformed

Name _____   Date _____

SYNTHESIZE THE UNIT

In your Evidence Notebook, make a concept map, other graphic organizer, or outline using the Study Guides you made for each lesson in this unit. Be sure to use evidence to support your claims.

When synthesizing individual information, remember to follow these general steps:
- Find the central idea of each piece of information.
- Think about the relationships among the central ideas.
- Combine the ideas to come up with a new understanding.

DRIVING QUESTIONS

Look back to the Driving Questions from the opening section of this unit. In your Evidence Notebook, review and revise your previous answers to those questions. Use the evidence you gathered and other observations you made throughout the unit to support your claims.

PRACTICE AND REVIEW

1. Order the objects from least to greatest momentum.

   _____ **a.** 1.0 kg ball moving at 500 m/s

   _____ **b.** 5.0 kg ball moving at 25 m/s

   _____ **c.** 20 kg ball moving at 20 m/s

   _____ **d.** 50 kg ball moving at 5 m/s

   _____ **e.** 100 kg ball that is stationary

2. A baseball with a mass of 0.155 kg travels toward a catcher at a speed of 35 m/s. The catcher's mitt brings the ball to rest in 0.25 s. The average force exerted on the ball is _____ N.

3. A 20 000 kg railcar traveling northward at 2 m/s bumps into a stationary railcar with a mass of 40 000 kg. The first railcar stops. After the collision, the speed of the second railcar is

   _____ m/s, and it is traveling in a _____ direction.

4. The brakes on a bike slow it from 5.0 m/s to a stop. The bike plus rider has a mass of 120 kg. Calculate each answer.

   The change in kinetic energy was –_____.

   If the brakes were applied over a distance of 50 m, the average force was –_____.

5. What forms of energy does an operating engine transfer to its environment? Select all correct answers.

   ☐ **a.** thermal energy   ☐ **c.** electrical energy
   ☐ **b.** kinetic energy   ☐ **d.** sound energy

6. A 24 kg child on a swing has 600 J of potential energy at the top of her arc, when her speed momentarily reaches 0.0 m/s. Calculate each value.

   As the child descends, she loses 100 J of potential energy. Her kinetic energy is now _____, and her potential energy is _____.

   When the swing's height has been reduced to half its starting value, her potential energy is _____. Her speed is _____.

7. If two objects with different temperatures come into physical contact, what can be said about the objects' final temperatures when they reach thermal equilibrium? Select all correct answers.

   ☐ **a.** The final temperatures will depend on the mass of each object.

   ☐ **b.** The final temperatures will depend on the density of each object.

   ☐ **c.** The final temperatures will depend on the heat capacity of each object.

   ☐ **d.** The final temperatures will be between the objects' initial temperatures.

Unit 2 Energy and Motion **173**

8. Sketch the path of a ball bouncing across the floor from the left to the right. How could an observer deduce the direction in which the ball is moving? Use this example to describe what happens to energy over time.

_____

_____

_____

9. A heat pump is similar to a heat engine, but it runs in the other direction. It takes in heat and work and outputs heat. Draw a diagram showing a hot reservoir and a cold reservoir with a heat pump between them. Add arrows to show the exchange of heat and work between the system (heat pump) and its environment. Remember to include the heat output. A perfect heat pump would move energy from the cold reservoir to the hot reservoir with no work. Show this perfect heat pump using a diagram, and explain why it violates the second law of thermodynamics.

_____

_____

_____

_____

10. Most cell phone users keep their phones in protective cases, which prevent their phones from being damaged if they are dropped or mishandled. How might these small plastic cases use the concept of deformation to keep cell phones safe?

_____

_____

_____

_____

UNIT PROJECT

Return to your unit project. Prepare a presentation using your research and materials, and share it with the class.

Remember these tips while evaluating:

- Demonstrate that your elaborate process works—energy input at one end will be passed along and perform the final task.

- Explain how your process includes several types of energy.

- Explain how energy is transferred and transformed in each step.

- Explain how energy is lost over the course of the process.

UNIT 3

Field Forces and Energy

Charge builds up as the wheel spins. The
force becomes strong enough to produce
a spark between the metal balls.

YOU SOLVE IT

How Can You Move Particles Using Electric Charge?

To begin exploring this unit's concepts,
go online to investigate ways to solve a
real-world problem.

FIGURE 1: Forces exerted at a distance can cause objects to hover.

In the photographs, a loop of metalized film hovers above a rubber balloon and a plastic pipe. There are no strings or air currents keeping the loop suspended. What makes the metalized film hover? A free-body diagram of the metalized-film loop would show an upward force balancing the downward force of gravity. Use your everyday experience and knowledge of physics to suggest possible sources of this upward force.

EXPLAIN What forces are acting on the metalized-film loop that cause it to hover?

_____

_____

_____

_____

_____

DRIVING QUESTIONS

As you move through the unit, gather evidence to help you answer the following questions. In your Evidence Notebook, record what you already know about these topics and any questions you have about them.

1. What field forces affect your everyday experience?
2. How do objects stay in orbit?
3. How do the relative strengths of gravitational and electric fields compare?

UNIT PROJECT

Go online to download the Unit Project Worksheet to help plan your project.

Hovering Toy

How can field forces be used to make an object hover? Test a variety of materials and designs to build a hovering toy. Describe how electric, magnetic, and gravitational fields are used to control the position of the toy.

Language Development

Use the lessons in this unit to complete the chart and expand your understanding of the science concepts.

TERM: inertia

Definition	Example

Similar Term	Phrase

TERM: gravity

Definition	Example

Similar Term	Phrase

TERM: gravitational field

Definition	Example

Similar Term	Phrase

TERM: field force

Definition	Example

Similar Term	Phrase

TERM: attractive force

Definition	Example

Similar Term	Phrase

TERM: repulsive force

Definition	Example

Similar Term	Phrase

TERM: electric field

Definition	Example

Similar Term	Phrase

TERM: magnetic field

Definition	Example

Similar Term	Phrase

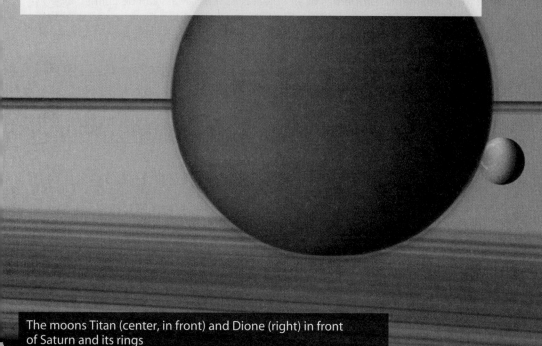

3.1

Mass and Gravitational Fields

The moons Titan (center, in front) and Dione (right) in front of Saturn and its rings

CAN YOU SOLVE THE PROBLEM?

Saturn's rings are composed of pieces of ice and rock ranging in size from specks of dust to large boulders. They orbit Saturn in bands thousands of kilometers across but less than a kilometer thick. Of Saturn's dozens of moons, many orbit in the same plane as its rings. Saturn's largest moon, Titan, is larger than the planet Mercury. It has enough mass to retain an atmosphere, visible in the image as a dark halo. Saturn's other moons are smaller than Earth's moon. Dione, shown in the image, is the fourth-largest moon. It orbits close to the planet, while Titan orbits about three times as far away.

Object	Mass ($\times 10^{21}$ kg)
Saturn	568 300
Titan	135
Dione	1.1

Think about the challenges of measuring the masses of these objects. A planet or moon can't be put on a two-pan balance or hung on a spring scale. Its mass must be measured by some other method.

INFER What kinds of observations can you or scientists make about objects in space? How might one of those observations help determine an object's mass?

_____

_____

_____

 Evidence Notebook As you explore the lesson, gather evidence about what observations are needed to determine the mass of an object in space.

Observing Gravity

One of the fundamental properties of an object is its mass. Mass can be defined as a measure of the amount of matter in an object. Often larger objects have more mass than smaller objects, but that's not always true.

INFER How can a small object have the same mass as a large object? Which do you think would be harder to pick up? Explain your answer.

_____

_____

Mass and Inertia

Another way to determine an object's mass is to observe the effect that a force has on the object. A greater force is required to accelerate, or change the motion of, an object with greater mass. This tendency of an object to resist a change in motion unless an outside force acts on the object is known as inertia. An object with a greater inertia than another object will also have a greater mass.

Observing inertia is something you do every day. When pushing an empty cart, you can accelerate it from rest relatively easily. However, accelerating a full cart from rest is much more difficult. The greater total inertia of the full cart makes the cart more difficult to accelerate. The items in the cart also have inertia and move forward with the cart. If the cart stops suddenly, the items' inertia keeps them moving forward, and they rattle forward in the cart. During a sharp turn, the items resist a change in direction, and they slide toward the side of the cart as the cart turns under them.

FIGURE 1: Animals with different masses, such as a rhino or rabbit, accelerate differently because of inertia.

a Rabbit accelerating

b Rhino accelerating

ANALYZE Which animal in the photos has greater inertia? How does this inertia affect the acceleration of each animal if the force changing their motion is the same?

_____

_____

Measuring Acceleration

Because inertia is a measure of mass, the relationship among inertia, acceleration, and force is the same as the relationship among mass, acceleration, and force. Constant acceleration results from a constant net force on an object. A constant force in an object's direction of motion, such as the force of gravity on a falling object, increases its speed.

Acceleration can be difficult to measure directly, because you must accurately measure two instantaneous velocities. One approach to finding acceleration is to apply Newton's second law of motion, $\mathbf{a} = \mathbf{F}/m$.

SOLVE Four balls of the same volume but different masses are dropped from rest. The table gives the mass of each ball and the force due to gravity on the ball. The vector arrow on each ball shows the magnitude and direction of the force of gravity on the ball. Calculate the acceleration of each ball, using Newton's second law of motion.

Explore Online ▶

Material	Rubber	Stone	Steel	Gold
$t = 0\,s$				
$t = 1\,s$				
$t = 2\,s$				
Force	9.31 N	28.42 N	54.88 N	137.2 N
Mass	0.95 kg	2.9 kg	5.6 kg	14 kg
Force/mass	_____ N/kg	_____ N/kg	_____ N/kg	_____ N/kg

EXPLAIN The balls have very different masses. Why did they fall with the same acceleration (calculated as force divided by mass in the table)?

_____

_____

Gravitational Force

Gravity is a familiar example of a force that provides an acceleration on an object. Gravity is the force of attraction between two objects. For smaller objects near a very massive body—such as objects near Earth's surface—the larger mass will dominate any interactions. While there is a force of attraction between a book and a pen, it is not observable because the interaction is dominated by the force of attraction of the Earth.

The force of gravity on a smaller object near the surface of a massive body is the weight of the object. Weight is related to mass, but they are not the same. Mass is a scalar value, with no direction. It is an inherent property, which means that it does not change when the system around a body changes. Weight, in contrast, is a measure of force. It is a vector, with a direction, and its value will change for objects depending on their distance from Earth's surface. The weight of an object, $\mathbf{F}_g$, can be calculated by multiplying its mass by the acceleration due to gravity: $\mathbf{F}_g = m\mathbf{g}$. Near the surface of Earth, the magnitude of the acceleration due to gravity, g, is 9.8 m/s^2.

FIGURE 2: The weight of a body on the surface of Earth's moon is about one-sixth its weight on Earth.

The moon is less massive and smaller than Earth, and the gravitational attraction between it and objects near its surface is also smaller. As a result, the acceleration due to gravity on the moon is lower, and objects weigh less on the moon. Larger planets, such as Jupiter, have a much stronger gravitational attraction between them and other objects.

ANALYZE How does the moon's smaller gravitational attraction compared to Earth affect the friction produced by the astronaut walking across the surface of the moon? (Assume all other factors are the same as on Earth.)

- ○ **a.** Friction is greater because of a stronger normal force.
- ○ **b.** Friction is greater because of a weaker normal force.
- ○ **c.** Friction is less because of a stronger normal force.
- ○ **d.** Friction is less because of a weaker normal force.

Though the mass of a golf ball is the same on Earth or the moon, the weight of a golf ball on the moon is much less than on Earth. On the moon, the golf ball can be hit farther. Astronauts need to adjust their walk to the weaker gravitational attraction of the moon. Astronauts who landed on the moon tended to move around by jumping short distances rather than taking steps, and they appeared to bounce across the surface.

EXPLAIN What properties do you think would be useful in the design of space boots that would help astronauts walk across the moon's surface? Explain.

_____

_____

_____

 Evidence Notebook A star is much more massive than an orbiting planet. How does the mass of the planet affect the gravitational force between them?

Representing Orbits

On Earth, the effects of gravity are obvious. Objects have weight and accelerate when dropped. But the effects of gravity can also be observed in space.

ARGUE What is a phenomenon in space that could be a result of gravity? Explain your answer with an example.

_____

_____

_____

Motion in Space

Though millions of kilometers away from Earth, Mars can be seen with the naked eye. The motion of planets in space is observable, even from a great distance. Mars, like Earth and the other planets, revolves around the sun. Each planet has an *orbit*, which is the path that a body follows as it travels around another body in space. Venus, Earth, and Neptune have the most circular orbits (they are not perfectly circular), while Mercury and Mars have the most elongated orbits. The orbits of the planets and the sun lie in a plane called the orbital plane. In this lesson, most orbits are shown as if looking straight at the orbital plane from a distant point in space.

INFER In the image below, only the first orbit is a circle. Which drawing do you think shows Earth's orbit? Which do you think shows Mercury's orbit? Use the labels E and M to indicate your choices. The sun is the yellow dot in the orbits below.

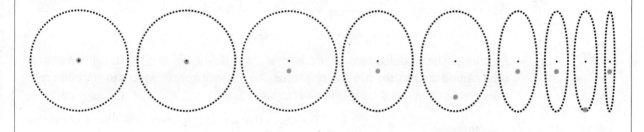

 Collaborate With a partner, discuss which of the shapes above are likely to be planetary orbits. Prepare a presentation to explain your reasoning.

APPLY How do you think the position of the sun in Mercury's elongated orbit compares to the position of the sun in Neptune's more circular orbit?

_____

_____

_____

The Shape of Orbits

Early attempts to model the patterns of planetary motion were based on circles. The moon seems to move in a near-circular orbit around Earth and as seen from Earth, the stars seem to move in circles around a point in the sky. However, these models did not adequately describe the complicated motion of the planets. Johannes Kepler used precise observations of Mars to determine that its orbit was best modeled as a shape called an ellipse. This model was used to make accurate predictions, and it also fit the orbits of other planets.

Language Arts Connection Research the history of astronomical research in the time of Kepler. Write an article about other astronomers and how their studies related to Kepler's.

Specifying Orbits

The planets have elliptical orbits that are nearly circular. Other orbits, such as those of many comets, are relatively long and skinny ellipses.

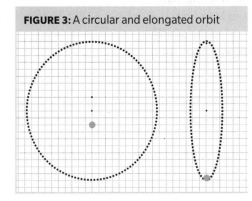

FIGURE 3: A circular and elongated orbit

INFER The orbit on the left in Figure 3 is a circular orbit and the orbit on the right is a more elongated orbit. The yellow dot represents the sun. How do you think the shape of the orbit relates to the position of the sun in the orbit?

_____

_____

_____

_____

An orbit can be modeled as an *ellipse*, an oval shape defined by two points called *foci*. In an orbit around the sun, the sun is at one focus. The distance from one focus to any point on the ellipse and then to the other focus is constant.

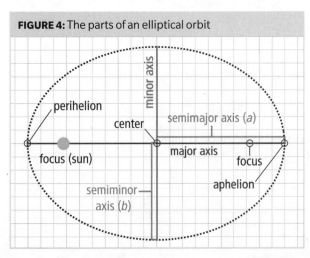

FIGURE 4: The parts of an elliptical orbit

The curve that a planet follows in its orbit around the sun can be described in terms of its elliptical shape. Ellipses have a long side and a short side, referred to as the major axis and minor axis. These axes can be used to describe the shape and average radius of an orbit.

Astronomers also describe orbits in terms of eccentricity, or how much it deviates from a circle. A highly circular orbit is said to have a low eccentricity while a narrower orbit has a higher eccentricity. Values for eccentricity vary between 0 for a circular orbit and 1 for a long, narrow orbit.

A planetary orbit can also be described in terms of how near or far the planet travels from the sun. A planet's closest approach to the sun is referred to as its perihelion. Earth's perihelion occurs in January, when the planet is roughly 147 million kilometers from the sun. A planet's farthest distance from the sun is referred to as its aphelion. Earth's aphelion occurs in July, when the planet is roughly 152 million kilometers from the sun.

✎ Engineering

Constructing an Ellipse

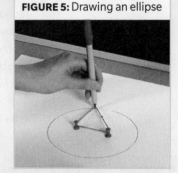

FIGURE 5: Drawing an ellipse

Engineers may use several different types of models to help them break a problem into smaller pieces. To use this approach, you might start with a physical model to understand how to construct an ellipse.

ANALYZE Select the correct terms to complete the statement about Figure 5.

The pushpins represent the minor axis | foci. The string connecting the pins has a constant | varying length. To model Earth's orbit, the pins should be farther apart | about the distance shown | closer together.

In a mathematical model, equations can define the points that make up an ellipse. Using x-y coordinates on the Cartesian plane, the equations are:

$$\frac{x^2}{a^2} + \frac{y^2}{b^2} = 1, \quad e = \frac{c}{a}, \quad \text{and} \quad b = a\sqrt{1 - e^2}$$

where e is eccentricity, c is distance between the center and the focus, and a and b are the semimajor and semiminor axes, respectively (longest and shortest distances from center).

These equations can be used to construct an ellipse in multiple ways. Substituting in numbers for a and b, the equation for an ellipse can be solved for y to generate x–y coordinate pairs to plot on a graph. Code can also be written that allows a computer to complete a drawing based on the equations. Adjusting the values of a and b in the equations for eccentricity and the semiminor axis will change the ellipse's size and shape. Adjusting other variables can rotate or shift the ellipse's position on the graph.

Kepler's Laws of Planetary Motion

In the early 1600s, German astronomer Johannes Kepler developed three laws that describe planetary motion. The first law states that planets follow elliptical orbits with the sun at one focus. The first law was a major shift in the understanding of the solar system. Most astronomers at the time thought orbits were circular, and many still thought that planets orbit Earth, not the sun.

Kepler's second law states that an imaginary line from the sun to a planet sweeps out equal areas during equal times. This means that the closer planets are to the sun, the faster they move. Kepler's third law states that the square of the period, T, of a planet's orbit is proportional to the cube of the orbit's semimajor axis, a. That is, $T^2 = ka^3$. The constant k depends on the masses of the planets and the sun.

Inertia and Orbits

 Language Arts Connection Consider this claim: *an orbit occurs when an object falls toward Earth but misses the ground.* Develop a presentation using drawings, video, animation, or a simulation that demonstrates this claim and shows how one object orbits another.

Think about the path of a projectile with an initial horizontal velocity, such as the cannonball in Figure 6. If no forces acted on the cannonball, it would keep moving in a straight line because of its inertia. But the force of gravity does act on the cannonball in the direction perpendicular to the ground and causes the cannonball's path to curve. A faster cannonball travels farther because of the curve of Earth's surface, as shown in the diagram by Isaac Newton. The force is toward Earth's center, so its direction changes. A cannonball with an extreme initial velocity would, in the absence of air resistance, continue falling all the way around Earth—it would continue to fall without ever hitting the ground. An orbit is explained by the same laws as projectile motion. An object in orbit has inertia that would keep it moving in a straight line, but gravity accelerates the object toward Earth's center, thereby keeping the object from traveling off into space.

FIGURE 6: A cannonball falls toward Earth's surface (left). If fired from a mountain with a greater horizontal velocity, it travels farther around Earth (right). With a high enough velocity, it could continue to fall in a closed loop.

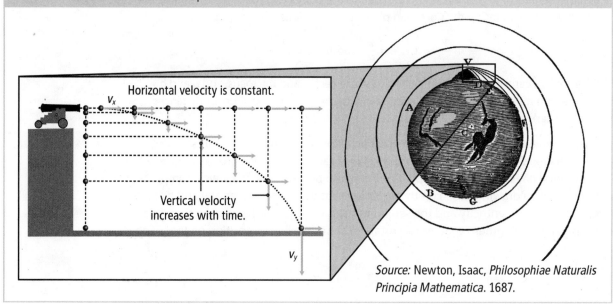

Source: Newton, Isaac, *Philosophiae Naturalis Principia Mathematica.* 1687.

EXPLAIN Select the correct terms to complete the statement about planetary motion.

The circular | elliptical | linear shape of a planet's orbit around the sun is related to projectile motion. The acceleration is always toward | away from | perpendicular to the sun. In theory, a planet moving closer to the sun is like an object near Earth flying | falling | floating —its speed and kinetic energy increase | decrease | stay the same as its potential energy decreases. The force and acceleration increase as $1/r^2$, so greater speed is needed for a smaller orbit to be stable.

 Evidence Notebook In what ways might the mass of an object affect its orbit around the sun? Would you expect to see a pattern?

Quantifying Gravitational Force

The sun is not the only object in space that has objects in orbit around it. Other stars in the universe have planets that orbit them, and some planets have moons orbiting them. Studying the orbits of various objects reveals patterns in their motion.

The Cause of Orbital Motion

Recall that an orbit can be described with variables, including its semimajor axis, a, and its period, T. When discussing orbits on the scale of the solar system, scientists often measure the semimajor axis and other distances in astronomical units (AU). One astronomical unit is equal to the average distance between Earth and the sun, or 1.496×10^8 km.

Figure 7 is a graph of the cube of the semimajor axis (a^3) versus square of period (T^2) and has lines for the planets around the sun, the planets around a star named Gliese 876, and the satellites around Earth. Note that this is a partial graph and some of the data used to determine these lines are not within the ranges included by the axes. Gliese 876 has a smaller mass than the sun, and Earth has a much smaller mass than either of the stars.

APPLY Select the correct terms to complete the statement about the graph.

On the graph, the slope is greater when the central object is more | less massive. Compare orbits along a horizontal line—those for a given distance a. The orbit around the sun would have a shorter | longer period than an orbit around less-massive Gliese 876. The speed of the sun's planets would be greater | less . A familiar force that depends on speed | mass is due to gravity. Earth's pull on an object near its surface is proportional to the object's mass. For orbits, the major component of the force is related to the orbiting | central object.

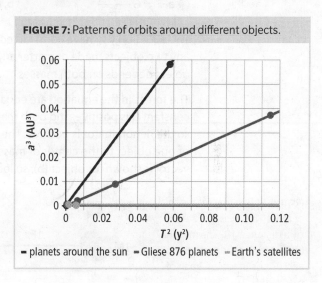

FIGURE 7: Patterns of orbits around different objects.

— planets around the sun — Gliese 876 planets — Earth's satellites

The inward pull of objects or materials due to mass is *gravitational force*. As an object orbits, it accelerates and its direction and speed change. Because of this acceleration, you can infer that it is being acted on continuously by an unbalanced force. At a given distance, a greater central mass produces a greater inward acceleration.

INFER Complete the equation to summarize how the force on an orbiting object depends on the mass of the central object, m, and on the distance between them, r. The symbol $\propto$ means "proportional to."

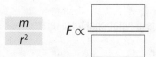

$$F \propto \frac{}{}$$

$\dfrac{m}{r^2}$

Newton's Law of Universal Gravitation

One of Newton's greatest ideas was to recognize the parallels between the motion of falling objects and the motion of orbiting objects.

APPLY Select the correct terms to complete the statement about gravitational force.

At Earth's surface, an apple falls from a tree. Ignoring air resistance, the apple moves toward | away from Earth's surface, and its speed increases | decreases | stays the same as it falls. This speed depends | does not depend on the mass of the apple. For a satellite in orbit around Earth, its path curves toward | away from Earth. If its orbit takes it closer to Earth, its speed increases | decreases | stays the same. This speed depends | does not depend on the mass of the satellite.

For an object near Earth's surface, the acceleration due to gravity does not depend on the object's mass. The force, however, does depend on the object's mass—a greater force is needed to lift a bowling ball than a tennis ball. The magnitude of the acceleration, g, is constant, but the magnitude of the force, mg, is proportional to m. Extend this thinking to objects in orbit.

MODEL The equation is a model of the gravitational effect of Earth, mass m_1, on a satellite or falling object, mass m_2. G is a constant. Determine where m_2 belongs.

○ **a.** $F = G \dfrac{m_1 m_2}{r^2}$ 　　　　　 ○ **b.** $F = G \dfrac{m_1}{m_2 r^2}$ 　　　　　 ○ **c.** $F = \dfrac{G}{m_2} \dfrac{m_1}{r^2}$

The equation you have constructed is Newton's law of universal gravitation and applies to any two objects made of matter anywhere in the universe. The gravitational force on each object depends on both masses.

The forces in the equation are equal in magnitude and opposite in direction. The scalar constant G is positive, and both masses m are greater than zero. The distance is squared, so the denominator is positive. The displacement **r** is measured from the center of mass of one object to the center of mass of the other object. In Figure 8, the displacement vector is shown for object (b), so look at the gravitational force exerted on that object.

FIGURE 8: Two masses, each of mass 1M, are separated by a distance 1R. The masses attract each other with equal and opposite forces, each of magnitude 1F.

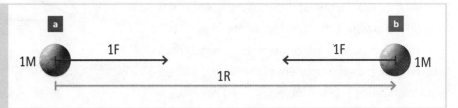

PREDICT How would the force between the two objects in the figure change if the radius between the objects was doubled?

_____

_____

_____

 Evidence Notebook How is gravitational force related to the design of a hovering toy in the unit project?

Calculating Gravitational Force

The value of G in the equation for force is called the gravitational constant, and it is equal to 6.674×10^{-11} N·m²/kg². The negative sign is added to the equation as a convention to indicate an attractive force.

$$F = -(6.674 \times 10^{-11}\, \frac{\text{N·m}^2}{\text{kg}^2}) \frac{m_1 m_2}{r^2}$$

You can use Newton's law of universal gravitation to explore how each of the variables affects the force. For example, if one mass is doubled, you would put the factor of two into the numerator. If the distance doubled, you would put the factor of two squared, or four, into the denominator.

SOLVE In the first row, the force between the two spheres is −1F, where F is a particular value of force. Determine the force in each of the other examples. A force twice as strong is −2F, where the negative sign is a convention that represent an attractive force.

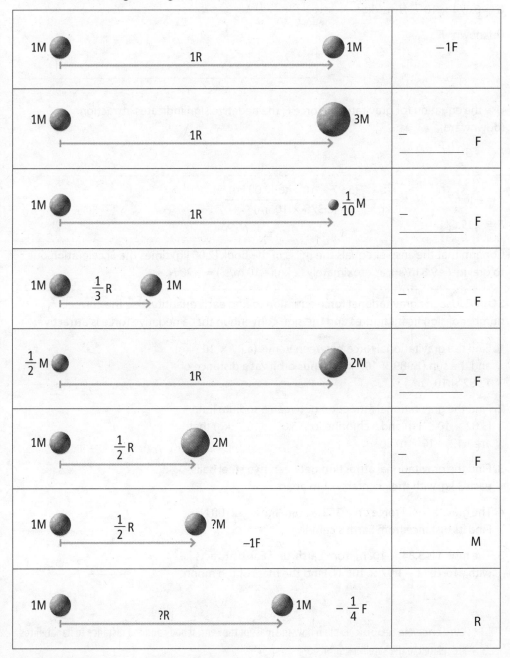

Problem Solving

Calculating Weight

SAMPLE PROBLEM The weight of an object on Earth's surface is a measure of the force of the gravitational attraction between Earth and the object. The distance is measured between the centers of the two masses. Earth's mass is 5.97×10^{24} kg. Its radius is 6.378×10^{6} m. Calculate the weight of a 2.00 kg textbook by using the equation for gravitational force.

ANALYZE Known:

$m_1 = 5.97 \times 10^{24}$ kg

$m_2 = 2.00$ kg

$r = 6.378 \times 10^{6}$ m

$G = 6.674 \times 10^{-11}$ N·m²/kg²

Unknown: F

MODEL Draw a diagram, and label the variables.

PLAN Use the equation for gravitational force F; the negative sign indicates attraction (downward).

$$F = -G\frac{m_1 m_2}{r^2}$$

SOLVE

$$F = -(6.674 \times 10^{-11}\ \frac{\text{N·m}^2}{\text{kg}^2})\frac{(5.97 \times 10^{24}\ \text{kg})(2.00\ \text{kg})}{(6.378 \times 10^{6}\ \text{m})^2}$$

$$F = -19.6\ \text{N}$$

CHECK YOUR WORK Confirm that the answer equals the mass of the book (2.00 kg) times the acceleration due to gravity (-9.8 m/s²), approximately (2 kg)(-10 m/s²) $= -20$ N.

PRACTICE PROBLEMS **SOLVE** Use the gravitational force equation to find each quantity. Use the correct number of significant figures and the sign convention that a negative force is attractive.

1. Find the gravitational force between Venus (4.87×10^{24} kg) and the sun (1.989×10^{30} kg). Venus orbits at a distance of 1.082×10^{11} m.

2. Find the gravitational attraction between a sodium ion (3.82×10^{-26} kg) and a chlorine ion (5.89×10^{-26} kg) that are 1.12×10^{-10} m apart.

3. Find the gravitational attraction between two steel balls, each 3 kg, with their centers 0.1 m apart.

4. The gravitational force on a 352 kg satellite is -2100 N. Find its distance from Earth's center.

5. The moon is 3.84×10^{8} m from Earth, and Earth attracts it with a force of -1.97×10^{20} N. Find the mass of the moon.

Evidence Notebook Explain how the mass of the central body and the distance to its satellites are related to the satellites' orbits.

Analyzing Gravitational Effects

Gravitational forces exist between objects that have mass. The forces pull objects together whether the objects are touching or are far apart. An unbalanced force can change an object's speed, direction, or both. A change in speed means a change in kinetic energy. An object's potential energy may also change.

Fields and Energy

In general, forces are classified as either contact forces or field forces. Contact forces are forces that can be exerted only between objects that are in direct contact. Field forces are forces that can act on objects at a distance. A field is an area where a force can affect an object. For example, the area surrounding a mass in which another mass would be influenced by a gravitational force is a gravitational field.

Like any unbalanced force, an unbalanced field force can change an object's speed, direction, or both. A change in an object's speed means that the object's kinetic energy also changes. Thus, when an object is in a field, its kinetic energy can change. The field can also cause changes in the object's potential energy.

ANALYZE Examine the velocity vectors for the orbiting object and the roller coaster. Think about how kinetic energy (KE) and potential energy (PE) change. Draw lines from the labels to the red dots to show where the maximum and minimum of each form of energy occurs.

max PE

min PE

max KE

min KE

EXPLAIN Select the correct terms to complete the statement.

A notebook lifted from ground level to a height of 2 m has gained kinetic | potential energy. If the notebook is dropped, it gains kinetic | potential energy as it falls and accelerates. A change in the notebook's position in the gravitational field—a change in the value of $r \mid m \mid g$ —can change the notebook's kinetic energy or potential energy.

When calculating potential energy, you can set the frame of reference to simplify the calculations. You might set zero to be the top of a lab bench, the floor, or some other height. For objects attracting each other across space, there is no natural zero. Gravitational force has infinite range—it is present even at great distances. The convention is to consider the potential energy of the system to be zero at infinite separation. It is then negative when the objects are closer together.

Surface Gravity

The gravitational field near Earth's surface is usually treated as uniform. Changing the height above Earth's surface makes very little difference to the magnitude of the gravitational force at that point—the force is treated as constant.

ANALYZE Think of m_1 as the mass of Earth and m_2 as the mass of an object at Earth's surface. Circle the terms in the first equation—the law of universal gravitation—that are combined into the constant, **g**, of the weight equation.

$$F_g = -G \frac{m_1 \, m_2}{r^2} \qquad\qquad \mathbf{F}_g = m_2 \mathbf{g}$$

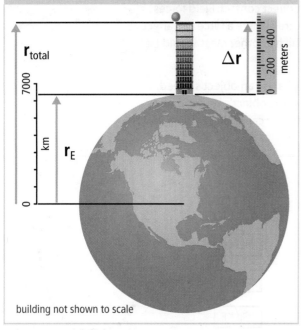

FIGURE 9: An exaggerated view of a ball balanced on a tower on Earth's surface

r_{total}

7000

km

r_E

Δr

0 200 400 meters

building not shown to scale

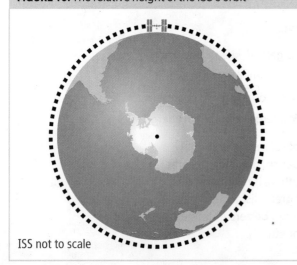

FIGURE 10: The relative height of the ISS's orbit

ISS not to scale

The G in the first equation is a constant and thus has the same value everywhere. However, for objects near Earth's surface, the separation r is nearly constant. Earth's radius, r_E, is so much greater than a height **h** measured from the surface that $r_E + \mathbf{h}$ is almost the same as r_E. The equation for potential energy, like the equation for gravitational force, can also be simplified by treating the force as constant.

SOLVE Earth's radius is 6378 km. The tower is 500 m high. In terms of Earth's radius, how tall is the tower?

- ○ **a.** $0.00000008\,r_E$
- ○ **d.** $0.8\,r_E$
- ○ **b.** $0.00008\,r_E$
- ○ **e.** $8.0\,r_E$
- ○ **c.** $0.08\,r_E$

For a spacecraft to escape Earth's gravitational pull, it needs reach a certain velocity. This velocity is called the escape velocity. The escape velocity is the same for any object, regardless of its mass, launched from Earth's surface. Using the equation for gravitational potential energy and kinetic energy, the escape velocity of the Earth's gravitational pull can be calculated. At that velocity, the kinetic energy and the (negative) potential energy add to zero.

INFER Select the correct terms to complete the statement about gravity in orbit.

The International Space Station orbits about 400 km above Earth's surface. This altitude increases the magnitude of $m_1\,|\,\mathbf{r}$ by about 6%. The acceleration due to gravity on the ISS is a lot | little less than what it is at Earth's surface. The sensation of weightlessness in orbit is | is not due to escaping Earth's gravitational attraction. Instead, it is similar to the experience of being in a car that goes over a sharp bump. For a brief time, you and the car are falling oppositely | together.

Hands-On Lab

Gravitational Field Strength

The gravitational force is stronger on Jupiter because Jupiter's mass is equivalent to the mass of 317.8 Earths. The strength of a gravitational field is related to how much force is exerted on a particular mass within the field. On Jupiter, your mass would be pulled with much greater force. Field strength is a measure of force per mass, measured in newtons per kilogram (N/kg). How do scientists make accurate measures of the strength of Earth's gravitational field?

In this lab, you will plan and carry out an experiment to determine whether gravitational field strength depends on the mass of an object within the field. To make sure that you obtain a true value of field strength, refrain from making your data take on values that you think you should get based on your assumptions about your results. An object's acceleration can be calculated using the equation $a = 2\Delta y/t^2$, where Δy is the distance the object falls and t is the time it takes to fall.

RESEARCH QUESTION What is the relationship between gravitational field strength and the mass of an object in the field?

MAKE A CLAIM

How do you think you can use careful measurements to determine whether the strength of Earth's gravitational field depends on the mass of an object in the field? How can you ensure that your methods are not influenced by previous measurements or understandings about gravity?

MATERIALS

- safety goggles
- balance
- meterstick or tape measure
- objects of various masses that can be dropped without damaging the object
- stopwatch

SAFETY INFORMATION

- Wear safety goggles during the setup, hands-on, and takedown segments of the activity.
- Immediately pick up any items dropped on the floor so they do not become a slip/fall hazard.
- Wash your hands with soap and water immediately after completing this activity.

PLAN THE INVESTIGATION

1. Consider the materials provided. Construct a system where Earth's gravitational field pulls on an object by allowing objects to fall freely.

2. How can you measure the gravitational field strength on objects that have different masses? Remember that gravitational field strength is related to how much force (F_g) is used to move an amount of mass (m).

3. Use a meterstick and stopwatch as measurement tools. Record their precision and how they could affect how you interpret your results.

4. Make at least five measurements for each mass with multiple trials. Multiple trials will get a more accurate measure of field strength. Average measurements for each of the different objects to reduce the effects of random error.

5. One type of bias in experiments occurs when researchers reject certain results because they do not confirm what they already know. This type of bias is called confirmation bias. How can you make sure that your experimental tests are not influenced by confirmation bias?

6. Write a procedure for your investigation in your Evidence Notebook. Include safety precautions, what materials you will need, and how you will measure quantities that can help you determine the strength of Earth's gravitational field. Make sure you explain how many trials you will perform for different tests and how you will avoid confirmation bias during the experiment. Construct a data table to record all your measurements, calculations, and observations.

7. Consult with your teacher. Once your procedure and safety plans are approved, gather your materials and begin testing.

CARRY OUT THE INVESTIGATION

Conduct your experiment. Record measurements carefully in the data table that you prepared. Because you are trying to implement a method free from bias related to previous understandings about gravity, make sure you record your opinions about the data that you collect.

CALCULATE

Calculate Earth's gravitational field strength on objects that have different masses. Show your work below.

ANALYZE

1. What do you notice about the values you obtained?

_____

_____

_____

2. What evidence do you have that your method for determining the gravitational field strength was not influenced by previous measurements or understandings about gravity? What steps did you take as a researcher to avoid confirmation bias?

_____

_____

_____

CONSTRUCT AN EXPLANATION

1. How did your measurement of the field strength of gravity on objects that have different masses compare to what you already knew about gravity? What might explain any differences?

_____

_____

_____

_____

_____

2. Why is it important for scientists to evaluate their testing methods to make sure they are not influenced by previous measurements or understandings?

_____

_____

_____

_____

_____

DRAW CONCLUSIONS

Write a conclusion that addresses each of the points below.

Claim How can you use careful measurements to determine the strength of Earth's gravitational field on objects that have different masses without allowing previous measurements or understandings to influence your results? Were your initial predictions about how to construct an unbiased method correct?

Evidence What evidence from your investigation supports your claim?

Reasoning Explain how the evidence you gave supports your claim. Describe in detail the connections between the evidence you cited and the argument you are making.

_____

_____

_____

_____

_____

_____

_____

_____

_____

 Evidence Notebook Compare and contrast the effects of gravity for the moon orbiting around the Earth and a ball being dropped on Earth.

Data Analysis

Gravity and Tides

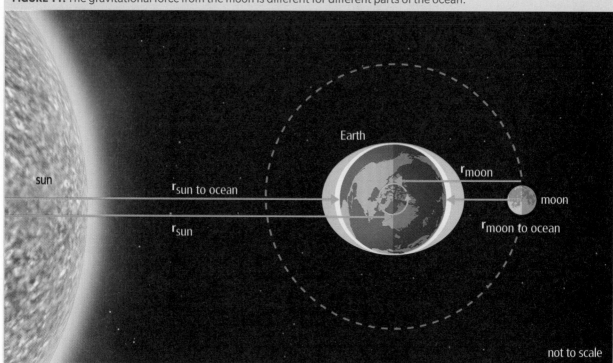

FIGURE 11: The gravitational force from the moon is different for different parts of the ocean.

The water in Earth's oceans bulges slightly in directions toward and away from the moon. Compare the gravitational force from the moon at Earth's center with the force at different locations on Earth's surface. The greatest force is on the side of Earth closest to the moon, so the ocean bulges toward the moon. Partway around Earth, the force is less. The water on the far side bulges outward because the moon attracts Earth's center more strongly than it attracts the more distant water on the far side. The contrast in force, called the tidal force, is proportional to $\Delta r/r$, where r is the distance from the center of the Earth to the center of the respective object (sun or moon) and Δr is Earth's radius—the difference in distances. You can multiply by m_1/r^2 to compare tidal forces from the sun and moon. Other factors are the same for both objects.

Tidal force is responsible for the periodic rise and fall of water levels at the seashore. A high tide occurs when a coastal region passes through the water bulge facing the moon or facing away from the moon. A low tide occurs when a coastal region is not within

one of the bulges. Most coastal areas experience two high tides and two low tides each day because of the difference in rotations of Earth and the moon. The sun's gravitational pull also causes tides on Earth, but because the sun is so far away, it has a smaller effect.

SOLVE Compare the results to determine the effects on Earth's tides for both the sun and moon.

Quantity	Sun	Moon
$r \ (\times 10^6 \text{ km})$	149.6	0.38
$\Delta r \text{ (km)}$	6378	_____
$\Delta r/r$	_____	_____
$m_1 \text{ (kg)}$	2.0×10^{30}	7.3×10^{22}
$(m_1/r^2)(\Delta r/r) \text{ (kg/km}^2)$	_____	_____

Proportional Force

FIGURE 12: Jupiter's moon Io

Instead of calculating the gravitational forces at different locations on Earth, you used a proportion. The fraction $\Delta r/r$ gave you an idea of the relative difference in force.

PREDICT Suppose a planet with the same mass as Earth but twice the radius is discovered that has a moon with the same mass as Earth's moon. It is orbiting at four times the distance that Earth's moon orbits Earth. About what fraction of the tidal force exerted by the moon on Earth would you expect the planet to experience?

○ **a.** 1/4   ○ **b.** 1/2   ○ **c.** 3/4

You can only use the value $\Delta r/r$ to compare the tidal forces exerted by objects on the same planet, as you did in the calculation of the sun's force on Earth and the moon's force on Earth. A calculation of tidal force for each object would have to take into account the mass of the planet.

If a planet and its sun have masses similar to those of Earth and the sun, the value $\Delta r/r$ could be much larger than the value for Earth and the sun depending on the value of **r**. This would indicate that the tidal force of the sun on the planet's water would be very large. The water bulges produced by the tidal forces would be so large that they would produce extremely high tides.

Tidal forces also act on Earth's atmosphere and on other bodies. Just as Earth's oceans are elongated along a line between Earth and the moon, other bodies are elongated. Figure 13 shows a planet being influenced by the tidal effects of a star. The star pulls on the planet and elongates its shape.

Jupiter and its nearby moons Europa and Ganymede cause tidal effects in another moon, Io. The directions of the tidal forces change, and the kinetic energy of the moving rock is transformed into thermal energy. Volcanic eruptions and new surface material on Io provide evidence of this energy.

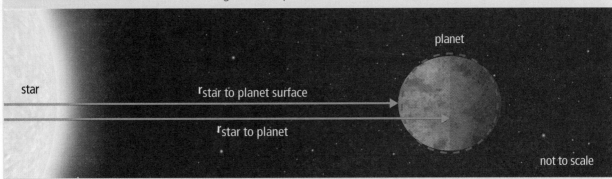

FIGURE 13: Tidal forces from a star can elongate a solid planet.

star

planet

^{r}star to planet surface

^{r}star to planet

not to scale

| ENGINEERING AN ELLIPSE | ORBITS AND OTHER ROTATION | GRAVITY ASSIST | Go online to choose one of these other paths. |

Lesson Self-Check

CAN YOU SOLVE THE PROBLEM?

FIGURE 14: The moons Titan and Dione in orbit around Saturn.

Think about how to find the mass of an astronomical object. A planet or moon can't be put on a balance or attached to a spring scale. The mass must be determined by other means. The approaches are based on how mass affects objects in space.

 Evidence Notebook Refer to your notes in your Evidence Notebook to make a claim about how observations could be used to determine the mass of an object in space, such as Saturn. Your explanation should include a discussion of the following points:

Claim What observations are needed to determine the mass of an object in space?

Evidence What evidence assures you that such observations would enable someone to determine the object's mass?

Reasoning How does the evidence you provided support your claim about the usefulness of specific observations to determine the mass of the object? For example, identify factors that can be ignored or ways that proportions might be used.

CHECKPOINTS

Check Your Understanding

1. Jupiter is about 5 times farther away from the sun than Earth and about 300 times more massive than Earth. The gravitational force between Jupiter and the sun is:

   ○ **a.** 60 times greater than the gravitational force between Earth and the sun

   ○ **b.** 60 times less than the gravitational force between Earth and the sun

   ○ **c.** 12 times greater than the gravitational force between Earth and the sun

   ○ **d.** 12 times less than the gravitational force between Earth and the sun

2. Mercury is 4.6×10^7 km from the sun at perihelion and 7.0×10^7 km at aphelion. Determine the length of the semimajor axis in order to specify the orbit.

   ○ **a.** 9.2×10^7 km   ○ **c.** 1.40×10^8 km

   ○ **b.** 1.16×10^8 ○ **d.** 5.8×10^7 km

3. The eccentricity of Venus's orbit is 0.01 and the eccentricity of Mars's orbit is 0.09. What does this mean about their orbits?

   ○ **a.** Mars's orbit takes it farther from the sun.

   ○ **b.** Venus's orbit takes it farther from the sun.

   ○ **c.** Venus's orbit is less circular than Mars's.

   ○ **d.** Mars's orbit is less circular than Venus's.

4. Select the correct terms to complete the statement.

   A small object of mass m_1 is a distance r from a large object of mass M and is subject to a force of strength F_1. The magnitude of its acceleration is a_1. The force exerted by the small object on the large object is different by m_1/M | the same (F_1) | equal but opposite. Then the small object is replaced by one with half the mass, $m_2 = (1/2)m_1$. The force on m_2 is $(1/4)F_1$ | $(1/2)F_1$ | F_1 | $2F_1$ | $4F_1$ and it has an acceleration of $(1/4)a_1$ | $(1/2)a_1$ | a_1 | $2a_1$ | $4a_1$ in a direction toward | away from the large object.

5. Mars has two moons. Phobos has an orbit with a period T of 0.3189 days and a semimajor axis a of 9376 km. For Deimos, $T = 1.2624$ days. What is a reasonable estimate of Deimos's semimajor axis?

   ○ **a.** 2700 km   ○ **c.** 23 000 km

   ○ **b.** 14 000 km   ○ **d.** 37 000 km

6. Select the correct terms to complete the statement.

   Saturn's moon Enceladus has an eccentricity and semimajor axis smaller than Saturn's moon Titan. Titan is many times the mass of Enceladus. Titan's distance from Saturn varies more | less than Enceladus's distance; therefore Titan's kinetic energy varies more | less over its orbit than Enceladus's kinetic energy.

7. Select the correct terms to complete the statement.

   A small object with the same mass as a large object will have less | the same | more inertia compared to the large object. It is difficult to increase an object's velocity | acceleration due to its inertia. Objects with the same volume but different densities will have different | similar inertia.

8. Round your answers to 2 significant digits.

   Earth's radius is 6378 km, and its mass is 5.97×10^{24} kg. The acceleration due to gravity at a point 10 000 km above Earth's surface is $-$_____ m/s^2. The force due to Earth's gravity on a 500 kg spacecraft at this distance is $-$_____ N.

9. A low-Earth orbit has a semimajor axis of 1.06 Earth radii and a period of 90 minutes, or 0.0625 days. A satellite in geosynchronous orbit stays above the same point on Earth, and so its period is 1 day. What is the length of the geosynchronous orbit's semimajor axis?

   ○ **a.** 0.15 Earth radii   ○ **c.** 11 Earth radii

   ○ **b.** 6.7 Earth radii   ○ **d.** 17 Earth radii

CHECKPOINTS (continued)

10. Mars's moon Phobos is only about 22 km wide. Your weight on Phobos would be 0.001 what it is on Earth. Its escape velocity is 11 m/s . This is the minimum velocity with which an object could be launched to leave the moon's surface and never return. You could launch yourself into orbit around Phobos with a strong, very fast jump. Compare this jumping speed to escape velocity, and describe what would happen if you jumped at an angle.

_____

_____

_____

_____

_____

11. The moon Io orbits Jupiter at a distance of 422 000 km, completing one orbit in 1.77 (Earth) days. Europa orbits Jupiter at a distance of 671 000 km in 3.55 days. Make a mathematical model of the relationship between orbital distance and period for a satellite of Jupiter. Explain or show your reasoning. Then use your model to predict the period of Callisto, which is 1 880 000 km from Jupiter.

_____

_____

_____

_____

_____

MAKE YOUR OWN STUDY GUIDE

 In your Evidence Notebook, design a study guide that supports the main ideas from this lesson:

The motion of the planets, and of other objects in orbit, can be modeled with Kepler's laws.

The force that produces orbital motion is gravity, and the equation for gravitational force predicts the motion of objects orbiting and of objects falling near the surface of a planet.

When an object changes position in a gravitational field, its kinetic and potential energy can vary inversely.

Remember to include the following information in your study guide:
- Use examples that model main ideas.
- Record explanations for the phenomena you investigated.
- Use evidence to support your explanations. Your support can include drawings, data, graphs, laboratory conclusions, and other evidence recorded throughout the lesson.

Consider how the motion of an artificial satellite around a moon, the moon around a planet, and the planet around the sun all follow the same few rules.

Modeling Electric and Magnetic Fields

A stream of water bends toward a comb.

CAN YOU SOLVE THE PROBLEM?

Keiko tries to recreate a phenomenon she saw in a video. On a dry day, she inflates a balloon. She then wipes a dry cloth over its surface. She turns on a faucet so that water flows out in a thin stream. As she moves the balloon near the water, the stream curves toward the balloon. Keiko also finds that she can use a plastic foam cup or a comb to bend the stream of water.

DESIGN Suppose you try Keiko's experiment. How might you straighten out the bent stream of water? List several ideas to test.

_____

_____

_____

_____

The challenge for this lesson is the following: Start with a situation similar to the second or third photo of Figure 1. Leave the balloon in place and unchanged. Without requiring anything that touches the stream of water, find a way to make it flow straight down, as it does in the first photo of Figure 1.

> **Evidence Notebook** As you explore the lesson, gather evidence to help you straighten out the stream of water in the challenge.

Explore Online ▶

FIGURE 1: The direction of a stream of water can be changed by a balloon.

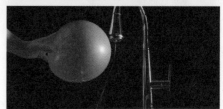
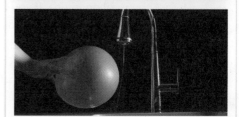

Exploring Magnets and Electric Charges

You have learned that matter produces gravitational force on other matter at a distance. Magnets and electric charges also can produce forces that affect objects at a distance.

Static Phenomena

Electrostatic phenomena are a special case of electric phenomena where electric charges or fields are at rest. The simple motion of charge from one place to another is often grouped with electrostatic phenomena. Simple interactions of magnets and materials are also considered static. In contrast, electric circuits and electromagnetic waves involve continually moving charges and changing fields; they are not considered static.

Types of Phenomena

FIGURE 2: Magnets and electric charge are part of many different phenomena and devices.

a Pollen sticking to a bee

b Screwdriver attracting metal

c Spire attracting lightning

d Toy parts sticking together

e Tools hanging on a strip

f Fringe strands standing apart

ASK Look at Figure 2, and then write a list of questions that you have about these phenomena. If you wish, you can include questions you might have about other magnetic or electrostatic phenomena.

_____

_____

_____

_____

You may have felt the pull of a magnet toward a refrigerator door. A magnet might pull on a steel refrigerator or on another magnet, or it might push on another magnet. Similarly, a charged object can attract or repel a second charged object, depending on whether the second object's charge is like or unlike the first. When clothes come out of a clothes dryer, a sock may cling to a sweater, yet individual strands of a scarf's fringe may repel and stand away from one another. An attractive force is a pull that can bring two objects closer together. A repulsive force is a push that can move them apart.

 Hands-On Activity

Observing Magnets

Look for patterns as you try simple tests with magnets.

FIGURE 3: A simple magnetic compass

POSSIBLE MATERIALS

- · safety goggles
- · bag of iron filings
- · bar magnets (2)
- · bowl of water
- · foam block
- · iron or steel objects, small

SAFETY INFORMATION

- Wear safety goggles and nonlatex gloves during the setup, hands-on, and takedown segments of the activity.
- Immediately wipe up any spilled water and/or iron filings on the floor so they do not become slip/fall hazards.

CARRY OUT THE INVESTIGATION

Record your observations and details of your procedure in your Evidence Notebook.

Part 1: Magnetic Compass and Fields

A compass responds to the magnetic field around it. Use a material such as polystyrene foam to float a bar magnet in a container of water. Record the initial position of the magnet relative to north, south, east, and west, as identified by your teacher. Then record what happens as you move a second magnet outside the container.

Part 2: Magnetizing Materials

Use a magnet to pick up paper clips or other small iron or steel objects. Then try to magnetize one iron or steel object by rubbing it repeatedly in one direction with one end of the magnet. Use an unmagnetized iron or steel object to test whether the first object is magnetized and stays magnetized. Record your observations.

Part 3: Visualizing Attraction and Repulsion

Move two bar magnets close together in various ways. Record your observations. Then arrange two bar magnets so that one north pole and one south pole are a short distance apart and the magnets stay in place. Abruptly set a clear plastic bag of iron filings over the two magnets, and then sketch what you see. Label the areas of attraction and repulsion.

INFER Based on your observations in Part 1 and Part 3, does the magnetic field around Earth's North Pole more closely resemble a bar magnet's north or south pole?

○ **a.** north pole   ○ **b.** south pole   ○ **c.** neither

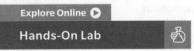

Magnetism Explore the forces and fields that exist between two magnets.

Exploring Magnets

If you hold a strong magnet close to a refrigerator door, you can feel the magnet pull your hand toward the door. As you move the magnet back from the door, this force diminishes. A few centimeters away, you may not detect any force acting between magnet and door. If you release the magnet when it is very close to the door, it moves toward the door and sticks to it. The magnet is pulled by the refrigerator, and the refrigerator is pulled just as hard by the magnet—the two forces are equal in magnitude and opposite in direction. However, the effect on the refrigerator's greater mass is less noticeable.

FIGURE 4: The north pole of a magnet is pushed toward the north pole of another magnet; the second magnet moves away continually. Explore Online ▶

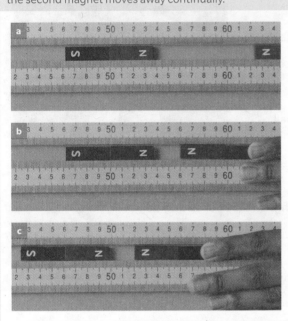

FIGURE 5: The south pole of a magnet is pushed toward the north pole of another magnet; the magnets move suddenly together. Explore Online ▶

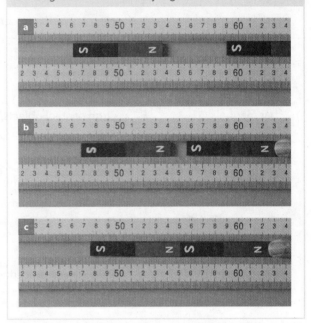

When the magnets shown are about 10 cm apart (Figures 4a and 4b), they have no visible effect on each other. Only when the ends are at a distance of roughly 2 cm does the magnet on the left start to move. The direction of the force between two permanent magnets depends on whether the poles closest together are like or unlike.

EXPLAIN In Figure 4 and Figure 5, think about how the magnet on the left moved as the magnet on the right approached. How do you think the forces between the magnets changed as they moved closer together?

_____

_____

_____

_____

The magnitude of the force between two permanent magnets depends on the strength of the magnets and the distance between them. In Figures 4a and 5a, the force between the two magnets is too small to overcome static friction. However, as the magnets get close, the force becomes stronger and overcomes static friction. The magnet in Figure 4 slides away until the magnetic force is small enough for friction to stop the motion. In Figure 5, the magnets move closer and so the force increases; the magnets snap together suddenly.

Exploring Charge

Electric charge is positive or negative and is measured in coulombs (C), or more often millicoulombs (mC) or microcoulombs (µC). A typical bolt of lightning can carry about 15 C of charge, so even 1 C is a large amount of charge. An object with equal amounts of positive and negative charge has no net charge—it is neutral. An object with more of one type of charge than the other has a net charge.

Electric charge is not something that you can usually sense directly. Instead, you might observe how a charged object exerts a force on other objects at a distance. For example, like charges can push strands of fringe or fur apart. As with magnetic force, electric force is weaker when charges are farther apart.

 Language Arts Connection Charge usually spreads over the surface of a metal object. Research how this scientific knowledge is used in the design of electroscopes, in which moving parts indicate the presence of charge. Use diagrams or a graphic organizer to summarize your findings.

Explore Online ▶

Hands-On Lab

Charges and Electrostatics
Make an electroscope, and then test how strong a charge is and whether it is like or not like another charge.

An electroscope uses repulsion to detect and measure static electric charge. You can build an electroscope that has two connected, metal leaves. You might protect the leaves within a container and connect them to a metal knob or plate outside the container. The leaves repel and stand apart when an object with electric charge is near the metal, whether the charge is positive or negative.

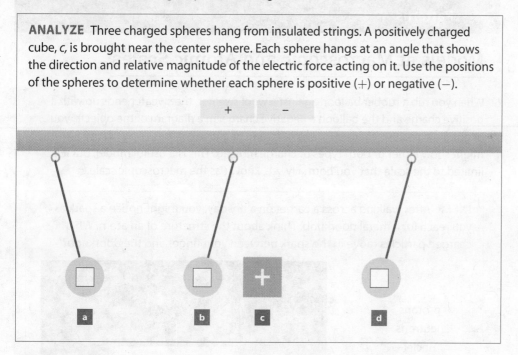

ANALYZE Three charged spheres hang from insulated strings. A positively charged cube, c, is brought near the center sphere. Each sphere hangs at an angle that shows the direction and relative magnitude of the electric force acting on it. Use the positions of the spheres to determine whether each sphere is positive (+) or negative (−).

INFER Select the correct terms to complete the statements about the charged objects.

Sphere d is attracted | repelled by the cube. It must have the same | opposite charge as the cube.

The cube pushes | pulls Sphere b, so the force between these like | unlike charges is attraction | repulsion.

Sphere a is attracted by Sphere b | Cube c | both b and c | Sphere d.

MODEL Label the visual model of an atom.

electron cloud   neutron   nucleus   proton

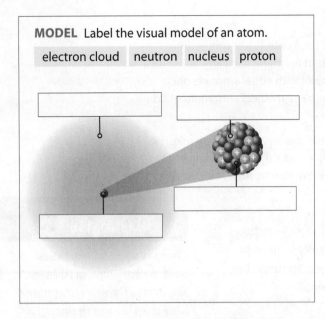

An object's charge comes from the particles that make up the object. Atoms are made of electrons, protons, and neutrons. Electrons are negatively charged. The charge of a single electron is -1.6×10^{-19} C, which is represented as $-e$. Protons are positively charged; each proton has a charge of $+e$. Neutrons have no net charge.

Electrons and protons are the source of electric charge. Neutral objects and atoms have equal numbers of protons and electrons. An object with more electrons than protons has a negative charge, and an object with more protons has a positive charge.

Electrons and protons, though tiny, are particles of matter. In the everyday interactions around you, they may be rearranged, but are conserved. Because charge comes from electrons and protons, charge is also conserved. Equal amounts of positive and negative charge appear when electrons and protons are separated, so the total charge remains the same. For example, walking across a wool carpet results in negative charge on your body and an equal amount of positive charge on the carpet, so the net charge on your body and the carpet together remains the same. Charge moves, but is not created.

 Patterns

Models at Macroscopic and Atomic Scales

When you rub a rubber balloon against a wool sweater, the sweater ends up with a positive charge and the balloon a negative charge. In a diagram of the objects, you might draw positive charges (+ symbols) and negative charges (− symbols), and you might show either or both types of charge moving. This is a useful model, but it is limited to the scale that you normally see, known as the macroscopic scale.

INFER After walking across a carpet on a dry day, you might notice a spark as you reach for a metal doorknob. Think about the structure of an atom. What charged particles move in the spark between your finger and the doorknob?

protons
neutrons
nuclei
electrons

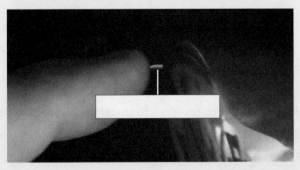

At the atomic scale, nuclei usually stay in place in solids. Electrons are typically the charged particles that move. In this model, an object gains a positive charge most often by losing electrons rather than by gaining protons.

Magnetizing Materials

EXPLAIN Figure 6 shows that a bar magnet held vertically attracts a paper clip, and then a second paper clip is attracted to the bottom of the first paper clip, and so on. What must have happened to the first paper clip?

○ **a.** It became a magnet under the influence of the bar magnet.

○ **b.** It was already a magnet before it was affected by the bar magnet.

○ **c.** It acted as a nonmagnetic spacer between the magnet and the second paper clip, similar to paper between a refrigerator magnet and door.

FIGURE 6: A magnet attracts a chain of steel paper clips.

Magnets can attract some materials that are not magnets, such as paper clips or a metal door. *Ferromagnetic* materials can become magnetized when in the presence of a permanent magnet. Ferromagnetic materials—such as iron, cobalt, nickel, and their alloys—have atoms that have magnetic fields. Normally, these magnetic fields are aligned randomly and cancel each other, so the material as a whole is not magnetic. In the presence of an outside magnetic field, however, the individual magnetic fields shift to align with the larger field, as if they were compass needles aligning with the field of a nearby magnet. When the outside field is removed, these materials may lose their magnetism immediately or may lose it gradually over time.

Charging Materials

In some materials, called *conductors*, electrons can move freely throughout the material. In other materials, called *insulators*, electrons may shift slightly but do not travel throughout the material. However, either type of material can become charged when electrons move onto or off of the material. A conductor is often used to make a connection to the ground or to another material that can supply or accept large numbers of electrons. Electrons then flow either way until the grounded object becomes neutral.

Polarization occurs when there is shifting or alignment of positive and negative charge within a neutral object, typically an insulator. The shift produces two regions within the object that have equal but opposite charge. Overall, the object remains neutral.

In Figure 7a, a comb with negative charge pushes the electrons in a bit of paper slightly away, leaving the near side of the paper with positive charge. The near, positive side is attracted to the comb more strongly than the far, negative side is repelled. When the charged comb is removed, the pieces of paper may stay polarized for a while. They become unpolarized over time.

FIGURE 7: Polarized pieces of paper and polar molecules show a shifting of charge.

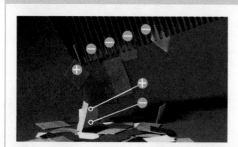

a A shifting of charge can be induced.

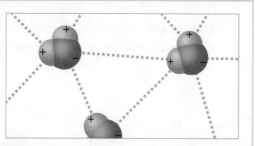

b Water molecules are polar but neutral.

Conductors can also become polarized by a nearby charged object. Electrons in the conductor move toward or away from the charged object. Conductors usually lose their polarization as the charged object moves away.

In contrast, a water molecule is naturally polarized and remains that way. The two hydrogen atoms each have a slight positive charge. Together, they balance the oxygen atom and its slight negative charge. Water molecules exert electric forces on one another (Figure 7b).

EXPLAIN Make comparisons between the ways polarized objects interact and the ways magnets interact.

_____

_____

_____

_____

 Engineering

Charging by Electrostatic Induction

FIGURE 8: Induce a charge.

The properties of insulators and conductors can be used to build up a large amount of charge on a conductor. When a highly charged insulator is brought near a conductor, a large separation of charge is produced in the conductor.

Suppose you attach foam cups as insulating handles on a material of each type: a conducting aluminum pie pan and an insulating foam plate. You put a relatively large charge on the foam plate by rubbing it with a cloth. You bring the negatively charged plate near the pan. Then you ground the aluminum pan—you touch it with your finger to enable charge to move from the pan, through you, to the ground.

APPLY To keep the aluminum pan charged, which would you do next?

○ **a.** Remove the grounding touch.   ○ **b.** Remove the charged object.

 Collaborate Draw a cartoon-like model that shows enlarged atoms, and show how the particles move in each of the steps described. Then work with a partner to reach agreement about what happens at the atomic scale.

 Evidence Notebook Use the behavior of positive and negative charges to explain how a balloon might bend a stream of water.

Mapping Electric and Magnetic Fields

You have observed that magnets and charged objects push or pull on each other. Magnetic and electric forces are produced by fields around such objects.

Visualizing a Field

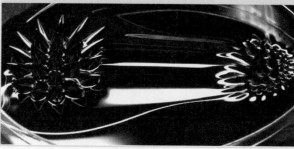

FIGURE 9: Spikes that form in a ferrofluid show the magnetic field at the ends of a bar magnet. One end is deeper in the fluid, so the pattern is not symmetric.

Magnetic force, much like gravitational force, is transferred through a field that surrounds a magnet. A magnetic field produces force on a magnetic test object, such as a small magnetic compass. Small particles of iron can also be used as test objects. In Figure 9, the peaks of an iron-containing ferrofluid show the shape of a magnetic field in three dimensions. The field is strongest at the two ends of the bar magnet. Iron filings form similar patterns and can even form lines that curve broadly from one end of a bar magnet to the other. Such two- or three-dimensional physical patterns can help you visualize a field. In a similar way, imaginary *field lines* can be used to model the strength and direction of a field in space.

A charged object is also surrounded by a field. An electric field produces force on a test object with a small charge. Visualizing or mapping an electric field can be done with such a test charge. A small positive test charge is pulled toward a negative charge or pushed away from a positive charge. The test charge tends to move along an electric field line.

In the photos of grass seeds in this lesson, such as in Figure 10, one or more charged rods touch the surface of a table sprinkled with grass seeds, which are neutral insulators. The tip of the rod, such as the one in the center of Figure 10, acts as a point charge on the surface. The electric field from the tip of the rod polarizes the seeds. The seeds line up roughly along the electric field lines.

INFER Select the correct terms to complete the statements about Figures 9 and 10.

- The higher, left end of the magnet is north | south | not identifiable with the information given.

- The charge of the tip of the rod is positive | negative | not identifiable with the information given.

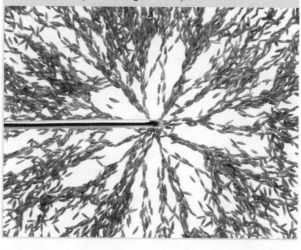

FIGURE 10: Grass seeds show the pattern of the electric field around a point charge—the tip of the rod.

The grass seeds around the charged rod form a radial pattern of lines. The force on a test charge, like the gravitational force on a satellite, lies along a straight line connecting the test object with the central object. In both cases, straight field lines can be drawn radiating from the central object. However, the field around an electric charge can be inward or outward, while the gravitational field is always inward because gravitational force is only attractive, not repulsive.

Hands-On Lab

Measuring an Electric Field

You will use the amount of displacement of a hanging sphere as a way of mapping an electric field. Then you will develop a way to use the field of a charged rod to move a hanging sphere to a specific displacement, reliably.

Research Question How can an electric field be used to move objects in a controlled way?

MAKE A CLAIM

Choose a target displacement, such as 2 cm, and record it in your Evidence Notebook. Describe what you expect to do to get the hanging sphere to be displaced by this amount. Include how you will be able to repeat that task even if one or more of the materials starts with an unknown charge.

_____

_____

_____

_____

POSSIBLE MATERIALS

- safety goggles
- cloth, wool
- rod, plastic
- ruler
- sphere, chargeable, suspended

SAFETY INFORMATION

- Wear safety goggles during the setup, hands-on, and takedown segments of the activity.

PLAN THE INVESTIGATION

Consider the following suggestions as you develop your procedure.

- Give the rod a specific amount of charge by rubbing it a known number of times with the cloth. Think about ways the amount of charge on an object can be varied.
- Gently run your hand over an object to remove charge.
- Test different ways to hold the rod: end- or side-on, below or to one side of the sphere.
- Use displacement as a measure of field strength to map the rod's electric field.
- Do one or more test runs to try out your procedure and equipment. Determine a good range for each variable. If needed, revise your target displacement.
- Consider what might go wrong. Plan to ensure the safety of yourself and your class.

In your Evidence Notebook, develop a procedure for your investigation. Make sure your teacher approves your procedure and safety plan before proceeding. As you test and refine your procedure, record your data and the details of your methods. If you need to change your methods, make sure your teacher approves the change.

ANALYZE

Record your responses in your Evidence Notebook.

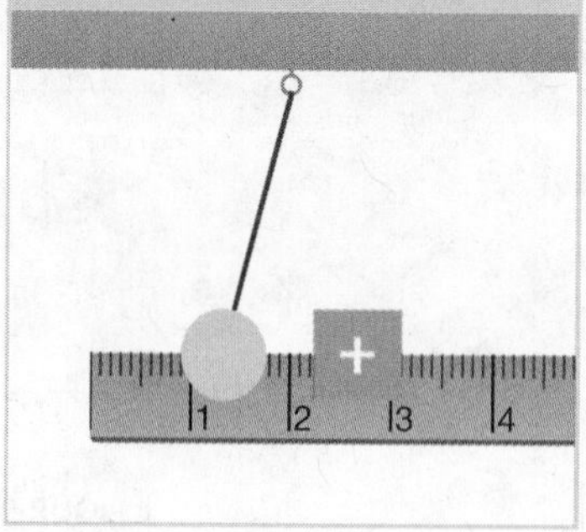

1. Sketch the field around the rod. Use the displacement of the sphere as a way of determining the strength of the field at different points around the rod.

2. Explain how you determined where the field around the rod was the strongest.

3. Summarize how you achieved the target distance reliably. Include how you addressed the possibility of an unknown initial charge on the materials.

4. What part of the procedure needed to be done the most carefully? Use the concepts of electric charge and fields to explain the need for care.

5. Suppose that, in a factory, a process gives different amounts of charge to good and to faulty items. How might you use electric force to sort the items into different bins?

FIGURE 11: Measuring the displacement of a sphere

DRAW CONCLUSIONS

Write a conclusion that addresses each of the points below.

Claim Refine your claim about how to achieve your target displacement reliably. Describe your method so that another person would be able to follow your directions to test your claim. Assume that the materials might have initial, unknown charges.

Evidence Give specific examples from your data to support your claim. Include a brief description of the field around the rod.

Reasoning Explain how the evidence you gave supports your claim. For example, describe the part of the field around the rod that you used to move the sphere and why that part of the field was effective.

_____

_____

_____

_____

_____

_____

_____

_____

EXTEND

Map the electric field of charged objects of other shapes and materials, such as a round balloon or a flat foam plate. Then compare the relative strengths of the fields of these different objects.

Representing and Mapping Fields

The pattern of the grass seeds in Figure 10 suggests lines in the field. You can model an electric field by drawing lines with arrowheads to show the field's direction. The closeness of the lines shows the field's strength. Next to a charge or a magnetic pole, the field is strongest, and the field lines are closest together. If you follow a line, you can see changes in the strength of the field and possibly the direction.

 Language Arts Connection Find one or more examples of lines used to show where a value is constant, such as the lines in a topographic map or lines of temperature or pressure in a weather map. How are these lines different from the lines used to represent fields? Explain your thinking to a partner, listen to your partner's explanation, and then refine your answer.

FIGURE 12: Electric fields around point charges

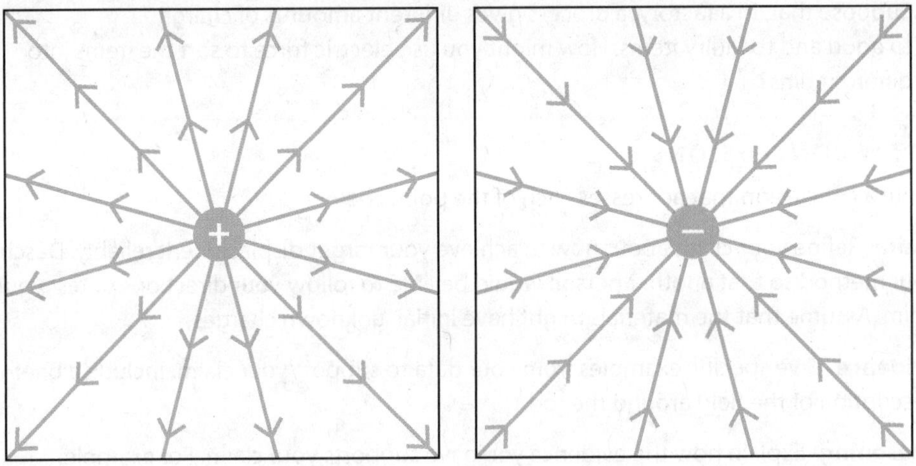

a The field lines around a positive charge   **b** The field lines around a negative charge

Explore Online ▶

YOU SOLVE IT

How Can You Move Particles Using Electric Charge?
Investigate how electric fields affect charged particles.

An electric field line, by convention, shows the direction of the force on a positive test charge. Field lines are continuous between charges—they do not stop or start in empty space. Electric field lines begin on a positive charge and end on a negative charge. You can see in Figure 12 that the lines are dense at a charge and less dense farther from an isolated charge.

PREDICT Show how you think the field lines between a positive and a negative charge would lie. Draw lines starting from at least six points all the way around the positive charge.

Field Strength

Potential energy is the stored energy due to position, such as the potential energy of an object in a gravitational field. The gravitational field can be described independently of the test object by dividing the gravitational force by the object's mass. Near Earth, the field is characterized by **g**, and so gravitational potential energy is *mgh*.

In a similar way, a small test charge can have electric potential energy because of its position in an electric field. The strength of the electric field at any point can be described by the force on the test object divided by its charge. Electric field strength is measured in newtons per coulomb.

APPLY Write the equations for the strength at a given point of a gravitational field and of an electric field. Use variables to represent the mass and charge of a test object, and assume you can measure the forces $\mathbf{F}_{gravitational}$ and $\mathbf{F}_{electric}$.

_____

_____

_____

_____

_____

The needle of a magnetic compass is magnetized. Such a needle can be used as a test object for a magnetic field. It shows the direction of the magnetic field at a location.

INFER Determine the polarity of the ends of the bar magnet. The arrowheads on the compass needles are north poles.

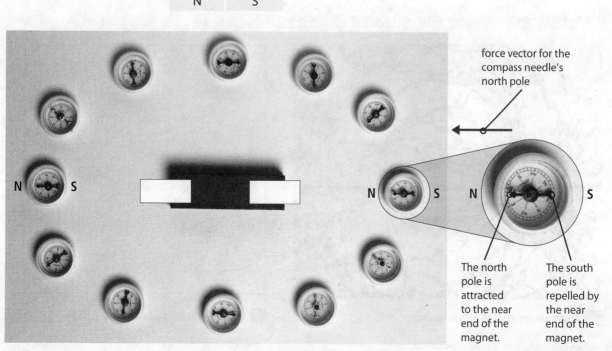

force vector for the compass needle's north pole

The north pole is attracted to the near end of the magnet.

The south pole is repelled by the near end of the magnet.

FIGURE 13: Magnetic field lines run from the north to the south pole of a magnet, indicating the direction that a compass needle would point at a particular location.

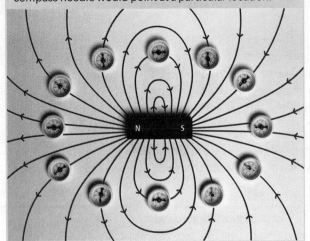

EXPLAIN If the compass needle to the right of the magnet were free to slide in any direction, how would it move? Use the direction and density of field lines to support your answer.

_____

_____

_____

The lines of the magnetic field are drawn from north poles to south poles and form closed loops. As with the arrows in electric fields, this direction is a convention. The density of the field lines shows the relative strength of the field. For simplicity, field lines are typically shown in two dimensions for a plane through the magnet. A more complex model might show the field around the magnet in three dimensions.

Combining Fields

The grass seeds in Figure 14a show field lines that curve between the unlike charges. Figure 14b shows more clearly how electric field lines stretch between a positive and a negative charge. Farther out, they make larger loops, much as the grass seeds do. At each point, the field is a vector sum of the fields from each charge affecting the space. The result is a single field of continuous lines from positive to negative charges.

> **Language Arts Connection** Explore simulations of electric fields and simulations of magnetic fields online, or use Figures 13 and 14b. Make a chart comparing the simulated field from a bar magnet with the simulated field from opposite charges.

FIGURE 14: The electric field lines curve and connect unlike charges.

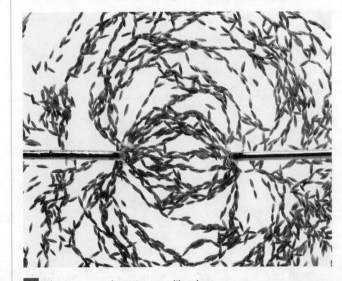

a The grass seeds connect unlike charges.

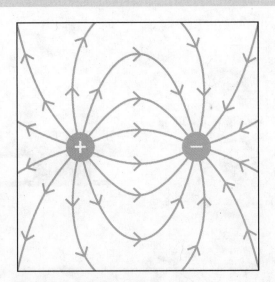

b Electric field lines point from the positive charge to the negative charge.

Cause and Effect

Dipoles

Think about a single polarized grass seed: one end has a net positive charge, and the other end has a net negative charge. Two equal but opposite ends, such as charges or magnetic poles, form a *dipole* when they are close but separated. Use Figure 14b to picture the electric field of the polarized grass seed. Imagine the ends of the seed as the two charges.

Now think about a seed near a positive rod in Figure 14a. The rod produces polarization in the seed. The negative end of the seed is closest and is attracted to the rod. The outward end of the seed has positive charge. It helps to polarize other seeds. It attracts the negative end of the nearest seed. As the pattern continues, the seeds form lines.

APPLY Assume that the end of the rod has a positive charge. Each seed becomes a dipole. Choose two seeds that are end to end. To one seed, add + and − labels to the ends to show how the seed is polarized in the electric field. Repeat for the other seed. You can label the photo directly or circle the seeds and redraw them.

Unlike an electric charge, a magnetic pole does not occur by itself. It is always part of a dipole or a more complex system. If you break a bar magnet, the broken ends are poles, and each piece of magnet forms a magnetic dipole. Within a permanent magnet are regions that act much like the grass seeds, aligning and carrying the field. On yet a smaller scale, an individual atom can be modeled as a magnetic dipole. The macroscopic magnet is the sum of many atomic-level magnets.

FIGURE 15: The magnetic field around a bar magnet and chain of magnetized paper clips

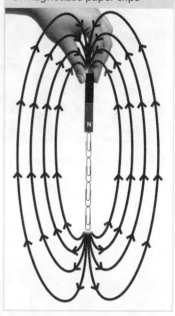

ANALYZE Compare the magnetic field lines shown in Figure 15 with those of a bar magnet that has the same length as the chain.

_____

_____

_____

_____

The alignment of dipoles may be easier to visualize as the chain of paper clips in Figure 15. Under the influence of the bar magnet's magnetic field, the magnetic fields around the atoms in each paper clip orient themselves to align with the strong nearby field. Each paper clip acts as a temporary bar magnet. The magnet and the paper clips together act as a single larger bar magnet.

Photographs, NYC; (b) ©Houghton Mifflin Harcourt

EVALUATE Compare the closeness of field lines between and around the like charges in these visuals with the pattern for unlike charges (Figure 14 or a simulation you may have explored). Remember how the lines show the field strength. Draw vectors to represent the force on a small positive test charge at each of the locations shown (A, B, and C).

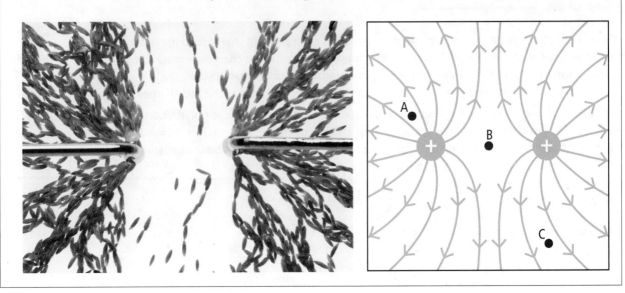

Like and unlike magnetic poles (Figure 16) produce magnetic fields in patterns similar to the electric fields you have just seen. The pattern of the small iron particles, or filings, resembles a pattern of field lines. In Figure 16a, the space between like poles is empty of iron filings. The pattern in the field shows the repulsion between the two north poles.

In Figure 16b, the iron filings connect the poles of the two magnets, suggesting dipoles that align. The pattern in the field shows the attraction between the north pole and south pole.

FIGURE 16: Iron filings show a two-dimensional representation of magnetic field lines.

a Iron filings show the field lines between repelling magnetic poles.

b Iron filings show the field lines between attracting magnetic poles.

 Evidence Notebook How might your knowledge of electric fields help you meet the challenge of straightening out the curved stream of water?

Quantifying Forces Due to Fields

 Collaborate With a classmate, write a list of the factors that affect an electric force and how they affect the force. For example, charge of a greater magnitude produces greater force.

The Inverse-Square Law

Electric field lines around a point charge are close together near the charge, but spread out as the distance from the charge increases. Greater density of the lines shows where the field is stronger. However, most diagrams show only a plane, which is a two-dimensional model. Real electric fields are three-dimensional. To use field lines to model the strength of the field quantitatively, three-dimensional space must be modeled.

ANALYZE Determine the number of field lines per unit area at distances of 1R, 2R, and 3R. If a line goes through a corner, count it as one-fourth (0.25) of a line.

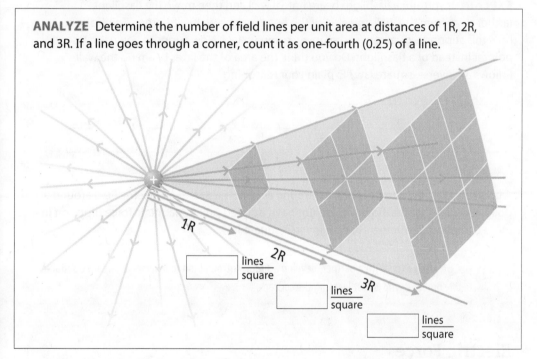

APPLY Select the correct terms to complete the paragraph about the inverse-square law.

Imagine a sphere with a radius, r, of 1 cm, centered on a point charge. Suppose the field is represented by 100 electric field lines starting at the center and passing through the sphere's surface. The surface area, A, is given by $A = 4\pi r^2$. If the radius of the sphere is doubled, the surface area of the sphere would double | triple | quadruple. This larger 2 cm sphere has fewer | the same number of | more field lines passing through its surface. At 2 cm, the electric field strength—represented by the number of lines per unit area—is the same as | one-half | one-fourth the electric field strength at 1 cm. The electric field is given in units of force per unit of charge. The electric force on a test charge placed at a distance of 2 cm is quadruple | double | one-half | one-fourth the electric force at 1 cm.

Inverse-Square Laws

$$F = -G\frac{m_1 m_2}{r^2}$$

Law of Universal Gravitation The attractive (by convention, negative) force of gravity between two masses, m_1 and m_2, is greatest when the distance, r, is small. G is the gravitational constant.

$$E = \frac{I}{4\pi r^2}$$

Electric Field Strength The strength of an electric field, E, around a charge decreases as the distance, r, from the charge increases. The quantity I in this equation combines the charge, q, with a constant.

$$I_{radiation} = \frac{P}{4\pi r^2}$$

Electromagnetic Radiation Suppose you have a light bulb emitting a certain amount of energy/time, or power, P. The intensity, $I_{radiation}$, of that light diminishes— the light gets weaker—as you move farther from the bulb (increasing r).

EXPLAIN If you aim a flashlight beam onto a wall and then move the flashlight farther away from the wall, the area of the beam on the wall gets larger. Think about how this supports, qualitatively, an inverse-square law. Now suppose you use a laser pointer instead of a flashlight. Do you think the area of the laser beam on the wall follows an inverse-square law? Explain your reasoning.

_____

_____

_____

A gravitational field can be modeled around a point mass, and an electric field around a point charge. Magnets, however, do not have isolated poles. Magnetic force drops off in a more complicated manner than an inverse-square law.

 Collaborate With a partner, develop a simple introduction to inverse-square laws suitable for someone who is first learning the concept.

Electric Force

Electric fields are like gravitational fields in some ways. You could draw gravitational field lines pointing straight inward toward objects with mass. Electric fields around negative point charges also point radially inward. The density of field lines is proportional to $1/r^2$, which indicates that the force on a test mass or charge follows an inverse-square law.

MODEL Complete the equation for Coulomb's law, which shows how two charges and the distance between them affect the magnitude of electric force. The symbol k is a constant equal to 8.99×10^9 N·m²/C².

| r^2 |
| q_1 |
| q_2 |

$$F_{electric} = k \;\frac{\boxed{}}{\boxed{}}$$

Attractive forces are negative by convention. In the law of universal gravitation, masses and distance are all positive, so a negative sign is included to indicate an attractive force. Electric force, however, can be attractive or repulsive.

ANALYZE When you multiply two charges, how do the signs of the charges affect the product? Summarize the pattern resulting from different combinations of positive and negative charge.

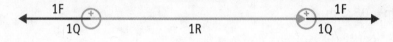

FIGURE 17: Two spheres, each with charge 1Q, produce a force of magnitude 1F as shown. The displacement of the rightmost sphere is shown as 1R.

Look at the repulsive force between the two spheres in Figure 17. For the rightmost sphere, the force is in the same direction as the displacement. The force is positive, and it tends to increase the displacement. You can see from Coulomb's law that two negative charges produce the same result. For unlike charges, the force is attractive. The product of the charges is negative, as is the sign of the force, and the displacement tends to decrease. The signs of the charges in Coulomb's law correctly determine the direction of the force.

APPLY Two charges of 1Q at separation 1R produce electric force 1F, as shown in Figure 17. For each additional example, determine the unknown force, charge, or distance. Use the sign convention for force.

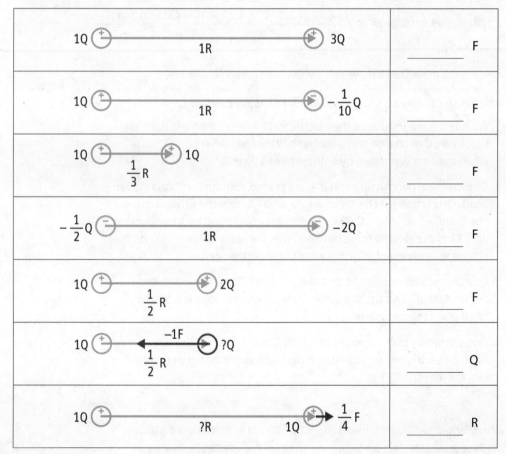

Problem Solving

Calculating Electric Force

On a dry day, two people each comb their furry pets with plastic combs. Laura's comb acquires -6.20 microcoulombs (μC) of charge. Jorge's comb acquires $-4.30\ \mu C$ of charge. What is the force on Laura's comb if Jorge's comb is placed 33.5 cm away?

ANALYZE

Known:

$q_1 = -6.20\ \mu C = -6.20 \times 10^{-6}\ C$

$q_2 = -4.30\ \mu C = -4.30 \times 10^{-6}\ C$

$r = 33.5\ cm = 0.335\ m$

$k = 8.99 \times 10^9\ N \cdot m^2/C^2$

Unknown:

F

> **ANALYZE** Draw the combs, charges, and force.

PLAN

Use Coulomb's law:

$$F = k \frac{q_1 q_2}{r^2}$$

SOLVE

$$F = 8.99 \times 10^9\ N \cdot m^2/C^2 \frac{(-6.20 \times 10^{-6}\ C)(-4.30 \times 10^{-6}\ C)}{(0.335\ m)^2}$$

$F = 2.14\ N$ (repulsive) on Laura's comb

CHECK YOUR ANSWER

Check to see if the calculated force gives the same separation of charges.

$$2.14\ N = 8.99 \times 10^9\ N \cdot m^2/C^2 \frac{(-6.20 \times 10^{-6}\ C)(-4.30 \times 10^{-6}\ C)}{r^2} = \frac{0.240\ N \cdot m^2}{r^2}$$

$r^2 = 0.112\ m^2$

$r = \sqrt{0.112\ m^2} = 0.335\ m$, which checks with given separation.

PRACTICE PROBLEMS

SOLVE Use Coulomb's law to solve the following problems.

1. What is the magnitude of the electric force between a glass ball that has $+2.5\ \mu C$ of charge and a rubber ball that has $-5.0\ \mu C$ of charge when they are separated by a distance of 5.0 cm?

2. Two identical conducting spheres are placed with their centers 0.30 m apart. One is given a charge of $+1.20 \times 10^{-8}\ C$, and the other is given a charge of $-1.80 \times 10^{-8}\ C$. The spheres are connected by a conducting wire. Find the electric force between the two spheres after the net charge spreads evenly. Ignore any charge on the wire.

3. Two charges are separated by a distance of 1.20 m. The magnitude of q_1 is 4.00 μC, and the attractive force on each charge is 0.500 N. What is the magnitude of q_2?

4. Two stationary point charges of $+6.00\ C$ and $+5.00\ C$ exert a repulsive force on each other of 17 500 N. What is the distance between the two charges?

Evidence Notebook Summarize the ways an electric force can be increased or decreased. Record what can be changed to make the biggest impact on the force on the stream of water.

Exploring Energy and Fields

A magnet or an electric charge, like a gravitational mass, exerts force through a field. The field can cause changes in the kinetic energy of another object.

Electric, Magnetic, and Gravitational Forces

Like other forces, magnetic and electric forces have magnitude and direction. When an object is pushed or pulled by more than one force, vector addition can be used to find the overall force on the object. Recall that vectors can be combined by breaking the forces into x and y components.

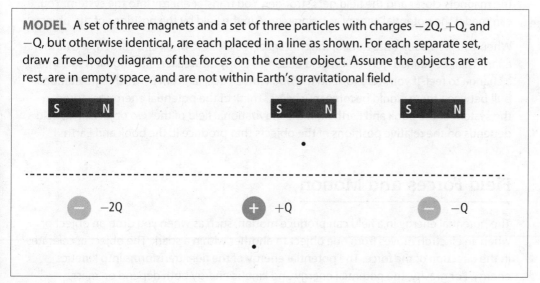

MODEL A set of three magnets and a set of three particles with charges $-2Q$, $+Q$, and $-Q$, but otherwise identical, are each placed in a line as shown. For each separate set, draw a free-body diagram of the forces on the center object. Assume the objects are at rest, are in empty space, and are not within Earth's gravitational field.

The gravitational forces on each center object from the side objects is very small and can likely be ignored relative to electric and magnetic forces. However, you can use your understanding of gravitational force to understand the effects of other field forces.

Field Forces and Potential Energy

You can use force as a way to become aware of the presence of potential energy. For example, think about the forces involved when you drop a book or lift it onto a shelf.

APPLY Select the correct terms to complete the statements about forces and fields.

An electron jumping from a hand to a doorknob is most similar to a book dropping | being lifted | being moved horizontally in the gravitational field near Earth's surface. The electron moves in | opposite to | perpendicular to the direction of the force.

Pushing the north poles of two magnets together is most similar to making a book move by dropping it | lifting it | moving it horizontally in the gravitational field near Earth's surface. You move the magnets in | opposite to | perpendicular to the direction of the force.

You can use the direction of force to evaluate changes in potential energy (PE). When a book falls, its gravitational potential energy decreases. You may treat this potential energy as a property of the book due to its height, PE = *mgh*. You think of the energy as stored in the book because of its position. Similarly, if you hold a paper clip close to a magnet, you can feel the tug and might think of the paper clip as having potential energy.

INFER When you push the north poles of two magnets together, where do you think the potential energy might be stored?

_____

_____

_____

For the two magnets, it does not work well to treat potential energy as a property of a magnet. Instead of thinking of PE as resulting from an object (one magnet) interacting with its environment, think of the system of objects and their combined field. You push the magnets closer and the field gets stronger. You transfer energy into the system. You can model the potential energy as being stored in the field by the positions of the objects.

When you lift a book onto a shelf, the centers of mass of the book and Earth move farther apart. Their combined gravitation field becomes a tiny bit weaker, although it is too small a change to feel. If you were to send the book into space, far from Earth, the gravitational pull between them would become much less. Think of the potential energy as stored in the system of the book and Earth or in the gravitational field of the two objects. The field depends on the relative positions of the objects that produce it: the book and Earth.

Field Forces and Motion

The potential energy in a field can produce motion, such as when you drop an object or when an electron moves from one object to another within a spark. The object accelerates in the direction of the force. The potential energy of the field transforms into kinetic energy. For gravity, the potential energy and kinetic energy both depend on mass.

APPLY Select the correct terms to complete the statements.

You can determine the electric force between two objects from their
masses | charges | magnetic dipoles and the distance between them. Their
masses | charges have no effect on the electric force. If one object is free to move and
you know the force, you also need mass | charge | mass and charge to determine its
initial acceleration. You need mass | charge | mass and charge, along with velocity, to
determine the object's kinetic energy.

 Evidence Notebook For your unit project, list ways to use electric fields and charge to balance the gravitational force on an object or to affect motion.

Fields are used in designs, such as the two applications shown Figure 18, to affect motion without direct contact. The field of a magnet acts through the glass to control a wiper on the inside of the fish tank. In electrostatic painting, the field produces force at a distance. Charged droplets or solid particles of paint repel one another but are attracted in a controlled way to the item being painted. The result is an even coating of paint on the item and little wasted paint.

FIGURE 18: A magnet outside of a fish tank moves a wiper that cleans the inside of the tank (a). Tiny charged paint droplets are attracted to grounded items to be painted (b).

a Magnetic control through glass

b Electrostatic paint control

Field Forces and Changes of Energy

Position affects the energy stored in field. A falling book loses potential energy as it gains kinetic energy. In a similar way, if the force from an electric or magnetic field causes the positions of objects to change, then the potential energy is reduced. If something acts against the field force to change the objects' positions, then potential energy is increased.

EVALUATE Which statements about kinetic energy (KE) and potential energy (PE) from fields are true? Use your knowledge of gravitational fields to help you make inferences about the other types of fields. Select all correct answers.

☐ **a.** When two objects in space pull closer together because of gravity, the gravitational PE in their field (or in the system) decreases.

☐ **b.** When a charged particle is accelerated by an electric field along field lines, PE decreases as it is transformed into KE.

☐ **c.** If two positively charged objects are pushed closer together, the system of the objects and fields loses PE.

☐ **d.** If the fields of two magnets cause them to snap together, the potential energy in the field between them decreases.

Ratio of Electric and Gravitational Forces

Coulomb's law shows how charge determines the strength of the electric force. Recall that mass affects how an object will respond to unbalanced forces. The ratio of charge to mass can be a useful property of particles. This ratio is useful in part because the ratio of electric force to gravitational force, $F_{electric}/F_{gravitational}$, is the same at any separation.

Think about two objects. Each force is proportional to $1/r^2$, which cancels out:

$$\frac{F_{electric}}{F_{gravitational}} = \frac{kq_1q_2/r^2}{Gm_1m_2/r^2} = \frac{k}{G}\frac{q_1}{m_1}\frac{q_2}{m_2}$$

The relative strength of the two forces does not depend on the distance between the objects. The relationship is proportional to the charge-to-mass ratio, q/m, of each object.

A mass spectrometer is a tool used in many fields of science. It uses the ratio between charge and mass to analyze the composition of a sample, to identify unknown substances, or to detect the presence of specific substances. For example, forensic scientists can use a tissue or blood sample to find out if a person has taken drugs or been exposed to toxins.

In a typical mass spectrometer, the material is first broken down into ions—charged atoms and molecules. The ions pass through a region of the spectrometer that uses the charge of each particle as a way to apply force. The force depends on the charge and changes the direction of each particle according to its mass. Deflections are larger for particles of greater charge or lower mass. Hydrogen ions, which have very small masses, might be deflected to one side while ionized complex proteins, which have much larger masses, travel nearly straight. The particles are counted as they hit detectors.

FIGURE 19: A mass spectrum is usually displayed as a graph. The computer may automatically label some peaks based on known charge-to-mass ratios.

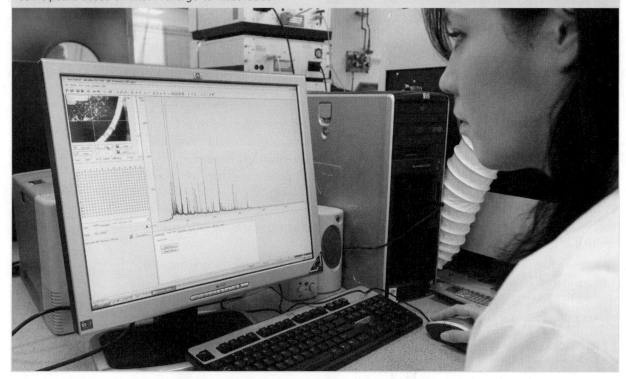

INFER Select the correct terms to complete the paragraph that describes how mass spectrometers can sort particles.

Mass spectrometers sort particles by their charge-to-mass ratio, or q/m. A particle with a charge Q and mass M would end up in the same place as a particle with 2Q and M | Q and 2M | 2Q and 2M because the charge | mass | charge-to-mass ratio is the same for both particles. A mass spectrometer could not be used to distinguish between particles with Q and 3M and particles with 2Q | 3Q | 4Q and 9M. If a particle can be ionized in different ways, such as by removing different numbers of electrons, then its mass spectrum would have a higher peak | pattern of peaks.

Evidence Notebook Review what you have learned about how field forces can affect potential and kinetic energy. Apply it to the challenge of the bent stream of water.

Guided Research

Electric Phenomena

Figure 20 shows motion from a video that was recorded aboard the International Space Station. Under free-fall conditions, such as in orbit, people and objects seem to have little or no weight. Gravitational force from Earth is present, but it has little effect in the reference frame of an astronaut. As a result, the effects of electrostatic force are easier to see.

In the video, an astronaut describes how he charges a knitting needle. He then uses a charged syringe to produce small charged water droplets near the knitting needle. He watches them move through the air. The droplets are attracted to the charged knitting needle. Some droplets spiral in and land on the needle quickly. Some droplets orbit the cylindrical needle, making helical paths up and down the needle. These orbits are not produced by a gravitational force, but by an electric force.

Search for videos and other supporting materials that are experiments in electrostatics or demonstrations of electrostatic phenomena. Explore some possibilities, and then select a topic:

• soap bubbles interacting with a Van de Graaff generator
• bees or other insects sensing electric fields
• electrostatic properties of spiderwebs
• volcanic lightning
• topic of your choice, if approved by your teacher

Take note of interesting videos and other visuals as you research your topic. You may wish to use them in your presentation.

Explore Online ▶

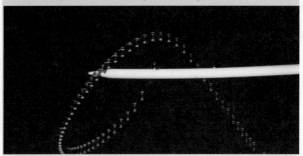

FIGURE 20: Aboard the International Space Station, water droplets orbit a charged knitting needle.

Language Arts Connection Research your chosen electric phenomenon. Gather information from multiple sources. Consider the reliability of the sources, and evaluate the information they provide—including completeness. Compare the information contained in the different sources. Also compare the information to the concepts you learned in this lesson. Focus on information that is relevant to electrostatic forces.

Prepare a demonstration of the electric phenomenon you researched, either as a multimedia presentation or a direct demonstration.

• Describe the locations and behaviors of the electric charge(s) involved.

• Explain any forces, motions, and changes in energy associated with the phenomenon.

• Your explanations may be qualitative, but if reliable quantitative data is available, include it as well.

Present your demonstration or multimedia presentation to the class.

| EXPLORING FIELDS | ELECTRONS IN WIRE | EARTH'S MAGNETIC FIELD | Go online to choose one of these other paths. |

Lesson Self-Check

CAN YOU SOLVE THE PROBLEM?

Figure 21 shows how a balloon can cause a thin stream of falling water to bend. To understand this pattern, think about neutral and charged objects. Think about the distribution of charge and about how different charges behave when they interact. Recall how charges behave in insulators and in conductors. Think about the causes and effects involved in induced polarization. Experiment with a balloon or other charged object.

In the challenge problem, a stream of water is bent by a charged balloon, as in the second and third photo of Figure 21. Find a way to cause the water to flow straight down, as in the first photo of the figure. Your solution should leave the balloon in place and unchanged, and it should not require anything to touch the stream of water.

Explore Online ▶

FIGURE 21: A stream of water bends as a balloon moves close to it.

Evidence Notebook Develop a solution to the challenge. You might test and optimize your method. Refer to your notes in your Evidence Notebook to propose a solution using a claim, evidence, and reasoning. Your written solution should address the following points:

Claim How would you straighten out the stream of water in the challenge? State your solution as a claim of what works; ensure that your answer has enough information for someone to test your solution.

Evidence Summarize the evidence you have gathered to support your claim. Include direct evidence, such as a picture or the data from an experiment, as well as any laws or patterns that apply to the situation. For example, if the sign of the charge on the balloon matters for your solution, you might present evidence that identifies the sign of the charge.

Reasoning Draw a model of the balloon and the stream of water. Show the charges you think are present. Use your model to illustrate your solution and to help explain why your method would straighten out the stream.

CHECKPOINTS

Check Your Understanding

1. Which of the following describe electrostatic phenomena? Select all correct answers.

   ☐ **a.** Clothing from a clothes dryer sticks together.

   ☐ **b.** Clear plastic wrap clings to a bowl.

   ☐ **c.** As a compass turns, its needle moves.

   ☐ **d.** A magnet sticks to a refrigerator.

   ☐ **e.** A polyester-fiber cleaning cloth picks up dust.

2. An object is tested by bringing it close to a neutral electroscope that has two conducting leaves initially together. As the object approaches, the leaves of the electroscope move apart. What can you conclude about the object's charge?

   ○ **a.** It is positive (+).

   ○ **b.** It is negative (−).

   ○ **c.** It is not zero (+ or −).

   ○ **d.** It is zero (neutral; no net charge).

3. Electric field lines point to the east. A negatively charged particle travels north into the field, slowly. What happens to the particle as it enters the field?

   ○ **a.** It is deflected to the east.

   ○ **b.** It is deflected to the west.

   ○ **c.** It continues traveling north.

   ○ **d.** It slows and then moves south.

4. Select all true statements about forces and fields.

   ☐ **a.** Electric forces and gravitational forces are each inversely proportional to the square of the distance between the particles.

   ☐ **b.** Electric, magnetic, and gravitational forces can each be attractive or repulsive.

   ☐ **c.** Fields can produce force at a distance from the source—the mass, charge, or magnet.

   ☐ **d.** A gravitational field, but not an electric field, extends in every direction from an object.

   ☐ **e.** Charge determines the strength of an electric force, but the acceleration depends on mass.

   ☐ **f.** Two masses can form a gravitational dipole.

5. A charge of magnitude Q is placed near each of three charges. The distance to and magnitude of each of the three charges are listed. Rank the magnitude of force from least (1) to greatest (3).

   _____ **a.** 2D, 2Q   _____ **c.** 2D, 4Q

   _____ **b.** D/2, Q/16

6. Suppose you push two objects, each positively charged, closer together. What happens to the energy stored in the field?

   ○ **a.** It increases.   ○ **c.** It decreases.

   ○ **b.** It does not change.

7. Two protons are separated by 1.00×10^{-10} m. How does the magnitude of the electric force compare to that of the gravitational force between them? Use $q_{proton} = 1.602 \times 10^{-19}$ C; $m_{proton} = 1.67 \times 10^{-27}$ kg; and the constants $G = 6.674 \times 10^{-11}$ N·m²/kg² and $k = 8.99 \times 10^9$ N·m²/C².

   ○ **a.** $F_{electric} = 6.88 \times 10^{-5} F_{gravitational}$

   ○ **b.** $F_{electric} = 1.24 F_{gravitational}$

   ○ **c.** $F_{electric} = 1.45 \times 10^4 F_{gravitational}$

   ○ **d.** $F_{electric} = 1.24 \times 10^{36} F_{gravitational}$

8. Two charges exert a force of 100 N on each other. If the charges are moved to a distance one-fourth of the original distance, what is the new electric force they have on each other?

   ○ **a.** 25 N   ○ **c.** 400 N

   ○ **b.** 100 N   ○ **d.** 1600 N

9. Two bar magnets are arranged in a line so that the north pole of the left magnet and south pole of the right magnet are close together: S-N S-N. In what direction would you draw the arrows on magnetic field lines in the space between the magnets?

   ○ **a.** to the left

   ○ **b.** to the right

   ○ **c.** splitting upward and downward

   ○ **d.** No field lines should be drawn here.

10. A charge q_1 of −2.3 μC (−2.3 × 10⁻⁶ C) exerts a force of 0.386 N westward on a charge q_2 of −5.6 μC (−5.6 × 10⁻⁶ C). Determine the distance and direction of q_2 relative to q_1.

    _____ m _____ of q_1

CHECKPOINTS (continued)

11. Imagine that the bar magnet shown is cut in half at its midline. The halves labeled N and S are pulled apart a short distance. Draw the two halves of the magnet and the field around and between them.

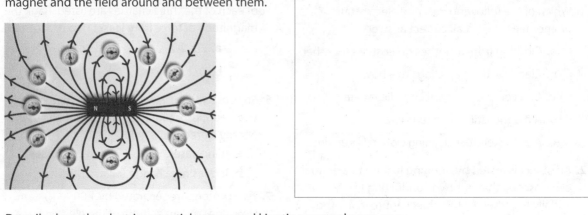

12. Describe how the electric potential energy and kinetic energy change as a positively charged particle is released from the surface of a positively charged metal sheet and moves toward a nearby negatively charged metal sheet.

_____

_____

_____

_____

MAKE YOUR OWN STUDY GUIDE

In your Evidence Notebook, design a study guide that supports the main ideas from this lesson:

Charges are of two types, positive and negative, and magnetic poles are of two types, north and south. Charges can be isolated, but magnetic poles do not occur in isolation.

Charged particles produce electric fields that act on other charged particles at a distance. Similarly, magnets produce magnetic fields that act on other magnets at a distance.

Unlike gravitational force, which is always attractive, both electric and magnetic forces can be attractive or repulsive. Like charges or poles repel, and unlike charges or poles attract.

Electric force can be described and calculated quantitatively. It is directly proportional to each amount of charge and inversely proportional to the square of the separation between charges.

Gravitational, electric, and magnetic fields can store and release potential energy.

Remember to include the following information in your study guide:

- Use examples that model main ideas.
- Record explanations for the phenomena you investigated.
- Use evidence to support your explanations. Your support can include drawings, data, graphs, laboratory conclusions, and other evidence recorded throughout the lesson.

Use patterns from the atomic scale (the model of electrons as the most common charge carrier) to explain patterns at larger scales, such as what happens when you charge an object.

Engineering Connection

Simulating the International Space Station (ISS)
Your experiences of how to drink water, cross a room, or toss someone an object are shaped by gravity. Within the ISS, the effects of gravity are small and hard to notice. The normal forces and friction that usually result from gravity are absent. A small force can launch an astronaut across a room. Astronauts need to learn to change their motion and expectations. They practice in training flights that produce a free-fall environment for a short time before they spend months in the very different environment of the ISS.

> Research how an airplane can be flown to give passengers the experience of free fall. Develop a presentation that includes photographs, diagrams, and explanations of the motion of the plane and the forces experienced by the passengers.

FIGURE 1: An astronaut's training includes spending time in an airplane that simulates conditions in space.

Art Connection

Defying Gravity Magic tricks rely on our everyday experience of how objects move. They surprise us when moving objects don't follow the rules. In movies, video games, and live shows, artists play with our perceptions. They challenge our expectations of how objects react to gravity and other forces.

> Research examples in which an object or person appears to violate the law of universal gravitation. Analyze either how the illusion is done or how the laws of physics would have to change for the effect to occur. Present your findings to the class as a demonstration.

FIGURE 2: Suspending objects in air is a popular magic trick.

Technology Connection

Touchscreens Many modern devices use touchscreens as a part of their user interface. Unlike buttons or switches, touchscreens can adapt to a variety of contexts, allowing people to use a single screen for a wide variety of functions. Many touchscreens use electric fields to determine what spot on the screen is touched. The electric fields allow the screen to register multiple touches with high precision, but also make screens sensitive to disturbances caused by other electronic equipment or water.

> Research a variety of touchscreen technologies, identifying the advantages and disadvantages of each mechanism. Choose one technology, and develop a presentation that includes a variety of media showcasing how electric fields are used in the technology.

FIGURE 3: A cell phone touchscreen

Center; (c) ©Trevor Williams/Photodisc/Getty Images; (b) ©LaylaBird/iStock / Getty Images Plus/ Getty Images

THING EXPLAINER BY RANDALL MUNROE

A BOOK EXPLAINING COMPLEX IDEAS USING ONLY THE 1,000 MOST COMMON WORDS

US SPACE TEAM'S UP GOER FIVE

The space boat that took people to the moon and back

You've learned the velocity required to attain orbit. Have you ever wondered how engineers design a vehicle capable of putting astronauts and cargo into orbit? Here's an explanation of what they designed and why it works.

RANDALL MUNROE
XKCD.COM

THE STORY OF TRAVELING TO OTHER WORLDS

THIS IS THE ONLY SPACE BOAT THAT'S LANDED PEOPLE ON ANOTHER WORLD.

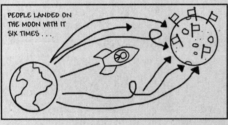

PEOPLE LANDED ON THE MOON WITH IT SIX TIMES . . .

...ALL ABOUT HALF A HUNDRED YEARS BEFORE THIS BOOK WAS WRITTEN.

AFTER THOSE VISITS TO THE MOON, WE STOPPED USING THIS SPACE BOAT TO GO TO OTHER WORLDS.

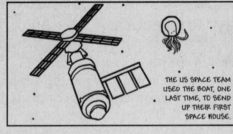

THE US SPACE TEAM USED THE BOAT, ONE LAST TIME, TO SEND UP THEIR FIRST SPACE HOUSE.

AFTER PEOPLE VISITED THE HOUSE A FEW TIMES, IT FELL BACK DOWN. PIECES OF IT LANDED IN A SMALL TOWN.

THE TOWN TOLD THE US SPACE TEAM TO PAY A FINE FOR DROPPING STUFF ON THE GROUND.

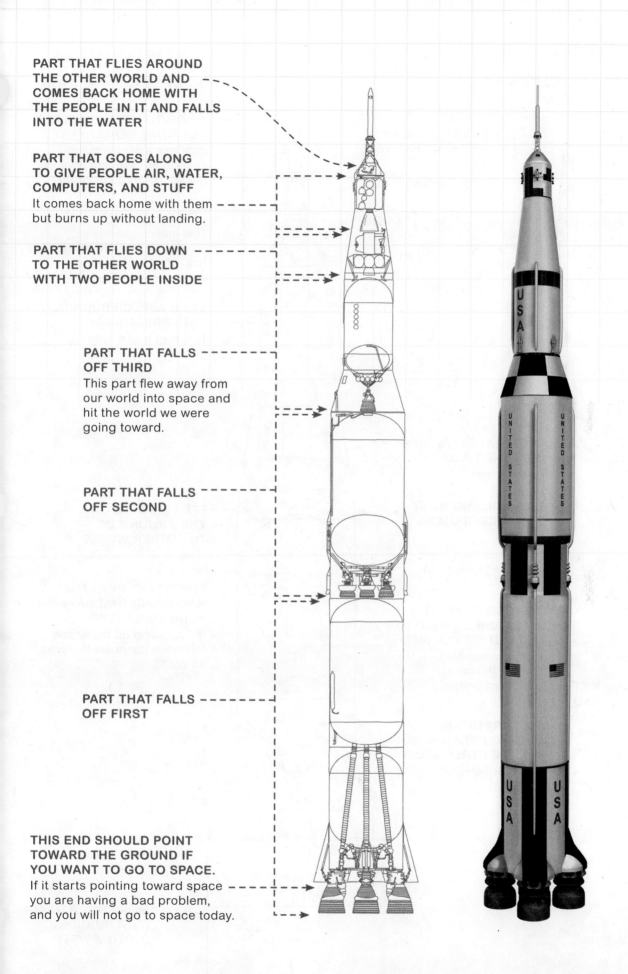

PART THAT FLIES AROUND THE OTHER WORLD AND COMES BACK HOME WITH THE PEOPLE IN IT AND FALLS INTO THE WATER

PART THAT GOES ALONG TO GIVE PEOPLE AIR, WATER, COMPUTERS, AND STUFF
It comes back home with them but burns up without landing.

PART THAT FLIES DOWN TO THE OTHER WORLD WITH TWO PEOPLE INSIDE

PART THAT FALLS OFF THIRD
This part flew away from our world into space and hit the world we were going toward.

PART THAT FALLS OFF SECOND

PART THAT FALLS OFF FIRST

THIS END SHOULD POINT TOWARD THE GROUND IF YOU WANT TO GO TO SPACE.
If it starts pointing toward space you are having a bad problem, and you will not go to space today.

USA

UNITED STATES

UNITED STATES

USA

USA

US SPACE TEAM'S UP GOER FIVE

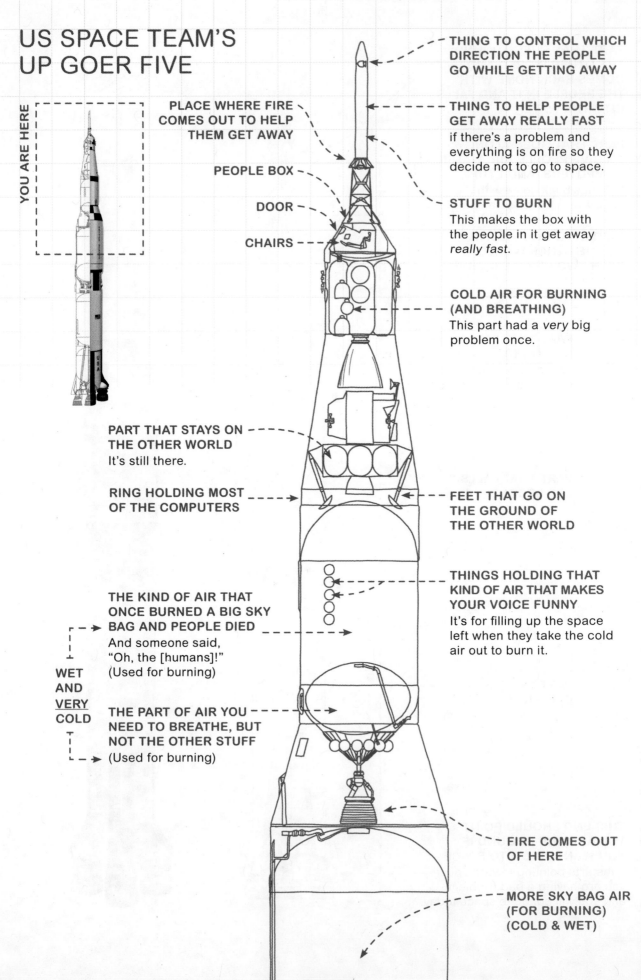

YOU ARE HERE

THING TO CONTROL WHICH DIRECTION THE PEOPLE GO WHILE GETTING AWAY

THING TO HELP PEOPLE GET AWAY REALLY FAST
if there's a problem and everything is on fire so they decide not to go to space.

PLACE WHERE FIRE COMES OUT TO HELP THEM GET AWAY

STUFF TO BURN
This makes the box with the people in it get away *really fast*.

PEOPLE BOX

DOOR

CHAIRS

COLD AIR FOR BURNING (AND BREATHING)
This part had a *very* big problem once.

PART THAT STAYS ON THE OTHER WORLD
It's still there.

RING HOLDING MOST OF THE COMPUTERS

FEET THAT GO ON THE GROUND OF THE OTHER WORLD

THINGS HOLDING THAT KIND OF AIR THAT MAKES YOUR VOICE FUNNY
It's for filling up the space left when they take the cold air out to burn it.

THE KIND OF AIR THAT ONCE BURNED A BIG SKY BAG AND PEOPLE DIED
And someone said, "Oh, the [humans]!" (Used for burning)

WET AND VERY COLD

THE PART OF AIR YOU NEED TO BREATHE, BUT NOT THE OTHER STUFF
(Used for burning)

FIRE COMES OUT OF HERE

MORE SKY BAG AIR (FOR BURNING) (COLD & WET)

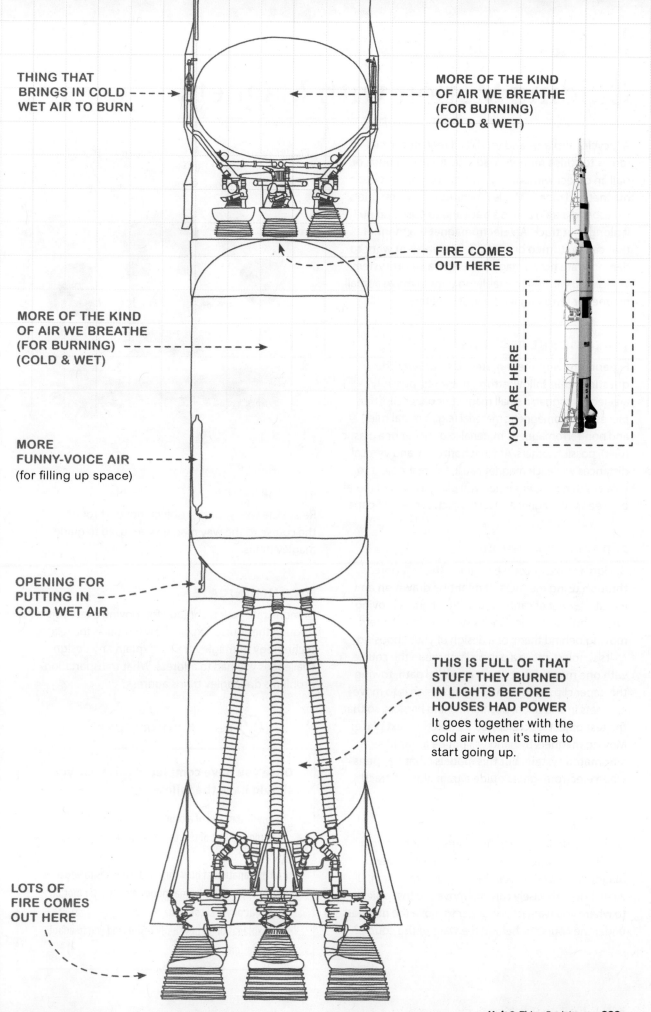

THING THAT
BRINGS IN COLD
WET AIR TO BURN

MORE OF THE KIND
OF AIR WE BREATHE
(FOR BURNING)
(COLD & WET)

FIRE COMES
OUT HERE

MORE OF THE KIND
OF AIR WE BREATHE
(FOR BURNING)
(COLD & WET)

MORE
FUNNY-VOICE AIR
(for filling up space)

YOU ARE HERE

OPENING FOR
PUTTING IN
COLD WET AIR

THIS IS FULL OF THAT
STUFF THEY BURNED
IN LIGHTS BEFORE
HOUSES HAD POWER
It goes together with the
cold air when it's time to
start going up.

LOTS OF
FIRE COMES
OUT HERE

Guiding Motion with Magnets

A bicycle, airplane, and forklift all rely on contact forces to cause motion. Magnetic force can push or pull an object without any physical contact between magnet and object. Maglev trains use electromagnets to suspend a train above a track and to push and pull it along that track. An electromagnet is a magnet that can be turned on and off. Imagine you want to demonstrate how a magnet-based transport system works. You will design a tabletop track to move a small magnet or ferromagnetic object 2 meters.

1. DEFINE THE PROBLEM

Experiment with these materials to answer the questions that follow: strong magnets, possibly an electromagnet; a small magnet or paper clip; thin pieces of ferromagnetic material (e.g., a metal ruler) and non-ferromagnetic material (e.g., paper or a plastic ruler); possibly others. At what horizontal and vertical distances will each magnet cause the test object to move? What happens when you place a sheet of metal between the magnet and test object? A sheet of paper?

2. DEVELOP A MODEL

Design a maze or course to guide the test object through using magnets. It might be drawn on an elevated sheet of cardboard, with magnets moving below; built of vertical index cards, with magnets moving behind them; or a design of your choosing. At its simplest, move a paper clip through the course with one magnet that traces a parallel path, towing the paper clip. A more challenging design is to move magnets in and out of position behind barriers, so that the test object is accelerated toward the next place. Moving magnets by hand will not be as rapid as an automated system, but this models what happens when electromagnets guide a train along a track.

3. DESIGN A SOLUTION

Refine the design of your first course based on your results. How often do you need to apply a new magnetic field? (For example, every 5 cm, 10 cm, 2 cm?) How precisely can you move the test object to where you want it? Is it better to move the magnets under the course or behind the walls of the course?

FIGURE 4: Iron filings are ferromagnetic and will align with a strong magnetic field. They are an example of how magnetic fields can move ferromagnetic materials.

4. USE A MODEL

Relate the way your test object moves through the course to the way magnets are used to guide maglev trains.

5. COMMUNICATE

Demonstrate your technique for moving a test object through the course. Explain how it models the related technology of maglev trains. Explain any design challenges you had to address. What transportation problems do maglev trains address?

✅ CHECK YOUR WORK

Once you have completed this task, you should have the following:

- a physical model of a course, through which you can move a test object using magnets that do not touch the object
- an explanation of how this model applies to larger-scale applications of magnetic fields to alter motion without physical contact
- an explanation of how early results led you to adapt your design

Name _____ Date _____

SYNTHESIZE THE UNIT

In your Evidence Notebook, make a concept map, other graphic organizer, or outline using the Study Guides you made for each lesson in this unit. Be sure to use evidence to support your claims.

When synthesizing individual information, remember to follow these general steps:

- Find the central idea of each piece of information.
- Think about the relationships among the central ideas.
- Combine the ideas to come up with a new understanding.

DRIVING QUESTIONS

Look back to the Driving Questions from the opening section of this unit. In your Evidence Notebook, review and revise your previous answers to those questions. Use the evidence you gathered and other observations you made throughout the unit to support your claims.

PRACTICE AND REVIEW

1. Earth's mass is 5.97×10^{24} kg, and $G = 6.674 \times 10^{-11}$ N·m^2/kg^2.

What is the acceleration due to gravity at a point 22 000 km from Earth's center? Report to two significant figures. _____ m/s^2

2. You give a balloon a negative charge by rubbing it on your clothing, and then you stick the balloon to the wall. What causes the balloon to stick to the wall? Select all correct answers.

- ☐ **a.** Positive charges are transfered from the wall to the balloon.
- ☐ **b.** Positive charges are transfered from the balloon to the wall.
- ☐ **c.** The balloon and the area of the wall next to it have opposite charges.
- ☐ **d.** Positive charge in the wall is repelled by the balloon.
- ☐ **e.** Negative charge in the wall is repelled by the balloon.

3. Two charges, Q and −2Q, are separated by a distance, R, with an electric force, F, between them. The charges are then changed to $\frac{2}{3}$ Q and Q, and the separation distance is reduced to $\frac{1}{3}$ R. What is the new force between the two charges?

- ○ **a.** F
- ○ **b.** 3F
- ○ **c.** −2F
- ○ **d.** −3F

4. Which are true statements comparing electric and gravitational forces? Select all correct answers.

- ☐ **a.** Both electric force and gravitational force can be attractive or repulsive.
- ☐ **b.** Gravitational force can act on objects at a distance, but electric force cannot.
- ☐ **c.** Electric and gravitational force are inversely proportional to the square of the distance.
- ☐ **d.** The gravitational force between two electrons is weaker than the electric force between them.
- ☐ **e.** Electric force acts only between charged objects, but gravitational force acts between all objects.

5. Select the correct terms to complete the statement about forces.

Electric and magnetic forces can only repel | only attract | repel and attract objects, while gravity can only repel | only attract | repel and attract objects. For each force, the arrows on | density of | width of the field lines indicate(s) the direction of the force on a test particle, while the arrows on | density of | width of the field lines indicate(s) the strength of the force.

6. An object in orbit around the sun moves faster when it is in the part of its orbit that is closer to the sun. How do the kinetic and potential energy of the object change throughout the object's orbit? How does the gravitational force between the object and the sun change throughout the object's orbit?

_____

_____

_____

_____

_____

_____

7. Compare the field around a point charge with the field around a magnet. Is there a scale at which the fields are similar? Explain your reasoning.

_____

_____

_____

_____

_____

_____

8. Compare electric potential energy with gravitational potential energy.

_____

_____

_____

_____

_____

_____

UNIT PROJECT

Return to your unit project. Prepare a presentation using your research and materials, and share it with the class. In your final presentation, demonstrate your hovering toy.

Remember these tips while evaluating:

- Clearly state what materials were tested and why you chose the material that was used in your final toy design.

- Describe how field forces (electric, magnetic, and gravitational) are related to your toy design.

- Explain any mechanisms used to make your toys hover. Include specific details of your toy design.

Electromagnetism and Generators

An electric arc is an electric discharge across a medium that is not normally conductive, such as air.

YOU SOLVE IT

How Can You Design a Wind-Powered Generator?

To begin exploring this unit's concepts, go online to investigate ways to solve a real-world problem.

FIGURE 1: A bicycle generator can transform kinetic energy into electrical energy.

A bicycle generator provides an opportunity to turn exercise into a source of electrical energy. The design captures energy to run a device or to be stored in a battery. Similar systems are found in hand-cranked radios and flashlights and in the braking systems in some electric cars. Bicycles, treadmills, and other exercise machines can be designed to operate without an outside source of electrical energy. They could also generate enough electrical energy to run electric displays or charge small devices such as cell phones.

EXPLAIN Based on the bicycle generator pictured here, how do you think the moving bicycle wheel allows for the generation of electrical energy?

_____

_____

_____

DRIVING QUESTIONS

As you move through the unit, gather evidence to help you answer the following questions. In your Evidence Notebook, record what you already know about these topics and any questions you have about them.

1. What causes electric current?

2. How are electric and magnetic phenomena related?

3. How do power plants generate electrical energy?

4. How can electrical energy be produced more sustainably?

UNIT PROJECT

Go online to download the Unit Project Worksheet to help plan your project.

Transforming Motion into Electrical Energy

In this unit you study electric generators that use kinetic energy from falling water, rising steam, and wind. How much electric current could you generate using your own kinetic energy as the input? Study designs of simple electric generators, and then build one. Use it to light an LED. Demonstrate your generator, and explain how the basic design could be scaled up to provide more energy.

Language Development

Use the lessons in this unit to complete the chart and expand your understanding of the science concepts.

TERM: electrical energy

Definition	Example

Similar Term	Phrase

TERM: voltage

Definition	Example

Similar Term	Phrase

TERM: electric current

Definition	Example

Similar Term	Phrase

TERM: electrical resistance

Definition	Example

Similar Term	Phrase

TERM: electromagnet

Definition	Example

Similar Term	Phrase

TERM: electromagnetic induction

Definition	Example

Similar Term	Phrase

TERM: electric grid

Definition	Example

Similar Term	Phrase

TERM: generator

Definition	Example

Similar Term	Phrase

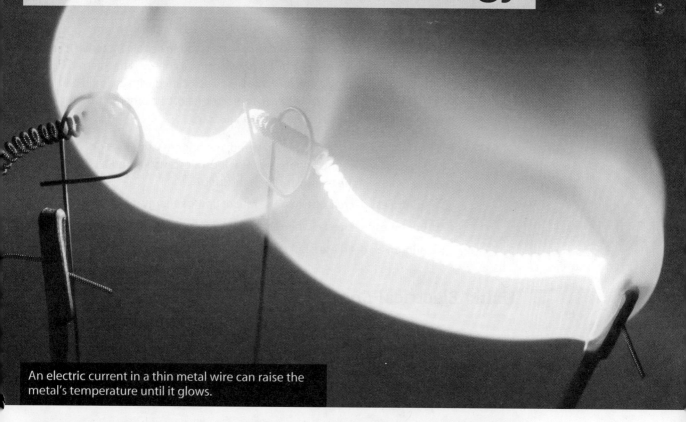

4.1

Flow of Electrical Energy

An electric current in a thin metal wire can raise the metal's temperature until it glows.

CAN YOU EXPLAIN THE PHENOMENON?

An incandescent light bulb contains a thin wire called a filament that glows when there is enough electric current in the filament. The tungsten filament in a typical 100 W incandescent bulb reaches temperatures over 2000 °C. A wire at this temperature would combust if exposed to oxygen, so the filament is encased in a bulb filled with an inert gas. Incandescent bulbs are used in warming lamps and incubators, where the energy released as heat is a benefit. When warming is not wanted, fluorescent or LED bulbs may be a more desirable choice of lighting.

GATHER EVIDENCE Can you think of any similar phenomena that could help explain why the filament glows when an electric current is in the wire?

_____

_____

_____

_____

_____

 Evidence Notebook As you explore the lesson, gather evidence to explain why a thin tungsten wire emits energy as heat and light when connected in an electric circuit.

Describing Electrical Energy

FIGURE 1: A dimmer switch changes the rate of flow of electrical energy in a circuit.

Electrons are negatively charged particles that, within certain materials, can move. The movement of electrons is how electrical energy is transferred in a circuit. Electrical energy is the form of energy associated with charged particles due to their positions and motion in an electric field. Like other forms of energy, electrical energy is measured in joules (J).

INFER When a dimmer switch is lowered, the brightness of the light bulb decreases. How does the brightness of an incandescent light bulb relate to the rate of flow of the energy through the bulb?

○ **a.** Brightness decreases when the rate of flow of energy decreases.

○ **b.** Brightness decreases when the rate of flow of energy increases.

○ **c.** Brightness decreases, but the rate of flow of energy remains the same.

Using Electrical Energy

Like a mass in a gravitational field, a charge in an electric field experiences a force that would move it from a position of higher potential to a position of lower potential. The electric potential difference between two points, voltage, is the amount of work needed to move a unit of electric charge between those two points. Voltage is measured in volts (V). A volt is equal to one joule per coulomb (J/C).

When charged particles move due to an electric potential difference, the electrical energy of the particles may be transformed into other forms of energy, such as thermal, radiant, or mechanical. People use these energy transformations to operate devices from toy cars to full-size electric vehicles, to light homes, or to entertain. Electrical energy may even be transformed into sound energy through electric speakers. Though the energy in a battery is stored in chemical bonds, it is often described as electrical energy because it generates a voltage.

FIGURE 2: Electrical energy can be stored in batteries. Electrical energy can be transformed into radiant energy and sound energy, as it is at a stage show for a music concert.

 Collaborate With a partner, discuss the ways that electrical energy affects your everyday life. Make a poster showing at least two different uses of electrical energy.

Electron Motion

ARGUE Metals have some electrons, called free electrons, that can move throughout the metal. How would one of these electrons move in a metal wire when there is no difference of electric potential across the wire?

○ **a.** It would not move at all.

○ **b.** It would remain in one atom.

○ **c.** It would move throughout a metal but stay in the same area over time.

○ **d.** It would move continuously in one direction.

Free electrons move quickly in different directions. When an electric field acts in the wire, the electrons' average positions slowly drift in a direction aligned with the electric field. The strength of the electric field determines the drift velocity. A stronger electric field accelerates the free electrons more. Because all of the electrons in the electric field experience a force from the electric field, all of the free electrons drift in the same direction at the same time.

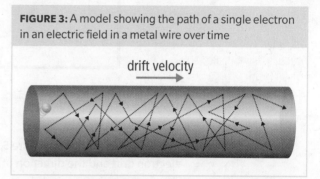

FIGURE 3: A model showing the path of a single electron in an electric field in a metal wire over time

drift velocity

Electric Current

EXPLAIN Electrons in a typical household circuit drift only about 1 cm per hour. Yet, when you flip a light switch to close a circuit, a lamp in the circuit will begin shining almost immediately no matter where it is in the circuit. Explain why the lamp turns on so quickly if the electrons drift so slowly.

_____

_____

_____

An *electric circuit* is a closed loop through which charge can move continuously. When a voltage is applied to a wire, an electric field is generated throughout the wire and a force acts on all of the electrons in the wire. While a single electron may move erratically, it is the net movement of charge in the wire that affects how a circuit behaves. If you measure the rate and direction in which charged particles move though a cross section of the wire in a circuit, you will notice a net flow of charge in one direction due to the electric field. The rate at which charge moves through this cross section is called electric current. Current is measured in amperes (A), or amps, where one ampere is equal to one coulomb per second.

FIGURE 4: A model of the motion of negatively charged electrons in an electric field in a wire

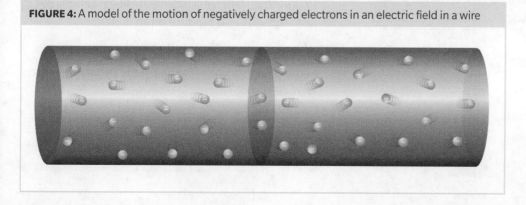

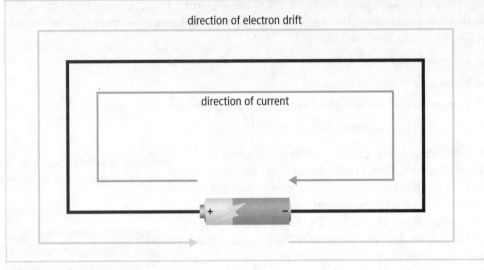

FIGURE 5: A model showing the directions of electron drift and electric current in a circuit in which the positive and negative terminals of a battery are connected by a wire.

direction of electron drift

direction of current

ANALYZE According to Figure 5, what is the relationship between the direction of electron drift and the direction of electric current?

○ **a.** They are the same.   ○ **b.** They are opposite.   ○ **c.** They are not related.

A battery in a circuit provides a voltage that generates an electric current in the circuit. When current was originally described, it was thought that the charge carriers moving in a circuit were positively charged. It was later discovered that the charge carriers were actually negatively charged electrons. However, the convention for the direction of current was maintained despite the discrepancy. Due to this convention, electrons actually drift in the opposite direction of the current.

 Language Arts Connection Research early descriptions of electric current. Make a timeline that shows key discoveries related to circuits, current, and electrons.

FIGURE 6: In a circuit, the field lines point from the positive to the negative terminal.

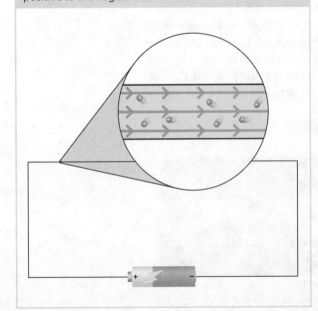

Direct Current

A battery has a negative and a positive terminal that provide a voltage in a circuit. Electrons continually drift toward the positive terminal in a circuit with a battery. When electric current flows in one direction only, it is called *direct current*. Flashlights and other portable electronics with batteries have direct current. Photovoltaic cells, which generate electrical energy from sunlight, also produce direct current.

INFER Describe what would happen to the current in the circuit shown in Figure 6 if the battery direction were reversed.

_____

_____

_____

_____

Alternating Current

An *alternating current* changes direction at regular intervals. Many electrical components, such as incandescent light bulbs, function regardless of the direction of the current. As long as electrons are moving through the circuit, it does not matter whether they are moving continuously in one direction or alternating between directions.

FIGURE 7: In alternating current, electrons accelerate back and forth around an average position as the voltage in the wire alternates.

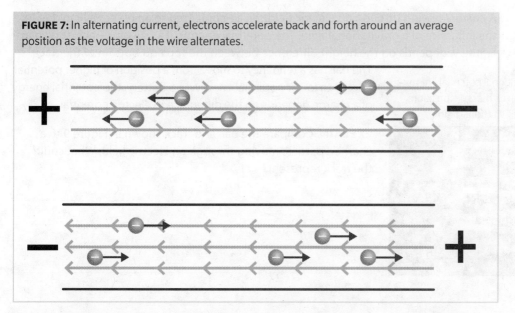

Recall that electrons follow an erratic path, but in the presence of an electric field, the net movement of electrons is in one direction. The net movement of electrons alternates in an alternating current. This high-frequency change of direction means that individual electrons actually travel very little. Rather, it can be more appropriate to say that they wiggle back and forth.

EXPLAIN Batteries discharge direct current. Wall outlets are a source of alternating current. Why might the adapter shown in Figure 8 between the wall outlet and the laptop computer be necessary?

FIGURE 8: A laptop battery requires an adapter to convert alternating current to direct current.

_____

_____

_____

_____

_____

 Evidence Notebook An electric generator, such as the one in the unit project, transforms mechanical energy into electrical energy. Does the type of current produced by a generator matter? Explain why or why not.

 Evidence Notebook Consider the motion of an individual electron in an electric field in a metal wire. Why does the electron move the way it does?

Controlling the Flow of Electrical Energy

A charge moving through an electric field can be compared to an object falling due to the influence of a gravitational field. The potential energy of a ball on a track, shown in Figure 9, depends on the height difference between the top and bottom of the track.

FIGURE 9: The gravitational potential energy of the ball depends on its mass, its position, and strength of the gravitational field.

The ball has a tendency to move from a position of higher potential energy to lower potential energy. In a battery, the potential energy of a charge depends on the difference in electric potential.

EXPLAIN Compare the ball and track shown in Figure 9 to a charged particle moving through an electric field. What could the track represent?

_____

_____

_____

_____

Generating Current

A difference in electrical potential energy produces an electric field. When the positive and negative terminals of a battery are connected by a wire, the electric field in the wire accelerates electrons through the wire, generating an electric current. This current can be measured using a device called an ammeter or visualized using a component such as an incandescent light bulb. An incandescent bulb glows brighter when more current is in the filament of the bulb.

FIGURE 10: The circuit on the right has a battery with twice the voltage of the battery on the left. The ammeter shows that current in the circuit on the right is double the current in the circuit on the left.

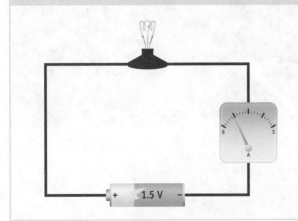
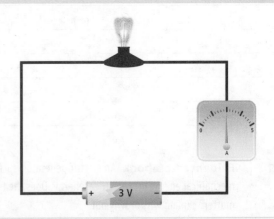

ANALYZE Compare the voltage and current of the two circuits shown in Figure 10. Assuming the pattern holds for other circuits, what is the relationship between current and voltage in a circuit?

O **a.** direct square   O **c.** inverse square

O **b.** inverse proportion   O **d.** direct proportion

The current in a circuit depends on the voltage of its energy source. The higher the voltage, the greater the difference in the potential energy of each electron between the two terminals of the battery. The greater the difference in potential energy, the stronger the electric field produced. An electron at the negative terminal of the battery will be accelerated through the wire toward the positive terminal by this field. As the electron moves, it repels other electrons in front of it. The direction of each electron changes when it collides with other particles, but the electric field causes all of the electrons in the field to drift in the same direction as they move. When the field strength in the circuit increases, the drift velocity of the electrons increases. As the drift velocity increases, the current increases.

Explore Online ▶

Hands-On Lab

Voltaic Pile Build a simple battery.

Limiting Current

Metals and metal alloys—such as copper and nichrome respectively—are good conductors of electrical energy because the free electrons in the metal can easily move throughout the material. In other materials, the electrons may be more strongly bound to their atoms, so the material does not have free electrons. These materials are insulators. Electrical energy does not move through insulators as it does through conductors. Conductors and insulators can be used to control the flow of electrical energy.

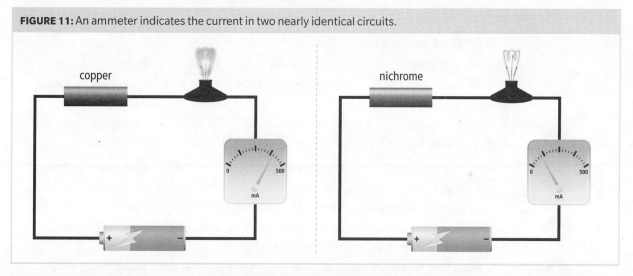

FIGURE 11: An ammeter indicates the current in two nearly identical circuits.

Figure 11 shows two circuits with only one difference between their components. In the circuit on the left, current passes through a wide copper cylinder. In the circuit on the right, the copper cylinder is replaced with one made of nichrome. The ammeter indicates that the current is lower in the circuit with nichrome than in the one with copper.

INFER The ammeters in the two circuits show that the current is higher in the circuit in which the electrons pass through the copper cylinder. Why do you think this is?

○ **a.** The electrons accelerate to a higher speed when they encounter the copper cylinder.

○ **b.** The electrons can escape from the nichrome.

○ **c.** The circuit on the left receives more energy from the battery.

○ **d.** The electrons move more easily through copper than through nichrome.

The difficulty in passing an electric current through an object is a measure of the object's electrical resistance. Resistance is measured in ohms. Copper has a low resistance compared to most other solids, which is one reason it is commonly used in wires. Resistance also depends on shape—the longer a wire, the higher its resistance. As the diameter of the wire increases, its resistance decreases. You can use wider wires to lower the resistance of a circuit.

Alan Spencer/Alamy

Hands-On Lab

Build and Analyze a Simple Circuit

A simple circuit consists of a voltage source, a component with resistance, and wires. In a circuit, current will exist in every resistor between the positive and the negative terminals.

RESEARCH QUESTION How are voltage, resistance, and current related?

MAKE A CLAIM

Given a relatively constant voltage source, such as a battery, how does changing the resistance affect the current in a simple circuit?

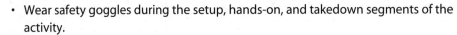
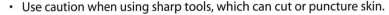
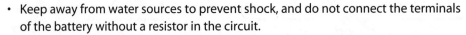

POSSIBLE MATERIALS

- safety goggles
- ammeter
- LED (optional)
- 9V battery
- switch (optional)
- resistors
- wires, copper, 30AWG, shielded

SAFETY INFORMATION

- Wear safety goggles during the setup, hands-on, and takedown segments of the activity.
- Use caution when using sharp tools, which can cut or puncture skin.
- Keep away from water sources to prevent shock, and do not connect the terminals of the battery without a resistor in the circuit.
- Wash your hands with soap and water immediately after completing this activity.

PLAN THE INVESTIGATION

In your Evidence Notebook, develop a procedure for your investigation. Make sure your teacher approves your procedure and safety plan before proceeding.

- Draw a diagram of a simple circuit that you can test to collect data about the relationship between voltage, resistance, and current. One or more resistors may be placed in series (one after the other in the circuit).
- Specify where the ammeter will be placed.
- Open the circuit after making measurements and before making any changes.
- Test at least three different resistance values.

COLLECT DATA

Collect and organize resistance and current data for your simple circuit in your Evidence Notebook.

ANALYZE

1. Make a graph of the current in the circuit for each resistance value.

2. Which equation best matches the relationship between voltage (*V*), current (*I*), and resistance (*R*) shown by your data?

    ○ **a.** $I = R/V$ ○ **c.** $I = VR$

    ○ **b.** $I = V/R$ ○ **d.** $I = 1/VR$

3. Is the current the same at every location in the circuit? Explain why this might be.

_____

_____

4. Explain whether or not you can use your data to predict what the current would be in the circuit if the 9 V battery was replaced with a AA (1.5 V) battery?

_____

_____

CONSTRUCT AN EXPLANATION

Predict how adding a resistor or other component, such as an LED, in series with a second resistor will affect the circuit? Test your prediction and explain the results.

_____

_____

_____

DRAW CONCLUSIONS

Write a conclusion that addresses each of the points below.

Claim Given a relatively constant voltage source, such as a battery, how does changing the resistance affect the current in a simple circuit?

Evidence Give specific evidence from your investigation to support your claim.

Reasoning Given your understanding of electrical energy and resistance, offer reasoning as to why your evidence supports the claim that you have made.

_____

_____

_____

_____

_____

Relating Current, Resistance, and Voltage

In most simple wire circuits, the relationship between current, resistance, and voltage is described by Ohm's law: the electric potential difference between two points in a circuit is equal to the current between the points multiplied by the resistance between the points.

$$\text{voltage} = \text{current} \times \text{resistance}$$

$$V = IR$$

V is measured in volts, I in amperes, and R in ohms. Current is directly proportional to voltage. For a component with constant resistance, when the voltage is halved, the current is also halved. Current varies inversely with resistance. For a component with a constant voltage, when the resistance is halved, the current doubles.

Ohm's law accurately relates voltage, current, and resistance in most materials. However, some materials do not follow this relationship. They are called non-ohmic materials. Temperature may affect the resistivity of a material. For example, the current through an incandescent light bulb stays relatively constant, even when the voltage across the bulb increases, because the resistance increases with the increasing temperature.

Problem Solving

Using Ohm's Law

SAMPLE PROBLEM

A circuit contains a battery and a 3.0-ohm resistor. The battery has a voltage of 1.5 volts. Find the current in the circuit.

ANALYZE

Known: $V = 1.5$ volts, $R = 3.0$ ohms

$V = IR$

Unknown: current I

PLAN

Solve Ohm's law for I. Substitute the values for V and R, and calculate I.

SOLVE

$V = IR$

$I = V / R$

$I = (1.5 \text{ volts}) / (3.0 \text{ ohms})$

$I = 0.50$ amps

CHECK YOUR WORK

Multiply: $IR = (0.50 \text{ amps})(3.0 \text{ ohms}) = 1.5$ volts, as expected.

PRACTICE PROBLEMS

SOLVE Answer the following questions:

1. Find the voltage in a circuit with a resistance of 15 ohms and current of 3.0 amps. _____

2. Find the current in a circuit with a resistance of 15 ohms and a voltage of 12 volts. _____

3. Find the resistance in a circuit with a voltage of 4.5 volts and a current of 1.5 amps. _____

4. How must the resistance in a circuit change for the current to remain constant when the voltage doubles? _____

Electrical and Thermal Energy

Current is a means of transferring electrical energy. If something resists that current—such as a high-resistance element in a circuit—some of the electrical energy is transformed into thermal energy. The electrical energy input into this system is equal to the sum of the electrical and thermal energy outputs.

When the accelerated electrons collide with the atoms of the wire, they impart more energy to the atoms, making them vibrate more, thereby increasing the temperature of the wire. The more moving electrons (current) or the higher the voltage across a component, the greater the energy transfer by the collisions, hence the greater the heat generated by the wire.

DESIGN Consider two different uses of electrical energy. Explain whether heat is a desired output for each use and whether a higher- or lower-resistance component is desired for the application.

_____

_____

_____

_____

FIGURE 12: Current in the metal coils of a toaster causes them to emit energy as both heat and light.

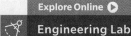

Explore Online ▶

Engineering Lab

Testing a Battery-Operated Heater Design a portable heater.

Influence of Engineering, Technology, and Science on Society and the Natural World

Electrical Energy and Society

Modern society depends on electrical energy to run many critical devices such as refrigerators and life-saving hospital equipment. Electrical energy is also commonly used in entertainment, from movies to video games. The development of the electric grid has made electrical energy widely available and the wide availability of electrical energy has led to more devices being designed to use this energy. Society's dependence on electrical energy has had many effects on society and the natural world.

FIGURE 13: Modern homes have many devices that require electrical energy to operate.

ANALYZE Which of the following are results of society's increasing use of electrical energy? Select all correct answers.

- [ ] **a.** increased greenhouse gas emissions due to electrical energy generation
- [ ] **b.** career opportunities focused on designing electrical devices
- [ ] **c.** new communication devices and increased information accessibility
- [ ] **d.** increased reliance on personal vehicles for transportation

---

📓 **Evidence Notebook** How do the microscopic interactions of electrons and the macroscopic behavior of current, voltage, and resistance explain energy transformations in an electric heater?

Spencer/Alamy; (b) ©Kevin Miller/Alamy

Case Study: Developing the Light Bulb

The need for human-controlled sources of light has existed for centuries. People need light to do work and stay safe. Some early solutions to meet this need were controlled uses of fire such as in candles and lanterns.

EVALUATE For each statement, state whether it describes a benefit, a cost, or a risk associated with using fire as a source of light.

FIGURE 14: A lantern uses fire as a portable light source.

cost   risk   benefit

Consequence of using fire as a light source	Cost/risk/benefit
Gas combustion releases toxins that pollute the air.	_____
Gas light also warms the room on a cold night.	_____
Unattended fires may spread.	_____
Candles and oil lanterns have a lifespan of hours.	_____
Candles are inexpensive and easy to store.	_____

Electric Lighting

In the early 1800s, scientists discovered that an electric current could pass over a small gap from one electrode to another, forming a bright arc. This discovery led to the development of arc lamps. The first arc lamps used a continuous spark between two carbon rods. Arc lamps needed a direct current to maintain the arc. They are very bright, but also very hot. They flickered and emitted sparks and made a buzzing noise. Despite their drawbacks, by the late 1800s arc lamps were used to light streets, department stores, and lighthouses, where their ability to light large areas was desirable. During operation, they emit UV radiation and can cause radio interference. Arc lamps are still used for specific applications where very bright light or UV radiation is needed.

FIGURE 15: During operation, an arc of electrical energy crosses the space between the electrodes in an arc lamp.

IDENTIFY CONSTRAINTS Most homes continued to use gas lanterns or candles for almost a century after the discovery of arc lamps. What obstacles existed that limited the adoption of electric lights in residential homes?

_____

_____

_____

_____

_____

Early Incandescent Light Bulbs

By 1900, a new kind of electric light bulb called the incandescent light bulb was available. These bulbs required less voltage than arc lamps, making them a safer alternative. In an incandescent bulb, a current in a thin filament causes the filament to become hot and emit light. The filament would burn quickly if exposed to oxygen, so the bulbs required the filament to be enclosed in a vacuum.

FIGURE 16: The incandescent light bulb was a safer, dimmer alternative to arc lamps.

Many scientists investigated different materials and manufacturing techniques to make an incandescent bulb that was safe, long lasting, and bright enough for practical use. The incandescent light bulb has been improved continually since its invention. Simultaneously, a reliable electric grid was developed, leading to widespread adoption of light bulbs.

Language Arts Connection Research Thomas Edison and his team to learn more about their role in the adoption of the incandescent light bulb. Make a digital presentation summarizing your research.

 Engineering

Optimizing the Light Bulb

Since it was first developed, the brightness and durability of the incandescent bulb has been improved. It was first demonstrated in the early 1800s that a thin platinum strip would glow due to an electric current, but the hot platinum quickly combusted with oxygen in the air. Soon, many scientists attempted to use this phenomenon to make a light bulb, but they had difficulty removing all of the air from the bulbs to prevent combustion of the filament. Thomas Edison's breakthrough was in being able to successfully remove all of the air from the bulb and doing so in a way that made manufacturing practical.

Edison and others continued to experiment with different filament materials and shapes to improve the brightness, efficiency, and lifetime of the incandescent bulb. Platinum, carbonized thread and paper, bamboo, cellulose, tantalum, and tungsten were all used to make filaments at one point in time. Today, tungsten is the most common filament material in incandescent bulbs.

EXPLAIN The filament in a modern incandescent bulb is a long thin strand of tungsten. This strand is tightly coiled and then shaped in a larger loop. This increases the surface area of the filament compared to using a single strand in a loop. How does changing the shape of the filament in this way affect the circuit?

_____

_____

_____

_____

_____

Improving Energy Efficiency

The brightness of incandescent bulbs is related to their power, or rate of energy use. Power is measured in watts (W). A watt equals 1 J/s. Because incandescent bulbs were the standard for so long, their power use is commonly used to describe their brightness. Brightness can be measured in lumens. A lumen (lm) is a measure of the amount of radiant energy emitted from a point source. A standard 60 W incandescent light bulb produces 800 lm. Different types of bulbs operate at different power levels to produce light of the same brightness. To compare the brightness of light sources, look at how many lumens they emit.

Approximate Power Usage of Light Bulbs				
Bulb type	450 lm	800 lm	1100 lm	1600 lm
Incandescent, standard	40 W	60 W	75 W	100 W
Compact fluorescent (CFL)	10 W	15 W	18 W	23 W
Light-emitting diode (LED)	7 W	11 W	14 W	17 W

EVALUATE Based on the table, which type of bulb is most efficient—produces the most light using the least power?

○ **a.** Incandescent, standard ○ **b.** CFL ○ **c.** LED

FIGURE 17: Each bulb type has a different lifespan, efficiency, safety, and price.

Comparing Light Bulbs

Energy efficiency is only one of the differences among the most common kinds of light bulbs. The potential lifetime also depends on the type of bulb. An incandescent light bulb can operate for about 1000 hours. Fluorescent lights may last 10 times longer than a standard incandescent, and an LED can last 15 to 25 times longer than standard incandescent light bulbs. Another important factor is safety. Incandescent and LED bulbs are similarly safe when their useful life is over. CFLs must be disposed of as hazardous waste because they contain small amounts of mercury. Broken CFLs should be swept up carefully, and the area should be wiped with a wet towel to remove traces of mercury.

 Collaborate With a partner, make a list of criteria and constraints that affect the choice of light bulbs for household use.

APPLY Like a house, the International Space Station (ISS) needs light sources. Describe different constraints and criteria that would likely apply to lighting the ISS.

_____

_____

_____

 Evidence Notebook Hatching chicks are kept under special lights to warm the air in the incubator. Explain what type of light bulbs might be used in an incubator and why.

Careers in Science

Electrician

FIGURE 18: An electrician installs wire in a building.

Every time you flip a light switch or plug in an electrical device, you can thank an electrician. Electricians wire, install, and test electrical systems in buildings. After the foundation is built and the walls of a building have been framed but not covered, electricians install the wires, light switches, and wall outlets, and they connect the public electrical lines to the circuit breaker of a building. Electricians also focus on maintaining existing systems. They troubleshoot problems and fix systems that are not working properly.

Electricians specialize in as many areas as there are uses for electrical energy. Many focus on residential, commercial, or industrial buildings. Electricians called line workers specialize in high-voltage wires that transmit electrical energy from power plants to buildings. Gaffers specialize in the electrical systems that support television and movie production. Auto electricians specialize in electrical systems in vehicles.

In addition to knowledge of electric circuit architecture and electrical components, electricians must also be familiar with codes and regulations related to their field of work. The wiring in buildings is regulated to minimize fire hazards and to ensure that connections to the electric grid are controlled.

Requirements to become a licensed electrician vary by region. Most electricians start out with a four- or five-year apprenticeship. Apprentice electricians work with a master electrician and often take additional formalized training. Apprentices must have a high school diploma and a good understanding of algebra.

> **Language Arts Connection** Research the diagrams used by electricians to describe the wiring for an item in a home, such as a switch, a ceiling fan, or a refrigerator. Select and print a diagram to use for a poster. Add labels to show the movement of electrons in the circuit. Then gather in groups to present and explain your posters.

ENERGY IN BATTERIES **VOLTAIC PILE** ⚡ **TESTING A BATTERY-OPERATED HEATER** Go online to choose one of these other paths.

Lesson Self-Check

CAN YOU EXPLAIN THE PHENOMENON?

FIGURE 19: When electric current passes through a thin tungsten wire, the metal emits energy as heat and light.

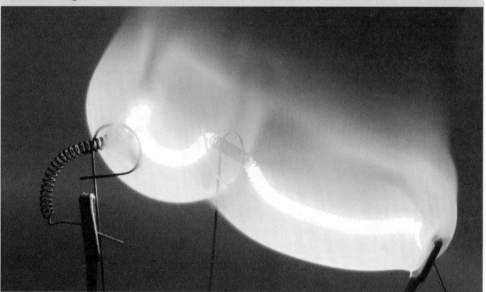

An electric potential difference generates an electric field, which causes a current in a circuit. Metals and metal alloys conduct electrical energy and are an important part of circuits. In a metal, free electrons can move throughout the metal. In the presence of an electric field, the free electrons drift in one direction over time, though collisions with other electrons and particles cause the electrons to move erratically. The shape, size, and structure of a material affects the resistance of the material. The more often electrons collide with other particles, the slower the drift velocity of the electrons. A slower drift velocity means reduced current.

 Evidence Notebook Refer to your notes in your Evidence Notebook to explain what energy transformations and transfers happen in a tungsten wire in an electric circuit. Use evidence and reasoning to support your claim.

Claim Why does a thin tungsten wire emit energy as heat and light when connected in an electric circuit?

Evidence Give evidence from the lesson and your observations to support your claim about a tungsten wire in an electric circuit.

Reasoning Describe in detail the connections between the evidence you cited and the claim you are making about a tungsten wire in an electric circuit.

CHECKPOINTS

Check Your Understanding

1. The table gives the voltage, current, and resistance in different circuits. Fill in the missing values using Ohm's law.

Voltage (volts)	Current (amps)	Resistance (ohms)
6.0	2.0	_____
6.0	0.50	_____
4.5	_____	1.0
_____	9.0	0.50

2. Select the correct terms to complete the statement.

A 1000 W microwave takes in 1000 J/s of electrical energy. A cup of water requires approximately 78 000 J to be warmed for tea. If the microwave is used to warm the cup of water, it will take less than | exactly | more than 78 s to warm the water because all | most of the original electrical energy input into the microwave will be transferred to the water.

3. Which are transformations that occur in an incandescent light bulb? Select all correct answers.
- ☐ **a.** electrical to thermal energy
- ☐ **b.** electrical to radiant energy
- ☐ **c.** chemical to electrical energy
- ☐ **d.** thermal to chemical energy
- ☐ **e.** mechanical to radiant energy

4. If the resistance in a wire greatly increases, what would you infer will happen to the motion of an electron in an electric field in the wire?
- ○ **a.** It will remain unchanged.
- ○ **b.** It will continue in a straight line.
- ○ **c.** It will have fewer collisions.
- ○ **d.** It will have more collisions.

5. Select the correct terms to complete the statement.

If the drift velocity of electrons increased, the current would increase | decrease | stay the same. If the voltage causing the electric field increased, the drift velocity of the electrons would increase | decrease | stay the same. If the resistance in the wire increased, the drift velocity of the electrons would increase | decrease | stay the same.

6. Electrons in a wire move in response to an electric field. What generates this field?
- ○ **a.** resistance
- ○ **b.** moving charges
- ○ **c.** the loop of wire
- ○ **d.** electric potential difference

7. Which of the following are accurate descriptions of voltage? Select all correct answers.
- ☐ **a.** the ratio of current and resistance
- ☐ **b.** the product of current and resistance
- ☐ **c.** the potential electrical energy
- ☐ **d.** the potential energy per unit mass
- ☐ **e.** the potential energy difference per unit charge

8. The voltage in a circuit is increased while the resistance remains the same. Select all correct answers.
- ☐ **a.** The electrical energy in the circuit increases.
- ☐ **b.** The electrical energy in the circuit decreases.
- ☐ **c.** The current in the circuit increases.
- ☐ **d.** The current in the circuit decreases.
- ☐ **e.** The energy that can be output by the circuit increases.
- ☐ **f.** The energy that can be output by the circuit decreases.

9. Select the correct terms to complete the statement.

Society regulates the efficiency of light bulbs to minimize | maximize energy use, because many sources of electrical energy have costs | benefits related to the environment.

CHECKPOINTS (continued)

10. Circuits in buildings are equipped with circuit breakers, which open a circuit to prevent too much current in the circuit. Why is it dangerous for large amounts of current to be in a circuit?

_____

_____

_____

_____

11. The invention of the light bulb led to a need for reliable electrical energy and the development of the electric grid. Give at least one example of how the electric grid has affected modern society.

_____

_____

_____

_____

12. A copper wire contains many free electrons, which can easily move throughout the wire. A potential difference is introduced between the two ends of the wire. What happens to an electron in the middle of the wire? How does it affect nearby electrons?

_____

_____

_____

_____

MAKE YOUR OWN STUDY GUIDE

In your Evidence Notebook, design a study guide that supports the main ideas from this lesson:

Electrical energy can refer to energy stored in a battery or to energy transferred by electric currents.

Voltage, current, and resistance in a circuit are related by $V = IR$.

Electrical energy can be transformed into other forms including thermal, radiant, and mechanical energy.

Remember to include the following information in your study guide:
- Use examples that model main ideas.
- Record explanations for the phenomena you investigated.
- Use evidence to support your explanations. Your support can include drawings, data, graphs, laboratory conclusions, and other evidence recorded throughout the lesson.

Consider how energy transforms from electrical to other forms and back.

Electromagnets and Inducing Current

A cell phone rests on a recharging station.

CAN YOU EXPLAIN THE PHENOMENON?

In some settings, connecting an electrical device and an energy source through a long wire would be difficult or unsafe. In wet environments, water can lead to a short circuit. If there is a lot of motion, the cord can dislodge. Users of wireless charging technology choose it for a broad range of reasons, including safety, convenience, and aesthetics. Wireless charging devices for small electronics, such as those for electric toothbrushes and cell phones, are gradually becoming more common.

EXPLAIN The battery of a laptop computer or cell phone can be recharged through a cord connecting the device to a wall outlet. When the connection is made, electrons flow through the circuit and recharge the battery. What could be used in place of the cord in this circuit as a way to transfer electrical energy?

_____

_____

_____

_____

_____

 Evidence Notebook As you explore the lesson, gather evidence to explain how wireless chargers use electric and magnetic phenomena to transfer energy without a physical connection.

Generating Magnetic Fields

EXPLAIN Identify two or more applications of permanent magnets, and explain what function they serve.

_____

_____

_____

Magnetic Fields and Transportation

Magnetic levitation, or maglev, trains use magnetic forces for propulsion. Both the attractive and repulsive aspects of magnets are used to levitate the train shown in Figure 1a, almost eliminating the friction between the train and its track. Magnetic attraction and repulsion are also used to accelerate the train forward and bring it to a stop.

FIGURE 1: Magnetic fields propel magnetic levitation trains and magnetically launched roller coasters.

a Maglev train

b Magnetically launched roller coaster

In the magnetically launched roller coaster in Figure 1b, a magnetic field along the start of the track propels the car. Unlike traditional roller coasters, magnetically launched coaster cars can continue moving higher after leaving the initial launch mechanism if the magnetic field propelling them is adjusted properly. Similar technologies are used to open and close sliding doors and move parts through factories.

INFER Maglev trains carry varying numbers of passengers and levitate at a consistent height even when passengers move around inside the train. Which of the following technologies could engineers use to keep a maglev train's motion stable?

○ **a.** very large magnets

○ **b.** single-pole magnets

○ **c.** very strong magnets

○ **d.** adjustable-strength magnets

Hands-On Lab
Electromagnets

Early experiments with electric current provided evidence of a connection between electric current and magnetic fields. You will investigate this connection.

RESEARCH QUESTION How is magnetism related to electric current?

MAKE A CLAIM

How do current-carrying wires affect objects that respond to magnetic fields?

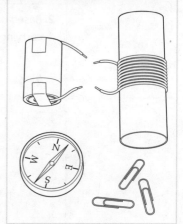

FIGURE 2: Insulated copper wire is formed into a coil and can be connected to a battery. Paper clips and a compass can detect a magnetic field.

POSSIBLE MATERIALS

- safety goggles
- balloon
- cardboard tube
- cloth, wool
- compass
- copper wire, insulated
- D-cell battery
- electrical tape
- iron nail or rod
- paper clips, metal
- wire cutters and wire strippers

SAFETY INFORMATION

- Wear safety goggles during the setup, hands-on, and takedown segments of the activity.
- Use caution when using sharp tools and materials, which can cut or puncture skin.
- Handle wires in the electromagnet by the insulated parts, so that your body does not become part of the circuit.
- This low-resistance circuit can become hot. Disconnect the battery each time you complete a set of observations. When the circuit is connected, do not directly touch the wire.
- Wash your hands with soap and water immediately after completing this activity.

PLAN THE INVESTIGATION

In your Evidence Notebook, develop a procedure for your investigation. Make sure your teacher approves your procedure and safety plan before proceeding.

- Refer to Figure 2 for a model of how to form the coil of wire.
- Strip a centimeter of insulation off the ends of a wire to form electrical connections.
- If you want to test the effect of a static electric charge for comparison, charge a rubber balloon and test its effects on the paper clips and compass.
- Plan to first investigate a coil of wire formed around a cardboard tube. Then, plan to conduct at least one investigation with a coil of wire formed around an iron nail or rod.

In your Evidence Notebook, sketch the designs of your circuits. Indicate the shape, position, and orientation of each component. Sketch at least two different configurations you will use for testing. Include any items used to detect the magnetic field.

ANALYZE

1. What evidence indicates the presence of a magnetic field when the circuit is connected?

_____

_____

_____

2. Based on your observations, draw the magnetic field lines around a coil of wire carrying current. The arrow indicates the direction of the current.

3. What happened to the magnetic field when you disconnected the battery?

_____

_____

_____

4. How did adding the iron nail or rod to your coil affect the magnetic field?

_____

_____

_____

DRAW CONCLUSIONS

Write a conclusion that addresses each of the points below.

Claim How can a magnetic field be generated using current? How does this compare to your initial claim?

Evidence What evidence from your experiments supports your claim?

Reasoning Explain how the evidence you gave supports your claim. Describe in detail the connections between the evidence you cited and the argument you are making.

_____

_____

_____

_____

Electromagnets and Permanent Magnets

An electromagnet uses electric current in a wire to generate a magnetic field. The field can be strengthened by increasing the number of coils or by increasing the current. Adding a ferromagnetic core, such as an iron rod, in the middle of the coils will also increase an electromagnet's strength. The magnetic field of the wire causes the magnetic fields of the atoms in the core to align, which produces a stronger magnetic field. An electromagnet's magnetic field can be varied by changing the current. Like the maglev train and the magnetically launched roller coaster earlier in this lesson, many technologies rely on electromagnets.

INFER Which of the following generates the magnetic field in electromagnets and permanent magnets?

○ **a.** voltage source

○ **b.** moving electrons

○ **c.** stationary electrons

The magnetism of permanent magnets, such as bar magnets or pieces of the mineral magnetite, arises from the motion of electrons within atoms. At the atomic level, all magnets are electromagnets. Individual electrons each spin in some way, causing each electron to generate a small magnetic field around itself. Electrons move and therefore generate an additional magnetic field. Whether these individual magnetic fields cancel or reinforce each other depends on the material. In most materials, these magnetic fields cancel one another out. In permanent magnets, the fields are aligned. In materials that can become magnetized, such as iron, the small magnetic fields can be aligned to match a large outside field. When a permanent magnet is removed from a piece of iron, some residual magnetism is observed in the iron.

 Cause and Effect

Causation and Correlation

Electric current and magnetism are related. The electromagnet in Figure 3 uses the connection between electric current and magnetism to move heavy magnetic objects. However, without empirical evidence, it can be difficult to determine whether one phenomenon is the cause of another or if they are simply correlated. For example, high ice cream sales are correlated with high sunscreen sales. If one occurs, the other is also likely. However, people do not buy sunscreen because they bought ice cream.

FIGURE 3: A powerful electromagnet

APPLY Scientists have determined that electric current causes a magnetic field. What evidence demonstrates this cause-and-effect relationship?

_____

_____

_____

_____

_____

Magnetic Field Direction

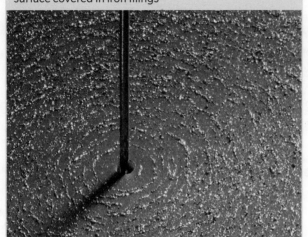

EXPLAIN In Figure 4, tiny pieces of iron called iron filings lie on a horizontal surface pierced by a vertical current-carrying wire. The iron filings, like compass needles, align themselves with the magnetic field. Describe the shape of the magnetic field. Why might the field be this shape?

_____

_____

_____

_____

A current-carrying wire generates a magnetic field. The field forms a circle around the wire. The direction of the field depends on the direction of current. Take, for instance, the wire in Figure 4. The current in the wire is directed downward. The direction of the magnetic field around the wire is clockwise when viewed from above. The direction of the magnetic field around a current-carrying wire can be modeled with a person's right hand. When a person points their right thumb in the direction of the current and coils their right fingers, their fingers point in the direction of the magnetic field. This method for modeling magnetic field direction is referred to as the right-hand rule. When applying the right-hand rule, recall that the direction of current is opposite that of electron motion.

ANALYZE Assume the electrons in a vertical wire flow upward. In what direction do the magnetic field lines point when viewed from above?

○ **a.** outward from the wire   ○ **c.** counterclockwise

○ **b.** in toward the wire   ○ **d.** clockwise

MODEL Using the right-hand rule, draw the magnetic field around the electron's path. Make a key for your drawing, indicating what symbols indicate field lines into and out of the page. What is the direction of the field at point **a**?

a

Evidence Notebook Explain the similarities and differences between permanent magnets and electromagnets.

Generating Current Using Magnets

A magnetic field forms around an electric current. This field affects compass needles, iron filings, and other test objects in the same way the magnetic field around a bar magnet does. This behavior indicates that magnetic and electric phenomena are connected.

PREDICT You determined that an electric current in a wire generates a magnetic field. Do you think a magnetic field can generate an electric current? Explain your answer.

_____

_____

_____

Energy Transformations in Generators

A bicycle generator is one way to produce electrical energy without connecting to an electric grid or a battery. Bicycle generators are stationary bicycles that use the motion of a rider's pedaling to generate electrical energy. When the pedals are stationary, no electric current exists in the circuit. When a rider pedals, electric current is generated in the wire. This current is sufficient to run or recharge small appliances.

EVALUATE A bicycle generator outputs electrical energy. What type of energy is input to the system?

○ **a.** electrical energy   ○ **c.** magnetic potential energy

○ **b.** gravitational potential energy   ○ **d.** kinetic energy

Figure 5 shows a diagram of the subsystems within a wind turbine. The electric generator highlighted in the figure has an input of kinetic energy in the form of rotational motion and outputs electrical energy. Generators can use other sources of kinetic energy, such as a flowing liquid like a river or tides. A human turning a crank can also act as the source of kinetic energy. The opposite energy transformation takes place in an electric *motor*, which is a device that has an input of electrical energy and outputs kinetic energy, usually as motion of a crank or shaft. Some generators can be adapted to function as motors, and some motors can be adapted to function as generators.

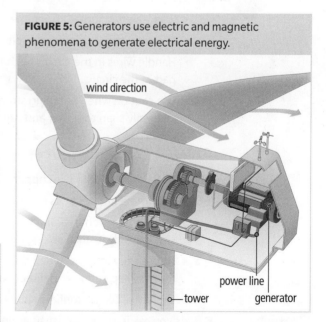

FIGURE 5: Generators use electric and magnetic phenomena to generate electrical energy.

wind direction

power line

tower   generator

 Evidence Notebook How might you use these ideas about sources of kinetic energy to help you determine what types of motion to use in designing your generator in the unit project?

Hands-On Lab
Inducing Current

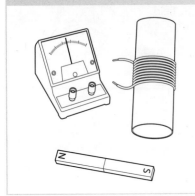

FIGURE 6: The wire coil from the Electromagnets lab, a bar magnet, and an ammeter to detect current

The modern world runs on electrical energy, but how does society generate and transfer this energy? You have seen that electric current in a wire causes a magnetic field around a coil. In this lab, you will investigate whether a magnetic field near a coil can generate an electric current in the coil.

RESEARCH QUESTION How do magnetic fields affect coils of wire?

MAKE A CLAIM

How might it be possible to generate an electric current with a magnet?

_____

_____

_____

_____

POSSIBLE MATERIALS

- safety goggles
- ammeter, analog with microampere resolution, or galvanometer
- magnet, neodymium or rare-earth
- cardboard tube

- magnet, standard bar, size that can fit one end inside the tube
- copper wire, enough to coil 60 times, ends stripped, wrapped around the tube with its ends free

SAFETY INFORMATION

- Wear safety goggles during the setup, hands-on, and takedown segments of the activity.
- Use caution when using sharp tools and materials, which can cut or puncture skin.
- Handle wires in the circuit by the insulated parts, so that your body does not become part of the circuit.
- Use caution when handling strong magnets. Some magnets are strong enough to suddenly snap together and cause injury.

CARRY OUT THE INVESTIGATION

1. Make a circuit with the copper wire coil and ammeter, but no battery.
2. Start the ammeter at its lowest setting, microamperes, to detect small currents.
3. Check the current reading when the magnet is far from the coil of wire, sitting next to it, sitting inside it, and moving near it. Try moving the magnet in different ways.
4. Notice the moments when the ammeter shows a current has been generated. Try to repeat the position and direction of the magnet to generate a predictable current.
5. Explore different configurations of wire coils, and make use of different magnets.

As you carry out your investigation, record your observations in your Evidence Notebook. Be aware of your procedure's limitations and make sure to use an appropriate level of accuracy when recording your measurements.

ANALYZE

1. What factors affect the current generated in the wire?

_____

_____

_____

_____

2. How can the procedure be modified to reverse the direction of the current?

_____

_____

_____

_____

3. In your investigation, you moved a magnet near a stationary coil of wire. What would happen if you held the magnet stationary and moved the coil of wire?

_____

_____

_____

_____

DRAW CONCLUSIONS

Claim How can a magnetic field generate current in a coil of wire? Was your initial claim correct?

Evidence What evidence from your experiments supports your claim?

Reasoning Explain how the evidence you gave supports your claim. Describe in detail the connections between the evidence you cited and the argument you are making.

_____

_____

_____

_____

_____

EXTEND

How can you increase the magnitude of the current generated?

_____

_____

_____

Relating Electric Current and Magnetism

Electric and magnetic phenomena are closely related and often discussed together as electromagnetism. Many modern technologies apply electromagnetism to transfer energy over a short distance.

Electromagnetic Induction

The presence of an electric charge, such as a balloon with a static charge, is not enough to generate a magnetic field. Similarly, a magnet laid near a wire will not cause a current. However, a moving charge will cause a magnetic field to form around the charge. In turn, a changing magnetic field near a wire will cause an electric field and generate a current in the wire. Electromagnetic induction is the formation of a voltage across a conductor in a changing magnetic field. When electromagnetic induction causes a current to form, it is said that current has been induced. A current can be induced in a coil of wire by placing it in a changing magnetic field with no need for physical contact between the wire and a battery. This method of transferring and transforming energy is crucial to the design of many electrical systems, including generators and the electric grid.

Electromagnetism and Force

A changing magnetic field exerts a force on a charged particle. This force affects electrons constrained within wires differently depending on the relative shape and orientation of the wire and the magnetic field. In some cases, this interaction induces a current in the wire, as in an electric generator. In other cases, it can cause the wire to move, as in an electric motor.

EXPLAIN Summarize the connections between electric and magnetic phenomena.

_____

_____

_____

Electromagnetism in Nature

All magnetism is caused by moving charged particles. In solids such as bar magnets, ferromagnetic materials, and electromagnets, this motion is confined to the movement of electrons. Magnetic fields can also arise from the motion of charged particles in a fluid or in space. Earth's magnetic field arises from the motion of charged particles in molten iron alloys within Earth's core. The regular circulation of these charged particles has similarities to the current in a wire coil.

 Language Arts Connection Select a star or a planetary body other than Earth. Research its magnetic field and the related internal processes. Make a poster comparing how the movement of charged particles generates the magnetic field of the body you researched and the magnetic field of Earth.

 Evidence Notebook Suppose you have a rechargeable battery, such as that in an electric car. Explain how you could design a charger for a garage or public parking area that would not require a cord.

Designing with Electromagnetism

ANALYZE What everyday phenomena rely on electromagnetism?

_____

_____

_____

Electromagnetism and Technology

Electromagnetic technology has wide-reaching effects on society. The fan in Figure 7a, mixers, and other motors use electromagnets to transform electrical energy into kinetic energy and are used to move air, mix materials, or move objects. The speaker in Figure 7b converts electrical signals into vibrations that produce sound waves using electromagnets. Streams of charged particles are directed by magnetic fields in electron microscopes. Electromagnetic induction, often just referred to as induction, is used to transfer electrical energy across an electric grid. These technologies facilitate entertainment, comfort, scientific research, and communications.

FIGURE 7: Fans and speakers are designed to use electromagnetism.

a fan

b loudspeaker

  Influence of Engineering, Technology, and Science on Society and the Natural World

Communication Using Induction

FIGURE 8: Cell phone tower

Understanding the connection between electric and magnetic fields made it possible to transmit information across great distances. This principle is applied in radio, telephones, wireless Internet, and other technologies. Messages that once took months to travel over land and sea are now transmitted and received in seconds.

  Language Arts Connection Research a means of communication that relies on electromagnetic phenomena. Make a poster that illustrates how this form of communication has influenced society.

Engineering a Motor

FIGURE 9: Toy car

Electric motors are integral to many everyday devices. Some are attached to fans and are used for cooling, heating, or drying. Others are used to propel machines, such as automobiles. All electric motors are devices that convert electrical energy into kinetic energy using electromagnetism.

Your company is designing inexpensive, battery-powered toy cars much like the one in Figure 9. There are many similar toys on the market right now, so your company needs a way to make your toy stand out. The Market Research department has identified that children between the ages of five and eight are primarily interested in fast-moving toys. Therefore, they have tasked you with designing an extremely fast spinning direct current (dc) motor for use in the toy cars. Recent budget cuts have impacted your Research & Development department. You do not have funding to purchase materials, so you must construct your prototype using only those materials already available in the warehouse.

DESIGN CHALLENGE Use the engineering design process to brainstorm, construct, test, and improve the design of an electric motor that can spin quickly and is made from available materials.

POSSIBLE MATERIALS

- safety goggles, heat-resistant gloves
- 1.5V AA batteries (4)
- 9V, C-cell, or D-cell battery
- battery holders (for 2 AA batteries or 4 AA batteries)
- cardboard, corrugated
- clay
- craft knife

- copper wire—copper, enamel-insulated covered (also called magnet wire)
- cylinders, assorted dimensions (could use batteries)
- duct tape
- magnets, neodymium and/or standard ceramic

- paper clips, large
- rubber bands, nonlatex
- sandpaper, for stripping ends of wire
- wire cutters
- wire leads with alligator clips
- wood or other material for a base

SAFETY INFORMATION

- Wear safety goggles and heat-resistant gloves during the setup, hands-on, and takedown segments of the activity.

- Use caution when using sharp tools, which can cut or puncture skin.

- Do not touch exposed current-carrying wire. While holding wires or batteries for any closed circuit, wear gloves that are thick enough to insulate from high temperatures and electric current, yet thin enough to allow for careful handling of materials.

- The wire coils may heat up rapidly during this experiment. If the device temperature increases too rapidly or becomes dangerously high, open the circuit immediately and allow the wire to cool.

- Make sure you disconnect wires from batteries after each test.

- Use caution when handling strong magnets. Some magnets are strong enough to suddenly snap together and cause injury.

CONDUCT RESEARCH

Use online and print resources to answer these questions.

1. Explain what a simple dc motor is and how it functions. Describe the field interactions that cause the motor's shaft to spin.

_____

_____

_____

_____

2. Describe the energy transformations that occur in a dc motor system.

_____

_____

_____

3. Research several different examples of simple dc motors. What properties are consistent across the motor designs, and what properties vary in different designs?

_____

_____

_____

DEFINE THE PROBLEM

Now that you have a basic understanding of the operation and structure of dc motors, it is time to engineer your own device.

1. Explain the design problem in your own words.

_____

_____

_____

2. Describe the criteria for a successful solution, being clear and specific so the criteria can be used to evaluate possible solutions. What criteria are specific to the intended user?

_____

_____

_____

3. Describe the constraints that limit possible solutions, being clear and specific so the constraints can be used to evaluate possible solutions. What constraints are specific to the intended user?

_____

_____

_____

DESIGN SOLUTIONS

1. As a team, brainstorm motor designs based on what you have learned from your research. Refer to your research notes for inspiration.

_____

_____

_____

_____

2. In your Evidence Notebook, make a decision matrix based on the criteria you identified. Use this decision matrix to evaluate at least three possible solutions. Also evaluate the possible solutions against the constraints you identified, recording your analysis. Select the most promising solution based on how it well satisfies the criteria and constraints.

3. Sketch a model of your design. Use labels to identify each system component and its role in the motor's operation.

4. In your Evidence Notebook, develop a plan for building your prototype. As you develop the plan, make sure to include the materials and technology you will use, as well as what safety precautions you will take. Have your teacher approve your procedure and safety plan before you build your prototype.

TEST

1. In your Evidence Notebook, develop a plan for testing your prototype. Write out a description of your plan, and make sure to include:

   - how you will test the system components
   - materials and technology you will need
   - necessary safety procedures
   - measurements you will use to evaluate the overall performance of the motor

2. Consult with your teacher to obtain approval for your testing procedure and safety plan before proceeding. Then, test your prototype to determine whether it meets the criteria and constraints for an effective and acceptable solution. Record your data and observations in your Evidence Notebook.

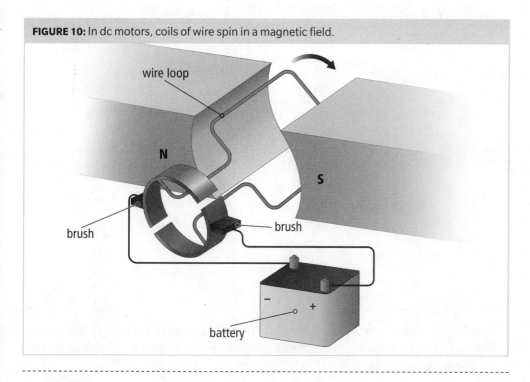

FIGURE 10: In dc motors, coils of wire spin in a magnetic field.

wire loop

N

S

brush

brush

battery

− +

OPTIMIZE

1. How might you determine the energy efficiency of your motor system? How might you use this information to optimize your motor?

_____

_____

_____

2. Compare your motor design to the model of a dc motor in Figure 10. Describe the similarities and differences between the two motors.

_____

_____

_____

_____

3. Share your design with other teams. Demonstrate your prototype, and explain how it meets the criteria for success. Elicit other teams' feedback on your design, and record the feedback you receive in your Evidence Notebook. Use their comments and critique to improve your prototype. You should also observe your classmates' designs and learn from their experiences. Provide constructive feedback on others' designs. Modify your prototype and test it again to identify which components of the system you might adjust to improve the motor's performance. Document your process, modifications, and test results in your Evidence Notebook.

4. Draw a labeled diagram of your final optimized design.

5. Describe the major changes you made from the initial design to the final design. Explain why each change improved the motor's performance with respect to the design criteria based on your understanding of electromagnetism.

_____

_____

_____

_____

_____

_____

6. If given fewer constraints, what additional changes would you make to improve your solution? Explain.

_____

_____

_____

_____

- -

COMMUNICATE

The Director of Marketing is excited to hear the results of your work. Prepare a presentation to share your motor design and test results with her. Be sure to highlight how your motor's performance contributes to the company's need for a fast-moving toy car marketable to children ages five to eight. Use digital media tools to add visual aids to your presentation.

 Evidence Notebook How could you apply this optimization process to a wireless charger? How do the improvements you made to the motor compare to improvements you could make to a wireless charger?

Careers in Science

Radiologist

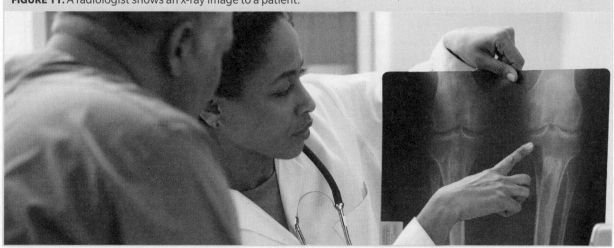

FIGURE 11: A radiologist shows an x-ray image to a patient.

Radiology uses medical imaging to diagnose and sometimes treat medical conditions. Medical imaging provides the physician with a visual model of the body's inner structure without the need for invasive surgery. Two familiar forms of medical imaging used in radiology are MRIs and x-ray imaging. Soft tissues are more easily examined with MRI, or magnetic resonance imaging, in which the patient is placed in a strong magnetic field from an electromagnet. Hydrogen nuclei within water molecules in body tissue act like small magnets and align with the field. When the electromagnet is switched off, the hydrogen atoms gradually return to their resting state. In this process, the hydrogen atoms emit radio waves, a type of electromagnetic radiation that can be detected by a receiver in the MRI. Different tissues undergo this process at different rates, allowing the receiver to determine what sort of tissue returned the waves. X-ray imaging exposes the patient to x-rays, another type of electromagnetic radiation. X-rays are absorbed and transmitted differently by bone, tissue, and air based on their differing densities. X-ray imaging is especially useful for diagnosing conditions affecting the bones (which are more dense than the surrounding tissue) or lungs (in which the air-filled spaces are far less dense than the surrounding tissue).

Language Arts Connection

Make a presentation that describes the careers, technology, and history of radiology. Include a section on how the fundamentals of electromagnetism are applied in that work. Integrate information from multiple sources.

Use the following questions to guide your research for your presentation:

- How do electric and magnetic phenomena intersect in the science of radiology?
- What training and education does a person need to work in radiology?
- How does radiology today differ from historic medical imaging practices?
- What forms of electromagnetic radiation are most prominent in radiology technology?

Physics in Your Community

Medical professionals from diverse backgrounds are responsible for contributions to radiology. Research a member of your community who works to apply or advance the field of radiology.

| GENERATING ELECTRICAL ENERGY | ELECTRIC CARS | THE IMPACT OF VISUALS | Go online to choose one of these other paths. |

Lesson Self-Check

CAN YOU EXPLAIN THE PHENOMENON?

FIGURE 12: A charger is connected to a household electric circuit. A device with a compatible rechargeable battery can be set on top to recharge without needing to be connected through a copper wire and open electrical contacts.

A battery is a way to store energy that can be transformed and used as electrical energy. When connected in a circuit, the electric potential difference will produce a current until the battery is depleted of chemical energy. A rechargeable battery, such as that in a laptop or phone, can be connected in a circuit with a voltage source and regain its potential difference.

Wireless chargers recharge a battery without a conductor connecting the device to the voltage source. Instead, wireless chargers transfer electrical energy through a field, without the need for a physical connection.

 Evidence Notebook Refer to your notes in your Evidence Notebook to explain how electromagnetic induction generates a current without a physical connection to the voltage source. Use evidence and reasoning to support your claim.

Claim How do wireless chargers use electric and magnetic phenomena to transfer energy without a physical connection? State your answer in the form of a claim.

Evidence Summarize the evidence you have gathered to support your claim. Include evidence such as models, sketches, or data from experiments, as well as any laws or patterns that apply to the situation.

Reasoning How does the evidence you cited support your claim? Explain how the results of your investigations and other pieces of evidence connect to the argument you are making.

CHECKPOINTS

Check Your Understanding

1. Which of the following can accelerate a stationary electron? Select all correct answers.
   - ☐ **a.** an electric field
   - ☐ **b.** a static magnetic field
   - ☐ **c.** a changing magnetic field
   - ☐ **d.** an electric potential

2. An electric current in a wire is directed from left to right when viewed from the side. In what direction is the magnetic field at a point above the wire?
   - ○ **a.** counterclockwise
   - ○ **b.** clockwise
   - ○ **c.** away from you
   - ○ **d.** toward you

3. Determine whether each variable affects the strength of an electromagnet, the magnitude of an induced current, or both. Check the correct response or responses in each row.

Factors in Electromagnetism		
Variable	Electromagnet strength	Induced current
Number of turns of wire in coil		
Distance between coil and moving magnet		
Strength of moving magnet		
Presence of an iron core in the coil		

4. In electromagnetic induction, how is energy transferred from the moving magnet to the circuit?
   - ○ **a.** through electrons that cross the gap
   - ○ **b.** through raising a weight
   - ○ **c.** through separating charges in an electrolyte
   - ○ **d.** through a changing magnetic field

5. What do you need to build an electromagnet? Select all correct answers.
   - ☐ **a.** a coil of insulated conducting wire
   - ☐ **b.** a voltage source, such as a battery
   - ☐ **c.** an ammeter
   - ☐ **d.** a compass
   - ☐ **e.** a magnet
   - ☐ **f.** a switch
   - ☐ **g.** a resistor
   - ☐ **h.** a coil of insulator

6. What do you need to induce a current by electromagnetic induction? Select all correct answers.
   - ☐ **a.** a coil of conducting wire
   - ☐ **b.** a power source, such as a battery
   - ☐ **c.** an ammeter
   - ☐ **d.** a compass
   - ☐ **e.** a magnet
   - ☐ **f.** a switch

7. An electromagnet is often made with an iron core. How does this improve the design?
   - ○ **a.** The heavier design makes the magnet more stable.
   - ○ **b.** An electric current is induced in the iron core, which opposes the current in the copper coil.
   - ○ **c.** An electric current is induced in the iron core, which increases the current in the copper coil.
   - ○ **d.** The iron core becomes magnetized, increasing the strength of the magnetic field.

8. Select the correct terms to complete the statement about magnets and electric current.

   For a magnet to induce a current in a coil of wire, the two must be moving | stationary with respect to each other. If the circuit is closed | opened, the current will stop. When you reverse the motion of the magnet, the current stops | starts | reverses.

CHECKPOINTS (continued)

9. How could you use the cause-and-effect relationship between electric current and magnetism to engineer a device that can generate a variable-strength magnetic field?

_____

_____

_____

_____

10. Draw a single loop of copper wire. Assume a battery produces a clockwise electric current in the wire. Use the right-hand rule to find the direction of the magnetic field just above the top of the coil, just below the top wire, just above the bottom wire, and below the bottom of the coil. Mark these on your drawing.

MAKE YOUR OWN STUDY GUIDE

 In your Evidence Notebook, design a study guide that supports the main ideas from this lesson:

Magnetic fields are generated by charged particles in motion.

At a macroscopic scale, the magnetic field formed around a current-carrying wire can be applied to construct an electromagnet.

An electric current can be induced in a wire by a changing magnetic field.

Electromagnetic induction can be applied to transfer a variable current from one place to another without an electric conductor.

Remember to include the following information in your study guide:

• Use examples that model main ideas.
• Record explanations for the phenomena you investigated.
• Use evidence to support your explanations. Your support can include drawings, data, graphs, laboratory conclusions, and other evidence recorded throughout the lesson.

Consider how empirical evidence supports the cause-and-effect relationship between moving electric charges and magnetic fields.

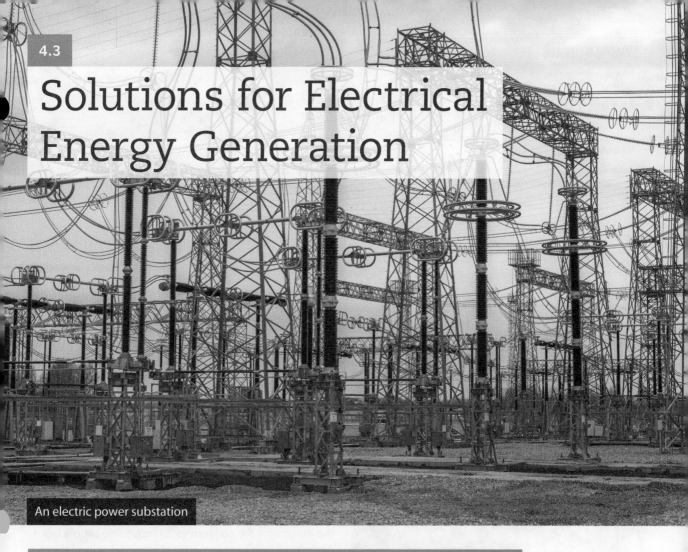

4.3

Solutions for Electrical Energy Generation

An electric power substation

Images Plus/Getty ImageT

CAN YOU SOLVE THE PROBLEM?

This morning, you may have woken to an alarm from a clock or phone that runs on electrical energy. You may have turned on an electric light, taken a shower with water warmed by an electric heater, donned clothes washed and dried with electrical appliances, and had a breakfast of foods cooked or kept cold with electrical energy, all before leaving the house. Clocks can run on mechanical energy and food can be heated or cooled in other ways, but rather than use a variety of power sources, most modern societies rely heavily on one.

EVALUATE What do you know about how the electrical energy you use is generated and delivered to your home?

_____

_____

_____

_____

_____

 Evidence Notebook As you explore the lesson, gather evidence to explain how the electric grid is able to provide a constant supply of electrical energy to regions that each have different natural resources and societal needs.

Producing Electrical Energy

Many forms of electrical energy generation use a changing magnetic field to induce an electric current. This involves harnessing some source of mechanical energy to move either a magnet or a coil of wire.

Generators

FIGURE 1: A basic generator design with a coil of wire around a rotating magnet.

EXPLAIN Describe one method you could use to generate an electric current in a coil of copper wire.

_____

_____

_____

_____

A generator converts mechanical energy into electrical energy. The motion in a generator does not have to be circular—magnetic fields can be changed by moving a magnet back and forth or in some other cyclical pattern. Because motion is relative, it does not matter whether the magnet or the coil moves. In fact, some simple lab generators use a moving coil of wire and stationary magnets to generate an electric current.

The wire in a generator is formed into a coil to magnify the amount of electromagnetic induction. One rotation of a 100-loop coil in a magnetic field induces a current in each loop, generating more total current than a single loop rotated in the same field. One basic design for a generator is a large coil of copper wire around a rotating magnet, as seen in Figure 1. Generators produce an alternating current because the pieces move in a cycle that causes the current to change directions regularly.

PREDICT Think about natural systems where energy is stored or transferred. How might one of these systems be used to produce electrical energy?

_____

_____

_____

_____

 Evidence Notebook What are the elements that you would need to include in order to design and build a functioning generator, such as the one in the unit project?

Electrical Energy from Mechanical Energy

In physics, *power* is the rate at which energy is transferred. Large facilities that generate electrical energy and transfer it to an electric grid are often called *power plants*. An electric grid is the system that distributes electrical energy. To supply electrical energy, a power plant must have a continuous source of energy to transform. To produce electrical energy from motion, engineers often seek reliable sources of mechanical energy. One method of transforming this mechanical energy into electrical energy is to place a turbine, a wheel with blades, in the path of either moving air, water, or expanding gases. The turbine is spun by the fluid, which then turns a magnet inside a wire coil.

Hydroelectric Dams

Hydroelectric plants can be installed in areas with sufficient flowing water. If a hydroelectric plant is built on a river, the river is usually dammed so that the flow of water can be controlled. The energy of a given volume of water is related to its speed. A narrow, fast-flowing river could produce as much energy as a wider, slower river. However, inconsistent water flow can affect the energy produced. Hydroelectric energy is renewable and does not produce atmospheric pollution. These plants may be expensive to construct, but are generally inexpensive to maintain. Damming rivers may negatively affect the flooded areas above the dams and the drier areas below the dams.

FIGURE 2: A hydroelectric plant uses fast-moving water to spin turbines.

INFER What effects might the construction of a new dam have on human and wildlife populations above and below the dam?

Wind Farms

Wind energy uses the flow of air to spin rotors connected to turbines, which generate electrical energy. A single turbine might supply enough energy to run an individual home, while a group of turbines in a wind farm might produce enough energy to contribute to the electric grid. Wind farms are suitable only for areas that have reliable and strong winds. Even then, they are highly dependent upon the weather, which can affect their reliability. Communities have also opposed wind farms for aesthetic reasons and because of concerns that the turbines may harm bird and bat populations.

ANALYZE Which of the following are true of both hydroelectric and wind plants? Select all correct answers.

- ☐ **a.** low maintenance costs
- ☐ **b.** require a continual fuel source
- ☐ **c.** need to be built in specific locations
- ☐ **d.** possibly inconsistent energy production

Explore Online ▶

YOU SOLVE IT

How Can You Design a Wind-Powered Generator?
Consider what the most important elements of a wind generator are.

FIGURE 3: Regular lubrication and maintenance are needed to keep a wind turbine performing efficiently.

Electrical Energy from Thermal Energy

When natural sources of mechanical energy are not available, mechanical energy can be produced by using another source of energy. One common method uses the expansion of a fluid when it is heated. Just as the lid on a pot of boiling water is moved by the expanding steam inside the pot, an expanding fluid can spin a rotor. Then, that rotor can be used to generate electrical energy just as a hydroelectric dam or a wind turbine would.

FIGURE 4: Thermal energy expands water into steam, turning a steam turbine that drives a generator.

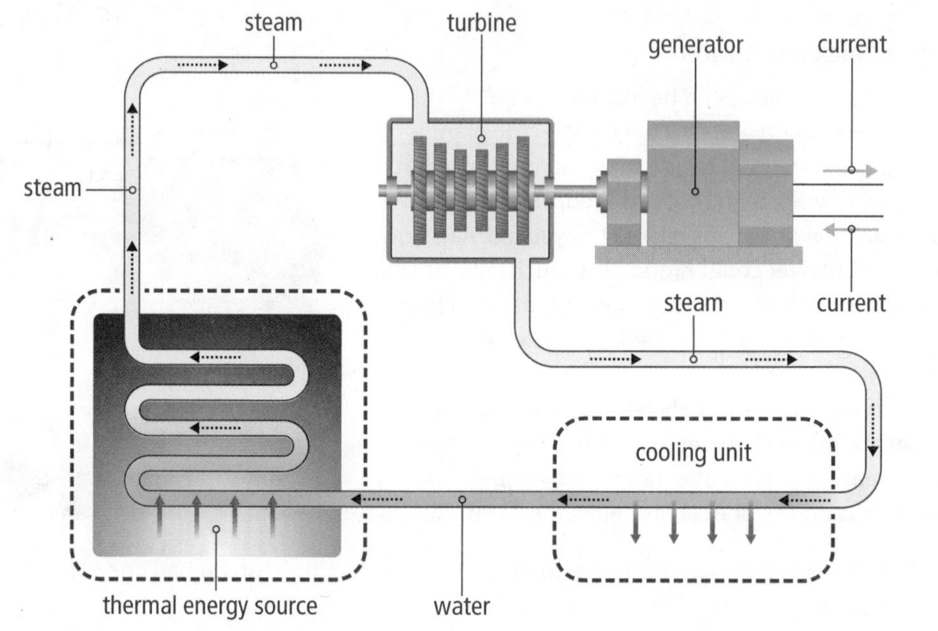

Unlike power plants that generate electrical energy using natural sources of moving water and wind, plants that use thermal energy produce their own flow of fluid. In these power plants, the fluid is water that turns to steam. Thermoelectric plants use a source of thermal energy to transform water into pressurized steam. The expanding steam spins the blades of the turbine to generate electrical energy. As the steam transfers energy as heat to the environment, it condenses back into water. When more thermal energy is added to the system, the fluid expands again, and the cycle continues.

APPLY What are some reasons a country might seek to replace power plants that rely on burning fossil fuels for thermal energy? Select all correct answers.

☐ **a.** to reduce dependence on a resource that is not available locally

☐ **b.** to increase the availability of fossil fuels for the citizens to make use of

☐ **c.** to reduce dependence on a resource that is being used faster than it is produced

☐ **d.** to protect public health by reducing pollutants that result from burning fossil fuels

☐ **e.** to counter global warming by limiting the carbon dioxide burning fossil fuels release

Power plants that use heat to produce electrical energy are called thermoelectric power plants. While some thermoelectric plants burn oil, coal, or natural gas to generate thermal energy, geothermal plants use Earth's internal thermal energy, and nuclear power plants use heat released by nuclear fission reactions.

Fossil Fuel Power Plants

Power plants that burn fossil fuels can be built anywhere, run at any time, and are often the least expensive way to produce electrical energy. The initial construction can be less expensive than other types of power plants. However, burning fossil fuels releases greenhouse gases, such as carbon dioxide, that are associated with climate change. Burning fossil fuels also produces airborne irritants such as heavy metals that can damage people's health. Ash from fossil fuel plants can contaminate local drinking water. Despite the health and environmental impacts, the reliability and low financial cost of using fossil fuels means that much of the world's electrical energy is still produced by burning natural gas or coal.

EXPLAIN What are local and global risks of burning fossil fuels to supply electrical energy?

_____

_____

_____

Nuclear Power Plants

Like power plants that burn fossil fuels, nuclear plants can run at any time. However, they do have to be located near sources of water so that they can be cooled effectively. These power plants make use of a process where radioactive atoms are split to consistently produce large amounts of energy. Nuclear fission does not require as much fuel as fossil fuels plants, but it produces long-lived, hazardous nuclear waste that is difficult to dispose of. While nuclear plants do not produce greenhouse gases, radioactive elements can pose serious hazards to humans and the environment. In mining the uranium commonly used in the fission reactions, radioactive radon gas is released, which can lead to lung cancer when inhaled. Spent uranium fuel is also dangerously radioactive and must be stored safely for tens of thousands of years. An accident can release damaging levels of radiation into the local environment, and the radiation is then spread by natural cycles. Enhanced safety systems can reduce the risk of an accident during operation but raise construction costs.

ANALYZE What are the environmental risks of uranium mining? What are the risks to the environment when a nuclear plant is in operation?

_____

_____

_____

FIGURE 5: The fuel rod assembly of a nuclear plant is engineered to withstand heat and radiation.

FIGURE 6: Uranium deposits near the surface can be mined with earth-moving equipment.

Geothermal Power Plants

Geothermal power plants require few inputs, but need to be located in areas with access to the heat released from Earth's inner layers, such as geologic hot spots, areas with volcanic activity, and regions along the edges of continental plates. Geothermal plants also require large amounts of water. Like hydroelectric dams or wind farms, geothermal plants makes use of a natural source of energy in a specific location. Geothermal plants can be economical when a geothermal energy source is close to the surface, but are infeasible in most locations. This form of energy is considered renewable, though it is possible to exhaust a source when heat is extracted faster than it is replaced. Drilling down in order to reach the high-temperature rock needed may have environmental effects such as releasing trapped greenhouse gases or contaminants. Some types of geothermal plants have also been associated with increased seismic activity.

FIGURE 7: A geothermal power plant uses heat from within Earth to convert water into steam and turn a turbine.

EVALUATE Unlike wind or solar energy, geothermal energy is available at all times. What is a limit on its more widespread use?

_____

_____

_____

_____

_____

_____

Electrical Energy from Light

FIGURE 8: Broad, flat leaves are similar to solar panels.

EXPLAIN What energy source does a leaf use to make the sugars that it needs to survive? How does it capture that energy?

_____

_____

_____

_____

_____

_____

_____

Solar Cells

Most methods of generating electrical energy rely on moving either a magnet or coil of wire, but radiant energy from the sun can be transformed using solar cells. A solar cell, also known as a photovoltaic cell, converts energy from light into an electric current. Solar cells utilize the photovoltaic effect, in which certain materials generate a voltage when they absorb energy from a light source.

The invention of the solar cell allowed for a wide variety of sensor technologies to be developed, but it also provided a new way to produce electrical energy. Solar cells do not require large moving parts to produce electrical energy like power plants that rely on generators and turbines do. This allows them to be used in many other circumstances. An early application of solar cells was to provide energy to spacecraft.

ANALYZE What are some ways that photovoltaic cells could be used? What advantages do they have over other ways to generate electrical energy?

_____

_____

_____

_____

_____

FIGURE 9: In the presence of light, photovoltaic panels generate an electric potential.

Getty Images

Influence of Engineering, Technology, and Science on Society and the Natural World

The Photovoltaic Effect

The photovoltaic effect was observed in the early 1800s. Early solar cells were very inefficient and were more for demonstration purposes than for use as a practical means of generating electric current. Once there was an increased understanding of how semiconductors could be used, practical solar cells started to be developed. Semiconductors are materials such as silicon and germanium that conduct electrical energy only under certain circumstances. By using different types of semiconductors, engineers can design a system in which electrons flow easily in only one direction. When light falls on the surface of the solar cell, it excites electrons in the top layer, which then begin to flow.

Language Arts Connection Make a presentation about how the development of photovoltaic cells has changed how they are used over the years. Research how past uses of these devices have corresponded with breakthroughs in their development or production.

Solar Panels

Photovoltaic cells can be connected into arrays called solar panels, and these panels can be combined into even larger arrays. A small solar panel might supply enough energy to run a calculator, while a larger panel could supply energy to a house or a satellite. The largest arrays can function as power plants. In certain conditions, solar arrays can allow for devices or buildings to use electrical energy without a connection to the region's electric grid. In such cases, it is necessary to have a way of storing electrical energy.

Solar Farms

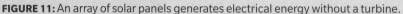

FIGURE 11: An array of solar panels generates electrical energy without a turbine.

Solar farms can work anywhere that the sun shines—the more sunlight there is, the more electrical energy is generated. Because the intensity of sunlight at Earth's surface is relatively weak, solar panels must cover a large area to generate significant amounts of energy. In fact, the panels used in solar farms are often tilted and adjustable to maximize their exposure to the sun. Solar farms do not produce pollution, though the production and installation of the panels can still have negative environmental effects. The price of installing solar panels has dropped in recent years and maintenance expenses are low, but some of the panels are fragile and must be protected from impacts. They require sunny conditions in order to operate and occasional cleaning to prevent dust and water from obscuring the sun's rays.

One advantage of solar panels is that they can provide electrical energy without depending on an electric grid. In areas with frequent power failures due to excess demand or to storms taking down transmission lines, solar panels and storage batteries could provide a more reliable source of energy.

EXPLAIN Which of the following are limitations of using solar energy? Select all correct answers.

☐ **a.** They can be damaged easily.

☐ **b.** They take up a large amount of space.

☐ **c.** Their operation produces little pollution.

☐ **d.** They only produce energy during certain weather.

Evidence Notebook Choose a method of energy generation, and explain its costs and benefits. When is this method a good solution, and when is it a weaker solution?

Storing and Distributing Energy

Almost every form of energy, including thermal, solar, and kinetic energy, can be transformed into electrical energy. However, electrical energy is useful only if it can be distributed easily and efficiently. The methods of storing and distributing electrical energy and the infrastructure to support its distribution are just as important as the ability to generate the energy in the first place.

 Collaborate With a partner, choose three types of power plants. Make a map showing the areas of your country where those power plants would be best suited. Then, identify areas that might need electrical energy distributed to them.

Distributing Electrical Energy

FIGURE 12: High-voltage transmission lines deliver current across great distances.

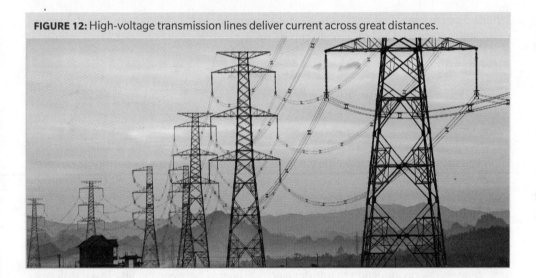

EVALUATE Nuclear plants, wind farms, and solar arrays that produce energy may be hundreds of miles from the communities where that energy is used. Using what you know about circuits, what problems might transferring electrical energy over these long distances cause?

_____

_____

_____

Transferring electrical energy across great distances requires minimizing energy losses. The power lost by wire carrying a current, I, is proportional to RI^2. Very high currents can lead to significant amounts of power loss in wires. If the current can be minimized, less power will be lost in its transfer. In a circuit, the power transferred is equal to the product of current and voltage. Thus, large amounts of energy can be transferred using small currents if the voltage is large enough. In situations where energy has to be transferred across hundreds of miles of wire, an alternating current with voltages as high as 500 kV is used to minimize the energy lost to the surroundings.

Getty Images

Transformers

FIGURE 13: Transformers step up or step down voltage as they transfer electrical energy between circuits.

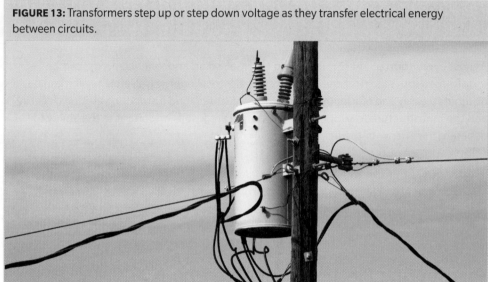

INFER Transformers that distribute electrical energy from the main power line to homes generally reduce voltage. Why might this be necessary?

_____

_____

_____

_____

High voltages can often be extremely dangerous. When you have a 9V battery, it can be safe to touch both of the terminals because your finger does not conduct electrical energy well. However, the higher the voltage, the more likely charges are to flow between the two terminals. The danger of high voltages is one of the reasons that large transmission lines are suspended high in the air. To make electrical energy safer for homes and businesses, _transformers_, which change the voltage and current of a wire, are used.

Transformers rely on induction to transfer electrical energy between circuits. In a transformer, the alternating current that flows through power lines is used to generate a changing magnetic field. This changing magnetic field is then used to induce a current in another wire. The number of coils in the transformer can be used to adjust the induced voltage. A transformer makes use of both electromagnets and induced current.

ANALYZE A power adapter plugged into an electrical outlet converts alternating current from a wall circuit into a lower-voltage direct current that a computer can use. How are power adapters and transformers similar?

☐ **a.** They reduce voltage.

☐ **b.** They increase current provided.

☐ **c.** They transfer electrical energy between circuits.

☐ **d.** They transform mechanical energy into electrical energy.

Storing Energy

EXPLAIN How can electrical energy be stored? Give an example of a device that does this.

_____

_____

_____

_____

FIGURE 14: A battery has a negative terminal (anode) and a positive terminal (cathode) separated by an electrolyte. Ions move across the electrolyte.

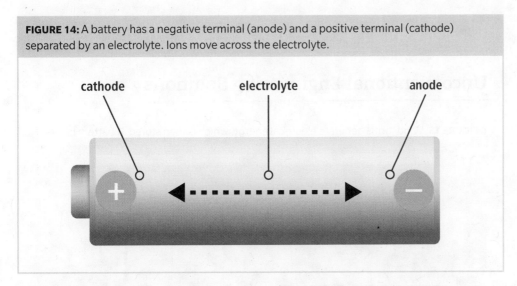

A battery is a device that transforms stored chemical energy into electrical energy. A battery contains an electrolyte, which is a material that conducts electric current in the form of positive and negative ions. The electrolyte separates the battery's terminals, which are where electrochemical reactions take place. When connected in a circuit, ions move across the electrolyte. In a typical design, the negative terminal of the battery is a metal that gives up electrons, and the positive terminal is a metal oxide that can accept electrons. A given battery can store only a certain amount of chemical energy, which limits the electrical energy that can be provided by the battery. In a rechargeable battery, the chemical process can be run in reverse by applying an electric field to the battery. This transforms some of the circuit's electrical energy into chemical energy within the battery.

Batteries are an extremely important part of the world's electrical distribution system. Consider all of the devices that you use that require batteries and how they would be affected if they had to be plugged into the wall. Batteries not only allow electrical devices to be portable and mobile, they also allow for the storage of electrical energy. With solar panels becoming widespread, there is a greater need to store energy for later use.

APPLY Do batteries provide direct current or alternating current? Why?

○ **a.** Direct current. Electrons move away from the negative terminal of the battery and toward the positive terminal of the battery.

○ **b.** Direct current. Electrons travel back and forth between the negative and positive terminals of a battery.

○ **c.** Alternating current. Electrons leave the negative terminal of the battery and travel to the positive terminal of the battery.

○ **d.** Alternating current. Electrons travel back and forth between the negative and positive terminals of a battery.

Electrical Energy Solutions

There are many methods for producing, storing, and delivering electrical energy. Production depends on the natural resources of each region, available technologies, and government policies. While the United States generates about 32% of its energy using natural gas, some countries use natural gas to produce almost all of their energy. Countries also have different electrical standards, which determine their supporting infrastructures. Because the United States uses 120V outlets and other countries use 230V outlets, travelers to some countries must use adapters for their devices.

Engineering

Unconventional Engineering Solutions

FIGURE 15: Wind farms generate electrical energy, which is then stored in battery banks.

An increased demand for electrical energy can lead to blackouts, rolling blackouts, and brownouts. A blackout is a loss of electrical energy; a rolling blackout is a deliberate series of smaller blackouts to prevent overload of the entire system; and a brownout is a drop in voltage, which causes a grid to deliver less energy.

A virtual power plant is a system that combines different types of power plants to produce a reliable overall supply of energy. These systems can rely on both traditional, large power plants and distributed, smaller plants, such as solar arrays and wind farms. When one component produces more energy than is needed at the time, that energy can be stored. This is often done using rechargeable batteries or by pumping water up into a reservoir and later releasing it to drive a hydroelectric plant.

EXPLAIN What are some additional benefits and drawbacks of virtual power plants?

_____

_____

_____

Evidence Notebook How do high-voltage power lines and electrical energy storage methods affect the use of certain types of power plants?

Evaluating Energy Solutions

Electrical energy production is a complicated problem that has many variables. Some methods can generate electrical energy at any time, while others can do so only under certain conditions. The financial costs can also vary wildly between different methods. An area that has tides or geothermal vents can use technologies that are impractical or too expensive to use elsewhere. Different methods can produce different amounts and types of waste products. In optimizing a solution to provide energy to a region, engineers almost always have to make tradeoffs between their criteria.

ASK What are some possible variables that you may need to consider when evaluating the type of power plants that could be built in your community?

_____

_____

_____

Differences in Communities

Every community has different needs and wants that affect how they interact with the electric grid. Urban populations use large amounts of energy each day to run lights and electrical devices, but they often use less energy per person than rural populations. Rural communities use less energy overall, but may value reliability and price more than cities. Without a large maintenance staff, a downed power line could leave people without electrical energy for long periods of time. Geography can also play a factor. For instance, cities in very warm climates may have high energy usage due to air conditioning.

Similar principles extend to the types of power plants that are built in communities. Factors such as the cost to operate, the health impacts, and the aesthetics of the plants can all determine the types of plants that are built in each region.

FIGURE 16: Different communities have a variety of energy needs that are based around their population, geography, and infrastructure.

 Language Arts Connection Conduct research to learn how electrical energy is produced in your region. What type of power plants have been built in your region, and is this energy used locally or sent to other locations? Write an article summarizing what you learned.

Impact on Human Health

FIGURE 17: Burning fossil fuels can release harmful pollutants and produce smog, which negatively affect human populations.

Power plants can have different effects on the health of human populations. Some types of power plants can pose immediate health hazards while others can cause health problems that may not appear for years. Burning fossil fuels release pollutants into the air, including greenhouse gases and harmful particles, that reduce air quality. Poor air quality contributes to respiratory diseases and is particularly dangerous for people who have asthma or cardiovascular health problems.

Nuclear plants release few pollutants into the air, but the radioactive wastes they generate remain dangerous for many years. Radiation causes cancer and other health problems, so waste disposal must be done carefully to protect living things. While nuclear plants are generally very safe, nuclear accidents have the potential to cause large-scale health crises if they leak radioactive material into the atmosphere, land, or water.

APPLY Describe an example of how an understanding of the impact on human health might influence power plant selection or construction.

_____

_____

_____

Financial Costs

FIGURE 18: Wind turbines have upfront costs, but not many ongoing costs.

Several factors determine how much money it costs to build and operate a power plant. Each type of power plant has a different mix of fixed and variable financial costs. Fixed costs include steady or one-time payments, such as paying for land, construction materials, or regulatory fees. Variable costs often depend on energy output. They include paying for fuel, labor, and maintenance costs, such as repairs and waste disposal. These will change due to the capacity and operating level of the power plant.

Energy production often involves tradeoffs between fixed and variable costs. For example, fossil fuel plants are relatively inexpensive to build, but they have high fuel and labor costs. In comparison, solar farms are expensive to build, but they require no fuel and fewer workers.

INFER Compare the fixed and variable financial costs associated with hydroelectric and nuclear plants.

_____

_____

_____

Environmental Effects

The construction and operation of power plants affect the environment in many different ways. Fossil fuel plants contribute greenhouse gases to the atmosphere. These gases absorb and reemit thermal energy, causing the atmosphere to warm over time. Rising temperatures often alter habitats faster than plants and animals can adapt, causing large-scale changes in populations.

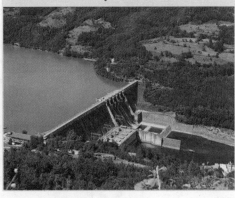

FIGURE 19: While hydroelectric dams are a form of renewable energy, they greatly affect a river's ecosystem.

Other types of power plants can have more local impacts. Fish populations are threatened when hydroelectric dams block their natural migrations. The light reflected from solar arrays can negatively affect bird populations, and drilling for natural gas can lead to groundwater contamination. While some power plants do have less impact on the environment than others, any large construction and ongoing activity will affect the environment.

EVALUATE Which type of power plant do you think has the least effect on the environment? Explain how you might compare impacts to decide which power plants have more negative or far-reaching effects on the environment than others.

_____

_____

_____

_____

Other Possible Criteria

There are many other factors that may influence power plant selection. Safety and reliability are considered alongside feasibility based on available land and natural resources. If the power plant is going to be located close to recreational or residential areas, the plant's aesthetics might become very important. Deciding which criteria are most important to meet the electrical energy needs and wants of the community helps decision makers choose among power plant types.

ASK Make a list of questions that decision makers could ask about the feasibility of building different power plants in a region.

_____

_____

_____

_____

PREDICT When might the appearance, or aesthetics, of a power plant matter to citizens in a community? Select all correct answers.

☐ **a.** when it operates day and night

☐ **b.** when it is located near residential areas

☐ **c.** when it must supply energy to a large population

☐ **d.** when it is located near parks or recreation facilities

Engineering

Choosing a Power Plant

You are on a board of an electric company and are helping to plan the construction of a new power plant in your region. You are tasked with deciding what type of power plant would best fit the region's needs and wants. Use what you know about different power plant types, possible criteria, and the region's constraints to choose the best solution.

EXPLAIN Which power plants are not feasible due to the constraints of your region?

_____

_____

_____

EVALUATE Decide on the quantitative and qualitative criteria that you will use to evaluate possible solutions as well as the weight for each criterion. Score each power plant from 0 to 5 for every criterion. Calculate the weighted scores for each power plant.

Power Plant Decision Matrix				
Design criteria	**Weight**	_____	_____	_____
_____	_____	_____	_____	_____
_____	_____	_____	_____	_____
_____	_____	_____	_____	_____
_____	_____	_____	_____	_____
_____	_____	_____	_____	_____
Total points				

ARGUE Based on your knowledge of power plants and your decision matrix, which type of power plant should be built in your region? Explain how the criteria and constraints affected your decision and if any tradeoffs had to be considered.

_____

_____

_____

_____

 Language Arts Connection Prepare a presentation to explain which power plant would be the best choice for your region. Include how you evaluated your solution.

 Evidence Notebook The electric grid draws from many types of power plants. How does this diversity benefit the overall system of electrical energy distribution?

Guided Research

Electrical Energy in Your Community

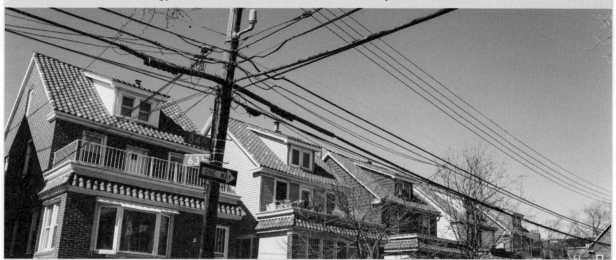

FIGURE 20: The electrical energy delivered to homes can come from a variety of sources.

In the early days of electrical energy distribution, hydroelectric power plants were more common than thermoelectric power plants. Hydroelectric plants were less expensive to operate. Around the 1930s, technical advances in the design of thermoelectric plants made them more competitive in terms of cost. At the same time, the difficulties of building hydroelectric plants in increasingly remote sites made expanding that power source less appealing. Thermoelectric plants that relied on nuclear energy or burning fossil fuels could be built anywhere, unlike hydroelectric plants that are limited to locations next to sufficiently large or fast rivers.

The economics of power plants can be evaluated in a number of different ways. For example, geothermal plants often have a high initial cost for digging the deep wells, but low operating costs once they are in use. Nuclear plants may be judged as less economical when life-cycle costs, including storage of radioactive waste, are included in the calculation. Fossil fuel plants are now viewed as less optimal when the long-term costs of air pollution and greenhouse gases are considered. Options that generate less air pollution, such as wind, geothermal, and hydroelectric, have other environmental costs.

Criteria may be weighted differently in different places or times. For example, if a primary goal is to get as much electrical energy to as many people as possible as fast as possible, well-established technologies are appealing solutions. Technologies that require a lower initial investment of money or time are also appealing. But if environmental and sustainability concerns are more heavily weighted, different technologies are viewed as optimal power-generation solutions.

Language Arts Connection Research the power plants that produce electrical energy in your region. What is the source of energy for these generating plants? How does your community power plant compare with the optimal local energy sources you rated and debated in the course of the lesson? Write a brief blog post or newspaper story that explains how electrical energy is generated in your community and what long-term changes might make sense for that system.

| WAR OF THE CURRENTS | NUCLEAR WASTE DISPOSAL | CALCULATE YOUR POWER USE | Go online to choose one of these other paths. |

Images Plus/Getty Images

Lesson Self-Check

CAN YOU SOLVE THE PROBLEM?

FIGURE 21: Electrical energy is generated at a power plant and then distributed using high-voltage wires.

Electrical energy can be generated in remote areas using solar cells, wind turbines, and other methods that do not require connection to an electric grid. However, most electrical energy is generated at a central location and then distributed to businesses and households through an electric grid.

Electrical energy can be generated in different ways, each with benefits and costs. The optimal method in one location may not work as well somewhere else. Some primary energy sources, such as fossil fuels, can be used anywhere that fossil fuels can be reliably transported to. Others, such as wind or geothermal energy, make sense only in a limited number of areas. However, fossil fuels produce more air pollution than other energy sources, and the supply of fossil fuels is being exhausted faster than it is replaced. Most countries do not depend on a single type of power plant. Often, multiple methods are used to generate electrical energy.

 Evidence Notebook Refer to your notes in your Evidence Notebook to explain whether or not it is a benefit for an electric grid to make use of many different types of power plants.

Claim How can the electric grid provide a constant supply of electrical energy to regions that each have different natural resources and societal needs?

Evidence What evidence supports your claim regarding how the electric grid can provide a constant supply of electrical energy to different regions?

Reasoning Describe how the evidence you provided supports your claim regarding how the electric grid can supply electrical energy to a regions with a variety of resources and needs.

CHECKPOINTS

Check Your Understanding

1. Select the correct terms to complete the statement.

Electrical energy generation often involves a magnetic field and a conductive wire. Current can be induced in a wire coil by a strong | changing | weak magnetic field. A current can also be generated by changing the orientation | material | temperature of the wire coil in the presence of a magnetic field.

2. Sort each type of power plant into the correct category.

| hydroelectric | fossil fuel | geothermal |
| solar | tidal | wind |

Can be used efficiently anywhere	Can be used only in certain places

3. What is an advantage of using coal rather than wind to generate electrical energy?

- ○ **a.** Coal is more efficient than wind power.
- ○ **b.** Coal is cleaner than wind power.
- ○ **c.** Wind power is not renewable.
- ○ **d.** Coal can provide energy at any time.

4. Select the correct terms to complete the statement.

A virtual power plant is an engineering solution to pollution | blackouts and can make up for inconsistencies in energy output from solar | fossil fuel | nuclear power generation.

5. Connect the method of electrical energy generation to its requirement.

Solar	○	○ Flowing water
Hydroelectric	○	○ Volcanic activity
Geothermal	○	○ Reliable, strong air currents
Wind	○	○ Large open area

6. In damless hydroelectric power, the mechanical energy of a river is harnessed by designs similar to waterwheels, or turbines inside dams. What are the chief advantages of this technology over existing dammed hydroelectric? Select all correct answers.

- ☐ **a.** People are not displaced.
- ☐ **b.** A slow, flat river can be used.
- ☐ **c.** Wildlife is not disrupted as much.
- ☐ **d.** More electrical energy is produced.

7. Put the steps for wind energy in order.

- _____ **a.** A changing magnetic field is produced.
- _____ **b.** Current is output by the generator.
- _____ **c.** The turbine produces rotational energy.
- _____ **d.** Wind blows across the blades of a turbine.
- _____ **e.** A current is induced in the coil.
- _____ **f.** Rotational energy spins a magnet.

8. The Mars Pathfinder rover had a flat solar panel on top. The later Mars Explorer rovers had solar panels on "wings" that could be angled. What was the likely reason for this design change?

- ○ **a.** Dust cannot affect tilted surfaces, only horizontal ones.
- ○ **b.** The rovers could use wind energy as well as solar for motion.
- ○ **c.** Increasing the number of solar cells increases the voltage.
- ○ **d.** Solar panels could be angled to maximize solar energy absorption.

CHECKPOINTS (continued)

9. A tidal stream generator uses a tidal flow to turn the blades of a turbine. A tidal barrage generator captures high-tide water behind a dam and uses the potential energy of the water to generate electrical energy, much like a conventional hydroelectric dam. Compare and contrast these ways of using tidal energy.

_____

_____

_____

_____

_____

_____

10. Describe the relationship between the power plants that generate electrical energy and the infrastructure that distributes this energy. Explain the role that energy storage serves in this system.

_____

_____

_____

_____

_____

_____

_____

MAKE YOUR OWN STUDY GUIDE

 In your Evidence Notebook, design a study guide that supports the main ideas from this lesson:

Electrical energy can be generated by turbines that rely on mechanical or thermal energy sources and by solar cells.

Induction is used to transfer electrical energy between circuits in an electric grid.

Batteries store electrical energy and provide direct current.

Different means of producing electrical energy have various costs and benefits, and may be well or poorly suited to different situations.

Remember to include the following information in your study guide:
- Use examples that model main ideas.
- Record explanations for the phenomena you investigated.
- Use evidence to support your explanations. Your support can include drawings, data, graphs, laboratory conclusions, and other evidence recorded throughout the lesson.

Consider how modern civilization depends on the reliable distribution of electrical energy.

Chemistry Connection

Chemistry of a Battery Batteries have two electrodes, the connections that conduct current in and out of a medium. The electrodes are separated by an electrolyte, a substance such as an acid, base, or salt that conducts electrical energy through the motion of ions. When in a circuit, electrons from the negative electrode flow through the wire toward the positive electrode.

> Single-use and rechargeable batteries are used to store and distribute electrical energy. Research the science that underlies alkaline batteries, one of the most common types of battery. Make an infographic of an alkaline battery in which you label the parts and indicate how energy is transferred through the battery.

FIGURE 1: Cutaway view of an alkaline battery

Music Connection

Electric Guitar Pickups A variety of mechanisms can be used to detect vibrations in a string. One device, known as a magnetic pickup, consists of coils of wire wrapped around several magnets. Magnetic pickups can detect vibrations in ferromagnetic strings and use that motion to generate an electrical signal.

> Research the design and functionality of one variety of pickup. Incorporate a sound recording of music made using this pickup into an oral or multimedia presentation, which should focus on the engineering design of pickups. Include how this pickup interacts with the instrument and how the pickup affects the use of the instrument.

FIGURE 2: This pickup—the black oval—consists of magnets in a coil of wire.

Technology Connection

Electric Circuits in Textiles Smart textiles include flexible electrical components. Garments made with these textiles might use energy from a battery, a solar cell, or other sources. Some applications are aesthetic—clothes that change color or light up. Other uses are practical, such as clothing that can produce extra warmth when it's cold or cool you when it's hot. Medical applications include fabric with optical fibers that can be used to treat infants with jaundice.

> Research smart textiles. Write a blog post that describes one way in which a smart textile is applied. Include the problem the smart textile is designed to solve and how the smart textile differs from other approaches used to address that problem.

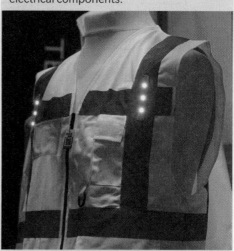

FIGURE 3: Smart textiles are embedded with electrical components.

Source: (c) ©Roger Fletcher/Alamy; (b) ©Ian Davidson/Alamy Live News/Alamy

THING EXPLAINER BY RANDALL MUNROE

A BOOK EXPLAINING
COMPLEX IDEAS
USING
ONLY THE 1,000 MOST
COMMON WORDS

FOOD-HEATING RADIO BOX

Waves that make pieces of water move faster

You know that microwaves are a high-frequency form of electromagnetic radiation. How does a microwave oven cook food faster and more efficiently than other types of ovens? Here's a look at what makes microwaves so useful.

RANDALL MUNROE
XKCD.COM

THE STORY OF HEATING FOOD WITH RADIO WAVES

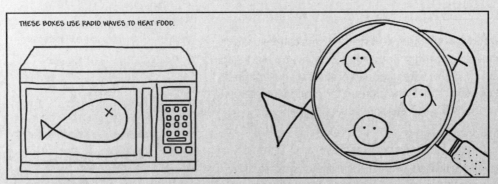

THESE BOXES USE RADIO WAVES TO HEAT FOOD.

RADIO WAVES PUSH ON THE TINY PIECES WATER IS MADE OF AND MAKE THEM GO FASTER.

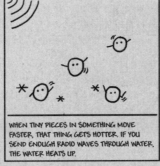

WHEN TINY PIECES IN SOMETHING MOVE FASTER, THAT THING GETS HOTTER. IF YOU SEND ENOUGH RADIO WAVES THROUGH WATER, THE WATER HEATS UP.

MINE DOESN'T LOOK GOOD . . .

TNK!

FOOD-HEATING RADIO BOXES CAN HEAT UP COLD FOOD YOU SAVED, AND LET YOU BUY FOOD THAT'S FULL OF ICE, KEEP IT FOR A LONG TIME, AND THEN HEAT IT AND GET RID OF THE ICE.

THESE BOXES MADE IT MUCH EASIER FOR PEOPLE TO EAT WITHOUT SPENDING A LONG TIME MAKING THEIR FOOD.

GREAT . . . NOW WHAT DO I DO WITH THE OTHER TEN HUNDRED OR SO MINUTES?

YOU CAN ALSO USE A RADIO BOX TO TAKE FRESH FOOD (LIKE FISH) AND HEAT IT UP AND TURN IT INTO DIFFERENT KINDS OF FOOD, JUST LIKE YOU DO WITH THE OTHER HEATING BOXES IN YOUR KITCHEN.

BUT IT CAN BE HARD TO USE FOR THAT, SO BE CAREFUL, ESPECIALLY WITH FOOD MADE FROM ANIMALS.

OK, WHO HEATED UP THE FISH IN THE FOOD-HEATING RADIO BOX??

Microwave diagram (left)

HOW LONG

OPEN

HOW LONG ← Time teller

TIME HEAT | HOW HOT | JUST BE A TIMER ← Controls you actually use

TEA | FISH | WINE
JUST ICE | LEAVES | PLASTIC FOOD
HAIR | LONG HAIR | SAND
OUTER SPACE | CAT EGGS | KNIVES
FLOWERS | GLASSES | MONEY
SHARE ON FACE BOOK | TEETH | FIRE

← Lots of other controls they always add even though no one ever wants them

ONE | TWO | THREE
FOUR | FIVE | SIX
SEVEN | EIGHT | THE NUMBER AFTER EIGHT
NONE

← Numbers (pointing at SIX)

NEVER MIND | START ← Starter

OPEN ← Door opener

RADIO

These radio boxes use exactly the same size of wave as the computer "hot spots" in your house. Different kinds of radio machines use different sizes of waves, but these two use the same size. There's a reason for that.

At the same time food-heating radio boxes started being used a lot, people were building more and more radios to send messages. Countries decided to leave the wave size used by radio boxes (about hand-sized) open for anyone to use, since radio boxes everywhere were already using it. When people started making computer radios, they used that size, since it was one of the few sizes of wave that anyone was allowed to use at home.

Now, the whole world sends messages from their computers using the food-heating radio box wave size. It works fine—the only problem is that if there's a hole in your radio box, it can make the movie on your computer stop for a moment while you make food.

COMPUTER "HOT SPOTS"

WHY IS THERE ICE IN HOT FOOD?

Radio boxes are good at heating water but bad at heating ice. They *can* heat ice, but it takes a long time.

When you put iced food in a radio box, after a while, parts of it start to turn to water. But since radio boxes are really good at heating water, those parts start to get hot really fast. They can even get so hot they start turning to air—before all the ice is even gone!

To get around this problem, you can run the radio box on low power, which will heat the food with lots of pauses in between. That gives time for the hot parts to spread out, and no one spot will get too warm.

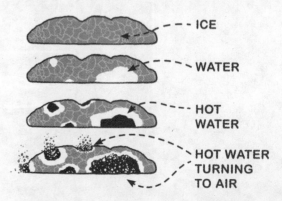

ICE

WATER

HOT WATER

HOT WATER TURNING TO AIR

FOOD-HEATING RADIO BOX

RADIO WAVE STOPPER
This stuff, which you see if you look inside the door, stops radio waves from getting out. They can't really hurt you—other than by slowly warming you up—but they could hurt other radios or make little flashes of light.

SPINNER
This spinner waves a metal stick to change the shape of the radio waves so the warm spots, which are places where the waves are strong, move around a little.

RADIO HALLWAY
This hallway carries the radio waves into the food box.

LIGHT

RADIO WAVES
The shapes they make are why food gets hot and cold spots.

REAL SIZE
This is about how big food radio waves are

This spinner turns the plate to try to give each piece of food some time in the hot areas.

FOOD PLATE

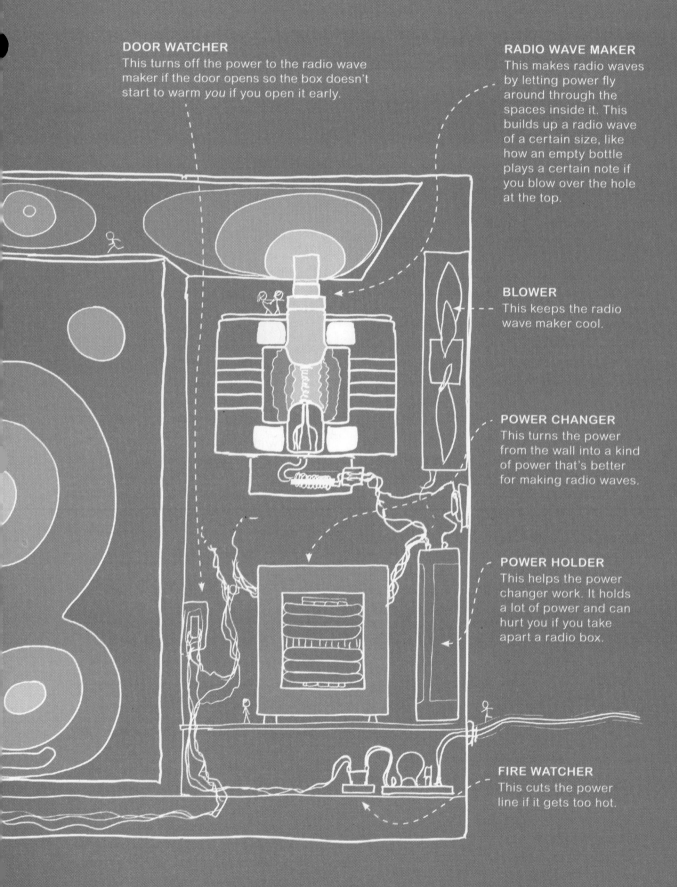

DOOR WATCHER
This turns off the power to the radio wave maker if the door opens so the box doesn't start to warm *you* if you open it early.

RADIO WAVE MAKER
This makes radio waves by letting power fly around through the spaces inside it. This builds up a radio wave of a certain size, like how an empty bottle plays a certain note if you blow over the hole at the top.

BLOWER
This keeps the radio wave maker cool.

POWER CHANGER
This turns the power from the wall into a kind of power that's better for making radio waves.

POWER HOLDER
This helps the power changer work. It holds a lot of power and can hurt you if you take apart a radio box.

FIRE WATCHER
This cuts the power line if it gets too hot.

Analyzing Materials for Circuits

One property of many metals is electrical conductivity, the ability to conduct electrical energy. However, conductivity is not the only factor in determining which metals should be used. Other factors must be taken into account, including the cost and availability of the metal and the environmental impacts of obtaining it.

In this activity, you will explore why particular metals are chosen for an application. You will use a multimeter to measure the electrical resistance across different types of metals that may be used to make a wire. You will also research how the use of certain metals affects their value in terms of economic impact, and you will explore how cost is a factor in decisions about what metals are used in different applications. Finally, you will research the disposal and recycling of materials widely used in electrical components.

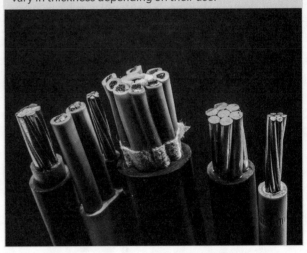
FIGURE 4: Wires may be made of different metals and vary in thickness depending on their use.

1. DEFINE THE PROBLEM

Select an application that requires a metal conductor. Describe how you will use a multimeter and research to explore which metal may be best for the application.

2. CONDUCT RESEARCH

Research the types of metals commonly used in home electric circuits or other components. Also look for other types of metals that could be used. Research the metals' economic history and environmental impact, as well as how the metals can be disposed of or recycled. Determine how to test the electrical resistance of a metal sample and how this value relates to conductivity.

3. CARRY OUT AN INVESTIGATION

Test the resistance of a variety of metals using a multimeter, and calculate conductivity for each sample. Measure conductivity for different wire types of similar diameter over short and long lengths, if possible.

4. ANALYZE DATA

Organize and analyze the measurements and observations you collected. Determine which metals may be best for use as wires in different applications. Remember that the cost of the metal may affect whether it is a good choice based on how much material is needed for an application.

5. COMMUNICATE

Prepare a written presentation in which you describe which metals may be best for a home electric circuit or other application. Describe how economic, environmental, and physical properties of a metal affect the choice of material for a given application. Include evidence from your research and investigation to support your argument.

CHECK YOUR WORK

Once you have completed this task, you should have the following:

- a method for measuring electrical resistance and conductivity
- an assessment of the costs and environmental impacts associated with the mining, purifying, and processing of various metals
- an explanation of the uses and applications of various metals in electric circuits and other electrical components
- a summary of information about certain metals and applications where they might best be used

Name _____

Date _____

SYNTHESIZE THE UNIT

In your Evidence Notebook, make a concept map, other graphic organizer, or outline using the Study Guides you made for each lesson in this unit. Be sure to use evidence to support your claims.

When synthesizing individual information, remember to follow these general steps:
- Find the central idea of each piece of information.
- Think about the relationships among the central ideas.
- Combine the ideas to come up with a new understanding.

DRIVING QUESTIONS

Look back to the Driving Questions from the opening section of this unit. In your Evidence Notebook, review and revise your previous answers to those questions. Use the evidence you gathered and other observations you made throughout the unit to support your claims.

PRACTICE AND REVIEW

1. Select the correct terms to complete the statement.

To transfer electrical energy with little loss of energy, it helps to raise, or step up, the current | voltage | resistance before transfer. At point of use, it is stepped back down. This is easily done with direct | alternating current because of the connection between constant | changing magnetic fields and electric current.

2. A magnetic field will form around a straight current carrying wire. Electromagnets instead use a design of tightly packed coils of wire. How does this improve the magnet? Select all correct answers.

☐ **a.** The field around each section of wire combines with that of nearby sections.

☐ **b.** Charge can only flow in loops.

☐ **c.** The magnetic field around each loop is in the same direction.

☐ **d.** The magnetic field around each loop alternates.

3. Some renewable-energy technologies insert a generator into a naturally occurring energy transfer or transformation. Order the forms of energy into the sequence that is used by a tidal power plant.

_____ **a.** electrical energy stored in battery

_____ **b.** gravitational potential energy

_____ **c.** electrical energy as current

_____ **d.** kinetic energy of water

4. What might happen when the voltage in a circuit is increased? Select all correct answers.

☐ **a.** The amount of electrical energy transferred to the circuit increases.

☐ **b.** If electrical resistance is held steady, current decreases.

☐ **c.** If electrical resistance is held steady, current increases.

☐ **d.** More current moves outside the circuit.

☐ **e.** The energy of electrons in the circuit increases.

5. Select the correct terms to complete the statement.

If the current in an electric circuit flows clockwise, the movement of negatively charged particles is clockwise | counterclockwise | both clockwise and counterclockwise. The movement of charge in an electric circuit is caused by a magnetic field | an electric potential difference | other charges in the circuit.

6. Correctly order the steps in the process of a coal-burning power plant.

_____ **a.** Coal is burned.

_____ **b.** Steam condenses to water.

_____ **c.** Steam spins a turbine.

_____ **d.** Water changes into steam.

7. Why is it preferred to transfer energy across long distances in the form of electrical energy, even in cases when the input and output are both kinetic energy?

_____

_____

_____

_____

_____

8. Draw a device that could use electromagnetic induction to illuminate a light bulb. Label the key components, and indicate which are moving and which are stationary. Clearly identify the energy input and output.

9. A small community is being planned in an isolated area, but its population is expected to grow over the next decade. Compare two different ways in which electrical energy might be generated and distributed for such a community. Choose one renewable and one nonrenewable source of energy. Identify any natural resources or features required for each of the two sources.

_____

_____

_____

_____

UNIT PROJECT

Return to your unit project. Prepare a presentation using your research and materials, and share it with the class. In your final presentation, demonstrate your electric generator. It should be able to make a light-emitting diode shine.

Remember these tips while evaluating:

- Explain how your model is similar to industrial generators.

- Describe any design features that you refined through trial and error.

- Explain how your model works. Include specifics such as why the magnet is positioned where it is, how to coil the wire, and the distance between magnets and coil.

UNIT 5

Wave Energy and Communication

YOU SOLVE IT

Is It Possible to Predict a Solar Storm?

 To begin exploring this unit's concepts, go online to investigate ways to solve a real-world problem.

In this photograph of a supersonic jet, areas of different air pressure appear as light and dark regions.

FIGURE 1: The ALMA radio telescope array in Chile is used to make astronomical observations.

When you gaze at the stars at night, you see only the narrow band of energy in the visible light spectrum. Stars emit light at other frequencies, which carry information about both stars and the intervening space through which the energy traveled. The design of radio telescope arrays—the shape and size of each dish and the number of dishes in an array—changes the amount of energy collected. Radio telescope arrays are usually located far from cities to avoid interference from other electromagnetic waves, such as radio and television broadcasts. ALMA was part of 8 telescopes and telescope arrays coordinated in a planet-sized array known as the Event Horizon Telescope, which produced the first direct image of a black hole's shadow and its surroundings in April 2019.

EXPLAIN How do you think the radio telescope array pictured is able to transfer the incoming wave energy from space into usable information?

_____

_____

DRIVING QUESTIONS

As you move through the unit, gather evidence to help you answer the following questions. In your Evidence Notebook, record what you already know about these topics and any questions you have about them.

1. Why are water waves spaced evenly apart?

2. What happens when waves interact?

3. Why can light waves be transmitted across empty space, while sound waves cannot?

4. What is the difference between analog and digital?

UNIT PROJECT

Go online to download the Unit Project Worksheet to help plan your project.

The Effect of Waves on Matter

People are exposed to many sources of electromagnetic radiation, such as the waves of radio and television broadcasts. Electromagnetic radiation is emitted by power lines that connect homes and businesses to the electric grid and by portable devices such as cell phones. Local wireless Internet is only possible if energy is always transmitted into the area. Some people worry about possible health effects of electromagnetic radiation. Research electromagnetic radiation and claims about its effects on human health. Determine whether scientific research tends to support or refute those claims.

Language Development

Use the lessons in this unit to complete the chart and expand your understanding of the science concepts.

TERM: mechanical wave

Definition	Example

Similar Term	Phrase

TERM: transverse wave

Definition	Example

Similar Term	Phrase

TERM: longitudinal wave

Definition	Example

Similar Term	Phrase

TERM: wavelength

Definition	Example

Similar Term	Phrase

TERM: frequency

Definition

Example

Similar Term

Phrase

TERM: amplitude

Definition

Example

Similar Term

Phrase

TERM: electromagnetic radiation

Definition

Example

Similar Term

Phrase

TERM: photon

Definition

Example

Similar Term

Phrase

Modeling and Using Waves

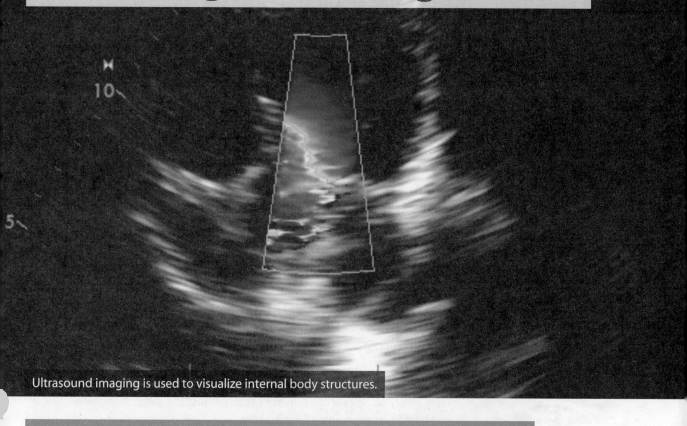

Ultrasound imaging is used to visualize internal body structures.

CAN YOU EXPLAIN THE PHENOMENON?

Ultrasound imaging is a medical scanning technique used to visualize soft tissue, such as muscles, organs, blood vessels, and the human heart shown in the image. It is sometimes used in conjunction with x-rays, which are good at imaging bone and the air-filled spaces in the lungs but poor at distinguishing between different types of soft tissue. Ultrasound imaging also has nonmedical applications, and it is used to analyze mechanical structures for hidden faults not visible on their outside.

APPLY How could sound waves help physicians see internal body structures?

_____

_____

_____

_____

_____

 Evidence Notebook As you explore the lesson, gather evidence to explain how the interaction of sound waves with matter is used in ultrasound imaging.

Classifying Waves

Waves rolling across a body of water may be produced when wind blows on the water's surface or when something such as a boat moves at or just below the water's surface. In other words, waves can be produced when something disturbs the surface of the water.

A series of water waves has high points and low points. A wave on the surface of a body of water is a curve with equal and opposite displacements above and below the equilibrium position, which is the level of the undisturbed water.

 Hands-On Activity

Waves in Water

FIGURE 1: A falling drop of water generates ripples when it lands.

Ripples, small waves on the surface of a liquid, form patterns that can give information about the disturbance that caused the ripples.

POSSIBLE MATERIALS

• container of water   • dropper or pipette

SAFETY INFORMATION

• Wear safety goggles and a nonlatex apron during the setup, hands-on, and takedown segments of the activity.

• Immediately wipe up any spilled water on the floor so it does not become a slip/fall hazard.

PLAN THE INVESTIGATION

• After filling the container with water, let any motion die down before observing the effect of adding droplets to the surface.

• Consider whether the shape of the container affects the appearance of waves on the water surface. Consider how you can change the energy of the falling droplet.

ANALYZE

1. Describe the pattern when a drop of water falls on still water. How does increasing the kinetic energy of a falling droplet change the pattern of ripples produced?

_____

_____

2. What happens to the kinetic energy from the water droplet when the ripples stop?

_____

_____

_____

Waves and Media

The world around you is full of waves. Some waves, such as water ripples and vibrations of a guitar string, are easy to identify. Others, such as sound and light, might not be easy to identify as waves. Waves can be classified as either mechanical or electromagnetic. A mechanical wave requires a medium through which to travel and is a transfer of energy through a medium by oscillation of the medium. Oscillations are back-and-forth motions around a central point. The generation of mechanical waves requires an initial input of energy. For water waves, this energy might come from wind or a passing boat. Electromagnetic waves are different from mechanical waves because they do not require a medium to travel. Energy from the sun travels as electromagnetic waves through the vacuum of space to Earth. Sunlight used by plants for photosynthesis and ultraviolet light that can cause sunburn are examples of electromagnetic waves from the sun.

 Evidence Notebook Different types of electromagnetic (EM) waves include microwaves, infrared waves, x-rays, and gamma rays. Where could you gather information about various types of EM waves for the unit project? Compare and contrast the various types of EM waves.

Waves and Motion

Mechanical waves can often take one of two forms. In transverse waves, the medium oscillates perpendicular to the direction in which the wave travels. In longitudinal waves, the medium oscillates parallel to the direction in which the wave travels. Imagine a bird floating in the water when a large wave passes by. The bird bobs up and down but does not seem to travel away with the wave. Surface water waves actually consist of both transverse and longitudinal waves, but the dominant motion of a floating object is up and down. The floating object's displacement is much larger in the vertical direction than in the horizontal direction. Because of this, a surface water wave is often simplified as an up-and-down oscillation of the water.

FIGURE 2: The up-and-down motion of a ball on the surface of the water as a wave passes

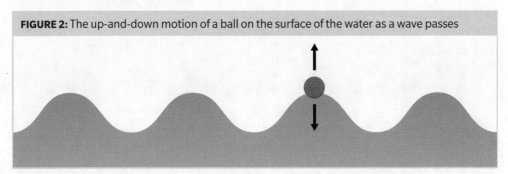

APPLY Which is the best description for the type of wave shown in Figure 2?

○ **a.** a longitudinal wave because the motion of the floating object is perpendicular to the direction in which the wave travels

○ **b.** a longitudinal wave because the motion of the medium is parallel to the direction in which the wave travels

○ **c.** a transverse wave because the motion of the floating object is perpendicular to the direction in which the wave travels

○ **d.** a transverse wave because the motion of the medium is parallel to the direction in which the wave travels

A transverse wave can be demonstrated with a rope attached to a wall. By holding the free end of the rope and moving it up and down, a wave will move through the rope toward the wall. As seen from the side, the tops of the waves are called *crests* or *peaks*, and the bottoms are *troughs*.

A longitudinal wave can be demonstrated with a popular child's toy, a long spring that is easy to stretch. Suppose the toy is extended along the floor between two people, stretched to several times its resting length. One person pushes forward on one end, compressing the first few coils. This area of compression will travel along the length of the spring as a pulse of compression or density.

FIGURE 3: A longitudinal wave travels along a spring.

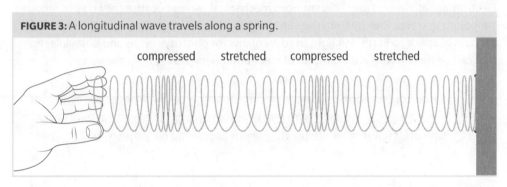

compressed   stretched   compressed   stretched

If the deformation of the coil is not a single pulse but instead a series of regular compressions and decompressions, it will generate a longitudinal wave. The regions of high coil density are the *compressions*. Between the compressions, there are regions with low coil density, known as *rarefactions*. Midway between each compression and rarefaction, the coil density is what it would be with no wave in the spring—the equilibrium density.

MODEL Draw a transverse wave and a longitudinal wave. Label each wave as either *transverse* or *longitudinal*. For each wave, label its direction and its parts (*crests* and *troughs*, or *compressions* and *rarefactions*).

ANALYZE Describe the ways that longitudinal and transverse waves are similar to and different from each other.

_____

_____

 Evidence Notebook Sound waves are longitudinal waves. Do you think sound waves are mechanical waves or electromagnetic waves? Explain your reasoning.

Modeling Waves

Sound waves begin with motion. For example, when a guitar string is plucked, transverse waves travel along the string. This vibration is transferred from the instrument to the surrounding air as a longitudinal wave, in which the compressions and rarefactions are areas of high and low air pressure, respectively.

INFER How is a person able to hear a sound from a guitar played across a room?

_____

_____

Sound Waves

Contrary to what is often shown in science fiction movies, no sound can travel through space. Sound waves are mechanical waves and require a medium in which to travel. Similar to waves on the surface of the water or along a stretched spring, the oscillating particles that carry a sound wave do not move very far from their starting positions. In a fluid, such as air or water, sound waves are longitudinal waves.

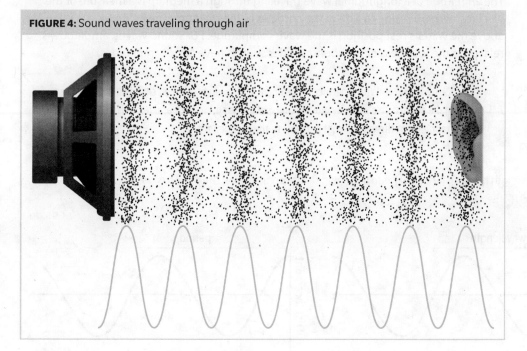

FIGURE 4: Sound waves traveling through air

EXPLAIN What do the dots and the blue line in Figure 4 represent?

_____

_____

In a solid, sound can be a transverse wave or a longitudinal wave. You can experience sound traveling through a solid with a tuning fork. Strike the fork, and then hold the handle against your jaw. You should feel small vibrations and hear a tone. The vibration moved along your jaw to the inside of the ear, rather than through the air to the outside.

EXPLAIN Suppose your friend played an instrumental version of your favorite song. How could you recognize your favorite song without the words? What properties of sound can help you identify it?

_____

_____

_____

Properties of Waves

Like all waves, sound waves can be described by their properties, which include frequency, wavelength, and period. Notes in a song have different pitches because they have different frequencies. The frequency of a wave is the number of wave maxima (or minima or any two corresponding points) passing a location per unit time. The units for frequency, f, are hertz (Hz), or cycles per second (s^{-1}). Frequency is related to wavelength, which is the distance from any point on a wave to its next consecutive point. For example, the wavelength of a longitudinal wave can be measured between two adjacent compressions of the wave, and the wavelength of a transverse wave can be measured between two of its adjacent crests. Wavelength is symbolized as λ and is usually given in meters. The _period_, T, of a wave is the time for a wave to complete one cycle and is usually measured in seconds.

The amplitude of a longitudinal wave traveling through a medium is a measure of the displacement from side to side of the particles in the medium. The height of a water wave above the water's rest position is the wave's amplitude. For sound waves, amplitude is related to the loudness of the sound: louder sounds have larger amplitudes.

 Collaborate With a partner, experiment with a long spring, each of you holding one end. Make a transverse wave by moving one end of the spring back and forth. Then increase the frequency of the wave. What happens to the wavelength?

FIGURE 5: The wavelength is the distance between matching points on the wave; the period is the time between those points.

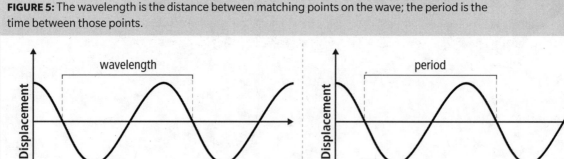

a Wavelength at a particular time

b Period at a particular location

Because all waves transfer energy from place to place, all waves have a wave speed (v). You can derive an expression for the speed, or velocity, of a wave in terms of its period or its frequency. Start with the fact that velocity of anything is equal to its displacement $\Delta\mathbf{x}$ divided by the time needed to undergo that displacement.

$$\mathbf{v} = \frac{\Delta\mathbf{x}}{\Delta t}$$

Then consider that, for waves, a displacement of one wavelength (λ) occurs in one period of the vibration (T) as shown in Figure 5.

SOLVE Select the correct terms to complete the formula for the speed of a wave in terms of its wavelength and period.

speed = wavelength | period × | ÷ wavelength | period

Imagine a young child walking with an adult. In order for the child to walk at the same speed, side by side with the adult, the child needs to take more steps per unit time. Both walk at the same speed but their number of steps per unit time (frequency of steps taken) are different. Now think about how much time it takes for each of them to take a certain number of steps. It takes the child less time to take that certain number of steps. In other words, a higher frequency means a shorter amount of time for one cycle (number of steps), or period. Mathematically, because frequency is equal to 1/T, you can write the formula for speed in terms of wavelength and frequency as:

$$v = \lambda f$$

The speed of sound in a medium depends on the medium's compressibility and its density. The less compressible (or more rigid) the medium, the faster the speed of sound. The greater the density of a medium, the slower the speed of sound. Because the density of a medium varies with its temperature, the speed of sound varies with the temperature of the medium through which it travels.

INFER Imagine you are in front of a musical band. Several instruments play at the same time, generating sound waves with different frequencies. All those sound waves travel the same distance to you, and you hear them at the same time, with no time lag between them. What can you infer about the characteristics of sound waves from that scenario?

_____

_____

Cause and Effect

Wave Speed in Different Media

Changes in temperature alter the medium through which a wave travels. When a given wave passes through a different medium, its frequency stays the same. In a magazine, you read a claim that the wavelength of thunder in air at a lower temperature is shorter than the wavelength in warmer air.

APPLY The speed of sound in dry air at 0.0 °C is 331 m/s. For every 10 °C increase in temperature, the speed increases by 6.0 m/s. The frequency of thunder, the sound associated with lightning, is about 100 Hz. Find the wavelength of this wave in dry air at 10 °C and at 30 °C. Report your answers to two significant figures.

_____

EVALUATE Use your answer to evaluate the magazine's claim. What do you think causes the change in wavelength as the medium changes?

_____

_____

Sound Waves

SAMPLE PROBLEM	A piano string tuned to middle C vibrates with a frequency of 262 Hz. Assuming the speed of sound in air is 343 m/s, find the wavelength of the sound waves produced by the string.
ANALYZE	Known: $f = 262$ Hz, $v = 343$ m/s Unknown: wavelength λ
PLAN	Solve the speed equation for λ. Substitute the values for f and v, and solve for λ.
SOLVE	$v = \lambda f$ $\lambda = v/f$ $\lambda = (343 \text{ m/s})/(262 \text{ s}^{-1}) = 1.31$ m
CHECK YOUR WORK	Check that the wavelength times the frequency equals the speed: $v = \lambda f = (1.31 \text{ m})(262 \text{ s}^{-1}) = 343$ m/s, as expected.
PRACTICE PROBLEMS	**SOLVE** Answer the following questions. Report your final answer using the correct number of significant figures.

1. Assume the speed of sound in water is 1500 m/s. What is the wavelength of a 262 Hz middle C under water? _____

2. The frequency of thunder is about 100 Hz. What is the period of a wave of thunder? _____

3. The lowest note on a piano has a frequency of 27.5 Hz. Find its wavelength in air. Use $v = 343$ m/s. _____

4. Find the period, in air, of a sound with wavelength 1.5 m. Use $v = 343$ m/s. _____

Sound Waves and Human Hearing

The average human ear can hear frequencies from 20 Hz to 20 000 Hz. Sound waves can have lower and higher frequencies, but these waves are not detectable by unaided human ears. Sound waves that have frequencies below 20 Hz are called infrasound. Infrasound can be heard by some animals, including elephants and pigeons. Infrasound sources include avalanches, earthquakes, volcanic explosions, and meteors. Sound waves with frequencies above 20 000 Hz are called ultrasound. Animals, such as dogs, bottlenose dolphins, and some insects, can hear ultrasound. Ultrasound imaging uses ultrasound waves. Bats, some whales, and some electronic devices produce ultrasound.

 Evidence Notebook The speed of ultrasound waves increases as they move from lung tissue to muscle. The frequency of the waves remains the same as they pass the boundary. How do you expect the wavelength of the ultrasound waves to change when they go from lung to muscle?

Case Study: March 2011 Tsunami

A wave transmits energy over distance, through matter or empty space, without transmitting matter over that distance. For mechanical waves, the wave temporarily moves the medium through which it travels. For example, sound waves travel through the air by the collision of air molecules. These molecules transfer kinetic energy in the direction of the wave's propagation and rebound toward their original position.

Ocean Waves

Like all waves, water waves transfer energy. In the ocean, most waves are produced when wind blowing on the water transfers kinetic energy to the water. The energy transfer is near the surface. The waves are confined to an area near the surface. To an observer submerged several meters below the surface, the waves are barely discernible.

In contrast, a tsunami is an ocean wave caused by a large displacement of water that can follow undersea earthquakes, volcanic eruptions, and landslides. Compared to regular surface waves, tsunamis have much longer wavelengths (sometimes hundreds of kilometers) and longer periods (anywhere from five or ten minutes up to one or two hours). In the deep ocean, the amplitude of the surface wave of a tsunami is small, perhaps less than 1 m. However, energy is being transmitted throughout the entire depth of the ocean, rather than being confined to a shallow area near the surface. Unlike regular surface waves, the speed of a tsunami wave depends on the water depth at the location where it is traveling.

A Tsunami in Japan

Just off the east coast of Japan on March 11, 2011, two colliding tectonic plates under the ocean floor caused an earthquake that lasted several minutes. The upthrust of this earthquake displaced the water above it, producing a tsunami that spread outward. Less than an hour later, the tsunami began to reach the Japanese shore. The tsunami caused massive destruction to buildings and damaged a nuclear power plant.

FIGURE 6: The March 2011 tsunami washed these boats onshore in Japan.

Getty Images

Rogue Waves

Tsunamis are not the only menacingly tall ocean waves. Rogue waves, once thought to be mythical, have been verified as isolated surface waves that are much taller than the average wave height for a region. Rogue waves do not have a distinct cause. Instead, rogue waves are thought to form when high winds and current conditions allow many waves to merge together to generate a very tall wave.

EXPLAIN Scientists using satellite radar images to study waves in the Indian Ocean discover a wave that is 25 meters tall. What evidence would the scientists need to determine if the wave were a tsunami or some other type of wave?

_____

_____

Energy and Amplitude

A boat on calm waters may bob up and down slightly over gently rolling waves. But the same could be tossed around by tall waves. The boat moves differently because the waves it encounters carry different amounts of energy.

Explore Online ▶

Hands-On Lab

Spring Toy Use a spring toy to demonstrate the motion of waves.

The energy of a wave is related to its amplitude. For a wave traveling through a medium, the wave's amplitude is the maximum distance that the particles of the medium oscillate from their rest position. For a transverse wave, amplitude is the distance between a crest (or trough) and the equilibrium position.

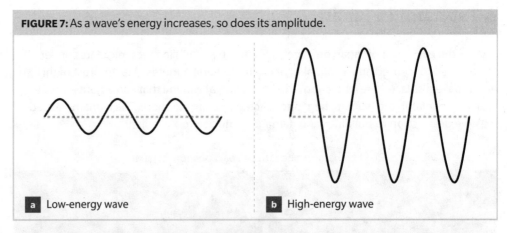

FIGURE 7: As a wave's energy increases, so does its amplitude.

a Low-energy wave

b High-energy wave

The energy of a wave is proportional to the square of its amplitude. Imagine two water droplets falling into water from different heights. If the second water droplet produces ripples twice as high as those produced by the first droplet, this means that the second water droplet has four times as much energy as the first one.

INFER Think about what happens to a water ripple as it spreads away from its source. What happens to the amplitude of the ripples? What can you infer about their energy?

_____

_____

ANALYZE As a tsunami approaches the coastline, it moves into shallower water. Write the descriptions on the image of how the wavelength (λ) and the amplitude (A) of the surface wave change with water depth.

shorter λ   longer λ   smaller A   larger A

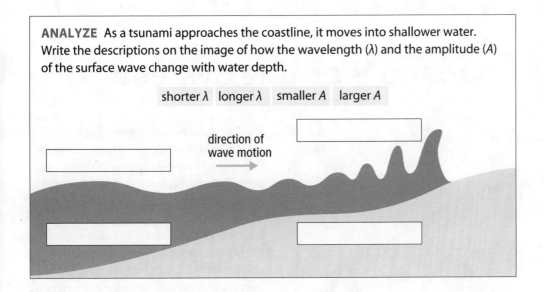

direction of wave motion →

Scale of Damage of the March 2011 Tsunami

The epicenter of the 9.0-magnitude earthquake that triggered the tsunami in March 2011 was located about 70 km east of the shore of Honshu, the main island of Japan. The tsunami traveled approximately 10 km in to shore and completely covered more than 500 km^2 of land. The 5–8 m displacement from the earthquake caused tsunami waves to reach run-up heights up to 40 m. Run-up is a measure of how high waves go above sea level and is similar to a measure of amplitude. The Japanese Police Agency reported that almost 300 000 buildings were destroyed, and a further one million damaged. Almost 4000 roads and over 70 bridges were also damaged by the earthquake and resulting tsunami.

PREDICT The March 2011 earthquake triggered a tsunami that propagated throughout the entire Pacific Ocean. Make a prediction of the wave height and level of destruction at locations along the California and Oregon coast.

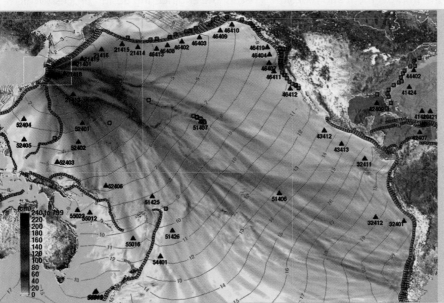

Explore Online ▶

FIGURE 8: The map colors indicate how the tsunami's amplitude changed as it spread out through the Pacific Ocean. The changing colors indicate changes in wave amplitude and energy. Darker colors (black and gray) correspond to higher amplitudes and energy, and lighter colors (yellow and green) correspond to lower amplitudes and energy.

Tsunami Warning Systems

FIGURE 9: The DART II tsunami warning system

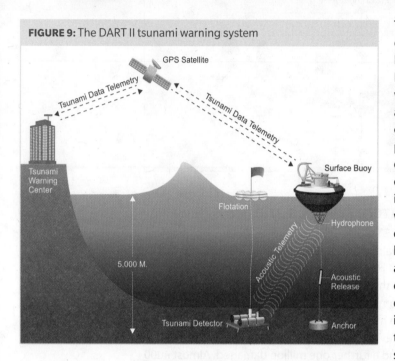

The Deep-ocean Assessment and Reporting of Tsunamis (DART) project is a network of buoys used to detect and report tsunamis. Because tsunamis travel fast in deep ocean water, quick and accurate warning systems are needed to save lives. DART I went into operation in 2003 and was a series of six pressure detectors at various locations on the sea floor, each with a companion communication surface buoy. A detector identified if a tsunami had passed over it when the pressure increased due to the extra height of water above it. Each surface buoy had one-way communication with a satellite that sent data to a warning center every 15 minutes. If a tsunami were detected, the buoy would automatically go into event mode and increase the reporting to every 1 minute. DART I buoy locations served to protect U.S. coastal areas.

After a devastating tsunami in the Indian Ocean in 2004, the importance of a global warning system became obvious. Engineers researched the requirements of a global detection system, assessed the deficiencies of DART I, brainstormed possible solutions, and improved upon DART I's design. DART II went into operation in 2005, and today it consists of a network of 39 buoys that use a two-way communication system with a satellite. The redesign allows scientists to manually put the buoys into event mode when a tsunami event is anticipated. This improvement allows the system to give earlier warnings so that people have more time to evacuate or prepare.

ANALYZE Improvement and redesign is part of the engineering design process. Which of these design improvements were made to DART I to help solve the global tsunami detection problem? Select all correct answers.

☐ **a.** one-way communication with satellite and buoy

☐ **b.** two-way communication with satellite and buoy

☐ **c.** increase in the number of detectors worldwide

☐ **d.** increase in the number of detectors at each location

☐ **e.** automatic event-mode reporting ability

☐ **f.** manual event-mode reporting ability

 Evidence Notebook Think back to the falling drops of water producing ripples. The ripples disappeared as their amplitude decreased. What does this indicate about the energy of the wave? Ultrasound imaging involves sending sound waves through various thicknesses of body tissue. How is the loss of wave amplitude related to the limitations of ultrasound imaging?

Wave Behavior

A waveform is a representation of a wave. Some waveforms can be easily seen, such as a transverse wave moving along a string. Others can be shown using a graph of some variable over time, such as the pressure over time for a sound wave. The sine graph is an example of a waveform.

 Collaborate With a partner, make a list of the characteristics of a sine graph, describing which features of the graph indicate that it corresponds to a sine function.

Wave Interference

Wave interference happens when two or more waves meet at the same point and combine into one wave. When waves interfere, the amplitude of the combined wave is equal to the sum of the amplitudes of the two waves. For transverse waves, if one has an amplitude of +5 cm and the other an amplitude of +2 cm, the combined waveform will have an amplitude of +7 cm at that point. If the second wave instead has an amplitude of −2 cm, the combined wave will have an amplitude of +3 cm at that point. To find the combined amplitude of a sound wave, you would combine the changes in pressure above or below the equilibrium pressure.

For simplicity, the illustrations in Figure 10 show the interaction of single pulses rather than longer waves. Each pulse is half a wavelength.

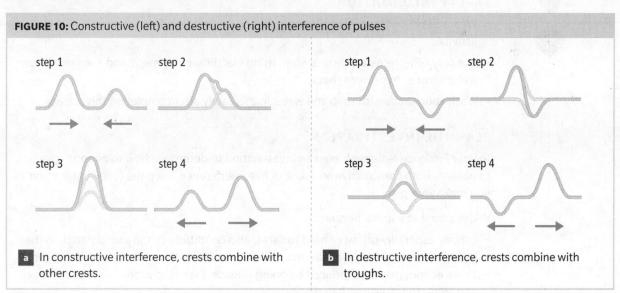

FIGURE 10: Constructive (left) and destructive (right) interference of pulses

step 1 step 2 step 1 step 2

step 3 step 4 step 3 step 4

a In constructive interference, crests combine with other crests.

b In destructive interference, crests combine with troughs.

INFER Two pulses travel toward each other in a rope. Use Figure 10 to describe what must be true for the two pulses to briefly cancel each other—that is, for the combined waveform to appear as a straight horizontal line.

_____

_____

_____

Interference of Sound Waves

In this experiment, you will use arrangements of two speakers and one observer to study constructive interference and destructive interference.

RESEARCH QUESTION

How can speakers be arranged to minimize interference that reduces sound clarity or loudness?

FIGURE 11: Destructive interference of two sound waves

MAKE A CLAIM

What determines how sound waves will interfere?

_____

_____

_____

POSSIBLE MATERIALS

- speakers (2)
- tone generator

SAFETY INFORMATION

- Wear safety goggles during the setup, hands-on, and takedown segments of the activity.
- Use only GFI-protected circuits when using electrical equipment, and keep away from water sources to prevent shock.
- Wash your hands with soap and water immediately after completing this activity.

PLAN THE INVESTIGATION

In your Evidence Notebook, plan an investigation to determine how to arrange speakers to observe both constructive and destructive interference. Keep the following in mind as you make your plan.

- Use a tone at a single frequency.
- Echoes, especially off flat or hard surfaces, also contribute to the sound heard, so the sound at a point will arrive from many directions rather than only from the speakers. These echoes might be reduced by going outside. Expect to produce zones of louder and softer tones, rather than silence.
- If the speakers are fixed in place, the observer can move to different positions.
- Research the wavelengths of audible sound frequencies, and relate this distance to reasonable distances between speakers and observer.
- Block one ear so that you are hearing the tone at only one position, not two.

Make sure your teacher approves your procedure and safety plan before proceeding.

ANALYZE

1. How did you arrange the two speakers and one observer to hear the two types of sound wave interference?

_____

_____

_____

2. When did you observe constructive interference of sound waves? When did you observe destructive interference?

_____

_____

_____

3. How strong was the effect you observed? What might account for this?

_____

_____

_____

4. In your Evidence Notebook, make a sketch of one of your setups, and note places on the diagram where you would expect to observe constructive and destructive interference.

DRAW CONCLUSIONS

Write a conclusion that addresses each of the points below.

Claim Think about the sound system you set up with two speakers and one observer. What determined how the sound waves interfered?

Evidence Give specific examples from your data to support your claim.

Reasoning Explain how the evidence you gave supports your claim. Describe in detail the connections between the evidence you cited and the argument you are making.

_____

_____

_____

_____

_____

_____

_____

_____

Reflection of Waves

At a boundary, a wave can behave in several ways. It can be transmitted, moving into the new medium. The wave can also be absorbed by the new medium, changing the medium's thermal energy (raising its temperature), or it can be reflected by the boundary between the two media. After a wave is reflected, it has the same speed, wavelength, and frequency as before.

Two types of reflection exist, and how a wave reflects affects how the wave and its reflection will interact. If the medium is fixed at a boundary, the wave will be reflected and inverted. If the medium is able to move along the boundary, the wave will be reflected without being inverted. Figure 12 shows both types of reflection of a pulse at a boundary.

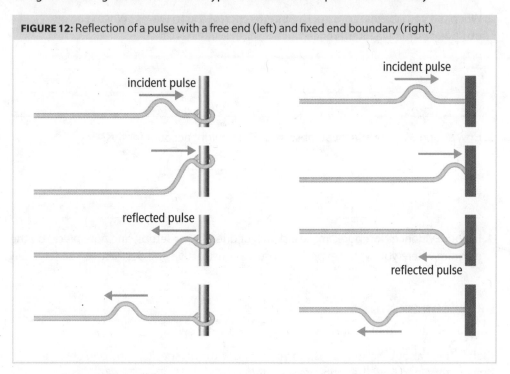

FIGURE 12: Reflection of a pulse with a free end (left) and fixed end boundary (right)

incident pulse

incident pulse

reflected pulse

reflected pulse

The concept of a fixed boundary can also represent a wave encountering a denser medium. Sound waves usually interact with a fixed boundary by reflecting off it. The incoming waves and reflected waves can interfere constructively or destructively.

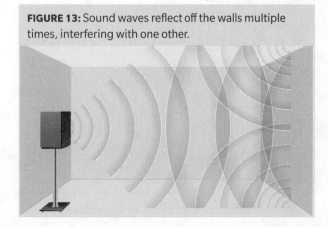

FIGURE 13: Sound waves reflect off the walls multiple times, interfering with one other.

SOLVE A wave of amplitude 0.30 m interferes with a second wave of amplitude 0.20 m. What is the largest displacement that may occur?

○ **a.** 0.60 m

○ **b.** 0.50 m

○ **c.** 0.40 m

○ **d.** 0.10 m

If the distance a sound wave travels before being reflected is long enough, the initial sound and its reflection will be heard at distinctly different times. The reflected sound is called an echo, and it can be used to measure distance. If you know the speed of sound in the medium and measure the time needed for a sound to go out and come back, you can calculate the distance the sound traveled in that time.

Bats, shrews, and other animals use echoes to find objects during a process called echolocation. Some people with visual impairments have learned to use echolocation to navigate around in their daily lives. They make clicking sounds with their tongues and listen for echoes that indicate if obstacles are in their paths. Some people are so successful at using echolocation that they can ride bikes and go hiking.

EXPLAIN Standing in a canyon, you clap your hands and hear the sound of the clap immediately, and then you hear it again 4 seconds later, after that sound has reflected off a canyon wall. How could you use this information to determine the distance to the canyon wall?

_____

_____

_____

FIGURE 14: Sound waves and their reflection

APPLY A sound wave reflects off a hard, stationary surface. What characteristics of the wave remain the same? Select all correct answers.

☐ **a.** amplitude

☐ **b.** frequency

☐ **c.** speed

☐ **d.** wavelength

Standing Waves

Explore Online ▶

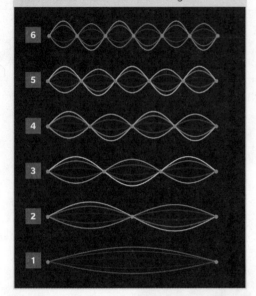

FIGURE 15: Standing waves occur in increments of one-half wavelength.

The note produced by a string depends on the string's mass, tension, and length. The mass and tension determine the speed of sound in the string. For that speed, a fundamental is the frequency of a note with a wavelength equal to twice the length of the string. The vibrating string will produce the bottom pattern shown in Figure 15, with two nodes at the ends and one antinode at the middle. The vibrating string will also produce the more complicated standing wave patterns shown. These higher frequencies, called harmonics, combine with the string's fundamental frequency to produce a complex sound.

The structures of stringed instruments are designed so the instruments can play notes of frequencies on certain ranges. On a stringed instrument, the strings are not the only parts that vibrate. The strings pass over a bridge, which transfers the strings' vibration to the hollow wooden body of the instrument. The vibration of the wood and of the enclosed air adds to the richness and volume of the sound.

If possible, with your class, test or make observations of the following scenarios. Observe as a musician plays a note, then tightens or loosens the string, and plays again. Compare the size and the different materials of the strings that produce different notes when stretched to the length used in an instrument. Pluck a stretched string that is not attached to an instrument, and compare the richness and volume of the sound.

ANALYZE

1. When the mass of the string increases, its fundamental note is at a lower frequency. What does this indicate about the speed of the transverse wave in the heavier string?

2. Consider the relationship between the pitch of notes produced by a stringed instrument and the length of the strings. Would you choose a longer or shorter neck for a stringed instrument intended to produce a very low frequency note?

3. A cellist presses down on a string, decreasing the length that can vibrate. Will the note become higher or lower?

4. Why do you think classical guitars are designed with strings made out of different materials, rather than simply varying the lengths of the strings?

 Evidence Notebook Ultrasound devices have a transducer that produces and detects ultrasound waves. How do you think an ultrasound imaging device works?

Applying Wave Behaviors

Patterns of sound echoes can be applied to map a surrounding area. Bats use echolocation to navigate and hunt, emitting sounds and detecting their echoes. They can determine both the position and the motion of potential prey. Dolphins use a similar system. Humans adapted the same principle in sonar, detecting the sound waves reflected off objects hidden underwater. The wave pattern is interpreted to determine distance.

In active sonar, such as that used by bats and dolphins, a pulse is emitted and then detected. In passive sonar, no signal is emitted by the detector. This gives less information—the time between emission and detection is unknown—but does not generate a signal that might be detected or might interfere with other signals.

Underwater Mapping

In sonar mapping, a ship emits an underwater pulse, or "ping," that travels through the water until it reaches a boundary and is reflected back. As a sonar device moves over an object, it maps its shape. An application of this technology is demonstrated by the map of the ocean floor shown in Figure 17. Maps with higher resolutions can be made using pings with shorter wavelengths.

APPLY The speed of sound in seawater increases when the water temperature increases and when the water's salt concentration, or salinity, increases. How would the pattern of sound detected by sonar change if the ship passed over a warm current? How would it change if the salinity decreased sharply near a freshwater stream flowing into the ocean?

_____

_____

_____

_____

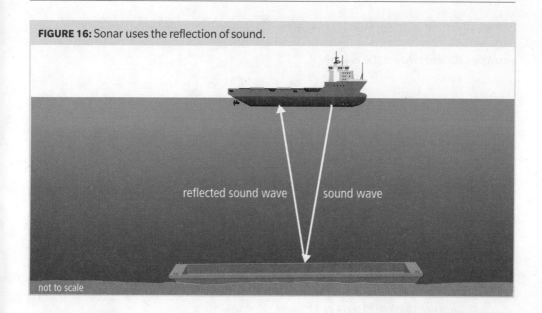

FIGURE 16: Sonar uses the reflection of sound.

reflected sound wave   sound wave

not to scale

FIGURE 17: A false-color image of the seafloor, created with sonar

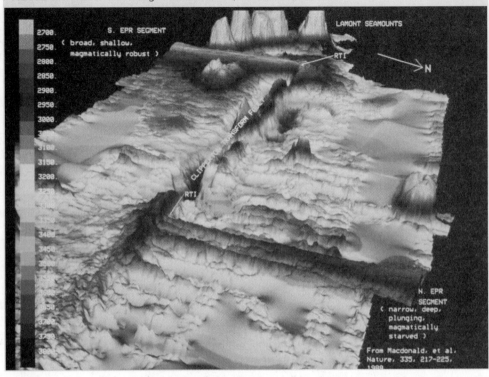

Architectural Acoustics

FIGURE 18: Music venue

Reverberation is the combination of an initial sound with its echoes. A perfectly absorbent room with no echoes would sound unnatural to an audience because it does not match our experience of sound. To limit reverberation, acoustic architecture is designed to make use of two basic principles. To absorb sound, walls may have perforated surfaces or panels covered with fabric. To scatter the reflections of sound and weaken echoes, surfaces may be curved or covered in specially designed acoustic diffusers.

APPLY The noise inside the cabin of a flying airplane can be very loud. How do you think aircraft manufacturers use architectural acoustics to minimize the noise from the airplane's turbines inside the cabin?

_____

_____

_____

_____

 Evidence Notebook An ultrasound wave encounters a layer of skin, a layer of fat, and a layer of muscle. The speed of sound in skin is 1620 m/s, in fat 1440 m/s, and in muscle 1590 m/s. What happens to an ultrasound wave as it encounters the layers?

Guided Research

Waves around Black Holes

Just as human ears detect only a small part of the spectrum of possible sound frequencies, human eyes detect only a small part of the light spectrum. Telescopes that observe in the infrared, ultraviolet, microwave, radio wave, and x-ray regions of the spectrum detect structures that are invisible to the unaided eye.

The top part of Figure 19 shows an x-ray image of the Perseus galaxy cluster. In the visible light spectrum, the Perseus galaxy cluster appears as a cluster of white blobs (individual galaxies) on a dark background. Not visible in these images is the cloud of hot gas that fills the galaxy cluster, nor the black hole at its center. Material spiraling in toward a black hole's event horizon emits x-rays. The white spot in the center of the photograph is not a black hole per se, but the radiation emitted by matter streaming into the black hole—somewhat like detecting an eruption at sea by observing the steam above it.

The bottom part of Figure 19 shows brightness differences when a special image-processing technique is used with the x-ray data. The blue areas in the image indicate a region filled with hot gas emitting x-rays. The black areas are cavities, formed by jets of material from the black hole pushing back the hot gas. The light and dark bands around the holes are interpreted as density waves passing through the gas—sound waves. The sound waves, initiated by the energy of the jets, carry energy through the gas, keeping it hot enough that it does not cool and fall into the black hole.

Hardly any of the radio signals that astronomers detect in outer space can be detected by humans. Astronomers can convert radio signals from outer space into sounds or colors that we can appreciate for comparison purposes. In April 2019, scientists used electromagnetic waves, specifically radio waves, to produce the first direct image of a black hole's shadow.

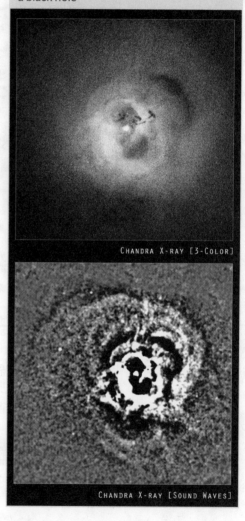

FIGURE 19: Sound waves in the gas around a black hole

CHANDRA X-RAY [3-COLOR]

CHANDRA X-RAY [SOUND WAVES]

Language Arts Connection Research videos and written communications about sound waves from outer space that have been detected in astronomical observatories and satellites. As you research the sound waves that have been detected to date, explore whether this phenomenon is unique to black holes or if there are other astronomical objects associated with the generation of sound waves. In your own words, write a brief article that summarizes the main findings.

| GRAVITATIONAL WAVES | NOISE POLLUTION, HEALTH, AND HEARING | SEISMOLOGIST | Go online to choose one of these other paths. |

Lesson Self-Check

CAN YOU EXPLAIN THE PHENOMENON?

FIGURE 20: Medical ultrasound applies the science of wave behavior at boundaries to generate images of hidden layers of tissue.

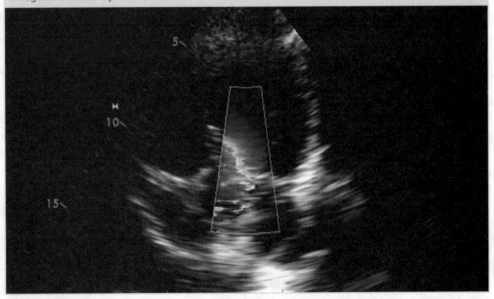

Medical ultrasound is a remote-sensing technique, a way to obtain information without physical contact. A transducer, or device that changes one form of energy to another, transforms an oscillating electric current into a mechanical oscillation at a frequency higher than human hearing. A receiver detects the ultrasound waves, and these signals are transformed into images.

Sound is a mechanical wave, meaning that it must be carried in a medium. At a boundary, such as the change in density between tendon and muscle, the wave can be reflected, transmitted, or absorbed. These types of interactions between a wave and matter depend on the combination of the characteristics of the wave, such as its frequency and wavelength, and the characteristics of the material, such as chemical composition, density, and compressibility.

 Evidence Notebook Refer to your notes in your Evidence Notebook to explain how ultrasound is used to detect the shapes of tissues inside the body. Use evidence and reasoning to support your claim.

Claim How is the interaction of sound waves with matter used in ultrasound imaging?

Evidence Give evidence to support your claim. Describe how sound waves interact with matter and what interactions are important in ultrasound imaging.

Reasoning Describe, in detail, the connections between the evidence you cited and the claim you are making about how the interaction of sound waves with matter is used in ultrasound imaging.

CHECKPOINTS

Check Your Understanding

1. Select the correct terms to complete the paragraph about waves.

A transverse wave is produced by oscillation parallel | perpendicular to the direction of propagation, while a longitudinal wave is produced by oscillation parallel | perpendicular to the direction of propagation. The distance between two consecutive crests is the wavelength | frequency | amplitude, while the displacement between a crest and the equilibrium point is the wavelength | frequency | amplitude.

2. Find the amplitude of the combined waves.

Wave A	Wave B	Wave A + B
−1	0	
0	1	
1	0	
0	−1	

3. In which materials can a sound wave travel? Select all correct answers.

☐ **a.** human tissue

☐ **b.** steel columns

☐ **c.** cold water on a lake

☐ **d.** lava from an erupting volcano

☐ **e.** the thin air at high atmosphere

☐ **f.** a sea of liquid methane on Titan

☐ **g.** the space between a comet and Earth

☐ **h.** the space between the walls of a vacuum thermos

4. The speed of sound in water is 1500 m/s. A sonar ping from a ship takes 0.80 s to be heard in the detector directly above the floor of the sea. What is the distance to the sea floor?

○ **a.** 600 m

○ **b.** 1200 m

○ **c.** 1900 m

○ **d.** 3800 m

5. The speed of sound in glass is 3950 m/s. Report your final answer using the correct number of significant figures.

What is the wavelength of sound in glass with a frequency of 1050 Hz ? _____

What is the wavelength of a rumble of thunder in glass, which has a frequency of 100 Hz? _____

What is the frequency of sound in glass with a wavelength of 0.47 m? _____

6. You are designing a room for watching television and movies. Which wall surfaces will be good choices to limit reverberation? Select all correct answers.

☐ **a.** concrete

☐ **b.** fabric

☐ **c.** foam

☐ **d.** glass

☐ **e.** metal

7. Select the correct terms to complete the statements.

A wave crashing on the beach is an example of absorption | transmission | reflection.

A sound heard through a closed window is an example of absorption | transmission | reflection.

An echo is an example of absorption | transmission | reflection.

A standing wave in a string is an example of absorption | transmission | reflection.

A glass vibrating in response to a singer's high C is an example of absorption | transmission | reflection.

Sound that hits a perforated wall is largely absorbed | transmitted | reflected.

CHECKPOINTS (continued)

8. When a sound wave reflects off an object that is moving toward the source of the sound, the compressions of the reflected wave are closer together than the compressions of the original wave. Explain how a bat might use this fact to determine the motion of an insect it is hunting.

_____

_____

_____

9. How do the differences between a tsunami wave and a wave produced by wind contribute to the destructive energy of the first compared to that of the second?

_____

_____

_____

10. Explain why sound in a room with perfectly absorbing walls will sound unnatural to a human ear.

_____

_____

_____

_____

MAKE YOUR OWN STUDY GUIDE

In your Evidence Notebook, design a study guide that supports the main ideas from this lesson:

Mechanical waves are a means of transmitting energy through the oscillation of a medium.

Waves can be longitudinal or transverse and can be described by their wavelength, frequency, amplitude, and speed.

Waves combine through interference and can be reflected at a boundary between media. These interactions explain standing waves and are applied during echolocation and when designing acoustic spaces and remote-sensing devices.

Remember to include the following information in your study guide:
- Use examples that model main ideas.
- Record explanations for the phenomena you investigated.
- Use evidence to support your explanations. Your support can include drawings, data, graphs, laboratory conclusions, and other evidence recorded throughout the lesson.
- Consider the relationship between the interactions of waves and matter, and wave energy.

Effects of Electromagnetic Radiation

Wireless communication transfers information through electromagnetic radiation.

CAN YOU EXPLAIN THE PHENOMENON?

While the term *electromagnetic radiation* may cause you to think of x-rays and dangerous high-energy particles, electromagnetic radiation is also produced by lamps, microwave ovens, and cell phones. In fact, most modern electrical devices utilize some form of electromagnetic radiation in their operation. While some forms of radiation can have serious health consequences, others are relatively harmless. Given modern civilization's reliance on electrical devices, there is ongoing debate about what forms and quantities of radiation are acceptable from the perspective of human health.

ARGUE What claims have you heard about the effects of electromagnetic radiation on human health? Do you think that these claims are accurate and trustworthy?

_____

_____

_____

_____

 Evidence Notebook As you explore the lesson, gather evidence to explain the effects of electromagnetic radiation on human health.

Electromagnetic Radiation and Matter

Electromagnetic radiation is the transmission of energy through electric and magnetic fields. Examples of electromagnetic radiation include visible light, high-energy gamma rays, and low-energy radio waves. Electromagnetic radiation is often modeled as traveling as waves called electromagnetic waves. Unlike mechanical waves, which can only travel through matter, electromagnetic waves can travel through matter or empty space.

Explore Online ▶

Hands-On Lab

Get in the Groove
Measure the groove spacing of a CD.

APPLY Electromagnetic waves usually travel much faster than mechanical waves. During a thunderstorm, you can count the seconds between a flash of lightning and when you hear the thunder. How could you calculate the distance between your body and the source?

_____

_____

_____

Matter's Effects on Electromagnetic Radiation

Electromagnetic radiation can interact with matter in many different ways. The waves that make up electromagnetic radiation can be transmitted through matter, reflected off matter, and absorbed by matter. A combination of these interactions often occurs when electromagnetic radiation encounters a new medium. For instance, your shirt may absorb some frequencies of radiation and reflect others.

Waves can also be diffracted, refracted, and scattered by matter. Diffraction is the bending and spreading of waves that pass through a small opening or around an obstacle. Refraction is the change in direction of waves that enter a transparent medium at an angle. When waves move from one medium to another, they may speed up or slow down, depending on properties of the new medium. This change in speed can cause the wave to change directions. Scattering is a special case of reflection, in which electromagnetic waves that strike a particle may be reflected in all directions.

FIGURE 1: Interactions of waves and matter

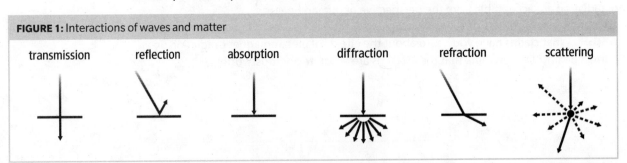

transmission   reflection   absorption   diffraction   refraction   scattering

INFER Which of these interactions do you think explains how you can see yourself in a mirror? What about the effects of looking through a magnifying glass?

_____

_____

_____

Electromagnetic Radiation's Effects on Matter

The interaction between electromagnetic radiation and matter depends on both the energy of the radiation and the properties of the material with which it interacts. Radio waves are transmitted through the walls of your school, so the walls are transparent to radio waves. On the other hand, visible light is not transmitted through the walls—it is reflected and absorbed. The walls are opaque to visible light. Your body is opaque to visible light but largely transparent to x-rays.

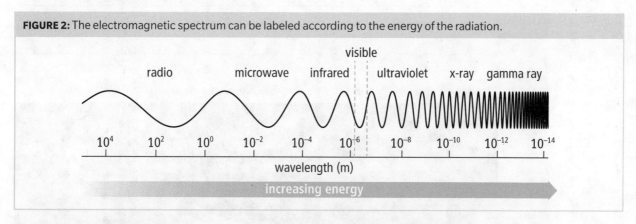

FIGURE 2: The electromagnetic spectrum can be labeled according to the energy of the radiation.

Electromagnetic waves can be described in terms of their wavelength, frequency, and energy. Frequency is correlated with energy. Radio waves have the longest wavelengths and the lowest frequencies and transfer the least energy. Gamma rays, in contrast, have the shortest wavelength and the highest frequencies and transfer the most energy. The entire range of electromagnetic wavelengths is called the electromagnetic spectrum.

When low-energy radiation interacts with matter, a small amount of energy is transferred to the material in the form of kinetic energy. As the energy is transferred, the average kinetic energy increases, and so the temperature of the material increases. Asphalt warmed by the sun and food warmed in a microwave are familiar examples of low-frequency electromagnetic waves adding to a material's thermal energy.

When high-energy radiation interacts with matter, the energy absorbed may be enough to separate electrons from their atoms, changing the charge of the atoms and disrupting chemical bonds. This kind of high-energy radiation is called *ionizing radiation*. Ionizing radiation can disrupt molecular bonds and is particularly damaging to living tissue. It can damage an organism's genetic material (deoxyribonucleic acid; DNA) and the DNA-repair mechanism.

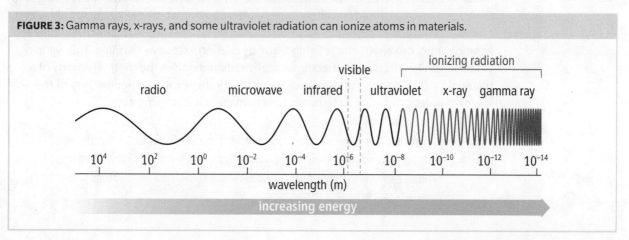

FIGURE 3: Gamma rays, x-rays, and some ultraviolet radiation can ionize atoms in materials.

Ionizing radiation comes from a variety of sources. It can be produced in nuclear processes such as radioactive decay and fusion reactions. Most ionizing radiation coming from the sun is absorbed by oxygen in Earth's atmosphere. When you want to deliberately produce ionizing radiation, x-rays can be produced by the rapid deceleration of beams of electrons.

INFER Why might you be asked to wear a lead vest when getting an x-ray taken?

_____

_____

_____

FIGURE 4: Sunscreen protects skin by absorbing ultraviolet radiation.

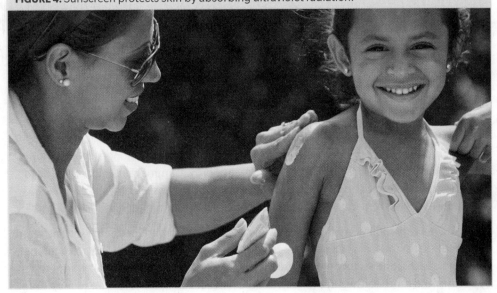

 Evidence Notebook In the unit project, you will research the effects of radiation on human health. How does the definition of ionizing radiation help you understand the possible effects of electromagnetic radiation on human health?

Nonionizing radiation still can be harmful to living tissue if it is energetic enough. Most ultraviolet radiation that reaches Earth's surface is not ionizing but can still cause changes to DNA. Sunburns are caused by cell damage resulting from this type of low-energy ultraviolet radiation. Exposure to high-intensity nonionizing radiation, such as microwaves, infrared, or visible light, can also damage living tissue by causing excessive warming. This warming occurs when low-frequency electromagnetic radiation raises the thermal energy of a material by causing the atoms or molecules to vibrate or rotate. The intensity of the electromagnetic radiation determines how damaging it is to living cells.

Language Arts Connection Identify three sources of information that describe the effects of electromagnetic radiation produced by modern technology, such as cell phones. Evaluate each source for reliability and validity. Make an infographic that summarizes your findings.

Hands-On Lab

Light and Color

You see objects of different colors every day. You might have noticed that the color of objects seems to change slightly under different lights.

RESEARCH QUESTION How does the absorption, transmission, and reflection of electromagnetic waves determine the color of objects?

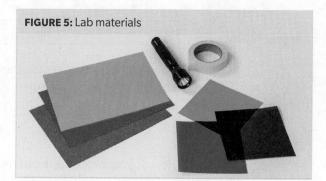

FIGURE 5: Lab materials

MAKE A CLAIM

What causes you to perceive objects as certain colors?

POSSIBLE MATERIALS

- safety goggles, nonlatex apron, nonlatex gloves
- construction paper (various colors)
- crayons (various colors)
- flashlight

- food coloring (various colors)
- glass or plastic squares (various colors)
- magazine with colorful photos
- paints (various colors)

- rubber band
- scissors
- small objects (various colors)
- squares of cellophane (various colors)
- tape

SAFETY INFORMATION

- Wear safety goggles, a nonlatex apron, and nonlatex gloves during the setup, hands-on, and takedown segments of the activity.
- Use caution when using sharp tools, which can cut or puncture skin.

PLAN THE INVESTIGATION

- Design and conduct an investigation to determine why objects have certain colors.
- Decide which light source you want to use for your investigation and how you will use it. Choose a way to produce any specific colors of light that you may require.
- Decide the objects you will observe. Think about how absorption, transmission, and reflection might affect perception of color. Be sure to choose objects of various colors.
- Decide what observations you will make and the best way to record them.
- In your Evidence Notebook, develop a procedure for your investigation. Make sure your teacher approves your procedure and safety plan before proceeding.

1. Use evidence from your investigation to explain why your prediction about what causes you to perceive objects to have certain colors was true or false. Explain your reasoning.

_____

_____

2. How did the filters affect the transmission of light? How did absorption, transmission, and reflection affect the colors you observed with the filtered light?

_____

_____

3. How do your procedures and results compare to those of other groups in your class?

_____

_____

CONSTRUCT AN EXPLANATION

Amber-tinted glasses help reduce eye strain by reducing the amount of blue-wavelength light that enters the eye from fluorescent lights. How can you use the results of your investigation to understand what "amber-tinted" means?

_____

_____

_____

DRAW CONCLUSIONS

Write a conclusion that addresses each of the points below.

Claim What causes you to perceive objects to have certain colors?

Evidence Give specific examples from your data to support your claim.

Reasoning Explain how the evidence you gave supports your claim. Describe in detail the connections between the evidence you cited and the argument you are making.

_____

_____

_____

_____

_____

_____

_____

_____

Matter's Effects on Color

The color of an object is not actually within the object itself. The color you perceive is the light reflected or transmitted by the object. Visible light consists of electromagnetic waves with a range of wavelengths, each of which corresponds to a specific color.

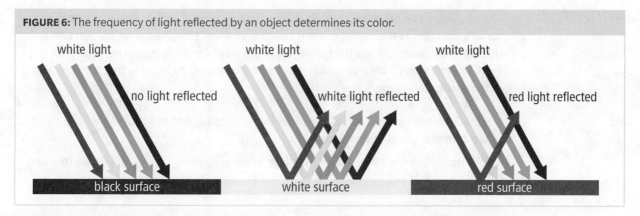

FIGURE 6: The frequency of light reflected by an object determines its color.

white light — no light reflected — black surface

white light — white light reflected — white surface

white light — red light reflected — red surface

Everyday objects reflect more than one pure color. An apple that appears red, for example, reflects more than a single wavelength of light in the red part of the visible spectrum. It reflects many wavelengths of light that together the eye perceives as red.

EXPLAIN Most plants contain chlorophyll, a substance that enables them to use sunlight to produce carbohydrates from carbon dioxide and water. How does the chlorophyll in plants interact with sunlight? How is this interaction related to the color of the plant?

_____

_____

Materials that appear transparent to the human eye allow one or more of the frequencies of visible light to be transmitted through them. Frequencies of light that are not transmitted by the materials are typically absorbed by them. The color of a transparent object is dependent on the frequencies of light that shine upon the object and the frequencies of light that are transmitted through the object.

INFER An object that is perceived as white reflects and scatters most visible light. An object that is perceived as black absorbs most of the incident visible light. Why, then, do some objects appear gray?

_____

_____

_____

Collaborate With a partner, discuss the following: In sunlight, a transparent, stained-glass window appears red, and an apple appears red. Why do each of these objects appear red? Explain how the absorption, reflection, and transmission of visible light by the objects are different even though both objects are the same color.

Evidence Notebook How do different types of electromagnetic radiation interact with matter? Which types do you think might be harmful to human health?

Studying Electromagnetic Spectra

The frequency and wavelength of electromagnetic waves, as well as the energy they carry, remain constant as the waves move through a vacuum. However, propagation into or through matter can change the properties of the waves and affect your perception of the light. Objects viewed through water may appear distorted by the way that light refracts when encountering the water's surface.

INFER Select the correct terms to complete the statement about the interaction of electromagnetic radiation with matter.

Waves may speed up or slow when they approach | enter | reflect off a new medium depending on the properties of the wave | medium.

Qualities of Electromagnetic Waves

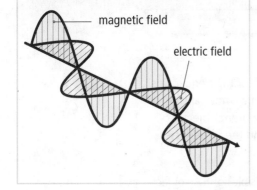

FIGURE 7: Electromagnetic waves are composed of oscillating electric and magnetic fields that travel away from the waves' source.

magnetic field

electric field

Electromagnetic waves travel through a vacuum in straight lines, but interactions with matter can change their direction. The path of a wave may be altered by refraction or reflection at the boundary of two media or by diffraction if the waves travel past an object or through an opening. If the waves are transmitted through matter, they will travel at the speed of light in the empty spaces between particles, but when they encounter a particle of matter, they may slow down as they are absorbed and reemitted by the particles.

Figure 7 shows a model of an electromagnetic wave. When a charged particle, such as an electron, vibrates, the electric field surrounding the particle oscillates. In the same way that you use a changing electric field to make an electromagnet, the changing electric field produces a magnetic field which oscillates at right angles to the electric field. The two fields will propagate away from their source.

APPLY What do mechanical waves and electromagnetic waves have in common?

○ **a.** Both are transverse waves.

○ **b.** Both wave types need a medium to propagate.

○ **c.** Both have oscillatory behavior.

○ **d.** Both are longitudinal waves.

EXPLAIN Order the statements from 1 to 3 to construct an explanation of how an electromagnetic wave might be produced.

_____ **a.** The changing electric field produces an oscillating magnetic field.

_____ **b.** A charged particle vibrates, causing the electric field around it to oscillate.

_____ **c.** As the magnetic field changes, it changes the electric field.

Identifying Matter by Its Spectrum

Electromagnetic waves that are emitted by matter can produce different types of spectra. A continuous spectrum consists of electromagnetic waves that contain all frequencies within a given range. Sunlight produces a continuous spectrum in the visible range. In addition to continuous spectra, many materials have unique spectra that provide scientists with clues about what they are made of.

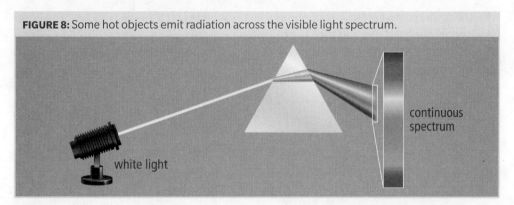

FIGURE 8: Some hot objects emit radiation across the visible light spectrum.

white light

continuous spectrum

An emission-line spectrum consists of distinct bright lines that correspond to electromagnetic waves of specific frequencies emitted by a substance. This type of spectrum is produced by the radiation emitted from atoms or molecules of a substance as they go from a higher energy level to a lower energy level.

An absorption spectrum consists of distinct dark lines that correspond to electromagnetic waves of specific frequencies that are absorbed by a substance. You can think of an absorption spectrum as the opposite of an emission spectrum.

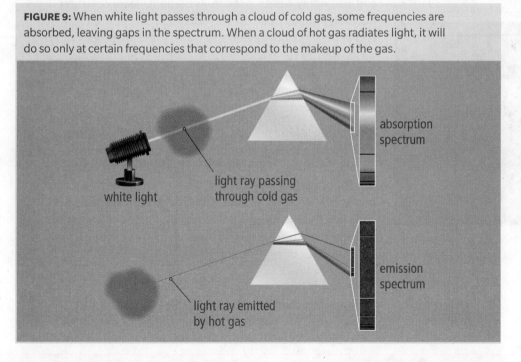

FIGURE 9: When white light passes through a cloud of cold gas, some frequencies are absorbed, leaving gaps in the spectrum. When a cloud of hot gas radiates light, it will do so only at certain frequencies that correspond to the makeup of the gas.

white light

light ray passing through cold gas

absorption spectrum

light ray emitted by hot gas

emission spectrum

ANALYZE Compare the absorption and emission spectra shown in Figure 9 for the gas. What do you notice about the two spectra?

Imagine that a star emits a continuous spectrum of electromagnetic radiation. If this radiation reaches a cloud of gas in space, most of it will pass through the cloud. However, the atoms and molecules of the cloud will absorb some specific frequencies. Astronomers observe this phenomenon as dark absorption lines or bands against the continuous background spectrum of the star. Because each element and compound has a unique absorption spectrum, astronomers can analyze the observed absorption lines and identify which elements and compounds are present in the cloud of gas.

ARGUE A source that emits a continuous spectrum shines on a low-density gas. The light is viewed through the gas, and then the gas is viewed from a perpendicular direction. Which types of spectra are observed in each case? Is there any position from which emission and absorption lines can be visible simultaneously?

_____

_____

_____

_____

Cause and Effect

Multiwavelength Astronomy

FIGURE 10: A false-color image of the sun in different ultraviolet frequencies

Stars emit radiation across the full electromagnetic spectrum, and astronomy is not limited to visible light. Radio wave and microwave telescopes collect radiation at the low-energy end of the electromagnetic spectrum. These telescopes can be located on Earth because low-energy radiation easily penetrates Earth's atmosphere. For direct observation of high-energy gamma rays, detectors must be placed on spacecraft or on high-altitude balloons.

An orbiting telescope, such as the Hubble Space Telescope, does not take images on photographic film but instead records incoming electromagnetic radiation. Filters can be used to record radiation of only certain frequencies, such as only infrared radiation, only visible light, or only ultraviolet radiation. If the data collected are of frequencies outside of the visible spectrum, false-color images are made from the data so that people can "see" what the sun or other astronomical objects look like in different parts of the electromagnetic spectrum.

INFER Why are some astronomical observations only possible outside of Earth's atmosphere?

_____

_____

_____

_____

© Houghton Mifflin Harcourt Publishing Company • Image Credits: ©NASA Goddard Space Flight

Spectra at the Atomic Level

The production of emission and absorption spectra is a direct result of the ways in which light interacts with matter. Matter is made up of atoms, which consist of a dense nucleus surrounded by electrons. In order to maintain stability, the electrons of an atom can have only specific quantities of energy, called energy states. The lowest energy level is called the ground state, and higher energy levels are called excited states.

Electrons move between energy states by absorbing or emitting energy. This energy is carried by a photon, which is a single, massless particle of light. The energy of the photon corresponds to the change in energy states.

When a photon with an energy that matches the difference in two energy states interacts with the atom, an electron can absorb the energy, moving it to the higher energy state. The excited states, however, are unstable, so the electron can return to the ground state by emitting a photon. The energy of photons absorbed or emitted by an atom corresponds to the frequency of an element's absorption and emission lines.

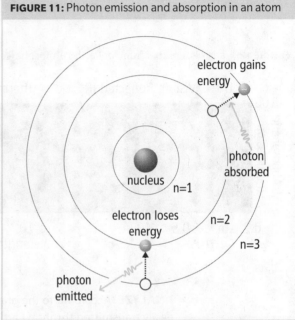

FIGURE 11: Photon emission and absorption in an atom

APPLY In absorption spectra, how are the lines that you observed generated?

- ○ **a.** ionization of atoms by losing electrons
- ○ **b.** ionization of atoms by gaining electrons
- ○ **c.** electrons moving to lower energy states
- ○ **d.** electrons moving to higher energy states

The electrons of molecules have specific energy states, just as atomic electrons do. Molecular energy states, however, are produced by the overlap of energy states of multiple atoms. Molecules have energy bands that produce broader absorption and emission features instead of distinct lines.

EXPLAIN When an electron moves to a lower energy state, the internal energy of the atom decreases. What happens to the energy?

_____

_____

_____

_____

 Language Arts Connection As new evidence is discovered, the models that scientists use to describe atomic structure are updated to reflect their understanding. Research two or more models of atomic structure that explain the locations of electrons in different ways. Be sure to study the electron cloud and Bohr models. Write a brief summary of the models, comparing them with Figure 11. Is the model presented in Figure 11 consistent with the models you researched? What are some limitations of the model shown in Figure 11? How is the model helpful?

Interaction with Earth's Atmosphere

Though Earth's atmosphere may appear to be completely transparent, it interacts with electromagnetic radiation that passes through it. Electromagnetic waves can be reflected or absorbed by gas molecules in Earth's atmosphere, such as oxygen, water vapor, and carbon dioxide. Visible light is easily transmitted through our atmosphere.

 Collaborate What forms of electromagnetic radiation do you encounter over the course of a typical day? With a group, make a list and compare the forms of radiation that you identified with those identified by other groups. Discuss why you included each form of radiation on your list.

FIGURE 12: Transmission spectrum for Earth's atmosphere

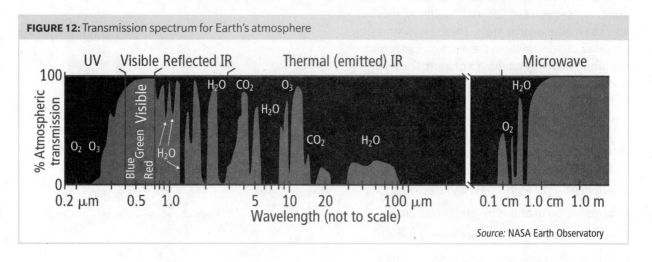

Source: NASA Earth Observatory

ANALYZE According to the graph in Figure 12, what types of electromagnetic waves are easily transmitted through Earth's atmosphere? What types are not? What frequencies might you use for wireless communication?

_____

_____

_____

_____

While most forms of high-energy radiation are absorbed by Earth's atmosphere, some ultraviolet radiation still reaches Earth's surface. Ultraviolet radiation is commonly divided into three bands that correspond to wavelength—UVA (314–400 nm), UVB (280–315 nm), and UVC (100–280 nm). While UVC is completely absorbed by the atmosphere, UVB is partially transmitted, and UVA is completely transmitted. The low levels of UVB that reach Earth's surface play a significant role in the development of sunburns and skin cancers. UVA, the lowest-energy form of ultraviolet radiation, has been shown to contribute to skin damage and DNA damage.

 Evidence Notebook How might the different types of radiation that pass through Earth's atmosphere affect human health?

Case Study: The Dual Nature of Light

Throughout history, many models have been proposed to explain how humans perceive light. Some early philosophers proposed that vision resulted from rays emitted by the eyes. The current model of light reflecting off an object into our eyes dates back to the work of Ibn al-Haytham in the 11th century. He also correctly proposed that refraction can be explained by light moving at different speeds in different media.

 Collaborate In a small group, discuss the path of light waves when someone looks at their reflection in a mirror. Draw a model of the path, showing both the light source and observer.

 Systems and System Models

Limitations of Models

A model is not an exact replica of a phenomenon. Instead, a model is an attempt to explain some aspect of the phenomenon. A model may simplify or ignore some parts of a phenomenon to make the model easier to grasp or more usable for making predictions. Models can be adapted and refined over time—or replaced altogether.

EXPLAIN You have seen light drawn simply as an arrow. As a model, what can this representation explain about light's behavior? Given what you've learned about the nature of light, in what ways do you think this model is limited?

_____

_____

_____

Early Models of Light

FIGURE 13: Newton studying light

In the 17th century, light was modeled as a particle by some scientists and as a wave by others. Isaac Newton was a proponent of the particle model, which explained light traveling in straight lines while waves do not. Christiaan Huygens supported the wave model, deriving rules for straight line reflection and refraction using waves traveling through a medium that he called aether.

INFER What evidence might have led Newton and Huygens to their conclusions?

_____

_____

_____

Wave Model of Light

In the 19th century, evidence for the wave nature of light became overwhelming. In 1801, Thomas Young observed that a beam of light passing through small slits forms an interference pattern on the screen behind it, as shown in Figure 14a. He explained this interference pattern as the result of wave crests and troughs constructively and destructively interfering with each other. Around the same time, Augustin-Jean Fresnel used Huygens's wave theory to explain the effects of diffraction.

The pattern of bright and dark lines observed by Young indicates that waves from the two slits interfere with one another. In Figure 14a, the bright lines indicate regions where constructive interference is occurring while the dark lines indicate regions where destructive interference is occurring. The pattern is regular, corresponding to the intersecting wave crests.

FIGURE 14: Young's experiment, in which light passes through two slits and forms an interference pattern

| a | Double-slit apparatus | b | Waves diffract and interfere after passing through two slits. |

INFER How do you think the image on the screen would look if particles, rather than waves, were shot through the slits?

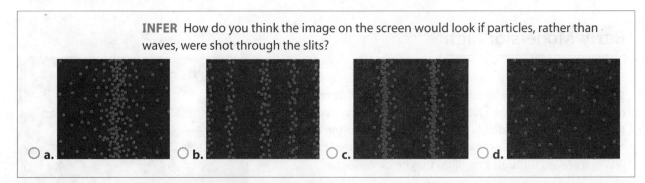

○ a.   ○ b.   ○ c.   ○ d.

Later in the 19th century, decades after Young's and Fresnel's respective breakthroughs, James Clerk Maxwell observed that the velocity of electromagnetic waves was similar to that of light. Maxwell realized that the two must be related. As a result, visible light was recognized as a part of a much larger electromagnetic spectrum.

Dual Model of Light

Though the wave model of light was the leading model for nearly a century, scientists observed phenomena that could not be explained by the wave model.

One topic that could not be explained by the wave model of light was the photoelectric effect. The photoelectric effect occurs when electrons are emitted from a surface when light falls upon it. According to the wave model of light, there should be a relationship between the kinetic energy of the electrons and the intensity of light that caused them to be emitted. However, this result was not observed. Instead, the photoelectric effect occurs only when light above a certain frequency falls on the surface This frequency is called the threshold frequency. In 1905, Albert Einstein solved this problem by proposing a model of light in which a particle, or photon, contained a fixed amount of energy. In this model, the photon transfers its energy to an electron when it strikes the material. The theory was confirmed in 1915.

FIGURE 15: In the photoelectric effect, electrons are emitted only when light above a certain frequency falls on a surface.

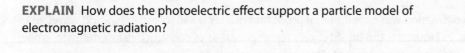

EXPLAIN How does the photoelectric effect support a particle model of electromagnetic radiation?

_____

_____

_____

 Language Arts Connection Search online for a simulation demonstrating the photoelectric effect. As you investigate the phenomenon, make note of the minimum wavelengths of light that are capable of causing electrons to be emitted from different metals. Make a short presentation explaining what these different wavelengths imply about the electrons in those metals. Include images from a simulation or your own visual presentation of the photoelectric effect.

EVALUATE Scientists claim that a dual model of light explains its behavior and ability to transfer energy and information. Evaluate this claim and describe whether particular phenomena can be explained by only the wave model or only the particle model.

_____

_____

_____

_____

Because of the development of the dual model of light, scientists began considering whether particles could exhibit wavelike characteristics. The idea that all matter has wavelike properties was proposed in 1924 by Louis de Broglie. The wavelength of a particle of matter became known as its de Broglie wavelength.

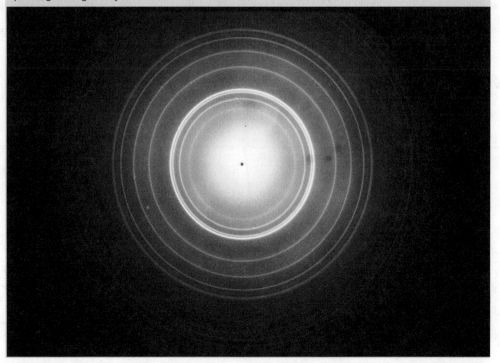

FIGURE 16: This circular diffraction pattern is the result of interference between electrons passing through a crystal.

Electron diffraction was experimental proof that matter is capable of exhibiting wavelike behavior. In Figure 16, the bright circles represent areas of constructive interference, while the dark areas represent areas of destructive interference.

Electron diffraction shows the wavelike nature of electrons and provides a tool to study matter at the molecular and atomic levels. Modern techniques use diffraction patterns of electrons to image and study the atomic structure of atoms. With a traditional microscope, the resolution is limited by the wavelength used to illuminate the object. Electron microscopes use a beam of electrons, which have much smaller wavelengths than light, to make images of objects. With this technology, much higher resolutions and magnifications are possible.

EXPLAIN Given the connection between energy and frequency in electromagnetic waves, how would you expect energy to affect the frequency of an electron?

_____

_____

_____

_____

 Evidence Notebook How does the photoelectric effect explain why exposure to high-frequency electromagnetic radiation is potentially more dangerous than exposure to high-intensity, low-frequency radiation?

Guided Research

Laser Diffraction Analyzer

Knowing the size of particles in solutions and powders is important for many applications. Manufacturers of cosmetics and paints, for example, monitor particle sizes to maintain uniformity of the products. Scientists studying lakes or soil composition may use particle size measurements as part of their analysis. A laser diffraction analyzer is a tool that uses the diffraction of laser light to measure particle size.

Both wet-dispersion and dry-dispersion measurements can be made with a laser diffraction analyzer. In a wet-dispersion procedure, a few grams of the sample particles are spread uniformly throughout a liquid. The liquid is then circulated through a small, transparent measurement container that is illuminated by the laser. The diffraction pattern that is produced is recorded and analyzed to determine the size of the particles. In a dry-dispersion procedure, a jet of powder is introduced through the sample container instead of a liquid.

A laser diffraction analyzer depends on scattering in which the particle size is larger than the wavelength of light. Laser light is useful because it is composed of light with a single wavelength and the light is coherent, which means the peaks and troughs of the waves are aligned. These properties result in less spreading of laser light, so the diffraction pattern is more focused. The analyzer does not directly measure particle size. Instead, it measures the intensity and angle of the diffracted light. A larger particle scatters light at smaller angles, so the diffraction pattern is smaller and brighter. A smaller particle scatters light at larger angles, so the diffraction pattern is larger and less intense. The intensity and angle measurements can therefore be used to calculate the particle size.

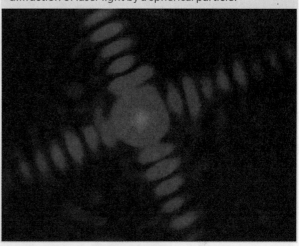

FIGURE 17: This pattern is produced by an ideal diffraction of laser light by a spherical particle.

Samples may contain just one size of particles or a combination of sizes, each forming its own diffraction pattern. Because particles are rarely spherical, measurements from multiple angles can be used to obtain a more complete understanding of a particle's dimensions. Sizes of particles measured with a laser diffraction analyzer can range from as large as a millimeter down to about 10 nanometers, or 10 billionths of a meter. A significant advantage of using laser diffraction analysis to determine particle size is that the measurements take only seconds to perform. Because the measurements are so fast, the process can also be used to make real-time measurements of changes in particle sizes.

 Language Arts Connection One type of diffraction analyzer uses red laser light for larger particles and blue light-emitting diode (LED) light for smaller particles, even though LED light is not as focused. Explain why the red laser light would not be as useful for smaller particles. Consider the claim that laser light is useful in evaluating the size of particles in many everyday substances. Write an evaluation of this statement based on the content of the passage.

ASTRONOMER   OPTIMIZING A RADIO RECEIVER   LASER SURGERY   Go online to choose one of these other paths.

Lesson Self-Check

CAN YOU EXPLAIN THE PHENOMENON?

FIGURE 18: Wireless communication transfers information through electromagnetic radiation.

As information transmitted through electromagnetic waves has become routine, humans have increased the amount of electromagnetic radiation in their environment. Short-wavelength electromagnetic radiation can damage cells by freeing electrons from atoms and molecules, while radiation with longer wavelengths can warm material that absorbs it. Because microwaves are easily transmitted through Earth's atmosphere, communication devices radiate at the longer wavelength end of the electromagnetic spectrum.

 Evidence Notebook Refer to your notes in your Evidence Notebook to construct an explanation for this question using a claim, evidence, and reasoning. Your explanation should include a discussion of the following points:

Claim What effects do different types of electromagnetic radiation have on human health?

Evidence Summarize the evidence that you have gathered to support your claim. What evidence is there that different types of electromagnetic radiation have varying effects on human health?

Reasoning Describe how the evidence you gathered shows that different types of electromagnetic radiation can or cannot contribute to health problems.

CHECKPOINTS

Check Your Understanding

1. Which is a property of electromagnetic waves but is not a property of sound waves?
   - ○ **a.** They can travel through a vacuum and through matter.
   - ○ **b.** They can be described by frequency and wavelength.
   - ○ **c.** They can transport energy and transfer it to matter.
   - ○ **d.** They diffract when they move through a small opening.

2. For each description, write *gamma rays* or *radio waves*, depending on what kind of waves the phrase describes.

   _____ high frequency

   _____ low frequency

   _____ high energy

   _____ low energy

   _____ long wavelengths

   _____ short wavelengths

3. Continuous, emission, and absorption spectra can be observed when materials interact with light. Select all correct statements about spectra.
   - ☐ **a.** Continuous spectra are unique to the material emitting it.
   - ☐ **b.** Absorption and emission spectra can be used to identify the chemical makeup of a gas.
   - ☐ **c.** Emission spectra are observed when white light passes through a gas.
   - ☐ **d.** Absorption spectra are visible as black lines on an otherwise continuous spectrum.
   - ☐ **e.** Continuous spectra show the complete range of visible light wavelengths.

4. Which statements correctly describe electromagnetic radiation? Select all correct answers.
   - ☐ **a.** It is composed of oscillating electric and magnetic fields.
   - ☐ **b.** It is produced when a charged particle vibrates.
   - ☐ **c.** The electric and magnetic fields oscillate in the same direction that they propagate.
   - ☐ **d.** Infrared waves have longer wavelengths than visible light waves.
   - ☐ **e.** Photons of ultraviolet radiation have less energy than photons of microwaves.
   - ☐ **f.** It never exhibits particle behavior but only wave behavior.

5. Select the correct terms to complete the statement about the photoelectric effect.

   A metal will not emit photoelectrons if the frequency of the incident light is above | below the metal's threshold frequency. Increasing the intensity of the incident light will | will not cause the metal to emit photoelectrons. This effect is evidence for the particle | wave model of electromagnetic radiation.

6. Select the correct terms to complete the statements about waves.

   Infrared | Ultraviolet waves have lower frequencies, so they interact with matter by ionizing atoms | increasing its internal energy. Infrared | Ultraviolet waves have higher frequencies, so they can interact with matter by ionizing atoms | increasing its internal energy.

7. How can you tell whether a spectrum is an absorption spectrum or an emission spectrum? Explain how each type of spectrum forms.

_____

_____

_____

_____

_____

8. The beam of a laser pointer is directed toward a white wall. A thin wire is then moved between the beam and the wall. What will the pattern of light shining on the wall look like? Evaluate whether the pattern supports a wave model or a particle model of light.

_____

_____

_____

_____

_____

MAKE YOUR OWN STUDY GUIDE

In your Evidence Notebook, design a study guide that supports the main ideas from this lesson:

Electromagnetic radiation includes a spectrum across different energy and frequency ranges.

The interaction of electromagnetic radiation and matter depends on the frequency and intensity of the radiation and on the properties of the matter with which the radiation interacts.

Light can be modeled as both a particle and a wave.

Remember to include the following information in your study guide:
• Use examples that model main ideas.
• Record explanations for the phenomena you investigated.
• Use evidence to support your explanations. Your support can include drawings, data, graphs, laboratory conclusions, and other evidence recorded throughout the lesson.

Consider how the models you have used in this lesson can be used to describe the interaction of electromagnetic radiation and matter.

5.3

Optimizing Information Technologies

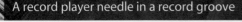

A record player needle in a record groove

CAN YOU EXPLAIN THE PHENOMENON?

The earliest version of a record player, called a phonograph, was invented by Thomas Edison in the late 1800s. It was based on the principle that sound can be produced through vibrations by moving an object over an etched surface, such as a wax cylinder in a phonograph. You may have noticed this phenomenon when traveling on some roads. The sound of a car's wheels varies with the grooves carved onto the surface of the road. Small grooves produce a higher pitch; wider grooves produce a lower pitch.

Vinyl records are made by turning vibrations of sound into grooves in a soft medium. The etches are transferred onto a metal master to stamp onto vinyl disks. People listened to music on vinyl records for most of the 1900s until cassettes began to replace them.

Analog technologies, such as the vinyl record player and cassette tapes, were very common until digital storage was developed. Compact discs (CDs) contributed to vinyl record players and cassettes falling out of use. Today, most of the music people listen to is stored digitally on magnetic hard drives or solid-state drives.

INFER Based on what you know about digital and analog storage technology, what are the advantages of digital and analog formats compared with the other?

_____

_____

_____

Evidence Notebook As you explore the lesson, gather evidence to determine why digital storage has replaced analog methods such as vinyl records.

Energy and Information

EXPLAIN How might the transfer of energy be connected to hearing the sound of a door closing?

_____

_____

_____

Energy Transfers

Every time a person hears a sound or sees an object, energy is transferred and transformed. Every piece of sensory input that reaches you is due to you absorbing energy. Your brain processes these energy inputs to identify important information. Often the information is interpreted as part of a pattern.

For example, a hot cup of tea has a higher temperature than your fingers. As you touch the cup, some of the thermal energy is transferred to the skin in your fingertips. The transfer of thermal energy causes an electrical signal to travel via your nerve cells to your brain. Your brain interprets this information, and you realize that the cup of tea is hot.

Water waves are mechanical waves that transfer energy across the surface of water. Although the open ocean may seem to be the same everywhere, those with the right training can interpret patterns in the waves. Many of the patterns last long enough to map and learn. A stick map, like that in Figure 1, shows such patterns. Stick maps were used by navigators from the Pacific Islands to show the relationship between the islands and the ocean swells. Some stick maps were used to travel between specific islands.

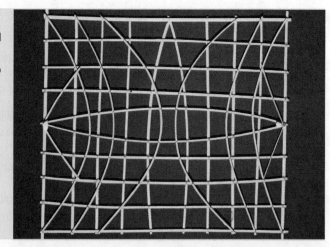

FIGURE 1: This stick map from the Pacific Islands is supported by horizontal and vertical pieces. Small shells are used to represent islands. The curved pieces represent the energy transferred by waves and currents.

Explore Online ▶

YOU SOLVE IT

Is It Possible to Predict a Solar Storm? Determine if information can be gathered to predict solar storms.

Ocean waves can convey information about the wind, currents, objects just below the surface, and objects out of sight beyond the horizon. This information is added to the waves when forces cause energy transfers. Winds interact with the surface of the water, causing waves. The size of a water wave depends on the strength of the wind and the time of the interaction.

Waves, Energy, and Information

ANALYZE What are some of the ways that you can transfer energy to communicate information?

_____

_____

Earthquakes involve powerful mechanical waves traveling through the ground. Seismic waves travel in all directions away from the source of an earthquake. These waves are recorded and analyzed to gather information about the earthquake as well as structures beneath Earth's surface. Scientists can map layers of Earth's interior because of the patterns of seismic waves interacting with the boundaries of the layers. This process is much like the way ultrasound pulses can be used to observe tissue layers inside the body. The transfer of energy from the waves contains information that can be useful to scientists.

Like water, sound, and seismic waves, electromagnetic waves carry both energy and information. Sunlight carries energy and contains information about the sun. Microwaves and radio waves, lower in frequency than visible light, can warm food in a microwave oven or carry information to and from satellites. The higher-frequency waves of ultraviolet rays, x-rays, and gamma rays carry enough energy to be hazardous to life on Earth. X-rays can convey information about what is inside the human body.

 Collaborate List three ways that waves are used to transfer energy. Compare your list with a partner's list. In each case, evaluate how that energy is transferred and transformed.

Waves in Technology

Detecting a mechanical wave requires that the detector absorb energy from the wave, such as how a sound wave makes an eardrum vibrate. In technology designed to detect mechanical waves, the wave often moves a component of the detector. For example, in both microphones and medical ultrasound devices, a diaphragm (similar to a drum skin) moves in response to sound waves.

FIGURE 2: Ultrasound can convey information from inside a beating heart or carry energy to break water into tiny droplets.

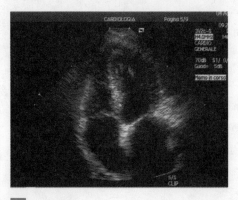

| a | Image of a heart | b | Machine that produces mist |

Photoelectric Effect

To gather information from an energy transfer, there needs to be a way to measure the energy transfer. With mechanical waves, it is often fairly straightforward to measure the movement caused by the wave. Electromagnetic waves can require more specialized equipment. The energy of light can be measured using the photoelectric effect. If enough energy from light is absorbed by certain materials, the material can emit electrons. This effect has been used to design devices that can measure the properties of light.

EXPLAIN Describe how you think the photoelectric effect could be used in a communication device.

_____

_____

_____

FIGURE 3: In a seismograph, a pen traces the amplitude of a seismic wave.

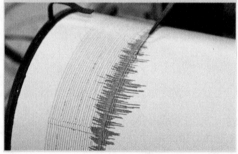

Medical imaging technologies, such as magnetic resonance imaging and x-ray imaging, produce electromagnetic waves to observe the human body. Other forms of technology only record naturally produced waves. A seismograph is used to record seismic waves during an earthquake.

Earthquakes are composed of several types of seismic waves. With seismographs, scientists can measure the time between the arrival of these waves. This time can be used to calculate the distance to the earthquake's origin, but not its direction. However, if this distance is measured from three different stations, the starting point of the earthquake can be calculated.

 Evidence Notebook Electromagnetic waves are used in various medical devices. As you work on the unit project, consider what effects different types of electromagnetic waves have on the human body and what kind of information can be obtained from these interactions.

 Language Arts Connection Communication devices emit and absorb energy in a variety of ways, but most modern devices make use of waves. Both mechanical and electromagnetic waves can be used to transfer energy and information without permanently displacing matter. Choose a communication device that uses the photoelectric effect, a diaphragm, or an antenna, and research in detail how it makes use of waves. Make a presentation that describes the process of how your chosen device transfers energy and information.

 Evidence Notebook What information is transferred by the details of the grooves in a vinyl record?

Communicating with Waves

When energy is transferred through waves, information can also be conveyed. This information can be used to communicate with other people.

ANALYZE List at least three different methods that you can use to communicate an idea.

_____

_____

_____

Encoding Information

Before information can be communicated through waves or other means, it must be recorded in a transferable format. Etching grooves into a vinyl disk to store music is similar to writing down your ideas on a piece of paper. Both are forms of encoding, the process of transforming information into a specific form for the purpose of communication, such as language, music, or flashes of light. Encoded information is recorded and transmitted in a different form. As a result, encoded information may take skill to interpret.

FIGURE 4: Information is encoded and transferred to a television.

There are many ways to encode information. Each method involves some kind of energy transfer or transformation. In speech, electric impulses in the brain are converted into sound. When typing, the keyboard transforms the kinetic energy of your fingers into electrical signals that are sent to a computer. Printing, cursive writing, and shorthand are all examples of encoding information through writing. Computers handle text in different ways. Plain text is a form of encoding that includes only the characters of a message and no additional information.

Computers use an encoding method called binary code, where information is recorded using just two stable, easy-to-distinguish states. These states are represented as a 1 or 0. A single unit of information, such as a 0 or 1, is called a bit. All information on a computer, from text to images, is encoded as strings of bits. For example, the letter A is represented as 01000001 in binary code. However, bits can be interpreted differently depending on their context. A string of bits could be interpreted as a character, an integer, a decibel level for a part of a sound, a single point of color on an image, or other kinds of data depending on the file type. While every computer uses binary code, additional encoding methods are used for different files.

APPLY Which of the following are ways that text is encoded? Select all correct answers.

☐ **a.** writing the lyrics to a song

☐ **b.** composing a poem

☐ **c.** painting a landscape with watercolors

☐ **d.** typing an email

Recording and Retrieving Information

Different methods of recording and retrieving information have benefits and drawbacks. Work with a partner to record a message by two methods, recording your voice and writing it as text. Compare the two formats.

RESEARCH QUESTION How does the way a message is recorded affect how fast it is stored and retrieved?

MAKE A CLAIM

What are the advantages of recording and transmitting information as text?

_____

_____

POSSIBLE MATERIALS

- devices to record and store audio and text notes
- message, 2–3 sentences
- timekeeping device

SAFETY INFORMATION

- Use only GFI-protected circuits when using electrical equipment, and keep away from water sources to prevent shock.

PLAN THE INVESTIGATION

In your Evidence Notebook, write a procedure to investigate the advantages related to using audio and text to record and retrieve a short message. Detail the methods and technology you will use to record and store both an audio message and a text message. When developing your procedure, consider the following:

- Both you and your partner need to time how long it takes you to record and play back the message and how long it takes you to write or type and read back the message.
- Write down a note or list you will use for your investigation. If you have extra time, you can try shorter or longer notes or lists.

COLLECT DATA

Conduct your experiment. As you carry out your plan, note any issues or new ideas that emerge during the investigation.

ANALYZE

1. Which method was faster to record, and which was faster to retrieve, copy, or transfer to someone else?

_____

_____

_____

2. What are some advantages and disadvantages of each method?

_____

_____

_____

_____

CONSTRUCT AN EXPLANATION

1. A sports statistician often has to record data quickly during live sporting events. What recommendations would you make to a sports statistician about how to record and retrieve information? Support your recommendations with evidence from your investigation.

_____

_____

_____

_____

2. Think about Internet search engines. Would they help you locate information as effectively if all online information were recorded as a sound file instead of stored in text form? Why or why not?

_____

_____

_____

_____

DRAW CONCLUSIONS

Write a conclusion that addresses each of the points below.

Claim What are the advantages of recording and transmitting information as text? Do the results of your experiment support your initial predictions?

Evidence Give specific examples from your data to support your claim.

Reasoning Explain how the evidence you gave supports your claim. Describe in detail the connections between the evidence you cited and the argument you are making.

_____

_____

_____

_____

_____

_____

Analog Information

Until about 50 years ago, most technologies used signals that varied continuously with the information that they were transmitting. For example, clocks represented time passing with the sweeping of the hour, minute, and second hands. Electric current was measured using a meter with a moving needle. Information transmitted in this manner has a continuous range instead of being divided into specific values. An example of a continuous range is your height. When you grow, at some point, you are every height between your initial and final height. Because this type of information is analogous to what is being measured, it is called *analog information*.

The information you transmit by your voice is also analog. When you speak, you transmit information via the words you choose, as well as information in your volume, pitch, and timbre. Waves are commonly used to transmit analog information.

APPLY Which of the following is an example of analog information?

○ **a.** a song recorded by a tape recorder

○ **b.** photos taken by a smartphone

○ **c.** the melody played on an electric keyboard

○ **d.** the words in a book of poetry

Digital Information

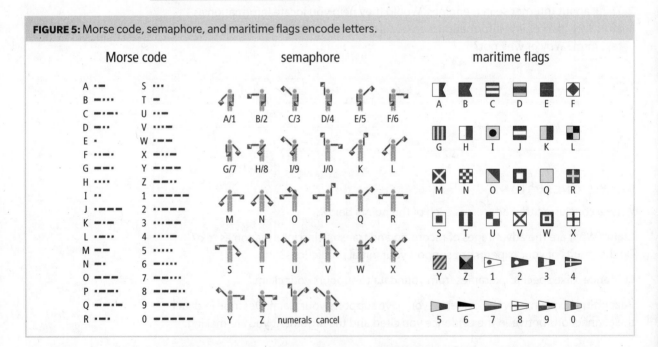

FIGURE 5: Morse code, semaphore, and maritime flags encode letters.

EVALUATE How is the information communicated through the encoding methods shown in Figure 5 different from analog information?

_____

_____

_____

When information consists of multiple discrete units, it is called *digital information*. For example, the number of people in a room would be digital information because when a person leaves or enters, the number changes by exactly one. Morse code uses digital information of sounds from short and long electric pulses over wires—dots and dashes. Digital information is encoded into the sequence of positions of semaphore flags or the sequence of maritime flags displayed on a line. The binary code used in computers is a type of digital information. Typically, it is easier to distinguish information in two distinct states at the expense of subtle details between those states.

INFER How might it be possible to convert between analog and digital information?

_____

_____

_____

Image Storage and Digitization

There are ways to represent most information in either digital or analog forms. Tiny silver halide crystals in each layer of film can store images by changing color when exposed to light of the right frequency. The size of the crystals determines the amount of detail of the image. A microscopic view of exposed film shows colored crystals.

FIGURE 6: Color film uses transparent layers, each sensitive to—able to record—one color of light.

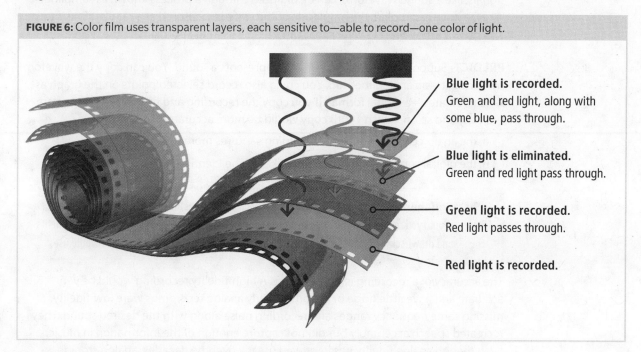

Blue light is recorded.
Green and red light, along with some blue, pass through.

Blue light is eliminated.
Green and red light pass through.

Green light is recorded.
Red light passes through.

Red light is recorded.

Information can be converted to a digital format through a process called digitization. Images on film can be digitized by dividing the image into a grid and measuring the crystals at each position. A smaller grid—one with closer positions—produces more detail. These images can be displayed on a screen by representing the different points of the grid as a pixel, the smallest unit of the digital image. Pixels are displayed as tiny dots or squares. From a distance, the pixels appear to form a continuous image.

Language Arts Connection Most photos are taken with a digital camera or smartphone. Research the technology used by digital cameras to record images; make labeled diagrams that describe one of the methods.

Sound and Waveforms

Sound is a continuous variation of frequency and amplitude. To produce early sound recordings, sound waves caused a diaphragm with an attached needle to vibrate. The needle would etch a pattern into metal foil. Later, wax and vinyl were used instead of metal.

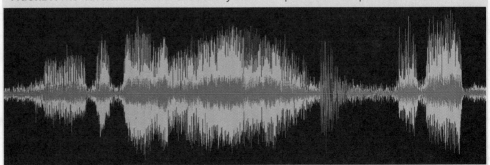

FIGURE 7: The waveform of a sound is usually more complex than a simple sine wave.

Most sounds are complex combinations of waves with different frequencies. These waves can be combined together to give a waveform, which shows the amplitude of the wave over a given time. A graph of the resulting waveform might look like Figure 7. Continuous signals, like a sound waveform, can be digitized through a process known as sampling. When a wave is sampled, the amplitude of the wave is measured at a regular time interval. This gives a list of discrete values that can then be used to approximate the waveform.

PREDICT Suppose you have a graph that represents a sound. You can copy the waveform by tracing it—an analog method. You could also record selected points on the graph as *x-y* coordinates—a digital format. If you copy the recording and then make a copy from the copy and so on, which 100th copy would be more accurate?

○ **a.** the analog copy, because the recording captures more detail

○ **b.** the digital copy, because copies are likely to be identical to the original numbers

 Collaborate Suppose you want to record a message for students 50 years in the future. Would you record your message in digital or analog form? Discuss with a partner the benefits and drawbacks of each method, and make a decision about which method you would use.

The accuracy of a recording is called *fidelity*. A high-fidelity recording would be very accurate and have little noise or distortion. Early analog recordings were low-fidelity, missing some frequency ranges and recording noise along with the desired sound. They recreated speech acceptably but did not capture enough of the information in music. Even though analog fidelity has improved greatly over the decades, analog storage becomes slightly damaged during each playback.

In a digital recording, waves with periods shorter than the time between the recorded points are not recorded well. This drawback can be overcome by increasing the number of samples taken in a given time period. As more points are recorded, fidelity increases, but more information must be stored. Accessing a digital file does not typically damage the file, and digital storage can often be physically smaller than analog storage.

 Evidence Notebook How is information encoded in a vinyl record, and how do you think information is encoded in a digital music recording?

Waves in Technology

INFER When designing a communication device, such as a radio or cable television, how do the criteria affect the type of wave chosen to use in the device?

_____

_____

_____

Choosing a Technology

Engineers weigh costs, benefits, and risks when designing communication systems. For example, encoding more information will increase the time it takes to transmit the signal. Transmission time can be decreased, but the technology required may have other tradeoffs, such as being more expensive.

FIGURE 8: Computers and cell phones transfer information in different ways.

One challenge for transmitting information is the range of a signal. Wireless signals, such as those used in cell phones and routers, diminish as they travel. These signals can get interrupted, and the signal can be lost. Using a wired connection can fix these issues. Wired connections tend to be more stable and can have greater ranges but require wires to physically connect the communication devices, which can be more expensive and less convenient.

Digital signals also have additional factors that must be considered. The format of a digital file can affect the amount of information that needs to be sent. Digital files can be compressed, or made smaller, by treating similar data points as equal. High-definition movies are much larger and take longer to download than more compressed versions. However, compressed files may require more processing to encode or decode and in some cases are less accurate. These tradeoffs need to be evaluated for each application.

Influence of Engineering, Technology, and Science on Society and the Natural World

Radio in Remote Regions

Many areas around the world do not have reliable Internet access. For instance, some people live in remote areas and rely on AM radio to transmit and receive information.

ANALYZE Suppose you want to broadcast news to remote communities. Consider the costs, risks, and benefits of transmitting news to a remote community using AM radio waves or cable television. Which would you choose and why?

_____

_____

_____

Hands-On Lab

Sending Signals

In this lab, you will design ways to send digital and analog signals. Evaluate the quality of each transmission, and explain tradeoffs related to accuracy, speed, ease, and complexity.

RESEARCH QUESTION What are the advantages and disadvantages associated with the transmission of analog and digital signals?

MAKE A CLAIM

Can digital or analog signals be sent more accurately?

POSSIBLE MATERIALS

- safety goggles
- devices for signaling with color or numbers
- device for signaling with light
- device for signaling with sound
- materials for tracing a shape
- waveforms from teacher

SAFETY INFORMATION

- Wear safety goggles during the setup, hands-on, and takedown segments of the activity.
- Use only GFI-protected circuits when using electrical equipment, and keep away from water sources to prevent shock.
- Leave circuit switches open (no current) when the circuits are not in use.
- Wash your hands with soap and water immediately after completing this activity.

PLAN THE INVESTIGATION

When developing your procedure, consider the following suggestions:

1. Develop a method to send an analog signal as well as two methods to send a digital signal. Record your procedures in your Evidence Notebook. Use the following to help guide your planning:
   - The signal you send must be received and decoded by a member of your group. Make sure the other member has a method to decode the received signal.
   - The waveform provided by your teacher will be presented on graph paper. You can use the squares on the graph paper to help design how to send the signal.
   - When sending the analog signal, make sure to account for time.
   - Make sure that your methods can transmit information accurately and consistently.

2. Choose one lab partner to be the sender and another to be the receiver. Test your signaling methods. Evaluate how quickly and accurately the signal could be sent and received using your method. Make adjustments to your method to improve the quality of the transmission.

3. Once you have effective methods to send analog and digital signals, show your plan to your teacher before proceeding.

ANALYZE

1. Compare the accuracy of your transmitted waveforms to the original waveforms. What could you do to make your transmissions more accurate?

_____

_____

_____

2. How could each transmission method be improved using automation?

_____

_____

_____

3. How did your transmission methods affect the way the digital signals were encoded?

_____

_____

CONSTRUCT AN EXPLANATION

Noise is a common problem when communicating. Noise can consist of anything that interferes with the transmission of a signal. For example, a very bright room might make it harder to send a signal using light. How did noise affect your transmissions? Were your digital transmissions or analog transmissions more affected by noise?

_____

_____

_____

DRAW CONCLUSIONS

Write a conclusion that addresses each of the points below.

Claim Can digital or analog signals be sent more accurately? Explain whether or not your results supported your initial predictions.

Evidence Give specific examples from your data to support your claim.

Reasoning Explain how the evidence you gave supports your claim. Describe in detail the connections between the evidence you cited and the argument you are making.

_____

_____

_____

_____

_____

_____

_____

Comparing Digital and Analog Storage

IDENTIFY CONSTRAINTS Depending on the type of information, storing information physically might be better than storing information digitally. Label each of the following with a *P* for physical or *D* for digital to determine which of the factors you think makes a storage type better for the storage of a text document:

_____ **a.** fidelity   _____ **b.** detail   _____ **c.** easy to copy

Paper and other physical storage may be destroyed or lost. You can detect information inscribed into stone and baked clay tablets from thousands of years ago, but you may not be able to read (decode) it. Similarly, digital information can be lost if the technology to decode it is discontinued. A decoding method is required to store any type of information.

Another important factor in data storage is security. While digital data are easy to store and copy, the data may also be easy to erase or steal. *More secure* generally means *less accessible*. However, more copies—physical or digital—generally mean that the information is less likely to be lost or destroyed.

Every day, enormous amounts of digital data are recorded automatically and stored in very compact physical forms. It would take a lot of time to search for a specific piece of information if the data were recorded on paper. It is much easier to organize, search, and analyze digital data. These digital technologies have shaped modern society.

 Language Arts Connection Choose two applications of digital information. Research how data may be encoded, stored, transmitted, and decoded in each. Make a presentation to show the advantages and disadvantages of using digital information for each application.

Engineering

Computers and Communication

FIGURE 9: A scan code

Modern computers can analyze images to look for an open path for a robot, convert printed text to a digital record, or identify a person in a photo. Computers can be used in a variety of ways to analyze and transfer information to improve communication. Recall that binary information is easy to read because it is in one of two distinct, stable states—black or white, 1 or 0, high- or low-voltage. Scan codes, such as the bar code on a product, have information encoded into black and white lines or rectangles and can be scanned by a moving detector and then interpreted using software. These codes allow people to quickly access information, such as the prices of different foods.

ANALYZE Suppose that you have a choice to communicate with a friend using a cell phone or a computer. What criteria and constraints would cause you to choose the computer over the phone?

_____

_____

Signals through Air and Wire

EVALUATE Which of the following represent ways information can be transmitted? Select all correct answers.

☐ **a.** digital music via headphones

☐ **b.** visible light sending music via a tall antenna

☐ **c.** streaming data via optical fibers

☐ **d.** radio waves broadcasting the news via a dish-shaped antenna

Signals can be sent through different media, and each has advantages and disadvantages. Wireless signals can be broadcast through air in all directions from a radio tower or in a particular direction from a dish-shaped antenna. Signals sent through metal wires and glass or plastic optical fibers can be transferred only through a physical connection. Air and optical fibers can carry many signals at the same time. Metal wires commonly carry only one signal at a time, though some signals can be temporarily combined.

The properties of waves affect how signals are sent. Bandwidth is the amount of data that can be transmitted per unit time. Because higher-frequency waves have more cycles per second; they can carry more information. However, increasing the frequency of a wave can shorten its range because it will lose energy more rapidly to its medium. Faster waves can also produce higher bandwidth because they reach the receiver in less time. A radio wave in air is faster than light in an optical fiber, which is faster than an electric pulse in a wire.

Noise is unwanted sound or any other unwanted disturbance mixed with a signal. Electric fields can interfere with wired and wireless signals. Because optical fibers are made of nonconductive materials, fiber-optic signals do not have this common type of noise. Any level of noise will change an analog signal. One major advantage of sending digital signals is that they can be designed to reduce the effects of noise. To affect a digital signal, the noise has to be so great that two of the discrete levels can be confused.

FIGURE 10: Wired and wireless transmission of signals both have advantages.

a Cables of optical fibers

b Cell phone tower

APPLY How might the properties of waves affect the speed and reliability of information transfer in a communication device?

_____

_____

_____

Information from Smartphones

EVALUATE What are two ways that phones are able to send and receive information?

_____

_____

_____

_____

FIGURE 11: Smartphones can be used in various ways.

A smartphone is one of the most complex devices people use in their daily lives. Smartphones are able to make phone calls but can also access global positioning data and make use of signals from wireless Internet networks, broadcast radio, and Bluetooth®.

For each type of signal, a smartphone can have different types of metallic antennas embedded within the case. The signal reaching each antenna is encoded according to the type of transmission and then processed using the appropriate decoding method.

Every year new smartphones come on the market with new features and improved performance. These changes are the result of collaboration between scientists and engineers during research and development (R&D) cycles. Engineers determine criteria that users may want and work with scientists to develop technology to meet those criteria. For example, smartphone users often wish to reduce the amount of data they use. During an R&D cycle, engineers and scientists may design a smartphone with radio receivers so that a user can listen to music without streaming it over the Internet.

 Language Arts Connection Research one of the methods that smartphones can use to transmit and/or receive information. Use technical texts to understand the details of the method you research. Prepare a presentation, including diagrams, to explain how it works to your classmates. Describe what need you think this particular method was designed to meet.

ARGUE Discuss with your classmates why you think smartphones were developed following the success of more simple cell phones. What are some of the advantages and tradeoffs of smartphones compared with more simple phones?

_____

_____

_____

_____

_____

 Evidence Notebook Make a table to summarize the advantages of the many ways that you can send, receive, and store sound information.

Guided Research

Information and Encryption

FIGURE 12: An Enigma machine was used to encrypt information during World War II.

Early forms of encryption involved a simple substitution of each letter of the alphabet with another letter. The first computer-based form of encryption involved a device called the Enigma machine, and it affected the outcome of World War II. One person would type the letters of a message into the Enigma machine, which would encrypt each letter into another one based on the position of a spinning rotor. The receiver would then type the encrypted text into another Enigma machine with the same settings to decrypt the letters.

Today, encryption keeps personal information secure when it is sent over the Internet. The sending device scrambles data before transmitting, and a receiving device uses the same program to unscramble the data. Devices such as routers are equipped with chips to allow encryption between a computer and a wireless network. The router scrambles your signal and uses the passcode for the wireless network as a key to unscramble it. Anyone not connected to the network can access the information, but it will be disorganized data unless the passcode for the network is used. Without encryption, information on an unsecured wireless network can be accessed freely.

 Language Arts Connection Research a modern method of data encryption used to secure information that is stored and transferred by computers. Prepare a brief report describing how your chosen method works. Include a comparison with the Enigma machine, and describe at least two applications where the modern encryption method might be useful.

| HISTORY OF RECORDING | DATA COMPRESSION | PACKETS AND PROTOCOLS | Go online to choose one of these other paths. |

Lesson Self-Check

CAN YOU EXPLAIN THE PHENOMENON?

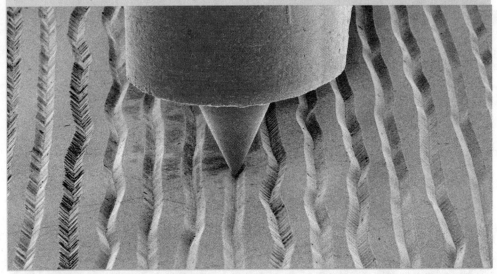

FIGURE 13: The pattern in a record's groove is an analog waveform.

Vinyl records store music as analog information. Though still used occasionally, this method of storing and retrieving music is not as popular today.

Not only have methods for storing music and other sounds changed over time, but the way people store information, such as messages and photographs, has changed. Most information that was once stored and transferred as analog information is now stored and transferred digitally.

Evidence Notebook Refer to your notes in your Evidence Notebook to make a claim about why digital storage has replaced storing recorded music on vinyl records. Your explanation should include a discussion of the following points:

Claim Why has digital storage replaced analog storage such as vinyl records?

Evidence What evidence supports your claim regarding the replacement of analog storage by digital storage?

Reasoning Describe, in detail, how the evidence you gathered supports your claim about why digital storage has replaced analog storage.

CHECKPOINTS

Check Your Understanding

1. Label each type of information as (**a**) analog or (**d**) digital.

    _____ **a.** an image on a screen made up of LEDs

    _____ **b.** an imprint of a hand pressed into clay

    _____ **c.** a sketch of a face

    _____ **d.** a code for a combination lock

    _____ **e.** a scan code

2. Complete the statement about storage of data by selecting the correct terms.

    Physical storage of information can seen in computer documents | old stone tablets. An advantage of digital | physical storage is the information can be found in less time and can be organized easier.

3. Which of the following are problems with wireless transmission of data? Select all correct answers.

    ☐ **a.** The frequency of the signal shifts as it moves into different media.

    ☐ **b.** The amplitude of the signal diminishes as it travels through the air.

    ☐ **c.** The signals are easy to decode.

    ☐ **d.** The signals can be affected by electric and magnetic fields.

4. Complete the statement about noise by selecting the correct terms.

    Noise affects digital | analog | both digital and analog signals. It enhances | interferes with the signal, adding unwanted signals or changing the existing signal. Low noise is an advantage of wire | air | optical fibers as a medium of transmission.

5. Historically, Morse code was often used to send a signal. What makes it well suited to this use? Select all correct answers.

    ☐ **a.** Dots and dashes are always better at relaying information.

    ☐ **b.** Morse code is never affected by noise.

    ☐ **c.** Morse code can communicate over long distances.

    ☐ **d.** Morse code can be encoded using distinct states.

6. Complete the statement by selecting the correct terms.

    Electromagnetic waves can carry energy and information. Optical fiber cables may use infrared waves | x-rays to transmit information. A water wave | radio wave is used to transmit information wirelessly.

7. Which of the following are ways energy is transferred via water waves? Select all correct answers.

    ☐ **a.** wind interacting with the surface of water, causing energy to be transferred to the water

    ☐ **b.** light shining on the surface of the water, transferring energy to the water

    ☐ **c.** an earthquake occurring under the ocean, causing a large amount of water to be displaced

    ☐ **d.** a boat displacing water as it propels across the surface

8. Complete the statement about data compression by selecting the correct terms.

    Data compression involves compressing a digital | analog file to reduce the storage size of the file. This compressed file can be transmitted faster | slower but the fidelity may increase | decrease.

CHECKPOINTS (CONTINUED)

9. In the early days of computer communications, computers transmitted digital signals over copper telephone wires. Why might this transmission method have been chosen? Why was it eventually replaced by others?

_____

_____

_____

_____

_____

_____

10. Cell phones use electromagnetic waves, such as radio waves, to communicate. Why do you think radio waves are a good means of transmission for cell phone signals?

_____

_____

_____

_____

_____

_____

_____

_____

MAKE YOUR OWN STUDY GUIDE

In your Evidence Notebook, design a study guide that supports the main ideas from this lesson: **Waves can carry information as well as energy.**

Information can be encoded and transmitted in analog and digital formats.

Digital and analog formats each have advantages and disadvantages.

Remember to include the following information in your study guide:
- Use examples that model main ideas.
- Record explanations for the phenomena you investigated.
- Use evidence to support your explanations. Your support can include drawings, data, graphs, laboratory conclusions, and other evidence recorded throughout the lesson.

Consider how systems can be designed to use wave characteristics to transfer energy and information.

Technology Connection

Mapping Information Geospatial technologies analyze data tied to specific places on Earth. The data might be demographic, such as the human population in specific places over time. The data might also be tied to geology or ecology, such as elevation or ground cover. A geographic information system (GIS) is a suite of software tools to manage and communicate data.

> GIS maps convey regional fire danger, changes in population, and other types of data. Choose a topic such as wildlife, water resources, or history. Use the U.S. Geological Survey or a similar national source to find GIS maps of your area. Research how electromagnetic radiation was used to collect or transmit the data. Develop a multimedia presentation about this information and how the GIS maps help convey it.

FIGURE 1: This GIS map shows sea surface temperature data during a hurricane, displayed with satellite imagery.

Social Studies Connection

Encryption and Decryption In World War II, the Germans' Enigma machine used electric wires and rotating wheels to change the encryption code after each letter was typed. Mathematician Alan Turing led the team who broke both the Enigma encryption—which used letters and Morse code—and the later binary Tunny encryption. The solutions used to manage and interpret this large set of data laid part of the groundwork for modern computing.

> Research how encryption and decryption are used in today's society. Write a brief blog entry that relates your findings to the history of encryption and explains the importance of securing data.

FIGURE 2: Alan Turing led the team of mathematician-cryptanalysts at Bletchley Park who broke the encryption of the German Enigma machine in World War II.

Archaeology Connection

Images from Underground Ground-penetrating radar works as a bat's echolocation does. Radar uses radio waves, which are lower in frequency than visible light. The device sends pulses of waves that are reflected back at boundaries—the ground's surface, changes in rock, underground streams, or caves. This technology can image the buried shapes of buildings, roads, and graves.

> Suppose you work for a company that offers ground-penetrating radar surveys of possible archaeological sites. A customer asks what sort of information can be found and whether the technology is well-suited to their site. Research this application of ground-penetrating radar. Prepare a short pamphlet that explains the technology: how it works, what it can detect, and limitations.

FIGURE 3: Ground-penetrating radar uses pulses of radio waves to detect shapes and boundaries beneath the surface.

A BOOK EXPLAINING
COMPLEX IDEAS USING
ONLY THE 1,000 MOST
COMMON WORDS

COLORS OF LIGHT
Light we can see and light we can't see

You know that the electromagnetic spectrum includes all light waves, not just those visible to the human eye. Electromagnetic waves have different properties due to their different wavelengths and frequencies. Here's a look at the different kinds of light.

RANDALL MUNROE
XKCD.COM

THE STORY OF LIGHT WAVES

LIGHT IS MADE UP OF WAVES, AND WE SEE LONGER WAVES AND SHORTER WAVES AS DIFFERENT COLORS.

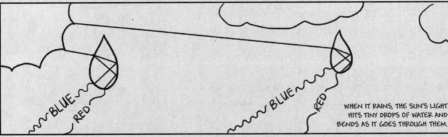

WHEN IT RAINS, THE SUN'S LIGHT HITS TINY DROPS OF WATER AND BENDS AS IT GOES THROUGH THEM.

SOME COLORS OF LIGHT BEND MORE THAN OTHERS, SO DIFFERENT COLORS REACH YOUR EYE FROM DIFFERENT PARTS OF THE SKY.

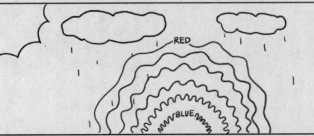

THESE SKY COLORS ARE SORTED BY HOW LONG THEIR WAVES ARE, FROM THE SHORTEST WAVES, BLUE, TO THE LONGEST WAVES, RED. BUT THE KINDS OF LIGHT DON'T STOP THERE! THOSE ARE JUST THE SHORTEST AND LONGEST WAVES THAT OUR EYES CAN SEE.

In real life, even if you could see longer and shorter light waves, you wouldn't see these colors spread out in the sky. There are three reasons for this.

FIRST

The Sun gives off most of its light in colors that we can see, and light that's a little shorter or longer. In colors that are *much* shorter or longer, the Sun is pretty dark!

SECOND

Lots of these kinds of light don't go through water, so they wouldn't go through the rain.

THIRD

The colors are sorted from long to short because short waves (blue) bend more than long waves (red). But there are some colors, kinds we can't see, where it goes the other way! That means that these colors wouldn't be spread out like they're shown on the next pages; they'd be laid in sheets over themselves—some parts top to bottom and other parts bottom to top—all in the same area of the sky.

COLORS OF LIGHT

HOW LONG ARE THESE WAVES?

A big country ----------

A small country --------

A city ------------------

A small town -----------

A building -------------

A truck ----------------

A dog ------------------

A finger ---------------

A computer key --------

These two black -------
spots:

A hair (the short way) --

A single bag of water
from your blood --------

A small thing that
takes over your body's
bags of water ---------

The dust in smoke -----

The larger pieces
everything is made of --

The smaller pieces
everything is made of --

The heavy centers
of those pieces --------

WHAT ARE THEY?

LONG WAVES

POWER WAVES

When you stick the end of something into the wall to power it, the power comes out in waves.

They're very long, slow waves, taking so long to change that our power lines aren't long enough to hold the "high" part of the wave and the "low" part at the same time. It might make more sense to say that the power turns on for a while, then turns off.

Light "turns on and off" too fast to count, but power waves only turn on and off a few dozen times each second.

RADIO

Radio waves and light are the same stuff. Radio is just longer. Our eyes can't see light that long, but we can build machines that can.

OLD RADIO

Cars use space radios for a few different things like . . .

NEWER RADIO

. . . finding where they are . . .
. . . and playing music

"SMALL" WAVES

REAL SIZE

Phones
Computer hot spots

Food-heating boxes are named after these waves. They use this color.

WARM LIGHT

Everything gives off light because everything is at least a little warm, and warm things give off light. Warmer things give off more light made of shorter waves.

Our bodies give off these colors of light because we're kind of warm, but not warm enough to give off light you can see.

If you wear special computer glasses that help you see these colors of light, you can see where people are in the dark using the light from their bodies.

Space heat from the start of time

LIGHT FROM WARM THINGS

Body heat

Sun light

LIGHT WE CAN SEE

RAIN COLORS

People say those rain lights in the sky show all the colors, but they don't really; there's no deep pink.

The more you learn about color, the more you find that almost everything people say about color is only sort of true.

BLACK LIGHT

This is the kind of light that burns your skin if you stay out in the Sun.

SPACE BITS

Sometimes, tiny rocks—going almost as fast as light—hit Earth. The air keeps us safe, but when they hit the air, they make a flash of high-power light. The air keeps us safe from that, too.

If any of these hit you, they could break down the things in your bags of water that tell your body how to grow. If you got enough of them, it could make your body start growing wrong.

When people go into space, where there's no air to stop these things, they sometimes see little flashes of light as the things from space hit their eyes.

That's one reason we don't let people stay in space too long—if they stay too long, their bodies might get hit in enough places that they start growing wrong.

LIGHT CARRYING A LOT OF POWER

These very "short" colors of light aren't really like waves at all. They're more like tiny rocks going very fast.

Not very many things make this kind of light.

CAN THEY REACH US FROM SPACE?

This side shows which kinds of light can get through Earth's air.

These long waves go through normal air, but can't get through a special layer of air near the edge of space. The air in that layer acts kind of like a mirror for radio, which is why you can pick up some kinds of radio messages from other parts of the Earth.

These radio waves go through air just fine. We use them for looking at stars and talking to our space boats.

These colors are stopped by the water in the air.

LIGHT THAT DOCTORS USE TO SEE THROUGH YOU

These kinds of light can't get through air.

FAR-AWAY FLASHES

About once every day, our space boats see flashes of very, very high-power light from somewhere far off in space.

We're pretty sure they come from huge stars dying, but we aren't sure exactly what happens in the stars to make the light.

FROM THESE IMAGES, IT LOOKS LIKE YOUR BODY IS FULL OF BONES.

OH NO! IS THERE ANY CURE?

This picture shows what other colors you would see if the rain colors kept going. (The picture isn't in color, but that's okay— they're not real colors, anyway!)

Light from the Sun can get through air. That's good, since we need it to see.

The Sun gives off light in these colors. The colors our eyes can see are right in the middle of that, which makes sense; eyes grew to fit the Sun's light.

A special layer stops some of the light that burns your skin. A while back, we learned that we had made a hole in that layer.

We didn't mean to. We're fixing it.

A BOOK EXPLAINING
COMPLEX IDEAS USING
ONLY THE 1,000 MOST
COMMON WORDS

PICTURE TAKER
Machines that turn light into pictures

You've learned that cameras convert straight lines (light) into images (photos) using basic principles of optics and chemical reactions. From simple pinhole cameras to sophisticated digital cameras, all use refraction to produce images. Here's an explanation that presents some complex ideas about photography in simple language.

RANDALL MUNROE
XKCD.COM

THE STORY OF MAKING PICTURES

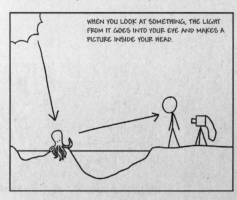

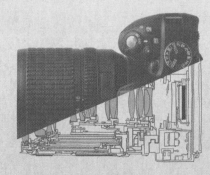

SHAPE

To make a picture of something, you need to control the light so that each part of the paper sees light from just one part of it.

One way to do this is by blocking almost all the light paths using a wall with a hole in it. (This makes a picture that's turned over, but that's okay—you can just turn it back.)

MORE LIGHT

The hole idea works, but a tiny hole doesn't let very much light through, so it takes a long time for enough light to hit the paper to make a picture.

To let in more light, you could make the hole bigger, but then the light from one spot starts to spread out on the paper, clouding the picture.

BENDING LIGHT

To make the picture less clouded, we need to bend lots of light from each part of the thing toward the spot on the picture that goes with it. We can do this by using things that bend light—like water and glass.

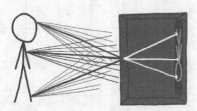
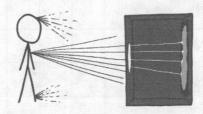
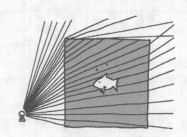

SPECIAL SHAPES

By cutting glass into the right shapes, we can make light benders that catch lots of light and send the light from each direction to a different part of the picture. This machine is good enough to take a simple picture, but it will be a little clouded and not very sharp or bright. To take a clearer picture, we have to add more benders to control the path the light takes more carefully. Most picture takers use glass, since it's easier to cut it into a shape than water.

Some people are trying to build computer-controlled benders that use water, which would let the benders change shape to control the light without using as many parts.

NOT AGAIN...

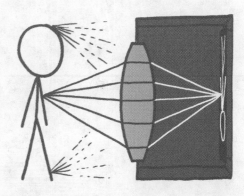

LIGHT PAPER

Some kinds of paper change color when light hits them. Picture takers used these for a long time.

This paper alone isn't enough to make a picture, though. When you hold the paper up to someone, light from every part of them hits every part of the paper, so your whole page will be all one color. (Unless you hold the paper so close to the thing that each part of the paper only sees light from one part of the thing, but that doesn't work very well.)

OKAY, SMILE!

BIG PICTURE TAKER

This machine is used to take sharp pictures, even of things that are small or far away.

Our eyes are better than most picture takers at seeing small and far-away things, but thanks to its very large benders that take in lots of light, this kind of picture taker can see even better.

LOOKER

The whole front end of the picture taker is for gathering light. The whole thing can come off, so you can use different lookers for different kinds of pictures.

WHY ARE THERE SO MANY BENDERS?

These light benders are here for different reasons, but one of the big ones is that some colors of light bend more than others when they go through glass. This can make some colors in a picture sharp while others are spread out. Different kinds of glass break up colors in different ways, so by sending the light through one kind of glass and then another, groups of benders can get the different colors to the same place.

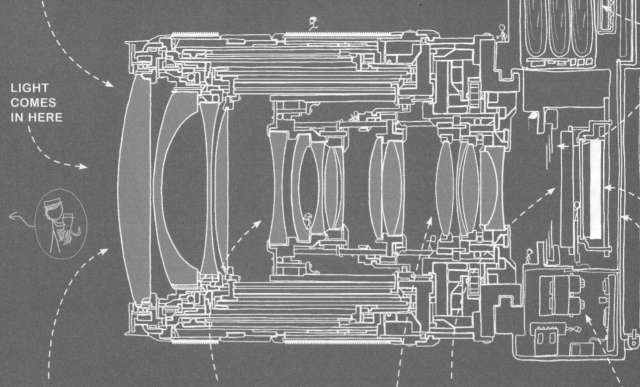

LIGHT COMES IN HERE

FRONT BENDERS

These grab all the light and start bringing it together so the other benders can do things with it.

FROM YOUR PICTURES, WE FIGURED YOU WERE JUST BAD AT USING CAMERAS.

NO, I'M ACTUALLY LIKE THIS.

CLOSE-OR-FAR BENDERS

These benders control how close up or far away the things in the picture look. They slide forward to look at small things far away, and back to see a wider view of the whole area.

PICTURE BENDERS

These light benders are the ones that bring the light together to make a picture on the light catcher in the back.

DUST SHAKER WINDOW

Even a tiny piece of dust stuck to the picture window can make the machine take bad pictures. In small picture takers, the picture window is locked inside and safe from dust. But on ones where you can take the big looker off to put on a different one, dust can get in. To keep dust from being a problem, there's a window in front of the picture window with a shaker on it. The shaker shakes the window very fast, throwing off any dust that sticks to it.

NO MIRROR

Nice picture takers used to have a mirror here, so you could look through a hole in the top and see through the looker, to see what would be in the picture. The loud "picture-taking sound" is the mirror moving out of the way to let light reach the back. Now, more and more picture takers are using screens to show you the view instead.

POWER BOX

Taking pictures can use lots of power, so picture takers usually need special power boxes.

MEMORY

This holds the pictures you take.

PICTURE WINDOW

This window opens and closes to let light through to the light catcher and take a picture. It has two sheets. When it starts taking a picture, the bottom sheet pulls down out of the way. When it's done gathering light, the top screen comes down to cover it. It uses two screens; if it used a screen that came up and then pulled back, then the top half of the light catcher would spend more time catching light than the bottom.

LIGHT CATCHER

This used to be made of paper, but on computer picture takers like this one, it's a flat sheet of computer light feelers. Each one checks how much light is hitting it, then tells the computer. The computer puts the messages together to make a picture.

SCREEN

This screen shows you what the light catcher is seeing. It also lets you look at the pictures you took and decide whether you want to keep them. Some picture takers have a hole you can look through, too, which shows you a view out the looker using a mirror (or pretends to, using another screen).

FLASH

If there's not enough light to make a good picture, this can light up the area for a moment while the picture window is open. The light can make the shadows in a picture look strange, though, so some people try not to use it very much.

Go online for more about *Thing Explainer*.

I HATE HOW EVERYONE TAKES PICTURES INSTEAD OF JUST ENJOYING THE VIEW.

...YOU SAY, INSTEAD OF ENJOYING THE VIEW.

CHANGING SHAPE

Picture takers have changed shape over time. The back parts are smaller, but some of the front parts of good picture takers have stayed big. The jobs done by the back parts, like saving pictures and storing power, are now being done by small computers. The front parts bend light, and computers can't do that yet. Soon, people might just use their hand computers as the back part, sticking them to a looker to take nice pictures.

LOOKER

HAND COMPUTER

Designing a Stringed Instrument

Stringed instruments are made in many cultures, using locally available materials. The strings are made to vibrate by plucking, bowing, or striking them. The sound is frequently amplified by a resonator, such as the body of a violin or harp. Design a stringed instrument that can play several notes. It should include strings of different thicknesses and perhaps different materials.

1. DEFINE THE PROBLEM

You will design a stringed musical instrument that can play several notes over the range of an octave (i.e., the highest frequency is at least double the lowest frequency). Use strings of different material, thickness, or both. The strings should be everyday items, such as twine, not ready-made guitar strings. State clearly the problem and the criteria and constraints for a solution.

2. CONDUCT RESEARCH

Research designs of different traditional stringed instruments. You may want to include handmade instruments constructed of found items. Identify a possible basic design and materials.

3. CARRY OUT AN INVESTIGATION

Test your materials, determining the range of sounds that can be produced. Examine how changing the vibrating portion of any one string affects the string's frequency. Measure the frequency, and graph it as a function of vibrating string length. Determine the relationship between frequency and string length.

4. DESIGN A SOLUTION

Use the results of your tests to build a prototype. Test the design: Can you play several different notes? Do they cover at least an octave? Refine the design based on testing your prototype.

5. IDENTIFY & RECOMMEND A SOLUTION

Demonstrate your stringed instrument. Explain how you adjusted the pitch to cover a full octave. Demonstrate how you can change the pitch of a string by changing its length or tension.

FIGURE 4: A musician plays a handmade instrument.

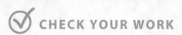 CHECK YOUR WORK

Once you have completed this task, you should have the following:

- an instrument with several strings, which can produce different notes
- a design record explaining how you adjusted the design from an initial sketch or prototype
- a presentation in which you play different notes on the instrument, explain how the vibrating string and any resonating pieces interact, and explain how you changed the pitch of the strings

Name _____   Date _____

SYNTHESIZE THE UNIT

In your Evidence Notebook, make a concept map, other graphic organizer, or outline using the Study Guides you made for each lesson in this unit. Be sure to use evidence to support your claims.

When synthesizing individual information, remember to follow these general steps:
- Find the central idea of each piece of information.
- Think about the relationships among the central ideas.
- Combine the ideas to come up with a new understanding.

DRIVING QUESTIONS

Look back to the Driving Questions from the opening section of this unit. In your Evidence Notebook, review and revise your previous answers to those questions. Use the evidence you gathered and other observations you made throughout the unit to support your claims.

PRACTICE AND REVIEW

1. Select the correct terms to complete the statements about waves.

   Compared with other water waves, a tsunami has a very long wavelength, corresponding to what sort of frequency? low | high

   What does this indicate about the time for one cycle of a tsunami swell? long | short

   A sonar ping returns more slowly than expected. What might this indicate? a hole | a ship

   Earthquake early-warning systems rely on sending a warning over electromagnetic waves, which travel much faster than seismic waves. If an earthquake is detected 30 km away from a station after 10 s, how long will it take the waves to reach a location 600 km away? 200 s | 600 s

2. A water wave with an amplitude of 5 cm interacts in phase with a second water wave with an amplitude of 3 cm. Which choice correctly describes the result?
   - a. a wave with a zero amplitude
   - b. a wave with an amplitude of 2 cm
   - c. a wave with an amplitude of 4 cm
   - d. a wave with an amplitude of 8 cm

3. Select the correct terms to complete the statement.

   A concert hall may be designed with flat | curved surfaces to focus | disperse sound waves. Sound is absorbed by surfaces that are soft or perforated.

4. Why do electron microscopes offer higher resolution than light microscopes?
   - a. Moving electrons have more energy than photons.
   - b. Moving electrons are easier to detect than photons.
   - c. Moving electrons have shorter associated wavelengths than visible light.
   - d. Moving electrons are slower than photons, capturing more detail.

5. Which of the following would increase the energy of a sound wave? Select all correct answers.
   - a. increasing the wavelength
   - b. increasing the amplitude
   - c. increasing the frequency
   - d. increasing the density of the medium
   - e. increasing the speed of the wave

6. An archivist chooses to copy an analog audiotape recording to a CD, which records the information as a digital pattern of 1s and 0s. What likely led to this choice? Select all correct answers.
   - a. improved fidelity
   - b. playback without abrasion
   - c. more information stored in a small space
   - d. easier to transmit digitally

7. Figure 5 illustrates a double-slit interference pattern of light that occurs when light is passed through two slits in a barrier. Is this an example of particle or wave behavior? The width of each slit is similar to the wavelength of the light. If the slits were 100 times as wide, would the behavior become more like that of a wave or like that of a particle? Describe your reasoning.

FIGURE 5: Double-slit interference pattern

_____

_____

_____

_____

_____

_____

8. Suppose that an interference pattern like that in Figure 5 were instead produced by sound waves. The slits are speakers about 1 m apart, emitting a tone of wavelength 30 cm. Explain where you would stand to experience the most constructive interference of the sound waves. How does this relate to the bright and dark bands in the pattern at the bottom right of the image? What would happen if you moved a microphone slowly across the room where the wave interference is occurring?

_____

_____

_____

_____

_____

9. Describe how a tsunami early-warning detection system uses energy and information from the disturbances that cause tsunamis.

_____

_____

_____

_____

UNIT PROJECT

Return to your unit project. Prepare a presentation using your research and materials, and share it with the class. In your final presentation, evaluate the strength of your hypothesis, data, analysis, and conclusions.

Remember these tips while evaluating:

- What is the premise of the argument?
- What empirical evidence supports (or counters) this premise?
- How did you evaluate this evidence?

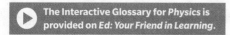

Index

Page numbers for definitions are printed in **boldface type**.
Page numbers for illustrations, maps, and charts are printed in *italics*.

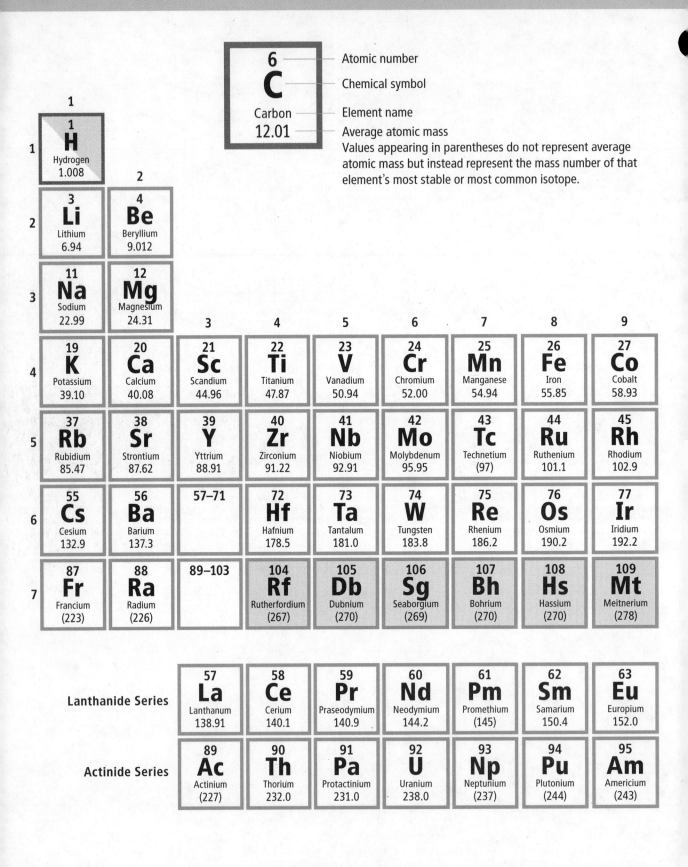

6
C
Carbon
12.01

— Atomic number
— Chemical symbol
— Element name
— Average atomic mass

Values appearing in parentheses do not represent average atomic mass but instead represent the mass number of that element's most stable or most common isotope.

Lanthanide Series

57	58	59	60	61	62	63
La	**Ce**	**Pr**	**Nd**	**Pm**	**Sm**	**Eu**
Lanthanum	Cerium	Praseodymium	Neodymium	Promethium	Samarium	Europium
138.91	140.1	140.9	144.2	(145)	150.4	152.0

Actinide Series

89	90	91	92	93	94	95
Ac	**Th**	**Pa**	**U**	**Np**	**Pu**	**Am**
Actinium	Thorium	Protactinium	Uranium	Neptunium	Plutonium	Americium
(227)	232.0	231.0	238.0	(237)	(244)	(243)

State of Element at STP

Solid
Liquid
Gas
Not yet known

							18
							2 **He** Helium 4.003

13	**14**	**15**	**16**	**17**	
5 **B** Boron 10.81	6 **C** Carbon 12.01	7 **N** Nitrogen 14.007	8 **O** Oxygen 15.999	9 **F** Fluorine 19.00	10 **Ne** Neon 20.18
13 **Al** Aluminum 26.98	14 **Si** Silicon 28.085	15 **P** Phosphorus 30.97	16 **S** Sulfur 32.06	17 **Cl** Chlorine 35.45	18 **Ar** Argon 39.95

10	**11**	**12**							
28 **Ni** Nickel 58.69	29 **Cu** Copper 63.55	30 **Zn** Zinc 65.38	31 **Ga** Gallium 69.72	32 **Ge** Germanium 72.63	33 **As** Arsenic 74.92	34 **Se** Selenium 79.0	35 **Br** Bromine 79.90	36 **Kr** Krypton 83.80
46 **Pd** Palladium 106.4	47 **Ag** Silver 107.9	48 **Cd** Cadmium 112.4	49 **In** Indium 114.8	50 **Sn** Tin 118.7	51 **Sb** Antimony 121.8	52 **Te** Tellurium 127.6	53 **I** Iodine 126.9	54 **Xe** Xenon 131.3
78 **Pt** Platinum 195.1	79 **Au** Gold 197.0	80 **Hg** Mercury 200.6	81 **Tl** Thallium 204.38	82 **Pb** Lead 207.2	83 **Bi** Bismuth 209.0	84 **Po** Polonium (209)	85 **At** Astatine (210)	86 **Rn** Radon (222)
110 **Ds** Darmstadtium (281)	111 **Rg** Roentgenium (281)	112 **Cn** Copernicium (285)	113 **Nh** Nihonium (286)	114 **Fl** Flerovium (289)	115 **Mc** Moscovium (289)	116 **Lv** Livermorium (293)	117 **Ts** Tennessine (293)	118 **Og** Oganesson (294)

64 **Gd** Gadolinium 157.3	65 **Tb** Terbium 158.9	66 **Dy** Dysprosium 162.5	67 **Ho** Holmium 164.9	68 **Er** Erbium 167.3	69 **Tm** Thulium 168.9	70 **Yb** Ytterbium 173.1	71 **Lu** Lutetium 175.0
96 **Cm** Curium (247)	97 **Bk** Berkelium (247)	98 **Cf** Californium (251)	99 **Es** Einsteinium (252)	100 **Fm** Fermium (257)	101 **Md** Mendelevium (258)	102 **No** Nobelium (259)	103 **Lr** Lawrencium (262)

Elements with atomic numbers of 95 and above are not known to occur naturally, even in trace amounts. They have only been synthesized in the lab. The physical and chemical properties of elements with atomic numbers 100 and above cannot be predicted with certainty.